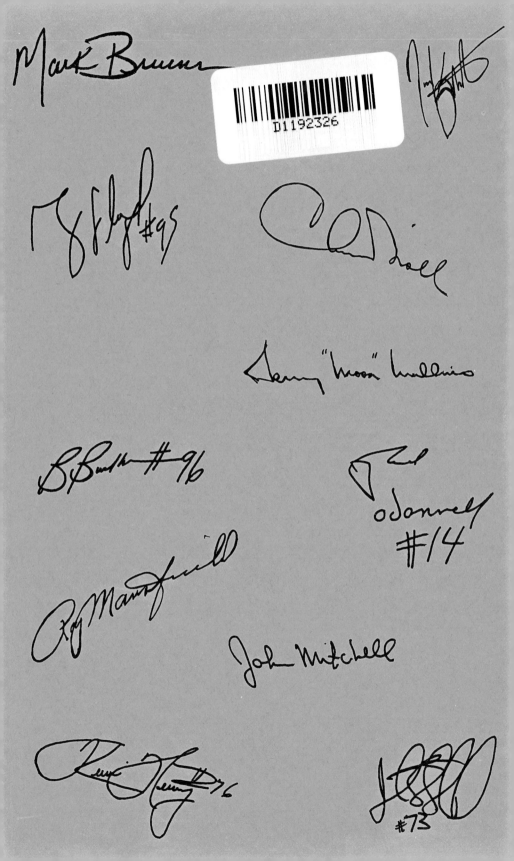

Keep the faith
and dare to dream.

Best wishes,
Jim O'Brien

KEEP THE FAITH

The Steelers of
Two Different Eras

By Jim O'Brien

*"You should earnestly contend for the
faith which was once delivered unto saints."*
— Jude 1:3

Bill Amatucci

Two outstanding cornerbacks from two different eras, Rod Woodson and Dwayne Woodruff, became disenchanted when their stature faded with the Steelers. It's a shame they had such short memories.

This book is dedicated to my wife, Kathie O'Brien, and our daughters, Sarah and Rebecca.

Copyright © 1997 by Jim O'Brien

James P. O'Brien — Publishing
P.O. Box 12580
Pittsburgh PA 15241
Phone: (412) 221-3580
        After Feb.1, 1998 (724) 221-3580

First printing, September, 1997

Manufactured in the United States of America

Printed by Geyer Printing Company, Inc.
3700 Bigelow Boulevard
Pittsburgh PA 15213

Typography by Cold-Comp
810 Penn Avenue
Pittsburgh PA 15222

ISBN 1-886348-02-2

Contents

5 Acknowledgements

10 Memos from Moms

12 Introduction

18 Behind The Scenes

29 Mike Webster

48 At the Hall of Fame

50 Bill Cowher

64 Kordell Stewart

81 Essay from Joy Hayes

85 Dr. Jekyll and Mr. Hyde

100 Jerome Bettis

109 Detroit

112 Bettis Family

122 Gladys Bettis

124 Will Wolford

137 Louisville

150 Ode from Don Shula

151 Tom Donahoe

161 Ray Mansfield

181 Steelers Alumni

185 Everything's different

194 Charles Johnson

212 Tim Lester

223 Collectibles

225 Elbie Nickel

230 Ernie Holmes

246 Mark Bruener

261 St. Vincent's

267 Levon Kirkland

282 Cowher's coaches

291 John Banaszak

298 Tim Lewis

317 Gains and losses

326 Jim Sweeney

342 Eric Ravotti

356 Guido Ravotti

358 Darren Perry

375 Baldy Regan

391 Tom Modrak

401 Joel Steed

417 Lloyd goes home

418 Joe Zombek

434 Kevin Henry

442 Bill Cowher and Arnold Palmer

447 Reviews of Dare To Dream

Books By Jim O'Brien

COMPLETE HANDBOOK OF PRO BASKETBALL 1970-1971

COMPLETE HANDBOOK OF PRO BASKETBALL 1971-1972

ABA ALL-STARS

PITTSBURGH: THE STORY OF THE CITY OF CHAMPIONS

HAIL TO PITT: A SPORTS HISTORY OF
THE UNIVERSITY OF PITTSBURGH

DOING IT RIGHT

WHATEVER IT TAKES

MAZ AND THE '60 BUCS

REMEMBER ROBERTO

PENGUIN PROFILES

DARE TO DREAM

KEEP THE FAITH

To order copies of these titles directly from the publisher, send $24.95 for hardcover edition. Please send $3.50 to cover shipping and handling costs per book. Pennsylvania residents add 6% sales tax to price of book only. Allegheny County residents add an additional 1% sales tax for a total of 7% sales tax. Copies will be signed by author at your request. Discounts available for large orders. Contact publisher (1-412-221-3580) regarding availability and price of all books in *Pittsburgh Proud* series, or to request an order form. This book will be printed only in a hardcover edition, and only hardcover editions remain of some of the earlier books. As of Feb. 1, 1998, the publisher's telephone number is (1-724-221-3580).

Acknowledgments
Postcards from Ireland

*"I asked him if you're
the real McCoy."*
— Art Rooney

rt Rooney, the late owner of the Pittsburgh Steelers, loved to
travel, and he especially liked going to Ireland. His family's
roots were important to him.

Wherever he traveled, he often sent me postcards. He sent postcards to family and friends and some sportswriters. He sent me postcards when I worked in Miami and when I worked in New York. He
was a faithful correspondent.

He sent me postcards from Ireland on more than one occasion.
One of them had a picture of a peasant farmer who was leading a
mule-driven rickety old wagon filled with hay. Mr. Rooney wrote on
the other side. "This guy says he's one of your relatives. I asked him
if you're the real McCoy, and he says you are."

On another occasion, Mr. Rooney sent me a postcard from
Ireland that pictured a mass being celebrated at a Catholic church
there. He said he offered a prayer there on my behalf.

Postcards and prayers and the friendship of a special man like
Art Rooney have helped me stay the course in my sportswriting and
family life. Art Rooney liked my name, James Patrick Joseph O'Brien,
and that my wife's name was Kathleen, the same as his wife and one
of his daughters-in-law, the wife of Art Rooney Jr., the second of his
five sons. He also liked that I grew up in Hazelwood, in the inner-city
of Pittsburgh. To him, I was a genuine Pittsburgh guy.

"Look at this dude from Hazelwood!" he hollered out to his oldest
son, Dan, when I strode into the Steelers' office in a new suit one day
when I was reporting on the team for *The Pittsburgh Press.*

Remembering one's roots, or where you come from, has always
been important to the Rooneys. That's why Dan Rooney realized a
long-time dream in the summer of '97 when he took his Steelers to
Ireland to play a pre-season game. They played the Chicago Bears,
owned by the McCaskeys, another proud Irish family, at Croke Park
in Dublin in what's been dubbed the American Bowl series. The
Steelers had previously played exhibitions in Spain and Japan.

Dan had been an organizer and activist in The American Ireland
Fund, and along with his good friend, Tony O'Reilly of H.J. Heinz Co.,
has raised money for Irish causes, and welcomed an opportunity to
travel to Ireland on several occasions to promote the game. Dan and
Bill Cowher, the head coach of the Steelers, had opportunities to play
golf on some of the great courses there, though Dan didn't think he
would play. Golf had its origins in the British Isles, specifically in
Scotland.

"The Irish claim *they* invented the game," said Dan Rooney. "They say the Scots were just better marketers, with all the stuff about St. Andrew's. The Irish are getting pretty good about marketing golf and sports themselves."

Bill Cowher's father is named Laird, which means Lord in Scotland, but his heritage is strictly German, just like his predecessor, Chuck Noll, who shared a stubborn streak. This book is about families and origins, where the Steelers come from, the kinds of people and communities that fashioned the football players who represent the Pittsburgh franchise. It is a sequel to my earlier book, *Dare To Dream*.

Art Rooney's role as a friend, mentor and patron is something I will always treasure. Time spent with him, in his office or on the sideline at Three Rivers Stadium, or in the early days at the Roosevelt Hotel and at the Fair Grounds in South Park, were part of the special appeal to work in sports.

I was standing on the sideline at the first day of the Steelers' mini-camp at Three Rivers Stadium on June 2, 1997, when Dan Rooney stopped by to chat with me and Norm Vargo, the sports editor of *The Daily News* in McKeesport and the dean of Steelers' beat writers. Dan was looking forward to the trip to Ireland. Talking to any Rooney on the sideline remains a special treat.

The turf was damp and there was a fine mist in the air in Pittsburgh that day. June was beginning where May had left off weather-wise. It had been the coldest May in Pittsburgh's history, and also one of the wettest. There had been flooding throughout the area. It was Ireland-like weather.

The Rooneys traced their roots to Northern Ireland, to Newry, and had some relatives there. Dan's brother, Pat, had a home in Ireland where he stayed when he went there.

"My father's father was Dan Rooney, and he left Ireland at age 12 to come to this country," said Dan. "My mother's mother was from Scotland, but she was also Irish.

"My dad was Art, and he named me, his oldest son, Dan. My oldest son is Art. And his oldest son is Dan. That's the way the Irish do it. You're a historian; you should know that.

"When we started The Ireland Fund, we went over there in 1975. This newspaperman is interviewing my dad, and he's asking him all kinds of questions about his background, about his heritage and his horses, how he got started in sports and all that stuff. When he was done, he thanked my dad. My dad said to him, 'You didn't ask me anything about the Super Bowl.' The writer looked at my dad and said, 'The Super Bowl? What's the Super Bowl?'

"So they've come a long way with football in Ireland. The Irish are great people. I like working with them."

None of us can get anything accomplished alone. Life is a team effort. I must thank my family, my wife Kathleen and our children,

Art Rooney, the founder of the Pittsburgh Steelers, and oldest son, Dan, the president of the Steelers, with political pals David L. Lawrence, former Mayor of Pittsburgh and Governor of Pennsylvania, and Tip O'Neill, former Speaker of the House, looking over their shoulders. There's also a photo, upper left, of Exposition Park (1891-1909) and a 1975 Super Bowl memento made for the "Prez."

Sarah and Rebecca, my mother, Mary O'Brien, who celebrated her 90th birthday while I was writing this book, and my sister, Carole Cook, for their love and assistance.

This is my 12th book, my ninth book about Pittsburgh sports achievement, and my seventh book in seven years, and I've been blessed with lots of boosters.

Special thanks for their help is extended here to Joe Gordon, who announced his retirement in April, 1997 after 28 years as a public relations executive with the Steelers, and his co-workers, Rob Boulware, Ron Miller, Lynne Balkovec Molyneaux, Renae McNabb, Mary Regan, Mike Miller and Matt Rohm. Michael F. Fabus, George Gojkovich, Jack A. Wolf and Bill Amatucci provided photographs.

I want to thank my dear friends and readers for their loyal support. Two in particular, Bill Priatko and Ron Temple, offered their thoughts and encouragement. Priatko's daily prayers were most appreciated by my family. So were supportive sermons on behalf of our books by Rev. Laird Stuart and Rev. Bob Norris of Westminster Presbyterian Church in Upper St. Clair.

Special thanks to my good friends, Alex Pociask of Stevens Painton Corporation and Tom Snyder of Continental Design & Management Group, and to John C. Williams and Peter P. Konczakowski and National City Bank of Pennsylvania, who have been most loyal in their support of my books. Patrons who have made these publishing projects possible include:

Dennis Astorino of LD Astorino Associates, Ltd.; Bill Baierl of Baierl Chevrolet, Inc.; Charles H. Becker Jr. of Johnson & Higgins of Ohio, Inc.; Jim Broadhurst of Eat'n Park Restaurants; Miles Bryan of Bryan Mechanical, Inc.; Everett Burns of E-Z Overhead Door Co.; Ray Conaway of Zimmer Kunz; Armand Dellovade of A.C. Dellovade, Inc.; Steve Fedell of Ikon Office Solutions; Mike Ference of Ference Marketing & Communications.

Ted and Barbara Frantz and TEDCO Construction Corporation; Frank Fuhrer of Fuhrer Wholesale, Inc.; Lloyd Gibson and John Schultz of North Side Bank; Daniel A. Goetz and Mike Hagan of Iron & Glass Bank; Ed Harmon of F.E. Harmon Construction, Inc.; Darrell J. Hess of D.J. Hess Advertising; David S. Jancisin of Merrill Lynch; Andy Komer and Bowne of Pittsburgh; Paul Lang of Bayer Corporation; Ron Livingston of Babb, Inc.; Dennis S. Meteny of Respironics, Inc.; Ronald R. Morra of Allegheny Club; George Morris of Norton Co.; Thomas H. O'Brien of PNC Bank Corp.; Ron Parkinson of J. Messner, Inc. and the Greater Pittsburgh Chevrolet Dealers Association; Jack Perkins of Mr. P's in Greensburg.

Charlie and Steve Previs of Waddell & Reed Financial Services; William J. Richardson and Herb Douglas of Schiefferlin & Somerset, Inc.; Lee Rowland and Steve Gagne of Merrill Lynch of South Hills; Patrick J. Santelli of Pfizer Labs; Jim McCarl and Robert W. Santillo of McCarl's Inc. of Beaver Falls; John T. Scalo and Jack Scalo of Burns & Scalo Roofing Co., Inc.; Stanley M. Stein of Feldstein Grinberg

Stein & McKee; Dick Swanson of P.R. Swanson Group, Ltd.; Tom Sweeney and Joe Reljac of Compucum, Inc.; Jim Roddey and Mike Fetchko of International Sports Marketing; Fred Sargent of Sargent Electric Co.; Tom Usher of USX Corporation; W. Harrison Vail of Three Rivers Bank.

This book is the handiwork of Bruce McGough and Tom Samuels of Geyer Printing, and Denise Maiden, Ed Lutz and Cathy Pawlowski of Cold-Comp Typographers. The cover design was refined and completed by Giuseppe Francioni of Prisma, Inc. This team has worked on all of my All-Pittsburgh books.

Two Pittsburgh guys, Baldy Regan and Jackie Powell, died while I was working on this book and they will be missed. They were bookends in the Steelers' press box for years, boosters at both ends of the booth, who made us all feel better. I thought of them and their smiles often while writing these stories. Two former Steelers, Ray Mansfield and Joe Zombek, also died during the same two-year span, as did two of the team's all-time fans, Joey Diven and Mossie Murphy. There are probably too many funerals in this book, but the Irish love a good wake.

All history is partial history, and all truth is the writer's truth, we're told, but we're pleased with this addition to our "Pittsburgh Proud" sports book series. I'm already at work on my next book. Thank you for your support.

Jim O'Brien

"Well, you told me to look back through my mind like it was a photo album, didn't you, yeah. I thought that was a good image. Childhood memories, memories of childhood, they are like that, it is like looking through an old photo album. You see people, groups of faces frozen a fraction of a second in time. You think to yourself, 'That's me, my parents, my brothers, but when was that, where was that? Who took it, why'd they take it, what does it mean?' "
— Studs Terkel,
A Life In Words
By Tony Parker

Memos From The Mothers

"That is a great book you came out with. I can understand why the Steelers wouldn't give it their official seal of approval. They are a business after all with their particular idea of what they want their image to be. Dare To Dream *is so full of life — good, bad, warts and all — it's probably too much for them. I've been enjoying it thoroughly — that is when I can get it back from friends and relatives I keep lending it to. Thank you for letting me contribute a small part to* Dare To Dream. *It's definitely a keeper."*

— Mary Strzelczyk,
mother of Justin Strzelczyk

"Thank you so much for your interest in our family. Dare To Dream *was such a great success in Youngstown and I must tell you that everyone loved it who was able to buy one before they sold out. Many people found them under their Christmas trees."*

— Nancy Olsavsky,
mother of Jerry Olsavsky

"It was nice to see our son, Carnell, and other family members in print and pictures. The book reminded me of many things I had forgotten about Carnell's early years. Carnell and his brother, Desmond, said that their schoolboy years in Culver City, California were the best and most memorable times of their youth. After reading Dare To Dream, *on game day when you saw the players mentioned in the book you experienced the feeling that you knew them on a personal basis.*

"Every parent wants their children to do well. I'm very grateful that Carnell is successful. Yet he still has a sense of humility."

— Elizabeth Ingrid Fields,
mother of Carnell Lake

"I'm waiting for you to write the book about what becomes of Mark and his teammates after they're done playing football, so we know what they've really achieved."

— Arlene Bruener,
mother of Mark Bruener

> *"To think about home eventually leads you to think back to your childhood home, the place where your life started, the place which off and on throughout your life you keep going back to if only in dreams and memories and which is apt to determine the rest of your life searching forever if you are not aware that you are searching."*
> — Frederick Buechner, Author
> *The Longing For Home*

Pittsburgh-born and bred writers John Wideman and Jim O'Brien were guest speakers at "Power of the Pen" seminar for high school students in the city's public schools held at Mercy Hospital in May, 1996. Wideman is a graduate of Peabody High School and O'Brien of Taylor Allderdice High School.

> *"If you don't tell your own story, no one will. Most people don't realize their dreams. It's wonderful to have people say they like your stuff. I wanted to write the books that weren't there. I wanted to write about my experiences with my family."*
> — Pittsburgh-born author John Wideman
> At "Power of the Pen" seminar for
> Pittsburgh public school students
> May, 1996

Introduction
Mothers know best

"They are somebody's children"

I was riding from Rocky Mount to Tarboro in central North Carolina. I was riding shotgun in a dark sedan driven by Minnie Thigpen, the proud mother of Yancey Thigpen, the premier receiver for the Pittsburgh Steelers during the 1995 season.

Minnie was telling me about her son, the youngest of three boys and the youngest of her six children, about her family and friends, and pointing out places on the landscape that helped shape Yancey Dirk Thigpen, which is his full name.

He may be the handsomest, if not the healthiest, of the Steelers, and like many of his teammates he's a "mama's boy." When you meet the mothers and sometimes the fathers of these professional athletes it hits home that we often overlook that these young men are, indeed, somebody's children. Yancey is a young man who merits interest and emulation because he's still a good kid, and his affection toward his family is just one reason he's so appealing.

Minnie was wearing a colorful orange, gold and brown pattern blouse and blue denim shorts, and I appreciated the fact that she kept her dark eyes on the dark country road as we headed for Tarboro because it demanded keen attention and astute driving skill. She was born August 1, 1942, three weeks before my own birthday. We had both turned 54 the month before and had many common references. It was easy for us to talk and share stories as we traveled through the night.

Tall pine trees were flattened on the ground on both sides of the road from Hurricane Fran which had swept through North Carolina and other coastal states with a vengeance a week or so earlier, giving the scene an eerie look earlier in the day when I was driving the main highway from Raleigh to Rocky Mount. A constant convoy of trucks filled the highway, carrying away the fallen timber. It was a memorable scene.

Minnie told me how to pronounce Conetoe — Co-nee-to, not Cone-toe or Con-a-to — the community where she lived just outside of Rocky Mount. When we entered Tarboro, she pointed out the Baptist church her family formerly attended, Yancey's elementary school, the railroad tracks he was told to stay away from as a child, and took me on a tour of her beauty shop, the Nu-Vision Hair Studio, a five chair set-up with posters of black women with different kinds of hairdos adorning all the walls.

She told me Yancey had been a big sports star and had graduated from Edgecombe High School in nearby Pine Tops. She said he had returned for a reunion there on May 23 of that year. There was a photo of Yancey on the wall of the beauty shop, which he had signed, "Best wishes to the NuVision Salon."

Her shop is in a small strip mall in Tarboro, next door to Hinton's Bar B Que, owned by Lonnie Hinton, whom I met during my visit.

The more Minnie Thigpen talked and told me of her son's history the more I thought I could appreciate the success story of Yancey Thigpen. She was troubled because Yancey kept getting injured and missing games, like he had during a brief stay with the San Diego Chargers, and battling one illness after another. She spent a lot of time praying on his behalf.

She was an active member of the Conetoe Chapel Missionary Baptist Church, and Yancey had her working overtime there.

"It's like a nightmare that won't end," Yancey Thigpen told people back in Pittsburgh. "I go to sleep, have a nightmare, and wake up; the next night I go to sleep and fall right back into the same nightmare."

Only the year before, Yancey had broken pass-catching records set by John Stallworth, snaring 85 passes for 1,307 yards and helping the Steelers get to Super Bowl XXX in Tempe, Arizona, where he even caught a short TD pass while eluding dandy Deion Sanders. Minnie Thigpen and her family were there to see it.

Yancey would have all kinds of physical ailments during the 1996 schedule and played in only six games, catching just 12 passes, quite a comedown from the year before.

I had been in Raleigh in late September, 1996, visiting my in-laws, Harvey and Diane Churchman, and drove across Rt. 64 East to reach Rocky Mount, about an hour's drive. Tarboro is ten miles farther east. The Tarboro River, named for its dark waters, according to Minnie, runs through it.

En route from Raleigh to Rocky Mount, I left Rt. 64 midway to go to Middlesex to see Sam Narron, a bullpen coach for the 1960 World Series champion Pittsburgh Pirates, whom I had visited several years earlier while working on a book about Bill Mazeroski and the '60 Bucs. I should have called in advance to express a desire to visit. Narron was not there. I learned from a neighbor that he was in a nursing home. He died a few months later. He was 83. I had so enjoyed my visit with him and his wife, Suzie, and they had been such a great couple and such great storytellers. Their attic, with all its baseball memorabilia, was like a wing of the Baseball Hall of Fame in Cooperstown, New York.

Minnie Thigpen was at home with two of her daughters, Valerie, 31, and Vickie, 34, when I arrived. Valerie is also a licensed beautician. I had a chance to say hello to Vickie during my visit.

Mrs. Thigpen was watching "Sports Center" on ESPN in the kitchen-TV room of her attractive but modest ranch home when I arrived that evening, September 25. She had been experiencing her own physical difficulties. She had back surgery in February and March.

13

"I have a spinal problem," she said. "All my life, always working on my feet, always standing."

There were framed photographs of Yancey and his family on the paneled walls of the multi-purpose room.

She said Yancey was not only injured, but also had been plagued with one ailment or another. She related a recent telephone conversation: "He said to me, 'Mom, I don't know what's happening to me. Every time I step onto the field, something happens to me.'

"He called me three times this past week. He was all stuffed up . . . had a cold. He was saying, 'Mom, what can I do for this cold? I'm hurting so bad.' He wanted some of the old remedies that he had as a child. He was saying, 'Mom, I just can't sleep.' He was pleading with me. I told him what kind of cold medicine to get. He called me the next morning to tell me he was feeling better."

The Steelers had played the Buffalo Bills on Monday the week before, and had a bye week when I went to Raleigh. Minnie told me one of those stories that we never normally hear about.

"Yancey called me at halftime of the game from Buffalo," she said. "At first, I was upset to get called away from the TV. When Yancey's on TV, you can be sure I'm watching."

The conversation went like this:

Yancey: "Did you see me? I was on the sideline standing next to the coach."

Mom: "Yes, I did."

Yancey: "Did I look kinda cute standing there?"

Mom: "You sure did."

Yancey: "Do I look like one of your children?"

Mom: "Yes, you do."

Yancey: "Do I look like you?"

Mom: "You certainly do."

Minnie Thigpen had to smile at her own recollection of Yancey's telephone conversation from the stadium outside Buffalo. I had to smile myself. On one occasion, when I was talking to Yancey in the Steelers' clubhouse, and asking him some questions about his mother, he pulled out a mobile phone and put me on with his mother back in Rocky Mount. Bam Morris had once linked me up with his mother in Cooper, Texas the same way.

"He's a good boy," Minnie Thigpen said. "He always has time to talk to me. All the time, he tells me, 'Mom, if you need something, please let me know.' I just hate to ask. He'll say, 'Mom, how am I going to know if you don't ask?'

"For Mother's Day, he couldn't make it home. He had always gone to church with me on Mother's Day. He wanted to make up for that. He said he was going to fly into Raleigh, and we could meet there. We got into a car and drove into Raleigh . . . he took us out to dinner, that's me and my two daughters.

"His oldest sister, Carolyn, is in Germany. Her husband is in the Marines. She'd let Yancey do anything. He couldn't beat her up, so he'd throw things at her, but she never got mad at him. He's the baby. He always has been.

"He has two older brothers, Keith, a captain in the Air Force, and Timothy, who had been in the military service but is now a police officer in Milwaukee. Yancey says Keith is my favorite, but all the kids say I favor Yancey. Kids are like that in every family. I tried to treat them all the same, but they say Yancey was my favorite.

"After Yancey's father, Edward, and I separated, Yancey was surrounded by women most of the time. We had a fire and we lost some photos in that, showing me and all the kids.

"We had it kinda rough at one point. I had such a large family to look after. I was married twice. I had five children to my first husband. Yancey was the only one by my last husband. Yancey's father is married a third time. He's from Rocky Mount, but he lives in Oak City now. I tried to keep us all together; I tried to keep them in church.

"We moved here, to this house, during the time Yancey was at Winston Salem State. He's dating a girl in Charlotte, and he's bought a house there. I went there to help him get his new house in order. At least he won't be that far away. We make the drive to Pittsburgh to see him play. It takes us about seven and a half to eight hours.

"When he played at Edgecombe High and at Winston Salem State, we went to all his games. We followed him. When he played, we were always there. Sometimes I was a little late getting there. He'd get nervous. He'd be asking, 'Where's my mom?' I'd get into the stands so Yancey could see me. He's always looking for me, even today.

"He loved all sports. And he was good at it. He liked Lynn Swann of the Steelers, and he always talked about him. It's funny how he ended up playing for the same team in Pittsburgh. We supported all his efforts. I told him, 'Don't ever forget where you come from.' I told all my kids something like that.

"I'm very fortunate. I never had any problems with any of my kids getting into any trouble. I'm glad my kids are all grown. But you miss them when you don't have them at home."

Most of the mothers I spoke to expressed thoughts like that. On May 10, 1997, on the eve of Mother's Day, I telephoned the mother of Ernie Holmes in Newton, Texas. Her son had been hospitalized in Beaumont two weeks earlier, complaining of chest pains. He was treated for severe angina. He was badly overweight and required a cane to get around.

Whereas Thigpen was a member of the Steelers of Bill Cowher's era, Holmes had been a standout defensive lineman for a brief spell with Chuck Noll's Steelers of the '70s. Holmes was hardly representative of the Steelers of that era. He had gotten into more than his share of jams with the law because of drug and alcohol problems and misbehavior.

15

Roxie Holmes talked about Ernie a lot differently than Noll, who got frustrated by Ernie's excesses, and had him traded to Tampa Bay.

"He was a good boy, never got in no trouble when he was young," said Roxie Holmes. I could hear her husband, Emerson, talking to her in the background while she was talking to me, coaching her about what to say. "Ernie was a quiet little boy. When he was growing up, he didn't have much to say.

"He was always lying down on the floor and watching the football games on TV. He said, 'One day, you're gonna be looking at me on the TV playing football.' He and his brother were playing football for two years before my husband or I knew about it. We didn't want them to play; we were afraid they were going to get hurt.

"When we discovered he was playing, he told us, 'I've been playing for two years and I haven't got hurt yet.' We agreed to let him play.

"His name was Ernest Lee, but everybody, including the state troopers, called him 'Fats' because he was a chubby boy.

"We raised hogs and cows and raised some crops here on our ranch. He just loved to eat. He might not have had a lot of clothing when he was a kid, but he always had a lot of food. Most mothers thought breakfast was a bowl of cereal. But I always cooked eggs and bacon, or eggs and steak for him. I'd cook a real breakfast for him, grits, steak gravy, and all. My kids were never hungry. He loved those big steaks.

"Ernie's feeling a little better. He has to go back to the hospital again. He's carrying too much weight. I'm scared for him, too. I hope he gets through this."

Holmes' heart problems prevented him from returning to Pittsburgh in April, 1997 for an appearance with his former linemates, Joe Greene, L.C. Greenwood and Dwight White, at Station Square on the city's South Side. I wondered whether there was any link between those steak-and-egg breakfasts of his childhood, and the severe angina that hospitalized Holmes as an adult.

In Pittsburgh, Steelers fans were worried about Thigpen's physical condition as well. Yancey had surgery on an ankle after the season. I saw him in May, walking on crutches through the Steelers offices. He improved and was able to join his teammates in workouts at Three Rivers Stadium for the team's minicamp at the outset of June. The Steelers needed him healthy and productive because the Steelers had lost Ernie Mills, thought they might lose Andre Hastings as well, and Kordell Stewart was going to concentrate on being a quarterback, so the Steelers were counting on Thigpen more than ever to regain his 1995 form.

This book is a look at some of the Steelers from two of the most exciting periods in Pittsburgh sports history, the Steelers of Chuck Noll and the Steelers of Bill Cowher. There are some striking similarities and contrasts between the individuals on both clubs.

Noll always said, "Strong mothers make for great football players."

Cowher considers his roots in Pittsburgh and his parents as a real plus in his life. "When you grow up here," he said, "there is such a strong work ethic. I was never a great athlete. I've had to work hard for everything I've accomplished. Taking pride in the little ability I had and trying to become the very best . . . that was something I was taught at an early age."

Coach Bill Cowher consoles Yancey Thigpen after pass drop.

Tiger Woods, giving his mom, Kultida, credit for his signature red shirts on Sundays:
*"Mom says it's my power color.
You've got to listen to your mother."*

Behind the scenes
Business as usual

"This is the game we have to play."
— Tom Donahoe

Friday before Super Bowl XXXI, and Dan Rooney and his oldest son, Art Rooney II, and Joe Gordon, the team's director of communications, were all in New Orleans. They were staying at the Royal Sonesta Hotel, the poshest inn on Bourbon Street. They were right in the midst of the madness that surrounds the Super Bowl.

No other Super Bowl site can compare to New Orleans, American's most European city. The Big Easy. I've covered two Super Bowls in New Orleans, and several other sports events — championship boxing and basketball — and it's the best. It's the most compact scene, everything within walking distance, great restaurants, interesting sights, great music, Royal Street, Café du Monde, The French Quarter, fresh clams and oysters on a bed of ice, Commander's Palace, Pat O'Brien's, Antoine's, jazz, gin fizz, over-priced drinks, tap dancers and musicians on street corners, exotic entertainment, in-your-face doormen and showgirls. Crescent City. The Big Hustle. And you're not far from the Mississippi River and paddlewheel boats or tourist attractions such as Jackson Square, St. Louis Chathedral, The Streetcar Named Desire.

That is definitely not Tom Donahoe's idea of an entertainment mecca. He would rather take a streetcar back in time to South Hills Catholic or to his parents' home in Mt. Lebanon, or go to mass at St. Bernard's Church, or a movie with his wife. He remembers his roots well, which is why he was happy to be in his office at the crack of dawn two days before the biggest football game in the land.

Yes, Donahoe was in his office at Three Rivers Stadium on January 24, 1997. He had been there since 7:30 in the morning, as is his custom, and now it was nearly 9 a.m. as we spoke in the media room. "I'm a morning person," he said. His office was a mess, with reports and files stacked high on every surface, which is why he didn't want to talk there, and preferred to meet in the media room. He couldn't wait to get to work, even when the boss was away.

"If you're not in the game, it's a waste of time," Donahoe said when asked why he had not gone to the Super Bowl. "I have more important things to do."

Donahoe recognized that the Steelers needed to be represented at the Super Bowl — better his boss than him — but he was busy trying to figure out how to keep the Steelers intact as best he could under the challenge of free agency and the salary cap in the National Football League, to do what he could do so the Steelers could return to the championship game. Then Donahoe would be happy to be there, sipping coffee in Jackson Square.

As director of football operations for the Steelers, it was Donahoe's job to oversee and coordinate the process.

There was only so much he could do. He knew he was going to lose more ballplayers than he could keep. That was the reality of free agency. It was certainly the reality of the Steelers' history in that regard.

"I hate this stuff," I protested.

"Hey, I don't like it, either," said Donahoe, a smile creasing his thin lips. "But this is the game we have to play. It's the system, and we have to live with it."

It's hard to write history when ballplayers come and go, when franchises come and go like the Cleveland Rams, the Cleveland Browns, the Houston Oilers, the Los Angeles Rams. I still miss the Chicago Cardinals and the St. Louis Cardinals and, most of all, the Baltimore Colts. You can't count on anything anymore. It's difficult for the fans. No team in Arizona should be called the Cardinals.

"You have to be flexible."
— Tom Donahoe

When I went to Cleveland in early February, 1997 to see the NBA All-Star Game, I stopped to check out the site by Lake Erie where Cleveland Stadium had stood. Now there was just rubble, mountains of brick, steel girders, wire and debris, a burial ground of memories. It seemed so strange. I had visited Cleveland two years earlier, three days after the townspeople learned that the Browns were leaving Cleveland in favor of Baltimore, and it was like visiting a city that had just been struck by an earthquake. I felt for those fans. It was wrong to let Art Modell move that team. The Browns belonged to Cleveland, not to any owner.

I also visited the nearby Rock 'n Roll Hall of Fame — I love that kind of nostalgia — and, to me, the highlight of the All-Star Game was seeing the "50 Greatest Basketball Players of All-Time" introduced at halftime, seeing Bill Russell reach down to assist George Mikan as he moved to the platform. The only player so honored not still living was "Pistol Pete" Maravich, whom I had met when he was a teenager. I love paying homage to old heroes, and I hate to see old ballparks leveled by wrecking balls. A new stadium and a new team would rise from the ashes in Cleveland before long, and order would be restored. A new "Mistake By The Lake" would become part of the city's skyline. And we could feel good again about telling jokes about Cleveland.

It was my third trip to Cleveland with my friends, Mike and Adam Ference, who were big fans of Michael Jordan. When I told Adam I had a clump of bricks from the wall of Forbes Field, he volunteered to climb over a fence to get me a brick from Cleveland Stadium as a souvenir. I advised him not to do that. I didn't want him or us to get arrested for trespassing.

Cleveland Stadium had once been a grand ballpark for baseball and football, but like Forbes Field, it had fallen on hard times and was badly outdated. Now some people in Pittsburgh were advocating that they tear down Three Rivers Stadium because it had outlived its usefulness. I don't buy that, and believe new ballparks won't be the panaceas to what ails sports or the general economic health of Pittsburgh. Ever since new ballparks had been built in Cleveland and Baltimore the stadium that opened in Pittsburgh for the 1970 season was no longer considered up to snuff.

Pittsburgh sports fans were threatened with the loss of the Pirates and the Steelers, and even the Penguins. Mario Lemieux said he was retiring. It was unsettling, to say the least. Owners and franchises were free agents, too. Free agency is good for football, as far as keeping it in the limelight on a year-long basis, but little else about it appeals to me. A pro football beat writer, like a volunteer fireman, is now on call 365 days a year.

People who follow the Steelers want to know their state of affairs every day of the year. A readership poll by *Sports Illustrated* indicates its readers would rather have off-season stories on football in the spring and summer than even baseball stories. Ed Bouchette of the *Post-Gazette* provides a "Steelers Report" on WTAE Radio five days a week on a year-round basis. It's unreal.

What was the game plan in Pittsburgh? What were Donahoe & Co. going to do to hold the fort, to improve the franchise and its football team? That would be a team effort, with Dan and Art Rooney, Bill Cowher and Donahoe discussing what was to be done.

"I'll sit down with Mr. Rooney, Art and Bill and talk about our team, and what we think our priorities are," Donahoe answered. "We'll have an idea of what we'd like to do, but it doesn't always work out the way you want. And you can't have a Plan B, Plan C or Plan D. The key is that you have to be flexible and patient. We have a chance to be successful at this. So far, we've been successful since the cap came into play."

Indeed, the Steelers had been to the playoffs the first five years since Donahoe and Cowher took over the team in 1992. They had a chance to win it all after the 1995 season, and it was there for the taking in 1994 and 1996. The Steelers blew golden opportunities to get to the Super Bowl both of those years. On the other hand, they got a lot farther than most teams. Maybe they just didn't have the best team. The city had been spoiled by its success in sports. The Steelers set a goal every year to get to and win the Super Bowl. So they can't blame their fans for being disappointed with anything less than the Steelers' stated goal. Fans feel a sense of loss when the team loses some of their favorite players in their prime.

> *"Decide what's right and then go ahead."*
> — Davy Crockett,
> Hero of the Alamo

21

"He wants to win."
— Tom Donahoe on
Dan Rooney

Donahoe said the league would be sending the Steelers a list of all the players available in free agency on February 15. It would be broken down by position and by team, with the telephone numbers for the players and their agents.

"We have a pro book on every team in the league and we try to make sure it's updated," Donahoe said. "We have a report on every player in the league. If we're interested in a defensive lineman, for instance, we can check to see who's available at that position and what we think of them. We share this information with the coaches, and we have the coaches look at the guys. They're always looking at films."

I mentioned to Donovan that I had just read a book called *All Madden* by John Madden and Dave Anderson, and that Madden mentioned that every team today had a front-office person who was called the "capologist" — who knew the ins and outs of working under the salary cap — someone who could crunch the numbers and work out the formulas for stocking a team and staying under the salary restrictions.

"Mr. Rooney is the capologist," said Donahoe, dryly. "He knows where everything is going."

Donahoe wasn't kidding. Anyone close to the Steelers knew that Mr. Rooney signed every check that came out of the Steelers' offices, even if it was to pay for staples and paper clips. He pulled all the significant strings in the Steelers' operation. The Rooneys have had a reputation for being cheap, but, in truth, the numbers don't substantiate that. They pay right up to the cap, even though their financial resources aren't nearly as bountiful as the Dallas Cowboys, New York Giants and San Francisco 49ers, for instance, or even some of the new NFL entries. They can be generous, they can be stingy. Rooney likes to keep a front-office staff that's lean and mean. He wants everyone to work hard, that's the idea. He was after city officials to find funding to build a new stadium for the Steelers so they could keep up with the Joneses in the NFL. Dan Rooney was, indeed, sounding more like Jerry Jones, the owner of the Dallas Cowboys, than Art Rooney, the founder of the Steelers, in his demands for what the city had to do if the Steelers were to stay in business, or stay in Pittsburgh.

While Art Rooney was regarded as one of the grand men of sports, and was universally popular, Dan had a different image. Somewhat shy and more of a dead-panned individual who retreats from most conversations, Dan Rooney deserves credit as the prime force for shaping the Steelers into one of the outstanding franchises in pro football. Before Dan took over the direction of the franchise, the Steelers floundered and fielded mostly mediocre teams. It was Dan

Rooney who hired Chuck Noll and then Cowher, and was steering the ship when the Steelers moved into Three Rivers Stadium and started operating like a major league enterprise. He lacked his father's charm and common touch, but he remained respected by his peers round the league. It was Rooney who turned to Donahoe to direct the everyday football operation, and Donahoe had done a great job.

"He's really a competitor," said Donahoe, defending his boss. "Outwardly, he might not show that. He wants to win. The business has changed, and he's changed along with it."

Then, too, Dan had suffered setbacks because of an auto accident and later an illness and surgery, and appeared frail. Was he strong enough to stay the course? How long would he remain as the head of the Steelers? He was readying his oldest son, Art II, a Pittsburgh attorney, to carry the torch. Art II was more like his father than his grandfather. He, too, would be a stern no-nonsense boss.

"We need to have good players."

The Steelers had 13 players who would become unrestricted free agents as of February 15, 1997. Everybody close to the scene had already conceded that the Steelers would not be able to sign Chad Brown, their best young defensive player, and others figured that the likes of Ray Seals, Deon Figures, Willie Williams and Jonathan Hayes would not be back. Jerome Bettis was thought to be the team's top priority as the player they could least afford to lose. No one knew what was going to happen with Rod Woodson, but the consensus was that the Steelers would ask him to take a significant cut from his $3.4 million annual salary.

Woodson was publicly bleating because the Steelers weren't in any hurry to offer him a new contract. They had paid him nearly $20 million for ten years of service. He was 32 years old now, damaged goods with a questionable knee, and the Steelers simply couldn't afford to pay him more than his current market value. They wanted Woodson, though, and they wanted him to complete his pro career in Pittsburgh. Woodson questioned the team's integrity and loyalty. These were the same Steelers who kept a roster spot open for him the entire 1995 season after he was injured in the opener so he could play in the Super Bowl. Had he forgotten that?

The players and their agents don't seem to understand that free agency works in their favor at the midpoints of the players' careers, and it can work against them at the tailend of their stay in the NFL.

"They're all critical," Donahoe said of the Steelers who were up for grabs. "We need to have good players to remain competitive, to be able to realize our goal of winning the Super Bowl. You know you can't keep them all. Good players will become available to us. We have to wait to see the fallout. The draft will be important, too. We've had good drafts the last five years and that's helped us stay competitive.

Michael F. Fabus/Pittsburgh Steelers

Tom Donahoe is flanked by Dan Rooney and Bill Cowher at summer training camp at St. Vincent College in Latrobe.

"We do it the way it's fair, the way it's right, really, in every respect, the way we have to do it to stay competitive. Bill's a great coach and you need players. Any coach will tell you that.

"There's good communication here and, while we may not always agree, we are here for the same reason. Everybody has input, a say-so. Everybody has control. I don't feel control is an issue here. Mr. Rooney runs the Steelers. Everybody is comfortable with that.

"Injuries were a big factor this season, but we can't use that as an excuse. You can't give players an out, and Bill's good at keeping the ship steered in the right direction, no matter what happens.

"We've gone after a lot of players, and some we haven't gotten. Maybe the most important thing to them has been the money, maybe we have been outbid. We have an idea in mind as to what we can pay a particular player without destroying our team. It still comes down to it's a team sport, and we feel you have to take that application to the salary cap.

"If you're going to give three or four people on the team all the money and one of these guys gets hurt, then you don't have anybody to go and replace him. Our approach has been more of let's take a team approach. The criticism may have bothered us the first year. But one thing that has been constant every year is the criticism, and the other thing that's been constant is we have a good football team."

The season had not ended on a positive note. The Steelers slipped badly in the stretch run, couldn't win on the road when it counted, and got blown away by the Patriots, a team they figured to beat.

"We're not geniuses."
— Dan Rooney

I mentioned to Donahoe that I had watched the Steelers practice at Three Rivers Stadium on the Thursday before their playoff loss at New England, and that I thought all three quarterbacks performed poorly. None of them inspired confidence. None of them completed many passes. Mike Tomczak and Jim Miller were off the mark, throwing high and wide, and Kordell Stewart kept bouncing the ball off the turf, short of his receivers. It was not encouraging. It was a prelude of what was to come in the fog at Foxboro Stadium, especially in Stewart's case. He was 0-for-10 throwing the ball against the Patriots.

"I've seen us practice and look awful and play great the next game," said Donahoe with a knowing smile. "I never know what practice means. I ask Bill how it's gone and he kinda shrugs his shoulders. Who knows?"

One day after the loss at New England in the playoffs, Donahoe told reporters, "I wish I had some answers, but I don't. I don't feel very smart today."

Dan Rooney added, when asked what happened, "We're not geniuses."

Following the Super Bowl, the St. Louis Rams called Rooney and asked if they could talk to Donahoe about filling their general manager's position. Rooney told Donahoe he could talk to one team, and that would be it.

Donahoe seemed surprised that someone was after him. "It's a compliment," he conceded. "It's also a distraction. I'm not looking to go elsewhere. They called me. I didn't call them. Why would anyone want to talk to me?"

The Rams were more than likely impressed with Donahoe for what he had accomplished at their expense during the 1996 Draft. Donahoe fleeced Jerome Bettis from the Rams in exchange for two late draft choices, and Bettis became the Steelers' MVP and one of the most productive running backs in the NFL. The Rams wanted to get rid of him, believing Nebraska bad-boy Lawrence Phillips was the answer to their prayers — why? — and the Steelers had gotten Bettis for next to nothing.   •

Donahoe had pulled off some magic in replacing departed players. The Steelers signed Kevin Greene when they lost Jerrol Williams, Mike Tomczak when they lost Bubby Brister, Ray Seals when they lost Donald Evans, Jonathan Hayes when they lost Adrian Cooper, John L. Williams when they lost Merril Hoge, Erric Pegram when they traded Barry Foster, Tom Newberry when they lost Duval Love, Norm Johnson when they lost Gary Anderson, Will Wolford when they lost Leon Searcy and Newberry, Bettis when they released Bam Morris. Donahoe had done it again and again.

Donahoe really wasn't interested in going anywhere, nothing came of the St. Louis overture, and he had not looked around to see what opportunities might exist for him elsewhere. His name had surfaced as a possible candidate for the athletic director's job at Pitt, but he insisted he had never inquired about the post, later filled by the hiring of Steve Pederson from the University of Nebraska. Donahoe firmly stated that he was happy to be where he was, working with the Steelers. "I've always been grateful to Mr. Rooney for giving me this job," he said. "I can't be critical of others for their lack of loyalty, and then jump at a job to go somewhere else. It wouldn't be me. That's not me."

His admirers believe Donahoe could command big money as a GM at another NFL franchise. People in the league have to recognize and appreciate his demonstrated ability to keep the team together in the face of injuries and free agency defections.

"If you want to define class it is Tom Donahoe," said player agent Joe Linton, who represents Jim Miller and Eric Ravotti. "He is always fair, honest and forthright. In this business, that's incredibly rare. Whatever he is worth in the open market, he is worth and then some."

On the flip side, there was also some flak — much ado about nothing as I saw it — that a rift had developed between Donahoe and Cowher in the aftermath of the defeat at New England. Donahoe had been disappointed in the Steelers' effort, and suggested they looked flat against the Patriots.

He was merely echoing what every Steelers fan felt and had already expressed. At a press conference in Pittsburgh the day after the game, a reporter repeated Donahoe's remark to Cowher to get his reaction. The coach bristled, and snapped, "Then talk to Tom about that!" Cowher was on edge to begin with, and he didn't want to hear any critical remarks from any source.

There's probably lots of tension at some of the meetings between Donahoe and Cowher and Rooney. They're all thin-skinned. Cowher, in particular, has a low boiling point. I've had an up close and personal experience in that regard, when I made the mistake of making a suggestion to Cowher on one occasion in his first year in Pittsburgh. My eyebrows were singed by the heat from Cowher's forehead. Cowher has all the answers. He doesn't accept counsel well. His assistant coaches have found him difficult, but that hardly makes him unique among head coaches in the NFL ranks or CEOs in the corporate community. Many of them are tough task masters. Cowher has done a fantastic job as coach of the Steelers, no question about that, but he should remember where he comes from, and feel blessed and lucky to have landed such a super job in his hometown where his parents can enjoy him and his handsome family. He is so popular with the Pittsburgh fans — he has no idea how much they adore him — and ought to be humbled by the regard with which they hold him. Cowher is quite the football coach, but he could be the complete package if he would lighten up a little, and respect people he deals with more consistently. In short, he could be nicer. Maybe he believes he has to project a tough exterior.

Donahoe does nothing to steal the spotlight from Cowher or his charges. Donahoe dismissed the stories that hinted at a fallout between him and Cowher.

"It's amazing how these stories get started," said Donahoe. "There is no rift. Bill and I get along fine. I say one thing, and people blow it out of proportion. I don't appreciate that. My comment was about the players not stepping up, not about Bill and his coaching staff or about the way they prepared the team for the game. They did a great job. The players play the game, not the coaches."

Cowher was just as eager to squelch the rumors of dissension in the management ranks. "We get along fine," Cowher said. "I have tremendous respect for Tom. Ours is a very professional relationship. We have mutual respect for each other."

"The problem is ego."
— Tom Donahoe

When the Steelers were seeking a coach after Chuck Noll announced he was retiring after the 1991 season, Donahoe interviewed Cowher, then the defensive coordinator of the Kansas City Chiefs; Dave Wannstedt, then defensive coordinator of the Dallas Cowboys; Mike Holmgren, then offensive coordinator of the San Francisco 49ers. All were tempting. All have done well. Holmgrem coached the Green Bay Packers to the Super Bowl XXXI championship.

After Noll retired, the Steelers also interviewed Rod Rust, the Detroit Lions' defensive coordinator; and NFL assistants such as Woody Widenhofer, Joe Greene, Dick Hoak and John Fox. They had all worked for the Steelers. Donahoe offered his impressions of the candidates to Dan Rooney, who made the final decision.

After he took over in 1992, Donahoe said, "We have a chance now for everybody to realize the No. 1 priority is the football team. If the football team isn't successful, none of us are successful, and this won't be a fun situation to be a part of. Everybody, and I do mean everybody, has a role to play. Everybody has a function, but you can't lose sight of the fact the No. 1 priority is the team.

"The problem, in my limited experience in pro football, is ego. People are sometimes hesitant to take their ego or their agenda and put it aside and say, 'This is what is best for the team.' If you don't have people who believe that and are willing to set aside their egos for the betterment of the group then you have a problem."

Cowher often echoes the same sentiments, insisting he does what is best for the team. Give him your best effort and he'll give you the best possible opportunity to succeed.

Donahoe and Cowher go back a long way. They competed against each other once upon a time on the Pittsburgh scholastic sports scene. Cowher, in his final game at Carlynton High School, returned an interception 24 yards for a touchdown and caught a pair of two-point conversion passes in a 47-7 victory over South Park on November 1, 1974. South Park was coached by Donahoe. "Cowher just killed us," recalled Donahoe. "It was scary." Cowher led Carlynton to a 7-2 record during his senior season, and South Park finished 1-5-3.

Donahoe and the Steelers staff were impressed with Cowher and Wannstedt more than any of the other candidates, and it was Rooney who made the final choice.

"The proper function of man is to live, not to exist. I shall not waste my days in trying to prolong them . . . I shall use my time."
— Jack London

28

Mike Webster
Strongest man no more

"All I did was go to work every day and do the best I could."

All seemed right in Mike Webster's world on Saturday afternoon, July 26, 1997, as he was inducted into the Pro Football Hall of Fame in nationally-televised ceremonies in Canton, Ohio.

Steelers' fans dominated the scene as they always do whenever one of their own is so honored, only 110 miles of interstate highway west of Pittsburgh.

Webster smiled when he heard the familiar chant of "Here We Go, Steelers. . .!" The fans yelled out to him by name. He squinted into the sun to see all the black and gold costumes, many of them wearing No. 52 on their authentic NFL-licensed jerseys, and the signs and banners that hailed him as "Iron Mike" and "The Iron Man" of the Steelers. Surely, some of those fans had been pumping Iron, or Iron City beer, in the parking lots around Fawcett Stadium to get into gameday form.

The Pittsburgh Brewing Company, in fact, had already signed a deal with Webster to issue a special commemorative beer can in honor of "Iron Mike" for the 1997 season. They had honored three of his former teammates, Andy Russell, Ray Mansfield and Rocky Bleier, by having their likenesses appear on Iron City cans the year before. It's not the Heisman Trophy, but in Blitzburgh it's close.

The fans in Canton were doing their best to make Webster feel like he was back at Three Rivers Stadium when the Steelers were the greatest team in the National Football League, and Webster was hailed as one of the greatest centers ever to play the game.

"I'm thrilled that Webby got in," said Steelers President Dan Rooney. "He meant so much to us as far as the things he did on the field and his leadership."

Webster was one of four enshrined that day, but his reception from the home crowd was greater than that afforded Don Shula, the winningest coach in NFL history with the Baltimore Colts and Miami Dolphins; Mike Haynes, a hard-hitting cornerback with the New England Patriots and Oakland Raiders; and Wellington Mara, owner of the New York Giants, and son of Tim Mara, the founder of the Giants and a charter member of the Hall of Fame.

Going to Canton for the Hall of Fame enshrinement ceremonies has become a rite of summer. I love to see all the greats of the game on that special weekend, and many Steelers' fans make the pilgrimage there each July no matter who is being honored. Many Hall of Famers show up each year, and it's like seeing your boyhood bubble gum card collection come to life when you see the likes of Pete Pihos, Y.A. Tittle, Arnie Weinmeister, Lenny Moore, Ray Nitschke, Marion Motley, Sam Huff, Dante Lavelli, Lou Groza, Chuck Bednarik and Otto Graham, and guys you met and got to know as a young sportswriter such as Larry Csonka, Larry Little, Bob Griese, Joe Namath, Gale Sayers and Dan Dierdorf and so many legendary Steelers such as Ernie Stautner, "Bullet Bill" Dudley and John Henry Johnson. It's great to rub shoulders with those outstanding individuals at different social events. When I go to Canton, I feel like a kid again.

Jack Lambert looked at it that way, too. He loved seeing the old uniforms and those flap-eared leather helmets, going there often during his youth from nearby Mantua, Ohio. Webster didn't share our enthusiasm in that respect, but said he was glad to be honored. He just never saw himself as important enough to have his bronze bust in the same building as Vince Lombardi, the coach of his favorite football team, the Green Bay Packers, during his youth in Wisconsin.

Webster starred at center for the Steelers of the '70s, and was a pivotal member of the fierce offensive line — they with the bare biceps — that intimidated other teams and won four Super Bowl titles. He was with the Steelers from 1974, their first Super Bowl year, to 1988, and finished his career in Kansas City with two seasons with the Chiefs.

He put in more seasons (15) and played more games (220) than any player in Steelers' history. He was known for dashing out of the huddle to get things going.

"I'm just excited," he explained back then. "I can't wait for the play to start. I'm like that all day before a game. The alarm rings in the morning and I sprint to the breakfast table."

Webster called out signals for the offensive linemen and spearheaded the offense as much as Terry Bradshaw. Altogether, he missed only four games in a 17-season career and his 177 consecutive games played (until an extended elbow sidelined him) is second in the Steelers' record books only to his predecessor and mentor, Ray Mansfield, who played in 182 straight games. Webster, Lambert and Joe Greene may have personified the Steelers of that era more than anyone else.

Webster was joining a distinguished list of former teammates who had already been inducted into the Pro Football Hall of Fame, namely Greene, Lambert, Bradshaw, Mel Blount, Jack Ham and Franco Harris. That makes seven Steelers from the '70s who have been so honored, plus their coach Chuck Noll. Webster had remained in pro football longer than anyone else on those four Super Bowl teams. Art Rooney Sr., the Steelers' late owner, also is in the Hall. Still standing in the wings awaiting the necessary number of votes for induction were Lynn Swann, L.C. Greenwood and John Stallworth, and some felt that Donnie Shell and Andy Russell from that era merited consideration as well.

Jim O'Brien

MIKE WEBSTER
Hall of Fame Class of '97

31

"I was surrounded by great athletes," said Webster. "All I did was go to work every day and do the best I could."

"I'm not sure I'm a Hall of Famer. I was there everyday and did everything I could to be as good as I could be.

"This is more a reflection of what happened in the '70s. It's beyond what you could hope to experience. It's an all-consuming award for the organization and the fans."

Bradshaw was picked by Webster to present him at the Hall of Fame induction ceremonies, which guaranteed greater TV exposure since Bradshaw was one of the stars of the Fox Sports team. By contrast, Shula had his two sons introduce him. "If Terry's there, I won't have to say much," Webster said in advance of the big day. Nobody plays to a crowd better than Bradshaw and he said the same sort of things about Webster that have drawn laughs before. During his stay in Canton, Terry told the people what a thrill it was to stick his hands under Webster's backside on every offensive play. Bradshaw swears that Webster had the perfectly shaped posterior, and that it warmed his hands on those cold winter days in Pittsburgh, Cleveland, Cincinnati and other NFL outposts. Of course, Bradshaw once said the same things about Mansfield. So it was fun in the sun for Webster. His wife, Pamela, and their family and friends were seated in a reserved section in front of the steps of the Hall of Fame, and his loyal and boisterous fans filled the hillside in the natural bowl setting at George Halas Drive. All appeared to be in place, so it seemed anyhow.

"I was never good-looking."
— Mike Webster

When Webster learned of his selection to the Hall of Fame, he was in Pittsburgh, staying at the Holiday Inn in Green Tree. His former teammate and good friend, Tunch Ilkin, was picking up the tab for Webster's stay in Pittsburgh.

Ilkin, of course, did not tell me that. Ilkin was reluctant to even discuss Webster's personal situation at all, which was true of most of Webster's former teammates and insiders with the Steelers. Earlier, the Steelers had picked up a $6,000 tab for Webster during a lengthy stay at the Hilton Hotel in downtown Pittsburgh. Webster had not left the team on the best terms — he had regrettably said some critical things about Noll and Rooney when he departed Pittsburgh in a huff — yet the Steelers still tried to help him. He later stayed at the Red Roof Inn.

The Steelers, sad to say, had gotten phone calls from officials at Amtrak saying that Webster was hanging around and even sleeping in the waiting room of their railroad depot in Downtown Pittsburgh. "I slept in a car for a year and a half," admitted Webster. "Yeah, I spent some time at the railroad station, too."

Ilkin and the Steelers were picking up the tab for Webster because he was virtually broke. It was difficult to comprehend. Why was he so down and out? Six years earlier, he was making $350,000 a year with the Chiefs. He made over $100,000 a year most seasons in the second half of his 15 seasons with the Steelers. Most of it was gone. He went broke. He lost his home. He sold his four Super Bowl rings. The Steelers were lining up Webster for paid appearances after his Hall of Fame selection, trying to help him make a comeback.

Webster was suing his former agent, Greg Lusteg, and investment counselors who had gotten him (and other former Steelers) into limited partnerships that went bust. Webster had lost his money in a series of bad investments, some as esoteric and ill-conceived as worm farms. Webster was hardly unique for losing money on limited partnerships — the great tax-saving investment of the '70s — but worm farms? He and his wife had separated, but he would visit his family often in Wisconsin, sleeping in the basement, and then take a train back to Pittsburgh where he was scuffling to put together some business ventures. He and Ilkin were looking into teaming up on some sports marketing efforts. Webster talked about a desire to create and sell some sports plaques, autographed prints and memorabilia. He mentioned big names like Kodak, Muhammad Ali, Dan Marino, Art Rooney, et al, in the same breath, but whether he had the contracts to deliver on same seemed vague. Too many people were already attempting to mine that field, and Webster had not shown he had the business savvy to make something like that succeed.

His health was also suspect. The word on the street was that he was ill. He didn't look good. He had lost a lot of weight, his ruddy complexion appeared withered and paler than one remembered. "I was never good-looking to begin with," Webster said. He had been to Allegheny General Hospital for check-ups and treatment. Rumors were making the rounds that he was having some physical problems associated with anabolic steroids he had taken — before their damaging side effects were known and before their use was banned by league officials — during his manic body-building developmental days with the Steelers. He was being treated by Dr. Jerry Carter, a psychiatrist at Allegheny General Hospital. Webster said he was waking up at night with convulsions and spasms. He had blackouts, and what Webster called "small heart attacks." Dr. Carter said Webster suffered from depression, which Webster blamed on abuse in his childhood. He denied that he had any serious health problems.

One of his former teammates and fellow weight-lifters, Steve Courson, had crusaded against the ill effects of steroids which he blamed for heart problems that had threatened his life. Courson was a candidate for heart transplant surgery at one point, but managed to miraculously correct his health problems with medicine, rigid diet and training regimen. Courson was suing the NFL for looking the other way, insisting the Steelers had been among those who ignored the players taking pills and drugs to enhance their performance.

Webster cursed those who were saying steroids were at the root of his distress, and felt this rumor is what kept him from being voted into the Pro Football Hall of Fame a year earlier, when he first became eligible five years after his playing career was completed. He insisted he never used steroids. Webster had been thought to be a shoo-in by most NFL observers. Coaches can be elected within a year of their retirement, as Shula and Noll were.

The Hall of Fame might have been a life raft for Webster. He needed to set sail on a new life. Shula and his wife were millionaires in their own right; so was Mara. Haynes had a job. Webster was in worse shape, in every respect, than everyone else in the Class of 1997.

Ilkin was in the crowd at Canton. A congenial man, Ilkin was doing well as an analyst on WPXI-TV's Steelers coverage and in a suburban construction business, and had settled in with his family in Upper St. Clair. Ilkin is a good man, a devout Christian who practiced what he preached, and he wanted to help an old friend. Ilkin came to the Steelers in 1980 and stayed till 1992, and missed the best days of both Noll and Bill Cowher. Ilkin was one of Webster's proteges, and he genuinely loved the man. "He was the hardest-working guy that I've ever played with," Ilkin said of Webster. "He outworked everybody. He had such a resolve and played hurt. He was just the best."

Soon after he retired from football, Ilkin had attempted to start a sports promotion and marketing business with another former teammate and offensive lineman, Craig Wolfley, but it didn't pan out. Wolfley's wife, Beth, walked out on him when he was struggling to get his post-football career together. This stunned their best friends. They appeared to be a well-matched Christian-committed couple.

According to Wolfley, who was citing statistics he said he read in a report from the NFL Players Alumni Association, 75 percent of NFL marriages fail these days, most of them coming apart in the post-football period. "There's a reason for it," said Wolfley. "Few couples are prepared for the change."

Wolfley was as reluctant as Ilkin, understandably, to discuss Webster's situation. Like Ilkin, he did not want to betray or embarrass a buddy. It was the way most Steelers of that era, and front-office officials of the Steelers, clam up when anyone asks about Webster or Sam Davis, a great guard on those Steelers' Super Bowl teams who lined up next to Webster. Davis was beaten to a pulp in his Gibsonia home in early September of 1991 for failure to pay off a business loan from the wrong guys, and had spent recent years in a personal care home in McKeesport. Teammates think he was beaten with a baseball bat, or some such instrument, and kicked senseless. It was whitewashed in local media reports that Davis had suffered head injuries in a fall down a stairway at his farmhouse.

While many former Steelers have been quite successful since leaving the game — people point with pride to Andy Russell, Mike Wagner, Dwight White, John Stallworth, Randy Grossman, et al — there are still some worrisome situations that give anyone who cares

Bill Amatucci

George Gojkovich

ebster sets the pace for "gassers", showing the ay for (left to right) Pete Rostosky, Craig Wolfley, ary Dunn and Terry Long at St. Vincent.

"Iron Man" behind the mask

George Gojkovich

Webster with Gerry Mullins, Rocky Bleier and Franco Harris after Franco scored TD vs. Bengals in 1978.

George Gojkovich

George Gojkovich

With Terry Bradshaw

Fending off Browns' Dave Puzzuoli

"You owe it to God, Mom and Dad."
— Mike Webster

about these guys pause for thought. Mike Webster should be doing better. There isn't a dishonest bone in his body. He was never accused of being a slacker. You gotta like this guy. He has no guile. And he gave all he had to give. But he seemed lost and disoriented without football, without the demands and structure football offered and demanded. His life's work was football, it's that simple.

When Webster was at his peak in Pittsburgh, a young lineman like Wolfley positively worshiped the ground on which he worked. "He was everything and what you would want to be," said Wolfley. "He was someone you idolized in a pure and good sense of the word. He set the standard for all Steelers. Every offensive lineman wanted to grow up to be Mike Webster."

Wolfley was divorced in 1994 from his first wife, Beth, a few years after his playing days were over. They shared custody of their children, Megan, 13, and Kyle, 11, both elementary school students in Upper St. Clair. Beth lived in neighboring Peters Township. Wolfley married Faith Lamb on November 8, 1996, and they operated the Martial Arts & Sports Complex in Bridgeville.

Other former Steelers who asked not to be identified offered a few reflections on Webster: "Appearances may be deceiving," they said of the family scene at Canton, "but they are better than reality."

"Mike has been tight-lipped about his situation," said another. "You can't get a straight answer. Those guys who see him as such an ironman don't want to think that he's not doing so well these days.

"You don't want to know there are clay feet there. You don't want to know. His own humanness and mortality brings it even closer to us."

Webster learned of his selection to the Hall of Fame on the eve of Super Bowl XXXI. Members of the media panel who pick the players for induction meet each year at the Super Bowl site, which was New Orleans this time. Many felt Webster should have been picked the year before when the Steelers were playing in Super Bowl XXX at Tempe, Arizona.

"It would be awful selfish to think I've done that on my own," Webster said when he learned of his selection. "First of all, I wasn't really a good athlete by professional standards. Second, my talent was God-given. He put me in this situation — to be able to play with great players on a great team."

The players so honored are first introduced as a group at halftime of the Pro Bowl in Honolulu, Hawaii. Mara missed that party, but Webster posed for photos with Haynes and Shula, with red leis around their necks.

Webster said he was sorry Ray Mansfield would miss his induction into the Hall of Fame. He and Mansfield had shared the position when Webster first joined the Steelers in 1974. Mansfield confessed that he had problems withdrawing from football, and missed the limelight. Mansfield had died at age 55 in November, 1996. "It's sad," said Webster. "I haven't dealt with what happened to Ray yet. He was a tough, tough football player."

36

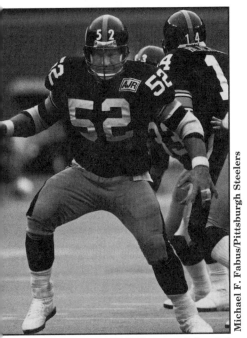

Mike Webster wears "AJR" memorial patch after Arthur J. Rooney died in 1988.

Mike Wagner, Sam Davis and Webster at Steelers' reunion at Melody Tent at Station Square in summer of 1990.

Webster, with left arm in sling, mixes with former teammates Larry Brown and Sam Davis at a Steelers' social gathering in 1990.

Webster was also named to John Madden's All-Time Super Bowl team that weekend of Super Bowl XXXI. No one liked tough, tough football players more than Madden. They didn't come any tougher than the kid from Tomahawk, Wisconsin.

As a youngster, Webster had admired the tough guys in pro football, such as Packers center Jim Ringo and linebacker Ray Nitschke, Bears end Mike Ditka and linebacker Dick Butkus.

Webster was joined by former teammates Stallworth, Swann, Blount, Ham, Lambert and Greene and by Joe Namath of Beaver Falls on the team selected by Madden, who was the analyst to Pat Summerall for the Super Bowl XXXI telecast.

"Baseball was holding me."
— Steve Blass

On the surface, Webster seemed to have so much going for him. He had made some bad decisions, though, and was no longer employed by any pro team, and had lost most of his money in business ventures gone sour. "Pro football players tend to think everyone wants to help them get rich," said Ilkin. In early July, 1997, just weeks before his Hall of Fame induction, ESPN revealed Webster's financial and family problems.

Webster always expressed great pride in his family and his Christian beliefs as a ballplayer, so one had to wonder what had gone wrong in his life. Nobody seemed more well-grounded as a ballplayer and he had never blown money on clothes, cars or appearances. Webster always looked like a farmer. He was football smart, but life dumb. When he was playing with the Steelers, Webster lived in McMurray, a suburb about 12 miles south of Pittsburgh. His home was the only one in the community with a blocking sled in the yard next to the swing set. Webster never stopped working at his game. It consumed him. It was his life. In truth, it was his wife.

He was the first player to report back to work at Three Rivers Stadium after the players' strike in 1982. I remember him passing Joe Gordon and me in a hallway at Three Rivers, telling us, "Got to get back to work." He sued the Steelers for failing to pay him what he thought was due him in salary that season. When players went on strike in 1987, Webster crossed picket lines, and took a lot of heat from veteran teammates. I remember seeing him after games where his knees hurt so much he had great difficulty moving around the clubhouse. I thought he was on his way to becoming another Jim Otto, the former Raiders Hall of Fame center, who had to get artificial knees in order to be mobile again. Webster held the football in his hand to start every play, but in a sense the football held him. Steve Blass, a former Pirates pitcher who lived in Upper St. Clair, recognized that he was obsessed by his sport. "I thought I was holding the baseball, but the baseball was holding me," said Blass.

Some insight was offered in *From The Dark Side Of The Game,* an insider's book by Tim Green, a former ballplayer with the Atlanta Falcons and at Syracuse University who had served as an analyst for Fox Sports:

"It comes down to a total lack of sophistication," wrote Green in his behind-the-scenes book that was published in 1996. "Most NFL players don't have advanced educations in law or finance, and they don't have the business experience to survive in the world outside football. They think that because they are big and tough, that no one would dare to rip them off. They don't know that the real world can be more cruel and more treacherous than even the football field. The adage is true more times than not: A football player and his money are soon parted."

During the family's stay in McMurray, Webster seemed to know what he wanted for his family. When his kids were pre-schoolers, he used to take them to a farm nearby.

"They feed carrots to the horses and feed the chickens," Webster said. "I'd like to buy some acreage, and get some animals. We had pigs. We used to ride them around the yard, and have a lot of fun."

He expressed a desire to get a farm of his own, like two of his teammates, Jon Kolb and Tom Beasley, who had spreads in Washington County.

Webster seemed best-suited to be making his living in football or farming. He could always get others to work hard.

"Habits," said Kolb, now an assistant football coach at Grove City College, explaining why Webster succeeded in pro football. "I used to tell players that the only time you have to be working is when Mike's working; which means you work all the time."

Football players respected Webster's zest and know-how. His football credentials were impeccable. Along the way, however, he had waffled on invitations to be an assistant coach in Pittsburgh, Green Bay, Cincinnati and had gone to Kansas City, in the first place, to serve as assistant coach to Marty Schottenheimer. He ended up playing instead simply because he was better than any centers in the Chiefs' training camp.

Webster had gone on record saying he didn't like the way they were playing pro football these days. Like Lambert, he hated wholesale situational substitutions. He stated publicly that he couldn't coach in modern day football. Ouch!

"My father was the reincarnation of Vince Lombardi."

I had a lengthy interview with Webster when he made a rare visit to the Steelers' offices late in the 1996 season. We sat down in Art Rooney's old office on opposite sides of The Chief's old desk.

39

"I used to look in here a lot to say hello to Mr. Rooney," Webster said. "I didn't stay long; I didn't want to overstay my welcome.

"When I first got here, Mr. Rooney was coming down the hallway for lunch. I got nervous talking to him; I waved my hands. I knocked coffee all over him. I thought I was gone."

Webster looked around the room, where there were photos on display from when Art Rooney held court there, pictures of pro football icons like Lombardi, Halas and Bert Bell. And team photos from nearly all the Steelers' seasons.

"This is only the second time I've been in here (the Steelers' offices) since I left the team," Webster said. "Last Friday was the first time."

He was looking for help from the Rooneys.

Art Rooney remarked at the team's 50 Seasons Celebration at the David L. Lawrence Convention Center in 1983 that, "I never had a player I didn't like. I never had a player I didn't think was a star."

Webster had worked in that environment. There was a photo on the nearby wall of all the former Steelers who attended that dinner. All wore black or dark business suits save for Webster, who wore a tan suede jacket with matching corduroy slacks and cowboy boots.

"I sure stick out; I didn't know we were supposed to wear black," Webster apologized once again. "No one told me to wear black. Every time I see that picture . . . those cowboy boots, I say, 'That's the idiot.' What a hick."

Webster was wearing a light green and white jersey, an off-white cowboy hat and a chagrined smile as he said this.

Webster knew Art Rooney Sr. was special and missed his presence. He missed football the way it was when he was playing for the Steelers when they were winning Super Bowls.

"I'm a helpless romantic," Webster said. "When they tear down Cleveland Stadium, I'll be heart-broken. As bad as that place was — like an indoor cattle facility — some powerful ghosts are in there. I left some skin and blood on that ballfield. Those locker rooms were awful, but you felt like you were playing football. If they ever tear this place down, I'll feel the same way.

"I loved to play at Lambeau Field in Green Bay. I grew up idolizing the Packers and Lombardi. You always felt he was there. My father was the reincarnation of Vince Lombardi. He wanted to be just like him.

"My father was very intolerant. But he could motivate us. He loved the Packers and Vince. My dad felt that type of discipline was essential for the development of character. That was Lombardi's trademark. His charm. I would love to hear him speak today. He was so charismatic.

"As a kid, I never went to see the Packers play. We couldn't afford it. In 1961 (December 31), when I was 9, I listened to the NFL championship game on the radio. The Packers clobbered the Giants, 37-0. My dad and his brothers were all there listening to it on the radio."

The year before, the Packers lost to Norm Van Brocklin and Tommy McDonald and the Philadelphia Eagles in the 1960 championship.

Thinking about those days, reminded Webster of his youth on the farm in Wisconsin.

"We had a crop farm, and hogs and beef cattle," Webster said. "We had plenty to do. My dad frequently worked 18 to 20 hours a day, getting fields ready for planting.

"My older brother and I did a lot of work. I rode on tractors at age 7. You'd start talking to yourself because you didn't always want to be working. You had to do it. Back then, no one talked about child abuse. You'd get a boot in the ass or a strap if you got out of line. I didn't do the same things with my kids."

What Webster was saying didn't sound right to me. I had met his father, Bill Webster, back in 1981 when he came to Pittsburgh to spend a week with his son and his family. I was reporting on the Steelers at the time for *The Pittsburgh Press.* I checked my files and found the clipping I had written about their reunion. Webster had a rosier view of his upbringing back then than he does now.

There was a paragraph that went like this:

"I remember during the summer we'd get up at 7 in the morning and, when I was 7 years old, I got to drive the tractor. Plowing the field was a real thrill to us. I think a farm is the only place to raise kids."

Quite a contrasting reflection, huh? Wonder what the real story is. Was Webster telling the truth in 1981 or was he telling the truth in 1997? What happened in the interim that changed Webster's story?

We're back in Art Rooney's old office in 1997, and our most recent interview:

"If my dad could have lived his life all over again, he would have been a football coach," Webster was saying. "When I was growing up, he was the kind of guy like Vince Lombardi, a real butt-kicker. He was a tough disciplinarian, and he taught me good values, and how to be mentally tough. He was affectionate, but strong and tough, too."

Most successful people were ones who were able to experience positive things in their childhood. Those subjected to trauma or abuse seem to carry scars. There are exceptions.

"But I wouldn't trade those days for anything," Webster said. "My dad taught us how to work. . ."

Back in 1981, Webster had said, "It was always a struggle. There were five of us kids and my dad sometimes worked two jobs. He'd have a night job to make some extra money. But he never complained. We always had something to eat and clothes on our back ."

Back then, his father felt he had made a bad choice in trying to make a living on that 640-acre potato farm. "It was the biggest mistake of my life," Bill Webster said. "When we'd have a good crop, so did everyone else and the price would be down. But we never had a crop failure."

He said it with the same sort of pride that motivated his son to excel on the football field. At heart, Webster was a potato farmer forever.

"I didn't play to be a legend or a hero."
— Mike Webster

Being in Art Rooney's office reminded Webster of the way it used to be, and the way it was different today. Even in his day, Webster was a throwback to an earlier era. In practice, for example, he wouldn't take water, no matter how hot it was.

"There are different types of training today," he said. "These guys are already bigger and quicker. We had a great weight program. We had a lot of maturity. It was a joke. We built up the image of it, the strongboys, the bare biceps business. We bared our biceps, in truth, so defensive linemen couldn't grab our jerseys so easy. Then they had those 'strongest man' contests."

And Webster won such contests, and so did Jon Kolb from that same club. Webster was asked what drove him to do it.

"To keep from failing, more than anything else," he answered. "There were lots of other reasons I was so driven, but that's kind of personal.

"There was definitely a fear of embarrassment. Everything we did was on film. Everything you did, others judged. You did all this to prepare to be successful. I didn't want to miss any games; it was great to go to work.

"I don't feel that way about football anymore. I have no desire to be involved. I don't even watch football."

To hear Webster, it sounds like he should have stayed with the Steelers. It was never as good elsewhere. "I should not have gone to Kansas City," he said. "It was definitely a mistake. I got caught up in making big money. I had been on the greatest team you could ever have. It would have been the final impression of me as a player.

"Mr. Rooney and winning Super Bowls, that's what was special about playing for the Steelers. I wouldn't trade that for zillions of dollars. Today, I wouldn't give you two cents for the way they play. How can you get into the rhythm of the game if you play two of eight plays? You're not a football player anymore. You just do everything as you're told. Coaches have so much control now. I don't like the West Coast offense. It's a piece of crap."

That's not the way it was with the Steelers of the '70s. "I have to go into the locker room here to feel the ghosts," Webster went on. "Chuck (Noll) was so disciplined. He was so focused. I see him now and I can't believe it. He's gotten 15 years younger since he retired. He looks like a young man. You had respect for him. You listened.

You have to work for a guy like that. He demands it and you want to anyhow."

Webster wasn't easy to understand when I spoke to him about the split in his family, and how he and Pamela had parted ways. They seemed to have a lot in common. During their days in Pittsburgh, Pamela called herself "just a housewife and a mother and I really enjoy it." She said their move from Pittsburgh was stressful for the family. Why didn't she get a job when times got tough? Webster's thoughts were somewhat disjointed. He rambled on, trying to sort it out, trying to make sense of it all. His commentary was confusing.

"People change," Webster said. "It was very traumatic. Now there are questions about who dad is? Where's our home now? I'm not going anywhere. What am I doing in Weirton? I have a friend there. I'm trying to get something going. I'd like some security. I want to be working for someone. You can't go back. There's just been a lot of changes. I spend a lot of time talking to people, trying to get something going. It's still traumatic. I missed 22 years in there somewhere.

"My kids are in Wisconsin. My wife and I get along great. She's a wonderful lady. I live in the basement when I visit. I want to be there for my kids. I see them whenever I can. Right now, I just want to be home. This is past and future business here. I don't like to be looked at. I didn't play to be a legend or a hero. I stayed too long. I played too long. . .

"My life is taking a turn. There are a lot of things I want to succeed at. I was never afraid to work. I'll straighten this out."

"I enjoyed the challenge."
— Mike Webster

Seeing photos from his past in the Rooney office may have prompted some stream-of-conscious thinking:

"I remember how great it was to work out with guys who were similarly motivated, who wanted to improve themselves, who wanted to get stronger, who wanted to succeed, who wanted the Steelers to be something special," said Webster, surveying the scene. "We used to get together a few days a week to lift weights. I miss that. I loved to do that.

"We had Steve Furness, Larry Brown, Ted Petersen, Jon Kolb, Steve Courson and Jim Clack. Craig Wolfley and Tunch Ilkin came along later. We worked out together at Washington & Jefferson College, and then at the Red Bull Inn in Washington, Pa. Lou Caringa, an avid weight-lifter, owned The Red Bull, and had a gym in the basement. The players ate at the restaurant as well.

"Lou and Jon were more dedicated and tougher than I was and more stubborn to a fault," Webster said. "We challenged each other.

43

I enjoyed the challenge. That's why I used to run the steps at Three Rivers Stadium."

Webster skipped around in his reminiscences. Often his thoughts would take him back to the farm. He was like one of those shiny steel balls in a pinball machine, bouncing here, there and everywhere, lights flashing, bells ringing.

"My mom's name was Betty and my dad was Bill. I had two brothers and two sisters. People had lots of kids in those days to work the farm. That's the way my dad grew up. My parents split up. My dad was married and divorced three times. It was a stormy situation. It was an alcoholic-dominated environment. Us kids were always shuffling around in rural northern Wisconsin. There were a lot of problems. After my parents split up, my two sisters lived with my mother, and my two brothers and I lived with my dad. It was a difficult childhood."

He spoke of attempts to kiss and make up with the Steelers after he went to Kansas City, but said he was unsuccessful.

"I wrote to Chuck (Noll), but he never responded. I had a proposal for him, an idea for a video tape production. It was pretty traumatic at the time not to hear back from him. Maybe he's still pissed at me for going to Kansas City."

Just as Mansfield knew that Webster was going to move him out, Webster recognized that Dermontti Dawson would be a better center than guard, where he was originally slotted with the Steelers.

"I'm the one who said, 'Put Dermontti at center. He can hold his own,'" Webster said. "He's a big Dwight Stephenson."

Webster was with the Steelers when they played the Hall of Fame game to begin the pre-season schedule in 1983. They defeated the New Orleans Saints that day. So he had seen the Pro Football Hall of Fame.

"I have no desire to go there," Webster said, not knowing he was going to be selected for the next class. "I walked through the building quickly, I remember. I'm not into that. I'm not worrying about whether or not I'll be elected. I'm already in there. There are photos of the Steelers of the '70s, the four championship teams. I don't need a bust of myself.

"I'm not the only former Steeler who should be in there. L.C. Greenwood should be in there, and so should some others I played with. Maybe you can't have too many Steelers. Al Davis is in there; it's funny who gets in and who doesn't.

"There's got to be something more important in your life than running helmets into each other. The ultimate joy is the people working together and doing something successfully with other people.

"There's only one Hall of Fame I want to be in. That's the Kingdom of Heaven. I'm not really interested in getting recognition in the secular world.

"It was enough for me to be looked upon as being dependable when I played here."

Webster squirmed in his seat, changed the position of his legs and made a face. "Can't sit too long," he said.

"I have good days and bad days. My knees hurt most all the time. My problem is calcium buildup, arthritis. My feet, they're totally ruined. My elbow. I've got big bones, cow joints.

"About 6-2, 265 pounds was the biggest I was. Today they wouldn't even look at me. Lot of teams play 6-5, 6-6 offensive linemen now. And everybody weighs 300 pounds. In some ways, that's a mistake. They don't move. They don't really block. What's allowed now doesn't require any technique. A lot of teams just get the biggest guys they can possibly get.

"I was always dependable. I always showed up and I never quit. I just kept going until the end. Just keep at it until you can't go no more. Physical collapse is your only excuse. I was never satisfied. I've never been satisfied with myself.

"Chuck Noll . . . he never offered many compliments. To him it might have been a compliment, but I didn't recognize it as such. The biggest compliment he paid me was keeping me that long.

"Noll never gave anyone that personal attention. Terry needed that. I'll tell you why Terry was so good. He had the ability to make the big play in the big games. In the third Super Bowl, Dallas covered our guys real close and Terry just threw the ball by them.

"In Kansas City, they always wanted me to tell stories about the Steelers."

Webster announced that he was retiring from the Steelers several times, and then changed his mind.

Back then he said, "I could never put on any jersey but a Steelers jersey. My special feelings for Pittsburgh will always be there."

He should have listened to himself. He never was that comfortable in Kansas City. "He had a hard time out there," Ray Mansfield said during Webster's stay in Kansas City. "He's not happy. He misses that era when he played with great teams."

Webster played in nine Pro Bowls, more than any other offensive lineman in NFL history. Through the years, Webster offered some thoughts about his approach to playing football and to life.

Webster's work ethic — report early, leave late, play hurt — is the major reason he earned the name "Iron Mike" and a reputation as one of the hardest-working guys in the game.

"No matter what you're up against, the No. 1 ingredient to life is that you continue to fight with everything you have. You have to fight the word 'can't.' You have to fight the word 'failure.' You can never give in to that. I'm on the way up, on the way back up. All I have to do is finish the game. As John Wayne said, 'I'll finish up, maybe not standing up.'

"I didn't do everything right. But I always tried to do everything the best I know how. I liked our approach to football in Pittsburgh. If you go back and check the tally board, the guys who ended up winning the most ran the football and played great defense,"

45

Webster watched John Wayne movies and memorized some of his lines. He'd say things like, "You owe it to God, Mom and Dad."

The family farm was actually in Harshaw, an old logging town with a population of 39 people, about 17 miles from Tomahawk.

"I grew up on a potato farm, lifting sacks of potatoes — hundreds of them — after school. We went to school and worked the farm before and after school. There wasn't much time for recreation and games or cartoons on TV. We were happy to just play a game of baseball on Sunday. Kids don't do that anymore. Once in a while we played a pick-up football game, three or four to a side.

"I was a running back, quarterback and wide receiver back when we played in the hayfields of northern Wisconsin. If you asked me back then, I would have said I had a heckuva lot better chance to become a farmer than a Super Bowler.

"My dad kept me working so hard that I wasn't able to play football until my junior year in high school."

At Rhinelander High School, Webster played football, wrestled, threw the shot and discus. In his senior year, he started lifting weights. The football season ended in mid-October. There was too much snow after that to play.

"If we didn't have the crops out on the first of October, we'd lose them to frost," Webster said. "And usually the ice doesn't come off the lakes until the first of May."

From there, he went to Wisconsin where he was a three-year starter and all-Big Ten as a senior. The computer rejected him as a high draft choice. The Steelers selected him on the fifth round in 1974. Pamela grew up in Lodi, a small resort community near Madison. Pamela worked in the athletic department at the University of Wisconsin, which is where she met Mike.

"There is more pressure and emotion involved in our family than in a normal family," she said when the Websters were living in suburban Pittsburgh. "When that happens, you have to give more of yourself to make the situation normal. We're quiet and stay home a lot. Everything we do is centered around the family."

Being the wife of a well-known professional football player had no special charm for Pamela Webster. Her thoughts might help explain why Pamela parted with Mike, when she filed for divorce in 1996. "We were broke," she said. "There were times I didn't have money for toilet tissue."

The Websters tried to distance themselves from the limelight in their Pittsburgh days. They both expressed a Christian attitude toward life and football, and Pamela promoted Mike as a terrific father and man.

"It might have been better if I had born a century ago," she said. "Sometimes, I don't feel ready for this day and age. I can see myself having a log house, a big horse farm and living outdoors most of the time.

"It would have been fun to be born in the horse and buggy days because it was a romantic, practical and very enjoyable era. I just can't see the glamour in this world of pro football."

Jim O'Brien

Mike Webster checks out photo of his idol, Vince Lombardi, on the Wall of Fame in Art Rooney's old office. Also pictured are NFL commissioners Paul Tagliabue and Pete Rozelle, and late NFL owners George Halas and George Preston Marshall.

"The difference between men is in energy, the strong will in the singleness of purpose and an invincible determination. But the greatest difference is in sacrifice, in self denial, in love and loyalty, in the fearless verve and humility and in the pursuit of excellence and in the perfect will, because this is not only the difference in men. This is the difference between great men and little men."
— Vince Lombardi

At the Hall of Fame

photos by Jim O'Brien

Penn State's greatest running backs, Lenny Moore and Franco Harris, share warm moments at Canton shrine on October 11, 1995.

Joe Namath, the pride of Beaver Falls, holds court with Pro Football Hall of Famers (left to right) Lenny Moore, Chuck Bednarik and Gale Sayers.

Former fullback foes, Larry Csonka and Franco Harris, have some laughs at Pro Football Hall of Fame ceremonies to mark opening of expanded facility.

Hall of Famer Lou "The Toe" Groza, the great Browns' lineman and place-kicker, poses with Bill Priatko of NFL Alumni Association at ceremonies on October 11, 1995 to mark expansion of the building on George Halas Drive.

Bill Cowher
Always looking ahead

"There will be adversity.
That's what life is all about."

Shortly before Bill Cowher came to work on a cool, rather dank Wednesday morning, April 23, 1997, the lobby of the Steelers' office complex at Three Rivers Stadium began to fill up with about twentysome young football players who were chasing a dream.

They were free agents, players who had not been selected in the NFL college draft the previous weekend. None of them caught the eye, or were particularly impressive looking. They were there for an orientation session, some to sign basic player contracts.

This was a time of the year when schoolchildren and their parents and teachers visit the Steelers' complex each day on spring field trips and, at first, some of these guys looked like they might have been leaders on a field trip. By the time they were all there, they looked, at best, like a Division III college football team. Pro teams need such players to properly conduct their training drills and scrimmages at summer camp. At St. Vincent College, in the sweltering heat of July and August, these young prospects would be called scrimmage fodder, or raw meat. Only two or three, at best, passed what former coach Chuck Noll called "the eye test." They were all hopeful, happy to be in the same stadium as the one where the Steelers and Pirates play.

Their chances of making the team were slim or none. One never knows, however. Cowher himself signed with the Philadelphia Eagles as an undrafted rookie in 1979 and was the last linebacker waived in training camp after playing in three pre-season games. He was invited to the Cleveland Browns as a free agent in 1980 and made the grade and put in five seasons as a player in the league, and had a job in the NFL ever since. Cowher could relate to the challenge these young men faced, and would give them every opportunity to prove themselves. He wanted to get lucky and find an NFLer or two to flesh out his football team.

On the wall on one side of the lobby were handsomely framed team photos of the Steelers' four Super Bowl title teams. Though it was unlikely any of those young newcomers might have been able to identify any of them, those photos included celebrated free agents such as Donnie Shell, Randy Grossman, John Banaszak and Sam Davis, who all became starters. Those four all had a hand in winning those four Lombardi Trophies that were displayed in a plexiglass case in the same area. Their success stories offer inspiration for all such long shots.

Only the Thursday before, that same lobby had been filled with raw sewage. There had been a blockage in the corroded pipes in the

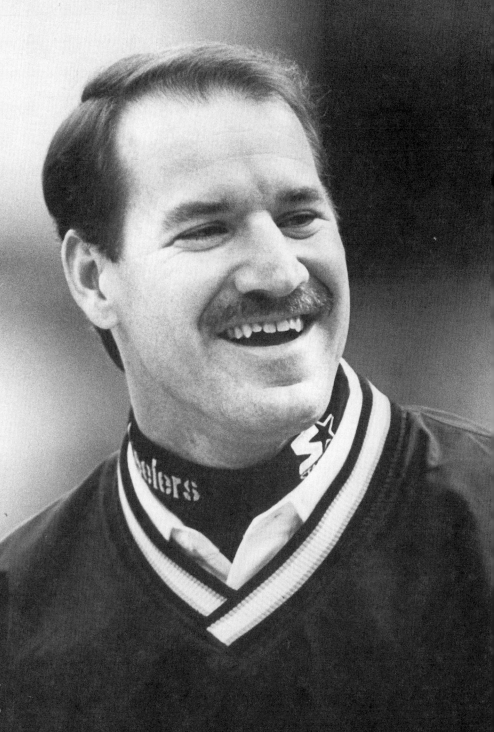

27-year-old Three Rivers Stadium and sewage had spilled out of the toilets and run through several offices, including Cowher's, the publicity and media rooms and the lobby. The Steelers' broadcast station, WTAE Radio, reported with great relief that the Lombardi Trophies had not been damaged. It did, however, stink out the joint — one day before a big crowd was expected for the NFL draft weekend activity — and stained and ruined much of the black carpeting. The carpeting had been ripped up and replaced, and the combination of aerosol sprays and large portable fans had camouflaged or eliminated most of the stink. So the newest signees who didn't arrive early enough to sit on the over-stuffed black leather couches and chairs in the lobby were sitting on new carpeting on the floor. The scene was reminiscent of a big city bus station on a holiday weekend.

The mess had been cleaned up, but it was still understandably unsettling for the Steelers' staff, and only made the brass more resolved to push for a new stadium for the Steelers on the city's North Side. They insisted Three Rivers Stadium was coming apart at the seams. They didn't want the Steelers to follow suit.

Cowher was keen on getting a bigger and better grass practice field as well, and improving the team's training facilities, and had appealed to Dan Rooney to do something to upgrade the Steelers' set-up. In the era of free agency, NFL teams must now compete for the attention of much-sought-after established players who have become free agents, and they must recruit the way college teams recruit by impressing their prospects with what they have to offer besides the money. They have to show them their workplace, their city, the communities where they might live.

This was an unsettling period in many respects. The Steelers had lost many of the players who had contributed to Cowher's excellent record of getting to the playoffs in his first five seasons as head coach of the Steelers. Already lost to other teams were Chad Brown, Willie Williams, Deon Figures, Ray Seals and Ernie Mills, newspaper stories strongly suggested Rod Woodson's days in Pittsburgh were numbered as well, and still up in the air was the contractual status of Jason Gildon, Bill Johnson and Andre Hastings. It looked like Jonathan Hayes would not be re-signed. Brentson Buckner had been dealt to the Kansas City Chiefs for a seventh round draft pick because Cowher had run out patience with what he perceived to be his easy-does-it disruptive ways. The year before, the Steelers had lost Neil O'Donnell, Leon Searcy, Tom Newberry, and Kevin Greene, all starters on their Super Bowl XXX team. There had been a major turnover of personnel in just two seasons. There was a big question mark at quarterback and concern about the comeback efforts of Greg Lloyd and Mark Bruener from injuries that sidelined them the previous season.

Chuck Noll used to say you never started a season with the same team that finished the prior season, but that was certainly more true now than when Noll was able to keep the core of his club intact, when as many as 22 players could claim four Super Bowl rings over a sparkling six-year span.

It was a chilly day, sprinkling here and there, and only 8,500 fans turned out that evening to see the Pirates defeat the Phillies at Three Rivers Stadium. Most of the city's sports fans were tuned in to what figured to be (and was) Mario Lemieux's last game at the Civic Arena in the fourth game of a best-of-seven first round Stanley Cup playoff series, with the Philadelphia Flyers winning the first three games. The newspapers, TV and radio shows had been saying goodbye for weeks to one of the city's all-time greatest sports performers.

It was going to be a nostalgic week in Pittsburgh. That same day, Pitt announced plans to retire the jerseys of three of its most famous football players, Marshall Goldberg, Joe Schmidt and Mike Ditka. They were to be honored in the same manner as Tony Dorsett, Danny Marino, Hugh Green and Bill Fralic had been earlier. Pitt's new athletic director Steve Pederson also discussed an aggressive season ticket selling program and kicked it off by selling the first pair of 1997 season tickets to Steelers' president Dan Rooney in a ceremony at a luncheon at the Pittsburgh Athletic Association, just across Fifth Avenue from the Cathedral of Learning.

There were ads in the local dailies promoting the latest appearance by the Steel Curtain Front Four from the Steelers' Super Bowl teams, namely Joe Greene, Dwight White, Ernie Holmes and L.C. Greenwood, at Station Square that coming Saturday. Following a reunion the previous summer, they had assembled several times for such public autograph signings. In Pittsburgh, there were always reminders of the high standards established by earlier teams in The City of Champions.

Cowher had grown up in Pittsburgh, in the middle class suburban community of Crafton, about 15 minutes from Three Rivers Stadium. He was aware of the winning tradition. He liked it that way. He had high expectations for himself and his Steelers. He welcomed the challenge.

"You keep seeing guys going out the door."

Bill Cowher could appreciate how Steelers' fans were feeling about the uncertainty of how the Steelers were going to fill the voids and field a championship contender for the 1997 season. He wore a comfortable-looking rayon black and white warmup suit as he sat in the refurbished black chair once occupied by Art Rooney, the beloved founder of the franchise, in a library/research room that remains a tribute to the late owner of the Steelers, and talked about his philosophies on football, his team, his family and himself.

Cowher would be 40 years old in a few weeks, May 8, 1997, and he had accomplished quite a bit in his first five years on the job, but he knew the Steelers had lost some of their best ballplayers, and it would be difficult to keep the Steelers atop the AFC Central Division and in the running for the Super Bowl. Cowher could empathize with the team's fans, and understand their concern.

"Absolutely, I know how they feel," said Cowher. "It's very frustrating. The type of coach that I am, I respect these players and I want to keep all of them. I try to get to know them as individuals. You build up relationships, you develop an attachment. You see them go . . . it's tough, it's frustrating.

"You get so close. You turn around and you keep seeing guys going out the door. At the same time, it's part of the business. It's the way things are now. I'm very happy for them that they have improved their financial situations, and signed contracts they're happy about.

"When things are going bad it's easy to get down about it. But you can't react that way. Each year, you have a new challenge. And I'm excited about that challenge.

"No. 1, you know there's going to be change every year. It's easy to say we've lost A, B and C, but how fair is that to D, E and F if we say we're not going to be very good? The other guys have prepared to play. They have an opportunity to show what they can do.

"We have that same approach when we lose players to injuries and whatever during the course of the season. We don't dwell on defeat or disappointments; we don't dwell on who we're missing and how much that might hurt us. As the coach, you *can* control the mindset of your team. That's my responsibility, to create that vision, that belief.

"If, out of my mouth, there comes a reason to fail, where is the reason to believe we can succeed going to come from?

"There will be adversity, there will be obstacles. That's what sports are all about. That's what life is all about, finding a way to overcome it, to deal positively with the challenge we're offered.

"I played on some bad football teams — I should say unsuccessful football teams — when I was in Philadelphia. I know what that's like. I was around Marty Schottenheimer when he dealt with some adversity at Cleveland and then Kansas City. So I know what that's like.

"When I grew up, I always had the fork-in-the-road mentality: if something didn't work out here, I'll go the other way. I've always tried to do the best I could do. I leave my hands in fate as to how it will all turn out.

"There's so much negativity that comes across in our society. We've tried to accent the positives here. Every problem is an opportunity to get something positive accomplished.

"I was never a great football player. I was a guy who tried to make the most of each opportunity I was given. When I was a special teams coach, I wanted to be the best special teams coach I could be.

When I was put in charge of the secondary, I wanted to be the best secondary coach. I talked Marty into letting me be the (defensive) coordinator, I tried to be the best coordinator. I never tried to solicit favor as a coach, but I took great pride in the accomplishments of the players I was responsible for."

When Chuck Noll retired after the 1991 season, following 23 years as the head coach of the Steelers, the Steelers interviewed some outstanding candidates to succeed him. Dan Rooney picked Cowher over two other top candidates, Dave Wannstedt, the defensive coordinator of the Dallas Cowboys, and Mike Holmgren, the offensive coordinator of the San Francisco 49ers. When Cowher came in for his interview, and knew of the possibility that he might be hired by the Steelers, was he wishing upon a star that he'd be selected?

"I don't ever put all my eggs in one basket," Cowher came back. "I wasn't anxious about the possibility, if you mean that. I knew someday I'd be a head coach. The Steelers' job wasn't something I aggressively went after. I tried to be myself. I wanted Mr. Rooney to know exactly what he was getting. I didn't try to show him someone else; I wasn't any different from who I am. I think you get into trouble when you try to be somebody else."

When Cowher said that, I found myself glancing at a photo of Bill Austin on the wall of what had been Art Rooney's office. Austin had come to Pittsburgh in 1966 from Green Bay, where he had been a valued offensive line coach for Vince Lombardi's great Packers teams. Austin tried to be like Lombardi and the players saw right through the masquerade. Austin gave way to Noll after the 1968 season in which the Steelers posted a 2-11-1 record. Austin returned to a successful career as a respected assistant coach with other NFL clubs.

"The most exciting thought about possibly coaching in Pittsburgh was coming back and being close to my parents, for our kids to be close to their grandparents," continued Cowher. "They were the first people I contacted when I was hired. It's been great for us and for them. It's given them a new energy."

I had visited Cowher's parents at their Crafton home the year before and felt immediately comfortable in their company. I couldn't say the same about being with their son. This was our first one-on-one meeting in four years, and the last one had not gone well, and ended abruptly. I prided myself on getting people I was interviewing to be at ease, but I couldn't get Cowher to relax. There was always a nervous edge about him and it was unnerving. I was careful with the way I phrased every question.

Cowher had so much going for him. He had returned to his home town to coach the Steelers, and had done so successfully, ranking right up there with some of the coaching greats of the game in taking his team to the playoffs in the first five years on board. He had no idea how popular he was with Pittsburghers and Steelers' fans everywhere. They loved this guy. When I was out signing books at shopping malls during the holidays, so many people offered high personal praise of the Pittsburgh coach. Cowher knew he wouldn't be as popular, however, if he wasn't winning. He knew he could count on his parents through thick and thin.

"As much as they've given to me, it's nice to be able to give them something back," he said. "My two brothers never really left Pittsburgh. Dale went to IUP and Doug went to Penn State, and they're both working in Pittsburgh. I was the guy who went off to N.C. State. I've been around the country since then playing and coaching in pro football. To be able to come back and spend the holidays — Christmas and Easter and days like that — with my parents is very special.

"The Super Bowl was something for my parents. It was my dad's choice to stay home with my mom and watch the game, and everything that preceded it on TV. He thought it was my day, and he didn't want to get caught in the middle. He thought he should stay home; it was his choice. (His father told me he wanted to be able to go to the refrigerator for a beer when he wanted one.)

"But I was able to make him so proud. To do that for him meant so much to me."

"He's a great role model."
— Bill Cowher
on Tiger Woods

Bill Cowher, who loves to play golf when he can find the time, had watched the Master's on TV the previous weekend, and was so impressed by the performance of Tiger Woods, who blew away the field, winning by a 12-stroke margin. He captured the imagination of sports fans all over the world with his winning ways. Woods set several records in seizing his game's most prestigious title in his first year on the pro tour. At 21, Woods was on top of the sports world. He was an African American/Asian American in a white man's game. He was handsome, charming and had a smile and enthusiasm that won over people who had never paid any mind to golf. He usually said all the right things.

Afterward, as he came off the 18th green, Woods smiled to the adoring crowd and gave his father, and then his mother, the longest and most earnest hugs a man could muster. He was thanking them for all that they had done during his developmental years. It was an emotional and moving scene. I had tears in my eyes, watching it all from the comfort of our family room couch.

"Watching that was so great," said Cowher. "That young man is so genuine. What you see is what you get. He's something that's so enlightening. He's a great role model. People will be after him. He should never change. He should be himself. He's doing so much for golf, so much for sports.

TIGER WOODS

"Every move has been calculated to make him the best person he can be. Your priority is the welfare of the child first. Who is he, and what is going to make him a good person, has priority over making him a good athlete."
— *Training A Tiger*
by Earl Woods, father of
golfing prodigy Tiger Woods

"To me, it's not a question of race. It doesn't matter what he is. What matters most is that, at age 21, he has the kind of maturity and the perspective he brings to his game.

"He captures everyone's heart. He competes so well under the most challenging of situations. He's not afraid to show emotion, and his relationship with his family, his demeanor — there's nothing phony about him — it's all so exemplary. We need more guys like that. It's great to see that. He has such a great presence. He's as genuine a sports figure as I've seen in many years."

There are Steelers' fans, of course, who feel the same way about Cowher himself.

"He's taken the game to another level," Cowher had to say. "It used to be that if you hit a 300-yard drive everyone was in awe. He averages 320 yards per drive. He has the total package. He has the aura and the heart to be so special.

"I love to play golf and I like to watch it, though I have a hard time relating to what somebody like Tiger Woods does with his clubs. It's hard to convince a household of women to watch a golf tournament. I live with four women so it's never easy to watch a golf tournament."

That brought up another subject. My wife and I have two daughters, and many people have asked me if I missed having a son. The answer for me is no, not in the least. I have served as a mentor and friend to many young men and derived a great deal of satisfaction from their success. So I could relate to Cowher's comments about his situation.

"I'm blessed," he said of his home situation. "I have three healthy, wonderful daughters, and they give me much love and warmth and pride as their father. My wife has competed in sports, and now my kids compete in sports, so we enjoy helping them and watching them grow up and have their own successes.

"I try to look at the total picture. This is still a job. I try to leave the job at work. It's nice to have young kids to go home to. They're not always aware of what's going on here, or what I'm up to. So it's a real relief to see them. They just see me as their dad.

"They're out playing in the yard when I come home. They're not sure what you did that day.

"In sports, I have lots of emotional highs and lows. That's really why you're in this game. When you lose the emotion for the game, it's time to get out. But we've always talked about perspective. My family, from my wife down to each of my three daughters, helps me keep my perspective."

I asked Cowher if he can keep things in perspective, considering he'd had such a great start and had been so successful as a coach with the Steelers. Did he realize he was putting up the kinds of numbers that can get you headed for the Hall of Fame? Cowher frowned at the idea.

"It's not time to sit back and reflect yet," he said, sounding a lot like Chuck Noll when I tried to get him to talk about his place in the game when he was in the midst of a training camp at St. Vincent College in Latrobe. "As far as I'm concerned, I'm in the middle of my career as a coach," said Cowher. "I know we're doing some good things, but I'm hoping we've only just begun.

"I'd like to think my coaching career has a long way ahead of it. I enjoy coaching. I really do. I have fun coaching. I'd love to work here for a long time. I love working for Mr. Rooney. I have so much respect for him. Talking about Tiger Woods; here's a 21-year-old who's genuine. Well Mr. Rooney is in his 60s and the only word I can think of to describe him is genuine. What you see is what you get.

"He has such a great feel for people. He has an aura about him. He's a Pittsburgh guy. And he has everything in its proper perspective. These are not qualities you find in a lot of successful people.

"I think the fans can relate to Mr. Rooney, as they did to his father. What we've accomplished as a football team has drawn them to our side. It's the biggest thing that they enjoy. They love this football team.

"This is a great place to play football on Sundays. It's a football town. That's no disrespect for the Pirates or the Penguins. But this is a blue collar town and they especially like their football. They enjoy all the sports teams here. When we have a game, it's not just the players . . . the fans of Pittsburgh wake up with a game face on.

"It's a happening. If you're not doing well, they'll be the first to tell you about it. If we're not doing well, we'll get booed, too."

Cowher was asked if he was aware of the specialness of coaching in his hometown.

"I guess when I really end up reminiscing is when I go with my oldest daughter to soccer games. Sometimes she's playing where I once played some sport. We were getting ready to play in a playoff game last year, and we were looking for a grass field to practice on for the New England game. I had Chet Furman look for a place.

"We ended up checking out the field they use at Northgate High. Northgate didn't mean much to me. Suddenly, I realized this was the old Bellevue field. I remembered playing football there when I was in high school. It was all coming back. 'Hey, I played here,' I said to Chet. 'I had a great game here.' We ended up not practicing there. We went to Duquesne University instead. But it was great being there, and all that it brought back to me. We go to places where our daughter is playing soccer and I go to places where I haven't been since high school or grade school.

"These are great reference points. I hope I'll never forget where I came up. You should always keep your roots. I never forget where I came from, and the people who gave me my first opportunities.

"We had a very close family. We don't have a big extended family. But my mom and dad and two brothers did a lot of things together. My dad really pushed us in sports. If you fell, you had to get up on your own. But my mom was always there if you were still crying. They both gave us a lot of stability.

"Growing up, we went through some tough stages. Through it all, thick or thin, they've always been there. It does come back to that. All my friends I had growing up around sports liked my parents as well. I was going from football to baseball to track and tennis. Everything revolved around going to camps all summer. Whatever I wanted to do, my parents were always there to support me, and boost me.

"Every Saturday when I was playing a home game at N.C. State, they would drive down for the game. I always knew my parents would be there. They'd get up around 4 on Sunday morning so that they'd get back to Pittsburgh in time to watch the Steelers on television.

"When I was younger and at home, me and my brothers would all be busy with sports and activities. My mom might cook dinner three different times. No matter when I'd come home, or with how many friends, my mother would come up with steaks or hamburgers for everybody.

"She always had a glow about her. No matter what happened, she made a positive out of it. My father had a lot to do with instilling the drive in me, but my mother was patient and loving and she was always a positive person.

"My wife, Kaye, helps me, too. She's a competitor. She comes from a hard-working background. She grew up on a farm. The only way she could have gone to college was through a scholarship. She has a great appreciation for where we are today. She views things objectively. She does a good job of giving me feedback about what I do and say, how I'm handling myself. She's my worst critic and my biggest fan."

"I had to be me."
— Bill Cowher

From the beginning, Bill Cowher has avoided comparisons to Chuck Noll, who had coached the Steelers the previous 23 seasons. Cowher kept telling people he hadn't accomplished anything yet — the Steelers were still seeking their first Super Bowl title under him — and that Noll was one of the game's legendary figures.

Noll's record had slipped in his last few seasons with the Steelers, though, so Cowher came in at a time when the organization and its fans were looking to get back to its glory days and winning ways. Cowher felt he could do that.

"It was not too tough to follow Chuck Noll," Cowher told us. "I didn't find it tough. What Coach Noll did, not many coaches have done. He was one of the all-time great coaches.

"I was just starting from scratch. I had to be me. When I retire, maybe then you can compare our records and see how we have fared. What Chuck's done would be hard for anyone to measure up to.

School days for the kid from Crafton

Brothers Doug and Bill Cowher sit in front of their mother, Dorothy, with their dad's sister, Aunt Mildred Smith, their father, Laird, brother Dale, and Uncle Herb Smith at the Cowher's Crafton residence.

"When I first came on board, there was so much I wanted to do to succeed here. Chuck was the farthest thing from my mind. I was looking at this as an opportunity for Bill Cowher. I was going to do everything I could do to be a winner here. I was going to do whatever I thought was going to work. I was happy for Chuck. He had such a great run and he looked like he was enjoying being retired. Every time I see him he looks younger.

"I have a tremendous respect for what he did as a football coach. He was himself. He did things his way. He didn't try to be like somebody else. When we got to the Super Bowl, I thought he might be willing to share some things that could be helpful to me. I asked to talk to him, and he obliged me, mostly telling me what it would be like, what the weeks ahead of the game would be like.

"We're all a product of what we are and where we've been. The Pittsburgh Steelers have a great tradition. What's been done here over a number of years has been most impressive. I think all the stuff around here that reminds us of those Super Bowl years is good for everyone. There's no reason for us not to be proud of that.

"I like to play golf in order to compete and for relaxation. I am not the kind of person who can run on a treadmill or ride a bike. I love playing golf. I love the competition and I love the opportunity to get away in the country, and walk the course. Who wouldn't love playing golf in Ireland, as I'm doing this July? I'm going to play with Arnold Palmer at the Family House Invitational at Oakmont in June. That's special. I love racquetball because of the competitiveness and because it helps me stay in shape. It's a workout.

"You have to win to keep your job. A lot of people in the NFL have lost their jobs this year, and in the years since I became the head coach here. I've worked with some great coaches along the way, in high school, in college and in the pros, both as a player and as a coach. You benefit from all of them. They all influence you some way.

"You have to worry about what's best to do with your team, what schemes might work, how to get good chemistry, all that. I'm thinking about what we might want to do in training camp, what we might want to change. At this time of the year, I try to balance that with my family life. It's time to recharge your battery and get back to basics, to relax a little while you have the chance.

"I'm getting excited about the coming season, the coming challenge. Every year is exciting for me. You have to take a step back and see what we've done, and what we hope to do the next time around.

"We have high expectations for this team. I'm turning 40 soon, but I still feel young. I enjoy what I'm doing. If I'm getting older, I hope I'm getting wiser. I'm not a guy who looks to be retiring any time soon. I enjoy what I'm doing tremendously. I love my children and my family. I'm looking forward to what they're doing and what they're going to accomplish as well. I worry about my family and the people I respect, the coaches and the players. I want to see them get some fruits from their labors. That's my greatest satisfaction. That's what I'm all about."

Steelers coach Bill Cowher is the tallest in his fearless fivesome at Family House Invitational at Oakmont Country Club June 23, 1997. The group, from left to right, included Frank Fuhrer III, of Fuhrer Wholesale Co., John Paul, executive vice president of sponsoring UPMC, Arnold Palmer and, at far right, Jay Juliussen of Ernst & Young.

Bill Cowher can't get away from media questioning wherever he goes. Stan Savran of Fox Sports wants to know how he feels about playing with Arnold Palmer, whom Savran got to interview for the first time in his broadcasting career.

Kordell Stewart
Some Slash/Dash/Cash

*"Quarterback is the position
I want to play, all the way
to the Super Bowl, I hope."*

Kordell Stewart was styling and smiling, and it's no wonder. For the second time in three months, Stewart was modeling a black and gold outfit and he looked fab-u-lous, as comic Billy Crystal might say.

Two months earlier, Stewart and teammate Jerome Bettis had modeled the Steelers' revamped uniforms at a coming-out party at the Pittsburgh Steelers' office complex at Three Rivers Stadium. The Steelers seemed to be showcasing Stewart at every opportunity. They had even sent him to Ireland a month earlier as a goodwill ambassador.

This time, at 10 a.m. on Tuesday, June 10, 1997, Stewart showed up in a shiny black-on-black striped double-breasted suit he had picked up in a men's boutique in Atlanta. He was wearing a businessman's conservative white shirt with a black and gold and white paisley tie that he tugged at with pride when Tom Donahoe came forward to offer a congratulatory handshake.

A sleek 6-1, 212 pounds, Stewart wears a double-breasted coat well. He didn't know the designer's name, but he said he thought it was "a nice double-breasted suit." He smiled when he said it, and did a model's turn to accent it.

"Don't I look good?" Stewart asked his boss, having some fun. "This is the way you gotta dress. I'm a black and gold man all the way. It's the only colors I want to wear."

Those are the colors at the University of Colorado as well, from whence Stewart came in 1995 as a second round draft choice to become a do-it-all offensive machine for the Steelers. He said he was going back to the Boulder campus the next day to take care of some unfinished business, and he wouldn't be back until July.

He was three credits shy of a bachelor's degree in communications at CU. Someday Stewart envisions himself as a sportscaster. The last Steelers' quarterback to follow such a career path was Terry Bradshaw. That was after he had won four Super Bowls.

"I want to go back to Colorado and do it right," said Stewart. "I want to get on the tube and talk. That's my cup of tea."

Stewart's smile was as gleaming as the diamond stud in his left earlobe. I'd never seen him smiling more, except after he had done something spectacular for the Steelers on the football field, dancing away from would-be tacklers on a long gainer or touchdown run. After such heroics, when they showed him, and then his coach, Bill Cowher, on the big screen atop Three Rivers Stadium, they were always smiling from ear to ear.

George Gojkovich

Steelers' fans swooned when they saw Stewart smiling.

Kordell Stewart, no question about it, was a big play guy. In 1996, he set an NFL record for the longest touchdown run by a quarterback with an 80-yard scamper. The first time he lined up at quarterback, Stewart rushed 16 yards on a sneak. He was definitely a first-down guy. Get him the ball and some way he would get the first down.

Stewart had just signed a new four-year contract to continue with the Steelers through the year 2000. The team had torn up the last two years of his original four-year contract, something they never used to do, and extended one that would be worth at least $9 million.

Things have changed. Dan Rooney, the president of the Steelers, used to take pride in saying the Steelers didn't re-negotiate contracts.

As a free agent and the team's most valuable asset, Bettis had signed for $14.5 million over the same span, but Stewart was moving into the same salary stratosphere, and Stewart had drawn even more attention from both local and national advertisers for endorsements. He was a young man who could be marketed.

His old contract would have paid him $780,000 over its remaining two years. Instead, he was getting a $2.5 million signing bonus, a salary for the 1997 season of $250,000 to keep his salary cap figure lower, while he would make at least $2.9 million. He would make $1.55 million in 1998, $2 million in 1999 and $2.5 million in 2000.

I can remember dancing through the hallways at Madison Square Garden, and hollering out to friends, after getting off the telephone and finding out I was going to be paid $65,000 a year to edit a national sports magazine. That was ten years earlier. I remember when I was the highest paid sportswriter on the staff of *The Miami News* at $200 a week, or $10,400 a year in 1969. How would it feel to sign the kind of contract Kordell Stewart had signed that day?

We'll never know.

"You've come a long way from Marrero, Louisiana," I suggested to Stewart as we passed in the hallway after the press conference.

"You've got that right, brother," said Stewart, smiling as he strode to the office of Dan Rooney at the other end of the complex. Rooney was calling from Ireland, where he had gone to do some more advance work on a Steelers-Bears exhibition set for Dublin in late July. Rooney wanted to congratulate the Steelers' young star.

The Steelers sent Stewart, Bettis and Mike Tomczak, the team's starting quarterback in 1996, to Dublin in early May as their representatives to help promote what was billed as the American Bowl.

Stewart wouldn't turn 25 until mid-October of the 1997 season, but he was now a certified millionaire. "I'm set for life," he said. Some in the room also thought he was set as the Steelers' starting quarterback to open the 1997 season, but Bill Cowher hadn't confirmed that publicly. Jim Miller, the third quarterback in the mix, was boiling mad about what he considered a premature judgment. You can bet that Tomczak was less than thrilled about being told he had been signed as a backup quarterback.

66

Miller had won the starting QB job at training camp the previous summer, but was yanked in favor of Tomczak after the third quarter in a loss in the season opener at Jacksonville.

"This is nice," said Stewart at his press conference, "but nothing's decided yet. I have to get out on the field and prove myself. In my heart and my soul, I know I'm very capable of leading this team. There's also a business side to this, and we had a chance to work out a new contract. And I'm happy about that."

He said he was also happy for Jim Miller the previous summer when Miller signed a contract extension that made him a happy man, at least that day. "I was happy for him, but I knew that I'd play," said Stewart. "I knew I'd get my opportunity."

Stewart and his high profile L.A.-based agent Leigh Steinberg, said a lot of things that played well in Pittsburgh, but had a hollow sound in some respects to anyone who had a sense of history. I couldn't help wondering what Steinberg had said at a similar press conference in New York when one of his clients, Neil O'Donnell, was introduced as the newest New York Jet a little more than a year earlier.

Sports agents don't come any bigger than Steinberg. He had succeeded the late Boston-based Bob Woolf as America's premier sports agent years earlier. Steinberg was, indeed, the prototype for the movie "Jerry Maguire," which had been nominated for an Academy Award. Hollywood darling Tom Cruise played the part of the hard-driving sports agent with a heart for his clients in the movie that was partly scripted and partly financed by Steinberg, who was making lots of money from the movie as well as the 24 NFL quarterbacks he represented in their contract negotiations.

When they asked the notorious thief Willie Sutton why he always robbed banks, he said, "That's where the money is."

Steinberg could say the same if asked why he concentrated on negotiating contracts for quarterbacks.

One thing Steinberg didn't say was "Show me the money!"

"You would be amazed by how many people come up to me and say that," said Steinberg, "as if they were the first person in America ever to say that to me."

Well, America is amazing in many ways.

"The Neil O'Donnell Story is not over yet."
— Leigh Steinberg

Steinberg brought a soft-leather satchel with him that was bulging with papers relating to his work as an agent — "the numbers on Kordell's contract are in there somewhere," he teased when asked about same — and there was a plastic natural water bottle that had been nearly drained, and two books he had brought with him to read on the plane between Pittsburgh and Los Angeles. He had all sorts of information in that satchel.

"I'll have to check, I'm not sure off the top of my head," said Steinberg, apologetically. "Too many contracts . . . too many time zones. . ."

He looked through the glasses he wore low on his nose to find what he was looking for. He had a gleam in his blue eyes, and he smiled as he searched for the information. In some ways, Leigh Steinberg looked more like Richard Dreyfuss than Tom Cruise.

Steinberg knows about as much, or more, of what's going on in the NFL than league commissioner Paul Tagliabue, another attorney who's fared well in the professional sports world. Attorneys and agents are the movers and shakers behind so much of what occurs in sports these days. Coaches and administrators have to stand in line to get a player's ear. Asked what he had heard about where Rod Woodson would wind up, Steinberg said he thought all along it would be the San Francisco 49ers.

"When the great players feel snubbed," said Steinberg, "they want to go somewhere where they can win right away, where they can go to the Super Bowl. He can do that in San Francisco. He can't do that in Cincinnati. Money becomes secondary. Then they feel like they're really sticking it to you. They want in the worst way to stick it to you. There, take that!"

Tom Cruise or even Cuba Gooding, Jr. couldn't have delivered that line with any more animation or gusto.

The Steelers were signing Stewart to this mega-buck contract even though no one could say with certainty that Stewart had shown he could play quarterback in a first-rate manner in the NFL.

In passing drills, exhibitions, and fill-in duty in regular season and post-season games, Stewart's showing strictly as a quarterback was held suspect. He had displayed some streaks of brilliance at quarterback in the last game of the 1996 regular season, a loss to the Carolina Panthers in Charlotte. School was still out on Stewart, the quarterback.

Slotted differently, with as many formations as offensive coordinator Chan Gaily & Co. could devise, Stewart was something special.

"Slash" Stewart seemingly could do it all. He was a quarterback/running back/receiver/punter, a quadruple talent like the Steelers hadn't seen since the days of "Bullet Bill" Dudley, Joe Geri, Lynn Chandnois or Mark Malone.

Stewart had shown that he could throw the ball, run the ball, kick the ball and that he was a superior athlete with a great attitude and confidence and, most of all, that he was a winner. He could probably be quite a defensive back and kick returner, too.

The Steelers were 3-4 and struggling at the start of the 1995 season. After they spotted Stewart into the lineup here and there, they came up with dreams and schemes every week to work him more into an offensive set that was sure to drive opposing defensive coordinators crazy, and the Steelers went on an eight-game winning streak, and finished the season in Tempe, Arizona at Super Bowl XXX.

Kordell Stewart compares notes with Jeff Blake, gifted quarterback of the Cincinnati Bengals

Michael F. Fabus/Pittsburgh Steelers

When pressed to specify Stewart's role, Cowher has commented, "I have not read the book that says what you should or should not do as an NFL head coach."

Cowher kept using the word "slash" when he described Stewart's situation, and the name stuck. "Slash" Stewart became a national phenom. Strictly as a quarterback, however, Stewart hadn't shown in two seasons that he was anything near Neil O'Donnell.

When Steinberg, in his opening remarks, said, "We consider that being quarterback of the Pittsburgh Steelers is a unique honor and one of the great positions in the world of sports . . . If Kordell's productive, he'll be here the rest of his career and that's that."

Hold on a minute. Isn't this the same Steinberg who once insisted that O'Donnell wanted to stay with the Steelers, then changed his mind when the New York Jets offered $25 million, or $7 million more than the Steelers, little more than a year earlier? Didn't O'Donnell and Steinberg turn their backs on that same unique position?

"There were extenuating circumstances," said Steinberg, when I asked him about that. "It was different. Neil was a free agent; Neil's father had died; his mother was living in New Jersey. It was a chance to get home with his family, and there was a lot more money. . ."

Later, outside of the press conference, Steinberg spoke more about the O'Donnell deal, and he wasn't defensive in the least. "He had two 'picks' (three interceptions, if you're counting) in the Super Bowl and they lost faith in him," said Steinberg. "I think Bill Cowher was consistent in his support of Neil, but the team let him get away, no matter how you look at it. They weren't all in agreement about his ability. The fans were a factor, too. You can't do much better than getting one drive away from winning the Super Bowl. The reaction to not winning it, in our view, was a little harsh.

"They didn't lose Neil O'Donnell when he became a free agent. They lost him the year before when they didn't lock him up when they had a chance to. I don't think they were sold on him at that time. After he got them to the Super Bowl, they changed their mind. After the interceptions against the Cowboys, they weren't as sure."

For the record, Dan Rooney was willing to pay the highest bonus ($4 million) and the highest average salary ($3.75 million) in club history to retain O'Donnell. The Steelers tried what they thought was their best, but in the end it wasn't good enough.

The Jets were in a different position. They needed O'Donnell, or so they thought, more than the Steelers to show their fans they were serious about doing something to stop the bleeding. After the Jets made O'Donnell an offer he couldn't refuse, Steinberg advised O'Donnell, "If you have one life to live as an athlete, why not live at least a part of it on center stage?"

The Jets had quite a tradition, too, though they had slipped badly from when they were one of the top teams in pro football, and had the highest-profile quarterback in Joe Namath to ever play the game. Being a starting quarterback in New York can be a unique position, too. Or in San Francisco. Or in Miami.

When someone asked Stewart if he had seen the light that it wasn't necessarily a good thing to go elsewhere for more money, Steinberg whispered something to Stewart, and he fielded the question instead of Stewart.

"The Neil O'Donnell Story is not over yet," said Steinberg. "To judge it in one year isn't right. Judge it over four or five years."

There were no Steelers officials sitting at the small table at the front of a room filled with Pittsburgh media, more than ever showed up for Steelers' football games before Chuck Noll turned the team around in the '70s. And this was just June!

Rooney was in Ireland. Bill Cowher was vacationing with his family in North Carolina. Dan Ferens, the business manager, who had negotiated the contract along with Art Rooney II, vice president and general counsel for the club, was in the back of the room, along with Donahoe, watching the proceedings. Neither felt comfortable in going to the front of the class. They dodge the spotlight whenever possible. Neither thought it was his role to sit up there instead of Cowher and Rooney.

So Steinberg and Stewart were a two-man show, and they said some insightful, heartfelt and also hard-to-swallow statements. Steelers' officials were proud of the way Stewart handled himself.

"It was a significant signing," said Donahoe later in the day, "because Kordell has proven he's one of the top players on our team. He's very unselfish. He's been able to contribute any way he could. Any time you have an opportunity to sign one of your best players it's a good thing to do."

Stewart said the "money wasn't a big deal," but it's unlikely he or Steinberg said anything like that during the discussions, which were initiated by Art Rooney II at league meetings in March.

"Kordell's a very poised young man," said Donahoe. "He has displayed that in the last two years. He's been able to make some big plays. Dan Ferens and Art II did a good job in signing him, and I liked the way Kordell handled himself today. It's something we felt we had to get done. The Rooneys like to pay people based on production."

Midway through the press conference, Steinberg repeated his statement that being the quarterback of the Steelers was a unique position.

In truth, being used in a multi-faceted manner was more of a unique situation than playing strictly quarterback. And "Slash" Stewart may have been more marketable than Kordell Stewart.

In any case, Stewart saw the Steelers' starting quarterback position as more unique than O'Donnell did. Whereas O'Donnell was coming off a Super Bowl disappointment when he sat down to discuss a new contract with the club, Stewart was coming off an 0-for-10 passing performance in the fog at Foxboro, Massachusetts, when the Steelers were upset by the New England Patriots in the second round of the AFC playoffs. Stewart threw short all afternoon, after he replaced Tomczak at quarterback, burying the ball repeatedly into the turf.

The Steelers were showing great faith in the future of Kordell Stewart when they signed him to this lucrative contract.

"I've shown that I can not only play quarterback, but that I'm also an athlete," said Stewart.

"It's not for the money."
— Kordell Stewart

Steinberg said bigger money was on the horizon. He voiced the opinion that the TV money available to be shared by NFL teams was going to double in two years, and that football players would be signing the kinds of contracts one sees more often in basketball and baseball. He said that whereas teams today were getting $40 million per team from their share of the TV money it would soon be $80 million.

If that happens, and Kordell Stewart is starting and shining as a quarterback for the Steelers, he will be paid in kind. He was confident the Steelers would pay the going rate at that time.

Stewart said he would leave such concerns to his agent.

He was looking ahead in a different way. His black hair was close cropped, coming to a point on his forehead in the fashion of Eddie Munster, the little boy in the old TV sitcom "The Munsters." To hear him talk about his dreams and plans, it was pointing Stewart and the Steelers to a future Super Bowl.

It was far more subtle than the arrow Ernie Holmes had cut out of his hair to point him in the proper direction.

"That's why we play," said Stewart. "Not for the game. Not for the money. We play to win championships, to get to the big one. I was fine before I reached this contract agreement. This just makes it better, beyond belief."

Somewhere in Carolina, Bill Cowher was smiling.

Stewart was glib and glad-handing everybody, even teasing Ed Bouchette, the beat writer for the Pittsburgh *Post-Gazette*, and someone with whom he has had a great relationship. I thought he was going to start tap-dancing.

Because of increased demands on his time and attention from an ever-growing national and local media, Stewart had restricted print interviews to Wednesdays only during the 1996 season. Sometimes he sparkled at such q. and a. sessions, and sometimes Stewart's spirit for same left a lot to be desired.

Sometimes he was sober and short with those who sought his thoughts on the State of the Steelers. He was young and maybe he would mature and realize he could be more of a statesman.

Kordell Stewart

Photos by George Gojkovich

"I feel I have the all-around package."
— Kordell Stewart

Steinberg is not as handsome as Tom Cruise — who is? — but he's just as engaging as Cruise appears on the giant screen. Steinberg is a sportswriter's dream. He spells out all the details of his players' contracts, whereas the teams prefer to say "terms of the contract were not disclosed" in their formal news releases.

Stewart said the Steelers were making a commitment to him — he said "obligation" — and he was excited about making Pittsburgh his home.

Asked why the Steelers were willing to re-work Stewart's contract at this time, Steinberg said, "My experience has been with Pittsburgh is that when they have a player they're really committed to, they want to sign and keep them here."

Left unsaid was that the Steelers were not fully committed to O'Donnell during those negotiations. The Steelers took a chance on O'Donnell's contract situation when they decided not to sign him before the final year on his contract. O'Donnell directed the Steelers to the Super Bowl. He was named MVP by his teammates.

"Except for that one negotiation, it's always been smooth sailing to work out a new contract with the Steelers," said Steinberg.

No matter what any of his detractors might say, the Steelers would have been better off if they had O'Donnell directing their attack in 1996, and possibly beyond.

Steinberg said it was difficult to draft quarterbacks who could come in save the day, and that no one was trading away top-notch quarterbacks, so the Steelers were smart to wrap up Stewart for a four-year period.

"Teams don't let established quarterbacks get away," said Steinberg. "No team lets a good quarterback go."

Steinberg says he is an "inveterate book reader," but he admitted to me that he had never read Murray Olderman's coffee table book, *The Quarterback*, or Bob Curran's book, *The $400,000 Quarterback,* or, what really hurt, any history books about the Steelers.

The Steelers had let more great quarterbacks get away than any team in NFL history. It began when Art Rooney dealt the draft rights to his pal George Halas and the Chicago Bears so they could select Sid Luckman of Columbia. The Steelers cut Johnny Unitas after drafting him in 1955, and later let Lenny Dawson, Jack Kemp, Earl Morrall and Bill Nelsen get away after playing briefly for the Steelers. You could add O'Donnell to that distinguished list. And they didn't draft Dan Marino.

Steinberg believes it was Joe Namath of Beaver Falls, the $400,000 quarterback in Curran's book about the early days of the

American Football League, who changed the economics and marketing of pro football.

"Namath signed a multi-year contract calling for $412,000," said Steinberg, "and O.J. Simpson signed one for $350,000, and those were the big contracts people talked about before I negotiated a better deal for Steve Bartkowski in 1975 with the Atlanta Falcons. Bartkowski, of course, was a quarterback, a pretty good one for a short spell, but not one who will ever be enshrined in the Pro Football Hall of Fame like Namath and O.J. When Namath guaranteed that the underdog Jets would beat the Baltimore Colts in Super Bowl III it changed the face of pro football forever.

No one in sports made more money or enjoyed a higher profile in professional sports back then than Namath in his prime.

"There has always been a premium price on quarterbacks," said Steinberg. "The quarterbacks jump out of the pack. I represented Troy Aikman when he signed with Dallas, and look what he did. He didn't do it his first year, and there was lots of criticism, but he certainly has earned his money ever since."

Steinberg said that Aikman and Stewart had the same quarterback coach in college, Rick Neuheisel, though at different schools.

"When I was sizing up Stewart's status as a pro prospect, I relied heavily on Neuheisel's opinion," said Steinberg. "And Neuheisel said Stewart was something special. He said Kordell's got it.

"At the point when we first met, Kordell was being pegged anywhere from a seventh to ninth round draft pick. He put together the most amazing pre-draft run I've ever seen.

"He played well in his bowl game appearance with Colorado. He played in the Hula Bowl and lit it up. The year he came out most of the quarterbacks didn't come to the combine in Indianapolis to be checked out. He did and he lit it up again. He took some chances which a lot of the established quarterbacks didn't take, and he lit it up.

"By the time he was through, there was a strong possibility he could have been a No. 1 draft choice. It was amazing."

The bowl game Steinberg was talking about was the Fiesta Bowl. Stewart led Colorado to a victory over Notre Dame, passing for 205 yards and rushing for 143 yards.

In the team's final game of the schedule, Stewart had captured the imagination of sports fans everywhere with his "Hail Mary" pass to Michael Westbrook to beat Michigan. The ball traveled 73 yards in the air before it landed in the grasp of Westbrook for the game-winning touchdown.

"The arm strength — that's just something I've been gifted with," said Stewart. "The running ability — that's something I've also been gifted with. I feel I have the all-around package as far as being able to throw, and when I get in trouble being able to run fast enough to get where I need to get and slide."

So Slash can slide with the best of them, too. He's stronger and swifter than Frank Tarkenton, that's for sure. So who knows?

Stewart grew up in humble circumstances as a kid in a community just across the Mississippi River from New Orleans. Yet he could say, "This isn't about money. The money doesn't make me happy. In order for me to achieve or justify those big dollars, I have to be a winner. That's what they're paying me to do.

"I don't need that much money. How can one person spend that much money? I'm going to share it with my family. Now I can help my father and I can help my brother. They're the most important people in the world to me. It's not about money."

No, people who have a lot of money can say that. "It's easier to say that when you've got it," Woodson once said.

"If you do well," said Stewart, "then you can enjoy making all that money. Winning comes first. Then you can get excited about all that money." Steinberg said he had clients who were making a lot of money who weren't happy because their teams weren't winning. The Pittsburgh media didn't want to spoil the day and ask if one of those clients was O'Donnell.

"It's just June now," reminded Stewart. "There's a lot of work to be done between now and the start of the season. I hate losing. I absolutely hate losing. I think we've lost some good players on our offense and our defense, but that's not going to stop us. Some of the young guys must step up. We've got the guys who can go all the way. We've got great camaraderie; I can see that already. The guys are enjoying themselves. That's my responsibility to make good things happen. I want to be happy doing what I'm doing. It's my hope to be the starting quarterback for the Pittsburgh Steelers.

"I've just been having fun. If having fun is going to cause me to make this much money, I'm going to keep on having fun."

Steinberg said he didn't believe the Steelers were signing Stewart to such a contract with the idea of having him be a backup quarterback or a wide receiver. "They haven't been paying their wide receivers that sort of money," said Steinberg.

"To me, it's obvious that Bill Cowher has told Kordell that he's the starter. It would be foolish to do otherwise." On July 11, just before summer training camp opened, Cowher named Stewart the starting quarterback.

"He's all too familiar with cancer."
—Leigh Steinberg

Stewart also announced that he was forming a Kordell Stewart Cancer Foundation to help raise funds for the American Cancer Society and their research efforts to find a cure for the disease that killed both his mother and his sister. His parents separated when Kordell was six years old. His mom, Florence, died of liver cancer six years later. Kordell was just 12 years old when his mom died. He moved in with his father, Robert Sr., who lived in Marrero.

"Kordell was so young," his brother, Robert Jr., recalled in an interview with Rob Ruck, a writer who has written several wonderful books about the black baseball leagues while teaching writing at the University of Pittsburgh. "He was suffering severely."

Ruck wrote about that episode in Kordell's life in a profile for *Pittsburgh Magazine* (October, 1996).

Florence Stewart had worked as a nurse and was finishing college when she learned she had cancer. She was sick for a year, and spent that time trying to prepare her three children — Robert Jr., Falisha and Kordell — for life without her. After she died, people in the family and community and at the family's church came to the support of the remaining Stewarts.

"Her death drew us even closer together," Robert Jr. related to Ruck. "That's all we ever knew, to stick together."

During the summer following his first season with the Steelers, Stewart went home to Louisiana to bury his sister, Falisha, who died from a respiratory illness linked to her cancer.

"Now there's no one more important to me than my father and my brother," claimed Kordell. "I'm glad I can help them. And I want to help some other people whose families have been challenged by cancer."

"Kordell is all too familiar with cancer," said Steinberg. "He's lost two loved ones because of it."

In his youth, Stewart was bolstered by the folks at the Nineveh Baptist Church, where he and his brother and sister sang gospel on Sundays. "Marrero will always be home," said Stewart. "Those are the people that I know will be there for me, regardless of what happens.

"I was brought up in the church, where there's a saying that things happen for a reason. That's the way I always look at it."

His father, 55 when his son signed his new contract with the Steelers, was a barber who could also do carpentry, sounding a lot like the fathers of Levon Kirkland and Kevin Henry. Robert Sr. taught his son how to cut hair, how to manage on his own, how to cook and clean up after himself. Teammates said Kordell's apartment was always spotless. He was single, but he was a disciplined housekeeper. He says he can't leave his apartment without making his bed. "I like things nice and in place," he said.

He doesn't drink or smoke. "All I have to do is keep my nose clean, and keep making progress as a quarterback," said Stewart at his press conference.

"I want to be the man here and get us to the Super Bowl as many times as I can."

He was close to C.J. Johnson, who was one of his receivers at Colorado, and they have played a lot of pitch and catch through the years, and Joel Steed, another CU alumnus. They had hooked up on some long bombs in a three-day mini-camp at Three Rivers Stadium a week earlier. Stewart would miss some of his neighbors in recent years, mainly two other Colorado alumni, Deon Figures and Chad Brown, as well as Willie Williams, who all signed elsewhere as free agents after the 1996 season.

77

He didn't mention them by name, but he would also miss two of the team's top receivers, Ernie Mills and Andre Hastings, and could only hope that Yancey Thigpen and Mark Bruener came back from disabling injuries and enjoyed good health, and that Johnson continued to blossom as an exciting pass-catcher.

"I'm a private person," Stewart told Ruck. "I want to stay Kordell Stewart, a normal guy. I've been brought up in the church. Just because you have a lot of money doesn't mean you need to wear a lot of gold around your neck. I'm just as normal as the guy walking down the street. On the field, I control the team. Off the field, I control myself."

In truth, Stewart is hardly like any guys walking down the streets of Pittsburgh. Stewart's statement was also made before he signed the big contract. He will be challenged more than ever to remain Kordell Stewart, the sweet kid from Louisiana.

Even if he never plays anywhere else but quarterback, he had become Slash Stewart. If he were able to keep smiling, Steelers' fans would follow in kind.

A walk on Woodson's sidewalk

Following the Stewart press conference, I decided to drive from the North Side to the South Side of Pittsburgh. I wanted to check out Rod Woodson's All-Star Grille at lunchtime to see how business was doing.

Whether he meant to or not, Woodson had offended many of his fans and patrons when he accused Pittsburgh sports fans of being racists in an article that appeared in a May issue of *Sports Illustrated.*

He had been booed when they showed his face on the big screen on the scoreboard at the roof of the Civic Arena during the Penguins' last playoff game of the 1997 season. Woodson said that black athletes who left Pittsburgh to play elsewhere were booed when they came to town, but that it didn't happen to white ballplayers. That simply wasn't true.

Pittsburgh sports fans boo everybody they think is a turncoat. Woodson later conceded that he knew they'd boo Neil O'Donnell whenever he came back to Pittsburgh. They already had, when O'Donnell didn't show up to receive an award at the Dapper Dan Sports Dinner after he'd jumped to the Jets.

Business fell off at Woodson's restaurant, and he quickly realized he had made a big mistake in his public outcry. So he started calling the Pittsburgh media, trying to make amends. Trying to control the damage.

I had never been to Woodson's restaurant, one of the biggest in town, a sprawling sports bar-restaurant that would be a challenge to keep going under the best of circumstances.

There were enough diners at the restaurant for lunch hour that would fill up most of the city's restaurants. But Woodson's restaurant was about one-sixth filled, and looked empty, kind of like Three Rivers Stadium when 5,000 fans show up for an afternoon game. It was quiet, and none of the Woodsons — Rod or his brother Joe, who looks after the place — were visible. Many customers come hoping to see a Steeler or some celebrity on the premises.

I checked out the sidewalk leading up to the front door from two different directions. It was called The Walk of Fame, and many of the foremost sports figures were memorialized in stars that were etched into the concrete. The stars were showing signs of wear and tear after only two years. Even so, it was reassuring, because only a few weeks earlier a large sports mural depicting some of the same superstars was destroyed when a Downtown building was imploded to make room for a future Lazarus Department Store. I watched it happen from a viewpoint atop Mt. Washington.

The names on the Walk of Fame honor roll were: Bill Mazeroski, Roberto Clemente, Bruno Sammartino, Billy Conn, Ralph Kiner, Jock Sutherland, Joe Paterno, Leon Hart, Floyd "Chip" Ganassi Jr., Chuck Noll, Pop Warner, Mike Ditka, John Galbreath, Honus Wagner, Art Rooney Jr., Pie Traynor, Bob Prince, Joe Montana, Terry Bradshaw, Bobby Lane (sic), Roger Kingdom, Maurice Lucas, Billy Knight, Norm Nixon, Jack Lambert, Willie Stargell, Franco Harris, Joe Greene, Johnny Majors and Art Howe. Art Howe? How did Art Howe get in that group? Yes, he had grown up in Pittsburgh and played for and managed the Houston Astros, but he hardly belonged in that kind of company.

"Sudden Sam" McDowell, a pitcher from Pittsburgh who starred in the big leagues, was a lot more qualified than Howe. Where was Arnold Palmer? I wondered why Jack Ham and Mel Blount weren't included, especially Blount, maybe the best cornerback ever to play for the Steelers, and a man by which Woodson and every cornerback in the future will be measured. In fairness, it's difficult to determine who should be so honored. No list would be complete.

How about Tony Dorsett and Mario Lemieux? Once inside the building, a mini-sports museum, one finds the autographed and beautifully displayed game uniforms of Dorsett and Lemieux and a lineup that is most impressive.

There are lots of photos, murals, memorabilia, dressing stall recreations to keep any sports fan fascinated before or after their dining experience. It's a pricey place; you're paying for the surroundings as well as the ample offerings. Critics tell me the fare is fair at best. You're also paying for the company you could be keeping.

The following are represented on the walls: Wayne Gretzky, Shaquille O'Neal, Oscar Robertson, Howie Long, Steve Young, Joe Montana, Lemieux, Jaromir Jagr, Jerry Rice, Dorsett, Greg Lloyd, Clemente, Mickey Mantle, Walter Payton, Johnny Unitas, Tony Gwynn, Randall Cunningham, Ronnie Lott, Michael Jordan. None of them would ever see a tab if they stopped by for a drink or dinner.

There were mementos of Woodson's football and track & field career at Snyder High School in Fort Wayne, Indiana, at Purdue University and with the Steelers. He opened this showcase restaurant in the fall of 1995. Now that he was no longer a Steeler, people were wondering when he would be closing it.

In late June, 1997, Woodson announced that he was going to sign with the San Francisco 49ers, as Steinberg had predicted. Woodson, at 32 and with seven Pro Bowl seasons behind him, wanted to go out with a Super Bowl contender.

Woodson had been offered $3 million a year on a contract by the Steelers the year before, but turned them down. He was offered one at a considerably lower number after the 1996 season, and turned that down as well.

Woodson was said to have discussed his situation with Franco Harris, who made a mistake by not signing with the Steelers for his final season. He must not have listened. He left Pittsburgh and the Black and Gold for San Francisco and the Red and Gold. No doubt, he left his heart in Pittsburgh.

George Gojkovich

Rod Woodson starred for ten seasons with the Steelers. He would be missed by fans who adored him. It shouldn't have ended this way.

Reflections on Dare To Dream

This essay was written by the mother of Jonathan Hayes, who played three years for the Steelers, but was not re-signed after he became an unrestricted free agent following the 1996 season. Mrs. Hayes was a schoolteacher for over 30 years. The Hayes family was from Bridgeville and Jonathan's coming to the Steelers after nine years with the Kansas City Chiefs was a true homecoming.

by Florence Joy Hayes

The fog has lifted and the Steelers' 1996 football season has come to a screeching halt. The sun has since come up over Western Pennsylvania and the world is proceeding as usual. Many of us have bruised egos, but this too shall pass. We should be proud to be AFC Central Division champions for four out of five years under Coach Cowher.

> *The credit goes to the man who is actually in the arena, whose face is marred by dust and sweat and blood; who errs and comes short again and again, who knows the great enthusiasms, the great demotions, and spends himself in a worthy cause; who at the best knows the triumph of high achievement; and who, at the worst, if he fails, at least fails while daring greatly, so that his place shall never be with those cold and timid souls who know neither victory nor defeat.*
> — Theodore Roosevelt

An unusual situation occurred in the Hayes family this year. It seems like only yesterday that Jonathan's younger cousin, Brandon Hayes, was attending the University of Iowa games with his dad to see Jonathan play. And today, Brandon Hayes — 6-5, 305 pounds — is playing football with the Carolina Panthers. My husband is so proud to have his nephew playing professional football.

As I read this interesting and inspirational book, *Dare To Dream,* I found the common thread among the players' stories to be that, despite their diverse backgrounds, they were determined to achieve success in our society. Many of their circumstances were horrendous, but with the ability to stay focused and persevere in their daily lives, and by receiving much love and support, they were able to overcome many situations. Each of them has developed a tough persona through blood, sweat and tears to arrive at this junction in their careers.

The old African proverb — "it takes a whole village to raise a child" — rings true throughout these chapters. These young men were encouraged by immediate and extended family members, citizens, coaches and friends through the good, the bad and the ugly. Many have overcome extenuating circumstances and I personally wish to commend them.

During my son's early years, we were the only black family in one area of South Fayette Township, just south of Downtown Pittsburgh. While things never got too far out of hand, we did have small incidents. Jeffrey, my oldest son, was the pioneer being the only black child at school. Jay, my second son, was the defender, always running interference for little brother, Jonathan. Here again, we see the strength of brotherly love and support one must have in any scenario.

> *Please don't curse that boy down there*
> *He is my son you see*
> *He's only just a boy you know*
> *He means the world to me.*
> *I did not raise my son, dear fan,*
> *for you to call him names.*
> *He may not be a superstar*
> *It's just a high school game.*
> *So please don't curse those boys down there,*
> *they do the best they can,*
> *They never tried to lose a game,*
> *They're boys and you're a man.*
> *This game really belongs to them, you see,*
> *You're really just a guest,*
> *They do not need a fan like you,*
> *They need the very best.*
> *If you have nothing nice to say,*
> *Please leave the boys alone.*
> *And if you have no manners,*
> *Why don't you stay at home!*
> *So please don't curse those boys down there,*
> *Each one's his parents' son*
> *And win or lose or tie, you see,*
> *to us, they're Number One!!!!!!*
> — Anonymous

However, Jonathan's dad — his first coach — assured him not to worry about being offended because the cream rises to the top.

As a high school senior and captain of the football team, a conflict arose over who should pay for Jonathan's football shoes because his feet were over a size thirteen and that was additional cost to the district. We were prepared to buy his shoes. I called the University of Pittsburgh Athletic Department and, ironically, the Steelers office to see where we could purchase his football shoes. We were directed to a store in Lawrenceville. At this same time, Jewett was president of the Quarterback Club, our booster group at South Fayette High School, and they gave us their full support in this regard. The issue was resolved in our favor before the school board meeting was held.

During Jonathan's senior year, he played football, baseball and basketball. The South Fayette schools played against the City League and the Catholic League in basketball. After putting in a full day of teaching, I would pick up my husband at the State Building in Downtown Pittsburgh. We usually ate dinner at Ritter's Diner. We always purchased extra sandwiches for the long trip home. It was not unusual for us to deliver players and cheerleaders to their homes in Morgan or Fairview. Otherwise, they would have had to return to school on the school bus, consequently getting home very late. Jonathan always assured everyone his parents would give them a ride home in our '78 Dodge Station Wagon. Guess what? We would! We made a commitment to our sons for their development, education and well-being, and I hope we came close to the mark!

We followed our sons no matter what sport and wherever they played and we still do to this day!

My husband is a no-nonsense dad due to his upbringing and his profession as a probation and parole supervisor. He dealt with difficult clients daily and knows first hand the pitfalls that can fall upon young men, especially young black males.

The interest we had in our sons' development extended to others in our church and community. Last year, Marvin Lewis, former Steelers' outside linebacker coach and Baltimore Ravens Defensive Coordinator, friend and church member, came to visit us. During our reminiscing, he told of how Jewett had taught him to swim. He was so grateful for this opportunity that today he, too, finds himself helping others, thus performing the mission of our church ("saved to save"). It really does take a whole village to raise a child.

These are issues I have shared just to make a point, but at the time they were quite significant to us. We often revealed to our sons that when you feel you are old enough to make your own decisions, you must be old enough to accept the consequences for your actions. Our sons had strong support from their church and extended family members. We were, and are grateful for this help.

The people of South Fayette Township have wonderful school spirit and community pride. It is almost a sin not to be wearing your school colors on game day. If you want to find "Lion Country," exit off Route 50 west to Miller's Run Road and follow those big paw prints all the way to our educational center. In our community, we have parents, neighbors and friends who are truly dedicated and devoted to the youth of South Fayette, and we are very thankful for them.

Jonathan, his teammates and coaches learned early on that you must play the hand that is dealt you. Being diagnosed with diabetes is certainly an obstacle. However, he has never used his diabetes as a crutch. Jonathan has been able to focus and dared to dream. When he wrote the book, *Necessary Toughness,* about his experiences of dealing with diabetes, he never dreamed he would have such an impact on so many people, especially young people. We are grateful that he has inspired others. It is important to remember that no matter what your situation, there is always someone who has experienced something similar and can empathize with you. *Dare To Dream,* young people and everyone. It's never too late! It takes patience, wisdom, perseverance and tons of faith. You can be whatever you want to be. Yes, *Dare To Dream* and, of course, *Keep the Faith.*

The Hayes men: Jeffrey, Jay, Jewett and Jonathan

Joy Hayes

Jay, Jonathan and Jeffrey Hayes

Jonathan sees Santa Claus during the holidays.

Photos from Hayes family album

84

Dr. Jekyll and Mr. Hyde
Figuring out the real Steelers

"My characters start generally when they are at the worst places in their lives. To improve themselves, they struggle; they struggle to understand their condition. I like that in people. I like to see people pull themselves out of whatever holds them from their best selves. You know, everybody really has a best self and a worst self; some people never fight their way to the best self. That is one of the worst sins in the world — to see the best self, to know it is there and to fail to try to achieve it."

> — Alice Walker, Author
> *The Color Purple*
> *Warrior Marks*
> *Living By The Word*

The two most dominant figures in the Steelers' locker room at Three Rivers Stadium during the 1994 and 1995 seasons were Greg Lloyd and Kevin Greene.

They were the two most popular players for the fans, ironically enough, and the two least popular players with the press and radio-TV people who reported on the team's daily activities. They were just so difficult.

They strutted about the room, always walking above the crowd, or, in the case of the media that assembled each midday in the middle of the room, through the crowd.

Lloyd loved to walk through the ten or twelve writers and sportscasters who had come into the room during the lunch break looking for willing interview subjects. They would be talking to each other, comfortable in each other's company, looking for a friendly face, an opening, someone who might like to speak to them about the state of the Steelers that day.

It was a strange Catch-22 setup because it was lunch time for the Steelers, and the Steelers would leave the locker room about the same time the media was arriving to go and get their meals that a catering service provided in the visitors' baseball locker room at Three Rivers Stadium. The Steelers would return with paper plates piled high with food, carrying a drink in their other hand, eager to sit down somewhere and eat their lunch. They wanted to eat, they wanted a break. The reporters were a nuisance for the best-hearted of the bunch.

The newsmen would assemble in the middle of the locker room, like an island, looking for players they might approach for an interview. They assembled at a spot that was midway between the shower room and Lloyd's dressing stall.

Lloyd would part them — like Moses parting the Red Sea — and pass by without a word, without a nod or wink or smile or any acknowledgment of any kind. It was as if they were not there. He was not out to make their day.

He would walk with his shaved glistening head held high, always the proud warrior, staring straight ahead with dark eyes. He always seemed to be glaring, daring anybody to get in his way. It was difficult to comprehend why he wanted to be so defiant, so distant, so difficult, so insensitive to anyone else's feelings. There was a volcanic heat in the depths of his dark eyes.

"He is so full of himself, so full of crap," said a former teammate, whom I had never heard say anything bad about anybody and never heard say a single cuss word. "I refuse to ever speak to him again."

Why couldn't Lloyd be more civil, considerate of those who sought his attention and thoughts about the latest game or an upcoming encounter? What was the big deal? How serious was all this stuff? Why couldn't he get real? I had never done anything to him to deserve his disdain. What did he care?

He appeared to have a big chip on his shoulder and dared everyone to knock it off. Why was he like that? What had happened to him in his career, as a child, as a college athlete, as an adult as one of the most-feared performers in the National Football League, that had fashioned his obstinate behavior? Then again, how would I deal with what he was dealing with? I remember my first boss, John Crittenden of *The Miami News*, once criticizing me and rebuking my miffed response back in 1968 by saying, "Someone must have kicked you real hard when you were a kid." I couldn't remember anyone doing that, not literally.

"The only thing that's
constant is change."
— Chuck Noll

During the 1995 playoffs, Lloyd would place a white towel on the carpet by his dressing stall, lie on it, do stretching exercises, talking or muttering to himself, ignoring the newsmen who passed by. He wouldn't talk to anyone, but he wanted everyone to see how dedicated he was to getting himself in the best possible shape for the challenge ahead. Some day, I thought, when he gets older and is removed from the game, he may realize that he missed out on something. These were great times, as good as it gets in sports, and he was in a constant snit, a personal fury, and failing to enjoy the moment. It seemed a shame. A big waste. He often rejected the requests of young autograph-seekers as well.

Greene would go in a different direction. He held his head equally high. He had let his blond hair grow long — it reached way below his shoulders as the season wore on — saying he would not cut it until the Steelers got to the Super Bowl. It got him a lot of attention.

He often brushed off media types like they were offensive tackles or bothersome ticks, constantly checking his watch or the clock on the wall, always in a hurry, too occupied to stop for an interview. When it suited him, Greene would pause and offer a few sound bites before rushing off to some important demands on his precious time. He'd talk about what was important in his life, say something like "God bless you" and leave you at mid-sentence. Somehow it did not all add up. Who was the real Kevin Greene? Where was the real Kevin Greene? Were there two different Kevin Greenes?

Greene always reminded me of one of those professional wrestlers the way he talked and walked, his chest pumped up, his arms pumping, like his boyhood hero, Hulk Hogan. He always looked like he was about to rush into a ring, jump over the ropes in a single bound and thump his chest and call out to the crowd at one of those Wrestlemania extravaganzas.

At first, it was a real turnoff. I had covered the Steelers on a daily basis for *The Pittsburgh Press* from 1979 to 1983, back when they had won the fourth of their Super Bowls and still had all the players of their glorious run of the '70s, and none of them had treated the media this way. Most of them were so accommodating, some more shy than others, but the majority were easy to talk to. Oh, in his rookie season, Mean Joe Greene spit into the face of veteran sports writer Pat Livingston. He later apologized, they became good friends, and Greene became the godfather of the Steelers' locker room, the man who most set the tone for a thoughtful work space. Jack Lambert gave a lot of reporters a tough time now and then, just for the hell of it, but was generally a good interview. The Steelers' clubhouse was a lot friendlier environment in those days. Lloyd and Greene set the tone, at first glance, for the Steelers' locker room of the '90s. Maybe it inhibited other Steelers from speaking too freely, or enthusiastically, lest they risk the wrath or baleful glares of Greene and Lloyd. Maybe I imagined all of this. This book is the truth, my truth.

Writers and publicists all approached most Steelers with some degree of trepidation, like they were wary of being rebuffed. Nobody sought rejection. So often, the media seemed to be walking on eggshells in the Steelers' clubhouse. Once anyone's lips started moving, there would be a swarm of writers and sportscasters, all thrusting their tape recorders toward the moving mouths, all eager to get the much-prized quotes, those often trite soundbites. There was a feeding frenzy, like a hog being tossed into a pool of piranhas. There was something messy about the whole process.

Goose Goslin of KDKA-Radio, in a q. and a. in *The Observer*, a Pittsburgh alternative weekly, was asked the following question: "Who do you hope never to talk with again and why?" His answer: "Kevin Greene, because of his arrogance."

"Everything changes."
— Joe Gordon

A lot had changed on the sports scene in 15 years. Chuck Noll had said the only thing constant about sports and life was change. Still, it was hard to deal with, if you thought it could be different, somehow better. The athletes were making so much money now and their attitudes about a lot of things, especially their responsibilities toward the media and the fans, had changed drastically. Their sense of self-importance, in many cases, had changed considerably. Art Rooney was dead. "When are you going to understand that everything changes?" said Joe Gordon, the team's spokesman who had known what it was like in the '70s, to rouse me from a deep sleep, as if I had gotten lost in the '70s. "The world has changed." Gordon, the greatest p.r. man the city and NFL had ever known, announced his retirement in the spring of 1997. He was no longer enjoying his job; the business had changed too much.

In truth, the media had changed, too. They had become more confrontational, seeking hotter stories, something that would seize a headline in the next day's newspaper or a teaser on that night's TV and radio newscasts. They were driven in that direction by their bosses back at the news desk. Sound journalistic judgment was lacking sometimes. Tabloid journalism was in vogue. Members of the media, especially those from out of town who descended on the dressing room during the playoffs in both seasons, would often begin an interview with a tough question, right out of the box, trying to elicit an angry, ill-thought retort from the assaulted athlete. ("So-and-so said you stink. What's your response to that?") I had always been taught to save the tough questions for last, lest you end up with an empty notebook. There was more of an adversarial relationship between the media and the teams and the athletes they covered.

In more peaceful times, I thought it was nice to get paid to stroll the sidelines at a Steelers' practice, swapping stories in the sunshine with Art Rooney. But I remember when I was 29, and new to *The New York Post*, and one of the veteran writers, columnist Milt Gross, said to me, in 1970, "I don't envy you. This business is not what it used to be. And it's going to get worse. The athletes have changed for the worse."

But there were still more good guys (and girls) than bad guys (and girls) among the media, and the same was true of the Steelers' family, yet there was this moat dividing the two sides from a better spiritual and emotional exchange. Both had something to learn from one another. Neither side was blameless.

"I just love the way he plays."
— A Greg Lloyd fan

Once you got past the impressions offered by Lloyd and Greene and got to know the Steelers' cast, it was obvious that the majority of the players were pretty nice guys.

They don't come any classier than Carnell Lake, Levon Kirkland, Dermontti Dawson, Darren Perry, Mike Tomczak and John Jackson. Leon Searcy was special in a dignified, quiet way. Ray Seals showed an inner strength and spirit in the wake of difficult personal challenges after his cousin Jonny Gammage was killed in an altercation with suburban police. Woodson was given The Chief Award by the media in 1994. It honored the memory of Art Rooney, and was given to a Steeler who had been especially cooperative with the media. But he was consumed by his efforts to rehabilitate himself so he could play in the Super Bowl if, indeed, the Steelers would get there, and said he did not want to be distracted with too many interviews. Kirkland won the same award in 1995.

It was special to watch the development of the young wide receivers, to see them mature and gain acknowledgment as gifted contributors after first being viewed as a weakness in the Steelers' line-up, and getting to know Yancey Thigpen, Ernie Mills, Andre Hastings and C.J. Johnson. Jerome Bettis was a breath of fresh air when he joined the team in 1996.

I was thankful for the cooperation of players like Jonathan Hayes, Jerry Olsavsky, Justin Strzelczyk, Kevin Henry, Brentson Buckner, Tom Newberry, Myron Bell, Bam Morris, Joel Steed, Erric Pegram, Chad Brown, Willie Williams, Deon Figures, Norm Johnson and Will Wolford. Neil O'Donnell was most decent, if not the most media responsive quarterback to ever hit town, and I would miss him, Searcy and John L. Williams. O'Donnell ducked the media for most of the work week, doing one mass interview per week, and I wondered whether he could get away with that in New York with fiercer demands from a much larger and often more critical media.

Kordell Stewart, the rookie phenom, could blow hot and cold, interested and disinterested, pleasant and aloof, and it was difficult to determine how he would find his way, if he could handle the attention. There were no doubts that he would become a big-time player at one position or another. He had great ability and great self-confidence.

Some of the spear-carriers had interesting insights to share, such as Steve Avery, Ariel Solomon, Kendall Gammon, Jason Gildon, Alvoid Mays, Fred McAfee, Jim Miller, James Parrish, Tim Lester, Jim Sweeney and Eric Ravotti. It looked like there would be an opportunity for Gildon and maybe even Miller to move up in stature.

Greene and Lloyd were an interesting duo. They were the outside linebackers for the Steelers' defensive unit, two of the best at their position in professional football. They were famous for sacking opposing quarterbacks. Nobody played any harder than these two, and that's why the fans at Three Rivers Stadium loved them. They could have cared less if their heroes had mistreated the media. What does that have to do with the outcome of a contest?

With Woodson sidelined most of the 1995 season after getting hurt in the opening game, they drew the most attention, cheers and banners at Three Rivers, and their jerseys — No. 91 for Greene and No. 95 for Lloyd — were the most popular jerseys worn by Steelers' fans. They were adored figures, and fans spoke of them in reverent terms at the tailgate parties in the parking lots outside the Stadium. "I just love the way he plays," a fan would say, in explaining why they were wearing one of their jerseys.

The fans had changed, too. I walked through the parking lots before the AFC title game with the Indianapolis Colts at the end of the 1995 season. Many of the fans had their faces painted in black and gold, they had hung Jim Harbaugh, the Colts' quarterback, in effigy. Fires were burning in barrels. Heat waves hung over the whole scene. There was a sustained roar and it was like being in an armed camp with Attila the Hun the night before his troops massacred all the inhabitants of a nearby village.

When Lloyd and Greene moved among their fans both were fabulous, good-hearted, warm-smiling fellows. A few fans spoke of disappointing experiences with them, as when they ignored them on the way to the locker room after a demanding practice at St. Vincent, but few saw their dark sides. I would see Lloyd and Greene outside the stadium signing autographs, and see them at shopping malls, and they were great ambassadors of goodwill for the Steelers. Each fitted the Dr. Jekyll-Mr. Hyde profile. There were, indeed, two different Greg Lloyds and Kevin Greenes.

Lloyd was lauded for his frequent visits and compassion with the kids at Children's Hospital. There were often letters about him in the Saturday sports pages, praising him or assailing him, depending on how he had treated a fan. Greene had come to the Stadium and mixed with fans who stood in long lines to purchase playoff tickets, even buying burgers and pizza for them. I saw him strolling through The Shops at Station Square the day before a playoff game in 1995, signing autographs for all who approached him. He looked like a happy tourist. He was not there on a paid gig; he just enjoyed being out there with the fans. Like Hulk Hogan, he fed on the public   adulation. I caught him after playoff games, in the company of his wife, Tara, talking to fans and signing autographs for an hour. Then he'd jump in his minivan and honk the horn and wave to his admirers as he drove off into the sunset.

"He gave Pittsburgh a lot, but then, I think Pittsburgh gave him a lot as well," said Steelers' coach Bill Cowher during the 1996 season after Greene had expressed some anti-Steelers' venom.

91

"They are such hypocrites."
— Steeler Insider

So why weren't Greene and Lloyd nicer with the newsmen? Both had been burned, as they saw it, by unfavorable reviews and stories during the course of the season.

Greene had gotten a lot of bad publicity during the team's summer training camp at St. Vincent College in Latrobe in 1995 for the seemingly unkind manner in which he had dealt with a young boy seeking his autograph.

Greene didn't like the way the kid had spoken to him, so he took a football the youngster had handed him to be signed, and punted it. Greene said it was a playful "pooch" punt. He was trying to make a point with the youngster. When the kid reclaimed the ball and handed it back to the Steelers' star, Greene again punted the ball away.

The kid's family wrote a letter of complaint that was reprinted in *The Post-Gazette*, and it set off a storm of criticism, and Greene and some of his teammates started catching some flak from local commentators and on the local sports talk shows. How could Greene be so insensitive? Greene felt he had gotten a bad rap. He apologized for his action, but insisted the kid had been out of line in his approach. He did his best in the weeks afterward to kiss and make up with the crowd. He felt, with good reason, that he had been as obliging to the fans as anybody on the team during his three years with the team. He wanted a good image.

Greene and Lloyd had both admonished many youngsters and adults for the way they went about seeking autographs. There's no question that some fans go about it in the wrong way, and for the wrong reasons. Greene and Lloyd said they wanted to be addressed politely, and called "Mr. Greene" and "Mr. Lloyd," and that they wanted the autograph-seekers to say "please" and "thank you" when their wishes were granted. It seemed like a reasonable request, that fans treat them with good manners and some modicum of civility.

"They are such hypocrites," said a Steelers' insider. "When was the last time they addressed anyone around here as 'Mr.' or said 'please' or 'thank you' to anyone?"

Lloyd had always been a reluctant interviewee, but he shut off the local media completely just before the third game of the 1995 regular season schedule, a game against the Miami Dolphins, because he insisted that he had been misquoted in remarks attributed to him regarding Dan Marino, the Dolphins' quarterback and a popular Pittsburgh sports figure.

Lloyd was quoted by the sports editor of the *North Hills News Record*, not a regular on the Steelers' beat, as saying while discussing Marino that he was "going to knock him into next week." None of the regular beat guys heard Lloyd make such a remark, and no one had it

Kevin Greene

Greg Lloyd

Bill Amatucci

Michael F. Fabus/Pittsburgh Steelers

Bill Amatucci

Defensive coordinator Dick LeBeau discusses strategy with Greg Lloyd and Kevin Greene, while defensive line coach John Mitchell, at far right, addresses his charges. Lloyd gave many of the Steelers' coaches the silent treatment, as he did the media.

on tape, and most of them questioned the veracity of the quotation. Yet all the newspapers and newscasts carried the remark without checking with Lloyd as to its authenticity. It made the national wires and newscasts.

During his career, Lloyd had made so many outrageous and controversial remarks, and had not backed down from any of them no matter the resulting fallout, so his insistence that he had never said any such thing had to be regarded with that in mind. Certainly he had said some things that suggested that he would be out to pillage Marino or any other NFL quarterback, so the attributed remark was certainly not out of character for him. As it turned out, he did injure Marino in the game and send him to the sideline.

But he shut off the local media after that, submitting to a select number of interviews from outside sources. Like Barry Bonds, who had been a similarly controversial figure with the Pittsburgh Pirates in a previous time, he turned on his best face and charm when the cameras from the TV networks wanted to give him some national attention. He was nominated by the Steelers for an NFL Man of the Year Award for community involvement. He and his wife Rhonda had been featured a year or so earlier in one of those heart-warming United Way ads for their activity in serving the community. It didn't add up. It was tough to understand why Lloyd and Greene wanted to give so many of the media a hard time while assuming different postures for other people. They were ticking off the image-makers.

I had seen Carnell Lake, for instance, in a shouting match with Lloyd one day, arguing about interpretations of Bible stories. It lasted a good 20 minutes. It was intense. I was talking to Darren Perry, doing my best to pay attention to what he was saying, but intrigued and distracted by the duel behind him involving Lake and Lloyd. Lake did not back down in the vociferous exchange. Perry laughed when he recognized my interest. "That's not new," said Perry. "You should see the way they get into it sometimes." This was not a fight or feud, I realized, just an ardent give-and-take among teammates who stood by their personal beliefs. Lloyd seemed to be baiting Lake, however, just to keep the debate going.

In many ways, Lloyd reminded me of Jack Lambert, the Steelers Hall of Fame linebacker, who went about his work on and off the field with a disdain similar to Lloyd's. They both were always playing the role, doing their best to be tough guys, working hard at gaining such an image. Lambert used to like to get under the fingernails of some of his teammates, and would incite arguments in the clubhouse just for the sake of a good argument. He would breathe a dragon's flaming breath on anybody who approached him with an annoying inquiry.

He and Dwight White didn't talk to each other for years because of a heated exchange they had in the training room at St. Vincent College early in their careers. I had gotten off to a bad start with Lambert when I began covering the Steelers in 1979, but we kissed and made up, and were able to work together for several years. There were many times when Lambert wouldn't let me up for air, and was determined to give me a difficult time, but I liked him and let him go on. Deep down, Lambert was a good guy, I thought, the real Jack Lambert, that is. Greene had some Lambert in him, too, the way he tried to jack up the crowd, the way he pointed a finger at opposing players and taunted them, the way he rallied the fans to the Steelers' side, the way he carried himself. Whenever I see Lambert today, he still does his best to Bogart me. It's part of his charm.

"I was thankful he didn't floss."

Deep down, Greene and Lloyd have a lot to offer people, too, in a positive sense. I know too many people I like and respect who have good things to say about them. I have met and spoken to Greene's family and regard them as good people, and they think Kevin Greene is the greatest. He would agree. I saw him with his wife, Tara, when he turned into a gentle giant, always protective, always leading the way for her. With her, in public, he was always the Southern gentleman.

With me, he was something less. I interviewed him one day and he was telling me how his parents had taught him to be polite. As he spoke, his blue eyes demanding my utmost attention, he spit chewing tobacco into a little paper cup he held a few inches from my nose. Another time, he brushed his teeth as he talked to me. I don't think he got any toothpaste on me. I was thankful he didn't floss, too.

He and Lloyd had a lot in common, more than they realized. They had both grown up in the Deep South. They had both been Boy Scouts, had military training in their college days, and had a militant manner. Greene was a fanatic about weight lifting, indeed, he had built himself into being a football player while in college. Lloyd had earned a black belt in Taekwondo, a martial art, in June of 1993. They liked to intimidate people.

I remember attending a press conference at Three Rivers Stadium at the conclusion of the 1994 schedule when Lloyd was named the team's most valuable player by his peers. Lloyd entered the media room, wearing a black cap backwards on his head, walked through the assembled media without a word, and sat down, petulantly, and leaned back in his chair, as far from the microphone as possible. Tab Douglas of 3WS Radio asked Lloyd if he could move closer to the microphone. Lloyd looked at Douglas with his most defiant glare — if looks could kill — and edged a millimeter toward the microphone. This was supposed to be a big day for Lloyd, recognition of his outstanding play for the Steelers, yet he chose to be a hard-ass, and resist any attempts at an honest question-and-answer, give-and-take session. He had lost his sense of humor; he didn't know how to have fun, at least not with the media.

The same Tab Douglas was the target for a post-game tirade after the Steelers lost the AFC title game to the San Diego Chargers. He asked Greene a harmless question about how he felt in the wake of such a disheartening defeat. Greene got into his face and shouted obscenities and embarrassed him in front of his colleagues. In short, he took out his personal frustration on the first person who got into his face. Douglas deserved better treatment.

It's too bad that neither Lloyd nor Greene had gotten to know Art Rooney, the late owner of the Steelers. He might have been a good influence on them; he might have drawn them out of their protective shells, the cocoons in which they chose to lock themselves, lest anyone get too close. If they had seen how he, one of the nation's biggest and most-admired sports legends, comported himself, how down-to-earth he was, eager to meet everyone and glad-hand everybody, how self-deprecating he was, how humble, how kind, considerate, Christian and all kinds of positive attributes. They might have learned something from him about public relations.

"It doesn't mean jack."
— Greg Lloyd

When Greene signed as a free agent with the Steelers prior to the 1993 season, his reputation as a quarterback-sacking, wild and theatrical linebacker with the Los Angeles Rams had preceded him. "It doesn't mean jack what he did out there," said Lloyd scornfully at the summer training camp. "All that matters is what he does here."

When Lloyd stepped on Greene's hand in a pileup and broke it in a pre-season game in 1994, Lloyd felt it unnecessary to say anything to Greene in the way of an apology. As Lloyd saw it, that was all part of the game. His seeming lack of compassion for a teammate was part of his sought-after image as one of the league's most menacing forces. He didn't feel any different when he leveled Green Bay quarterback Brett Favre in a pre-season game before the 1995 schedule. Lloyd didn't draw a penalty flag for his hard hit, but he did get a $12,000 fine from the league office. The league was picking on Lloyd, as he saw it, protecting those pansy quarterbacks, as usual. Greene and Lloyd were at extreme ends in the four-linebacker scheme the Steelers employed, but they drove each other to excel, to stay one step ahead of the other.

The Lloyd-Greene act was often a comic parody. Quake and Quiver were like Frick and Frack. Like Billy Crystal and Whoopi Goldberg in a joke-off. During practice sessions at St. Vincent, they were both always posturing and parading around, flexing their muscles for the madding crowd. It was some show.

Both wore different outfits from most of their teammates. They both wore those tight-fitting Spandex knee-length pants. Greene favored black and yellow striped Spandex, while Lloyd liked a black and white model, or a plain black one. Both wore their ballcaps back-ward on their heads. Both liked to wear black jerseys with cut-off sleeves to show off their biceps and both bared their well-muscled midriffs as well. It looked like Lloyd had rubbed himself with body lotion as well as he positively glistened before he would even break a sweat. Mel Blount had been the most physically impressive specimen at the Steelers' training camps in the '70s. Lloyd held that honor in the '80s and '90s.

Greene and Lloyd would both distance themselves from their teammates on the sideline, going to the extreme ends. They would sit on their helmets and look so seriously at the proceedings. They could easily be caught on camera because they were apart from the pack. They often went through the same routine on the sideline at regular season games. When they would start parading around it was fun to watch them, wondering whether they might bump into each other and fall down in a heap. When Dick LeBeau joined the staff as a defensive backfield coach, Lloyd didn't speak to him for three months. Lloyd gave the same silent treatment to Mike Archer, the linebacker coach, and Jim Haslett, the defensive coordinator, when they came on board. Unbelievable, huh?

While most of their teammates admired their approach to the game and their all-out efforts on the field, they sniped at their theatric shenanigans, how popular they remained with the fans despite often showing them disdain in one-on-one encounters, and they tired of Lloyd's loud tirades and personal attacks on their manhood during the games. They thought Lloyd was aware that cameras were catching his every move and word. The act got old, they said.

James Parrish, a self-described "journeyman" ballplayer, had the dressing stall next to Lloyd in 1994 and 1995. There were only two dressing stalls between two doorways, so they were somewhat isolat-ed. The Steelers' clubhouse was the eighth Parrish had called home during a four-year itinerant career. He had spent time with the San Francisco 49ers, Dallas Cowboys, Miami Dolphins, Indianapolis Colts, San Diego Chargers, London Monarchs, and Barcelona Dragons.

He picked up a Super Bowl ring from the Cowboys in 1993, even though he didn't suit up for the big game. He did play in the NFC title game, which he said was "the real Super Bowl."

"When I came out of college, I thought pro teams would be 50 some brothers, all pulling together, but it's not that way," said Parrish, a likable fellow even though Dennis Rodman was one of his role models. "Everyone has their own agenda. I'm interested in people's motives; why they're doing what they're doing.

"Every dressing room is different. Individual stars or key players set the tone for each dressing room. Greg Lloyd is looked upon by most as a leader, sort of, so players take their cue from him. They don't want to be out of line or favor with him. Wherever you go, certain guys are very aware of where the cameras are; it was especially that way with the Cowboys. The 49ers had more of a corporate atmosphere. The Steelers have a pretty good atmosphere in their locker room."

"He was as showbiz in his approach as Deion Sanders of the Cowboys."

Super Bowl XXX provided an interesting stage for Lloyd and Greene and it was interesting to see how they dealt with an international showcase situation.

Lloyd was late for most of the scheduled interview sessions with the 3,000 media types who descended onto the scene in Arizona in January, 1996. He and Greene were among some of the 20 or so Steelers who missed one session altogether because of some misunderstanding. The Steelers drew a $25,000 fine from the league office for that oversight.

I was among those waiting in a tent for Lloyd one day a few days before the meeting with the Dallas Cowboys. We sat and stood around the table with his namecard on it, and waited about 15 minutes before he showed up for what was to have been a 45-minute session. Another Steelers' linebacker, Jerry Olsavsky, a great comeback story, sat largely ignored at the next table. The media were missing out on a good story and a likable subject.

When Lloyd arrived, he sat down and began whispering answers to the questions posed for him. Lloyd has a wonderful deep baritone voice. He sounds so good on the radio and TV whenever he does talk. But he was whispering. The writers and sportscasters were leaning toward Lloyd, trying to capture his words. It was a pathetic scene. Once again, Lloyd had to play his game.

Less than two weeks earlier, in the jubilant dressing room, Lloyd used the F-word while shouting out to teammates. He had just been solicited for an interview by a TV network sportscaster, but insisted later that he didn't know he was on live television. "We're going to the F-ing Super Bowl," he shouted ever so slowly, enunciating each word to get fullest effect. That, too, set off a controversial week of reactions in the newspapers and sports talk shows. Shame, shame.

Lloyd didn't use the F-Word in the press conference in Scottsdale. "You know, you can do a hundred great things, but do one thing that people don't like, and it's like you have 6-6-6 etched in your forehead," said Lloyd when someone mentioned the recent flap over his post-game remarks.

"That was locker room talk. It wasn't the first time people have heard that word coming from me. People have made more of it than they should have. They wanted it to overshadow the actual win.

"My apology goes to any parents whose kids heard me say that. But my obligation is to my kids. It's up to parents out there to tell their kids, 'That man may be a big football player, but what he said was wrong.'

"At home, my kids don't see that No. 95. They don't see all that nasty stuff. They just see daddy. At this point, I don't care what the public thinks about me as a role model. My job is not to raise America's kids. Kids should be like their parents."

Greene got into the spirit of the occasion at Super Bowl XXX. He had left the team the first night in Scottsdale to fly to Las Vegas to participate in a wrestling show. He was pictured in newspapers the next day, posing in a wrestling ring with Hulk Hogan and Randy Savage after the Clash of Champions. This drew a critical eye from many of the media who wondered what he was doing in Vegas when the Steelers were ensconced in Scottsdale, getting ready for the biggest game of their lives.

Greene gave the media quite a show. He was loud and enthusiastic, bright-eyed, animated, offered expansive good stories, kidded them, playfully rebuked them when they asked what he regarded as an inappropriate question, challenged them, you name it. He was pictured on the front pages of newspapers across the world, and was on TV everywhere.

He was as showbiz in his approach as Deion Sanders, the Prime Time $35 million man of the Dallas Cowboys. Standing next to each of them, in the post-Super Bowl media interview tent, it was difficult to determine which one was putting us on the most. With their mouths moving, it was suddenly a spiritual revival tent. They were both harmless.

Greene left the Steelers after the 1995 season to sign with the Carolina Panthers as a free agent. He took a serious cut in pay, but he was reunited with Dom Capers, the former defensive coordinator of the Steelers, who had left the year before to become head coach in Charlotte. Playing outside linebacker in the same 3-4 defensive scheme, Greene led the league with 14.5 sacks, earned some bonus money, playoff money, and contributed mightily to the Panthers getting to the NFC championship game before losing to the eventual Super Bowl champion Green Bay Packers. Greene was named to the Pro Bowl in Hawaii. Lloyd signed an extension to his contract in 1996, and looked to be in great shape for his Steelers' future. He ripped up his left knee in the season opener at Jacksonville and was sidelined the entire 1996 schedule. He had played in five Pro Bowls, making him one of the greatest linebackers in team history and one of the team's most popular players.

He was not popular with the Pittsburgh press, however, and some snickered when they knew he was out for the season. He wasn't talking to them, anyhow, and now that wouldn't be a problem in their efforts to properly cover the club. If Lloyd were to go down with another injury, some would snicker again. Out of his view, of course.

"We don't have to lose to win, don't need to prove ourselves in the no-win race game."
— John Wideman,
Author

Jerome Bettis
A real Pro Bowler

*"I learned quickly
to follow rules."*

Jerome Bettis is a beautiful person. He is just fun to be around. He has a bubbly personality, for starters, and there is a natural warmth about him that invites company. He has slits, like extra smiles, where other people have eyes. He has a grin and thin beard that goes ear to ear on his broad face.

During his first season with the Steelers, he was usually in a cheerful mood, even when hobbled, nursing hurts and injuries. Bettis was simply an upbeat guy, a real sweet man. Bettis came to the Steelers in a trade on Draft Day, 1996 and became an instant hit in Pittsburgh. He was, as they say, a breath of fresh air.

Myron Cope kept calling him "The Bus" during Steelers' radio broadcasts and it caught on.

The media loved Bettis. He always had time for reporters. He was friendly, not full of himself, quick to promote teammates like Tim Lester who led the way for him when he ran the ball, and willing to make dates to discuss matters at more mutually convenient times. In short, he was a considerate, thoughtful individual, and a good interview, qualities respected in any workplace.

Lester liked to say good things about Bettis, too. "He was always a nice person who took his job seriously and treated people nice," allowed Lester.

Bettis may have been the best media-friendly running back of stature on the Steelers since Rocky Bleier, though Erric Pegram was pretty good in that regard, too. Franco Harris has always been a pleasant person, but was often guarded, reluctant to relate his personal thoughts, preferring a slight smile or shrug in response to most inquiries. Harris was a private person, and often spoke in a near-whisper.

"Jerome's a great guy," opined Pegram, even though he lost playing time to the workhorse Bettis the way he had the previous year to Bam Morris. "I mean just a *great* guy, even better than Bam, and Bam was a nice guy. We have a ball."

Bettis was there to talk about the ballgame no matter how well or how poorly he might have played. "Sometimes you don't have big games," he said after a rare substandard performance. "Sometimes you've just got to pound away and earn your pay. You just have to strap it up and get ready to go the next time."

Strangely enough, Bettis was said to have an attitude problem when he played in St. Louis the previous year. The Rams got rid of him in exchange for a second-round pick in 1996 and a fourth-rounder

Jerome Bettis is a happy camper with Steelers. George Gojkovich

"In the end, manners are about treating others as if they matter."
— Ellen Goodman, Columnist
The Boston Globe

in 1997. Of course, why they thought Nebraska badboy Lawrence Phillips would be less of a problem is beyond comprehension. Phillips arrived with a rap sheet, and it had nothing to do with hip-hop music.

Bettis is brief in dismissing the disappointment of his short stay in St. Louis:

"I was upset at the way I was perceived to be," said Bettis. "That was the hardest thing for me. I knew I was a quality individual. All I did was praise everyone and keep on going. For them to say I wasn't a team player and things like that made me a little bitter. But time soothes and heals all kinds of injuries."

Joe Moore, who was the line coach at Notre Dame during the years Bettis played there, was among those who boosted Bettis to the Steelers. Moore, who grew up in Pittsburgh and coached at Upper St. Clair and Pitt, was an old friend of the Steelers' Tom Donahoe, the director of football operations.

"He's a real friendly kid," said Moore. "He's engaging off the field, easy to get along with. He has a nice personality."

Obtaining Bettis at a bargain basement price turned out to be the Steal of the Year for Donahoe and the Steelers. Bettis could not have had a better attitude than the way he comported himself on the Steelers' scene.

Bettis had a clause in a revamped contract he signed with the Steelers that enabled him to become a free agent if he gained 1,200 yards in a season — talk about incentives — and he did just that and then some. He virtually carried the Steelers on his back while rushing for 1,431 yards.

Bettis had rambled for 1,419 yards on 294 tries in his rookie season with the Rams, and rushed for 1,025 yards on 319 tries in his second season in Los Angeles. In St. Louis, after the Rams relocated, he rushed for only 637 yards, but he carried the ball only 183 times.

It looked for a while after the 1996 season that the Steelers might not be successful in re-signing Bettis, but management recognized they needed him back more than any of the other free agents and, finally, came up with a deal that Bettis liked. Then, too, his mother had made him promise he would give Pittsburgh the last chance at signing him. And Bettis, even at age 25, was a young man who listened to his parents.

Pittsburgh had been good for Bettis, and he had been good for the Steelers and their fans. It was a mutual admiration society. Bettis recognized how good he had it in Pittsburgh, but money talks and players walk wherever they can get the most money. The Bettis Watch was a nervous period.

Steelers fans would have been crushed if Bettis had left town. They had embraced this jubilant widebody running back more than any of the other players who had departed in recent years via the free agency escape route.

Fans loved how hard Bettis ran, and how he'd get up quickly and punch the sky or pump his legs, like he was rarin' to go again. Some ballplayers' on-the-field antics are turn-offs, but Bettis managed to do his thing in a turn-on manner. Somehow it wasn't offensive, at least not for Steelers' fans. He moved tacklers out of the way and he moved fans out of their seats.

The Dallas Cowboys even hired one of their former players, Calvin Hill and his wife, Janet, the parents of Detroit Pistons' model star Grant Hill, to improve the behavior of their players. The Steelers might consider hiring the parents of Jerome Bettis. They brought him up the right way.

Steelers' fans love the guy. It didn't hurt him in Pittsburgh, western Pennsylvania or the tri-state area, for that matter, that he had played his college ball at Notre Dame. Anyone associated with the Fighting Irish has an instant appeal in these parts.

"I was surprised how they responded to me so early," said Bettis. "Me being a newcomer, I thought it would take a while for me to gain their respect.

"The minute I got out there, they were behind me a hundred percent. It's to the point where it's almost unimaginable. They're sending me so much mail. I can feel it when I'm talking with kids. One kid sent me $3 to help me stay here. Out of his own pocket!"

I came to appreciate just how popular Bettis had become with Pittsburgh sports fans one night at an unusual venue. I was invited by Sergio Franyutti of Bayer Corporation to come to Sewall Center at Robert Morris College to check out a Pro Bowlers Association (PBA) tournament, the final stop on the national tour, back in early November, 1996. Bayer, which provides the polyurethane to Brunswick for bowling balls, sponsored the event.

Bettis had been invited as well. He has been an ardent bowler since his boyhood — he has a 300 game to his credit at a celebrity event — and he was asked to participate in a similar pro-am event that preceded the tour competition on lanes set up on the basketball floor at Robert Morris. Bettis wasn't able to bowl because he was nursing some leg hurts, but he showed up to watch the pro bowlers because some of them are among his favorite sports people. He sat in the crowd of over 3,000 fans to see the pros do their thing up close in what is called arena bowling competition.

When the TV camera caught Bettis in the crowd and the p.a. announcer cited his presence, the crowd went ballistic. Not only was Bettis a Steelers' star, but he was a bowler — one of them! Lynn Swann, a former Super Bowl MVP for the Steelers, drew a more modest applause when his presence was announced. International hurdles star and two-time Olympic gold medalist Roger Kingdom, who had made his home in Monroeville and had attended Pitt, finished a distant third on the applause meter. Why Kingdom continued to live in a city that had always taken track and field for granted was puzzling. He'd have gotten a much more enthusiastic reception in Paris, London, Rome or Atlanta, where his accomplishments are more appreciated.

103

Swann and Kingdom were two of the most attractive and articulate athletes ever to grace the Pittsburgh sports scene, but Bettis had become even bigger in the public's what-have-you-done-for-us-lately mind.

Pro football and bowling are both big in Pittsburgh — for years Pittsburgh was one of the few cities in the country where ABC TV's Saturday pro bowling show was shown twice in the same day — so Bettis was fast becoming one of the city's favorite sons.

Bettis had been a Pro Bowler running back in his first two seasons with the Rams when they played in Los Angeles. When they relocated in St. Louis, something got lost in the shuffle. He became an overweight running back with foot problems and was playing in the wrong system. So he sulked and was hardly himself. Until the Steelers swapped a draft choice for him during the 1996 college draft.

How long did it take to become a Pittsburgh Steeler?

"It took me a training camp," said Bettis. "I knew what this team meant, what it was all about, what the city was all about. I fit in pretty good. I was from a blue collar town. I knew what it took to be successful. All they want here is a person who works hard. That's what they do every day of their lives."

Jerome, talking about his popularity in Pittsburgh: "It makes me feel good that the fans here appreciate me. It spurs me on. It's not flashy, it's not the glitter. It's hard-nosed, the blue collar work I do between the tackles. I prefer mixing it up in there and pounding away."

With the Steelers's two-back set, he gets the ball closer to the line — not as a deep I-back — and he gets better blocking up front. In Pittsburgh, he was reunited with fullback Tim Lester, who led the blocking for him out of the backfield during his earlier Pro Bowl years, and they were a magic tandem once again. When Bettis got back to the Pro Bowl in January of 1997, he took Lester along for a complimentary ride to Hawaii.

"He's my man," Bettis said of Lester. "I took Tim to the Pro Bowl in Hawaii the last time I went there and I supported him while he was there. It cost me a pretty penny, too. Tim eats like a horse."

Bettis also took his family, something he does for every game on the Steelers' schedule.

His family was good to him when Bettis was growing up, always there for him, always supportive, and he's returning the favor now that he can afford to be kind to them. With the contract he signed in late February of 1997, worth $14.4 million over four years, including a $4 million signing bonus, Bettis should be able to continue his kind ways with his family. He signed the contract one day after his 25th birthday. What a belated birthday present! He had become the highest paid player in Steelers' history.

"He's a good football player and he means an awful lot to our team," said Steelers president Dan Rooney. "We think it's the start of keeping us in the direction we want to be."

Pro Bowler Jerome Bettis (No. 36) looks ahead to great days with Steelers, following blocking of his buddy Tim Lester (No. 34) now that he has signed new four-year contract. He rushed for 1,431 yards in 1996 season.

Michael F. Fabus/Pittsburgh Steelers

Jerome Bettis fights for yardage and for his breath as he battles Jaguars and asthma in humid Jacksonville in 1996 season opener.

Bettis weighed nearly 250 pounds when he was at St. Louis. His agent, Lamont Smith, had Bettis work with a personal trainer in Denver during the offseason before he reported to the Steelers' training camp. He had trimmed down. The transformation was unreal. The extra effort certainly paid dividends; Bettis was well advised by his agent.

San Francisco and Houston had both expressed interest in Bettis when the St. Louis Rams were shopping him around.

When Houston used their No. 1 draft pick to get running back Eddie George of Ohio State, the Heisman Trophy winner, they weren't interested in Bettis anymore.

The Steelers made sense to Bettis. He liked how featured backs had fared in the Steelers' offensive scheme. Barry Foster, Leroy Thompson, Bam Morris and Erric Pegram all ran the ball well in the Steelers' system. Then, too, Lester was there, ready to succeed the departed John L. Williams as the principal blocking back. Bettis liked Lester and he liked what he had done for him in LA.

"It's definitely a running offense, a big running back offense," Bettis said. "It's where you pound the ball in there, take the ball 25, 30 times, and just wear a team out, and I think I can do that."

The Steelers also had one of the best offensive lines in the league, and certainly one of the premier centers to show the way.

"He doesn't need much, just a crack," said Dermontti Dawson, the Steelers' perennial Pro Bowl snapper. "He's such a big back, and you don't see guys that big who can move like that."

Bettis likes to boost the guys who block for him, and even took them all out to dinner one night at Morton's Steak House in downtown Pittsburgh where the bill came to about $2,500.

"These guys can make anybody look good," said Bettis. "They're the best. These guys give it their best every game, no matter what. There are a couple of All-Pros up there, as they make the rest play up to that level. I don't think there's a better offense in the league."

"A 300 game seemed unattainable."

Bettis wouldn't be happy with this book if you didn't hear about the 300 game he once bowled. His 300 game was accomplished in Muskegon in a pro-am celebrity bowling tournament. He had thrown 11 straight strikes, and some of the pros came over to check him out . . .

Listen to Bettis talking about the highlight of his bowling career:

"By the time I got to the 12th frame, I was ready to pass out. I had never gotten that far before. A 300 game was something that seemed so unattainable to me. Everybody in the whole building was watching, tons of people were standing and rooting for me, including a few pros. I tried to control the hook while releasing the final ball.

"I'm just hoping and praying. You're not sure where you're going to put the ball. You just put it out there and hope it comes back."

106

He drilled the pocket cleanly, hitting every pin. "I went nuts. It was bigger than anything, bigger than scoring a touchdown."

"This guy comes to work every day."
— Dick Hoak

I spoke to Bettis after the playoff disappointment at New England. Bettis did his best to play that day, but he wasn't physically up to it. He had a severe groin pull and a gimpy ankle. He ran 13 times for 43 yards and limped off the field in pain.

That same week he was back in the clubhouse at Three Rivers Stadium, doing his best to get healthy so he could play in the upcoming Pro Bowl in Hawaii.

"That was frustrating," said Bettis of his inability to play up to his own high standards at New England. "I knew I normally had the ability to contribute, to make a difference. Not being a hundred percent hurt. The team needed me to play well."

Did Bill Cowher ever consider not using him at New England? "No," Bettis came back. "He knew I wanted to play and that I wanted to play well.

"That's tough to do that when you can't make a play. I could feel it (in his injured thigh). When I was running straight, I could tell I wasn't running as fast as everyone else. Everyone was running faster than I was. If I had made a breakaway run, I couldn't have sustained it. I probably would have gone down like I was shot or something.

"Mentally, it really hurt. Here you had an opportunity, had a perfect situation you couldn't draw up any better. But you go out and lay an egg."

Instead, the day belonged to Curtis Martin and Keith Byars and Drew Bledsoe and Terry Glenn. Martin was the most productive running back and scored two touchdowns to open the early lead against his hometown team.

I asked Bettis about Martin, who had matriculated from Taylor Allderdice High School and Pitt to play in the pros, passing up his final year of college eligibility.

"I hear good things about him," said Bettis. "He has a great attitude and he's humble. He'll go a long way. He's gracious in defeat, too."

Asked for his thoughts about playing for Bill Cowher, Bettis offered:

"It's great to play for him. He was like a breath of fresh air. I'd come from a situation where I was an outcast, put in exile. He embraced me. I was going to be one of their main guys.

"He motivated us and gave us something to play for. He found ways, creative ways, to find something for us to play for."

Cowher had respected Bettis as an opponent. "I saw a guy that ran over us when we played them," commented Cowher. "I think he looks at this like a new lease on life."

What did Bettis think of Dick Hoak, the Steelers' laidback backfield coach? "He has a different way of getting excited," said Bettis, smiling as he tried to explain his position coach. "He gets excited by you doing well. He's proud like a parent. He likes to see you progress. His knowledge. He's played the game and he's been around, he's seen it all. We have the ultimate respect for him. We ask him about the guys like Harris and Bleier."

Dick Hoak coached Harris, Bleier, Foster, Thompson, Morris and Pegram and now Bettis and played with John Henry Johnson. "He's as good as anyone in the league right now," Hoak said of his newest charge. "In training camp, you could see he was a guy who would run over people. He causes them to miss. He has good feet, good balance. He's not just a power runner."

Whereas Foster was a complainer, and Ban Morris had bad habits on and off the field, Hoak had no negatives to offer about Bettis.

"This guy comes to work every day," said Hoak, a former Penn Stater from Jeannette, who's lived in Greensburg all during his stay with the Steelers. "He's like Franco was; he's not up one day and down the next. He's not a moody guy. He enjoys football, coming here, sitting in meetings. He's the same every day. He enjoys playing."

He was named MVP by his teammates after his first season with the Steelers, but it didn't give Bettis a big head.

"I'm an ordinary guy who likes ordinary things," he said. "Hopefully, I can help the team get back to the Super Bowl game."

"Civility has become a catchword in the past year, as if Americans experienced some great, late, collective awakening to the coarseness of public discourse, the rudeness of private life. There is talk of spitting ballplayers, swearing lyricists and dirty-warring politicians. In some odd twist, incivility has even become an accusation for combatants to throw at each other."
— Ellen Goodman,
Syndicated columnist,
The Boston Globe

Detroit
Some memories of Motor City

*"This town makes Pompeii
look alive at night."*
— Jimmy Cannon

Detroit brings many images to mind. Motor City. Motown. That's where they make many of America's automobiles. Diana Ross and the Supremes came out of its city projects. I was all set to move there and work there in 1970, after I received an offer from the *Detroit Free-Press*. I remember my wife, Kathie, and I staying at the Book-Cadillac Hotel when we were there to check out the city. It reminded us of a larger version of Pittsburgh.

I had been recommended by *The Miami Herald*, a sister newspaper in the Knight-Ridder chain. I changed my mind after initially accepting an offer to go to Detroit, and ended up instead going to *The New York Post* that year.

I had worked the previous year for *The Miami News*, covering the Miami Dolphins. The Dolphins were 3-10-1 in George Wilson's last season as the head coach.

Don Shula came in and turned the Dolphins completely around. The Dolphins finished 10-4 in Shula's first season. The following year they would play in the Super Bowl in the first of three consecutive appearances, the only team ever to do that. In 1972, the Dolphins would become the only undefeated team in National Football League history with a 17-0 record. Hard to believe that was 25 years ago.

Most of the players I had known from the 1979 team that went 3-10-1 were key contributors to the Dolphins' fantastic success, Hall of Famers like Larry Csonka, Bob Griese, Larry Little, and Dick Anderson, Nick Buoniconti, Manny Fernandez, Mercury Morris, Jim Kiick, Howard Twilley, Larry Seiple, Norm Evans, Bill Stanfel and Lloyd Mumphord.

I missed that successful run, though, because in 1970 I moved to New York, where the Mets and Jets had just won championships, and where the Knicks, Nets and Islanders were about to become champions as well. I also got to meet Muhammad Ali and cover several of his championship fights, which helped me not to feel too badly about missing out on the Dolphins' Super Bowl days.

When I was talking to Bettis about Detroit and his boyhood memories it made me think about what it might have been like to have worked in Detroit during the '70s.

"I hear you're going to Detroit," Larry Merchant of *The New York Post* told me one night at Madison Square Garden where I'd gone to cover a basketball game while completing my stay at *The Miami News*. "You're going to be out of the mainstream in the Midwest. Why don't you come here?"

109

Merchant, now an HBO boxing analyst and wordsmith, introduced me to Ike Gellis, the sports editor of *The Post* that same night, and Gellis offered me a job on the spot. So I went to New York instead of Detroit.

Detroit was the city of Joe Falls and Jerry Green, two of the best sports writers in the business. I was offered different mixes of teams to cover, but it could have included the Pistons, the Lions and the University of Michigan. I could have filled in on occasion with the Tigers and Red Wings as well.

I visited Tiger Stadium in downtown Detroit a few times with the New York Yankees. Every press box in baseball boasted of something special — it was the crab cakes in Baltimore — and I recall they had great ice cream in the press box at Tiger Stadium. When I think of the Tigers, I think of Al Kaline, Harvey Kuenn, Norm Cash, Willie Horton, Rocky Colavito, Denny McLain, Mickey Lolich and Billy Martin. I had a chance to interview all of them.

That's where the Lions played. The Lions of the '50s, as well as the Browns, the two best teams at the time, are a team from my youth that won't go away. The Lions of that era won five division crowns and three league titles. Buddy Parker, who later came to the Steelers, was their coach. They had such magic names on those teams, beginning with Dick "Night Train" Lane.

Then, too, there was Bobby Layne, Doak Walker, Bob "Hunchy" Hoernschemeyer, Tom "The Bomb" Tracy, Dick Stanfel, Marty Wendell, John Henry Johnson, Les Bingaman, Howard "Hopalong" Cassady, Jug Girard. The names run through my mind and it's fun just to say those names aloud again, to remember them as the bubble gum cards they were for a kid growing up in Pittsburgh, about three to four miles from the ballparks and stadiums of the Pirates and Steelers. The cards were as close as I came to big league sports in those days.

The Lions had Cloyce Box, Jim Doran, Jim David, Dorne Dibble, Jack Christiansen, Lou Creekmur, LeVern Torgeson, Thurman McGraw, Joe Schmidt from Brentwood, Pa., Harley Sewell, Charlie Ane, Gene Gedman from Duquesne, Pa., Pat Harder and Yale Lary. Dick Le Beau and Mike Lucci came along later. All magic names that roll off the tongue. Like Lem Barney and Mel Farr, they just sounded like Lions.

I think of Gordy Howe, Alex Delvecchio, Ted Lindsay and Terry Sawchuck of the Red Wings, the legendary boxer Joe Louis, and Dave Bing and Bob Lanier and Ray "Chink" Scott of the Pistons. Detroit was a good sports town. Bettis reminds you it was a great bowling town, too.

I remember going there to cover a heavyweight boxing championship bout between Joe Frazier and Bob Foster. Frazier caught Foster flush on the forehead and opened a cut which bled profusely. Some of the blood spurted onto a woman who was working for Western Union at ringside. It was her first ringside assignment.

When the blood flew her way, she fainted dead away on top of her machine.

One night before the fight, I was walking through the dark streets of downtown Detroit with two of my favorite sports writers, Jimmy Cannon, a nationally-syndicated columnist from New York who used to delight me with stories of his days in Paris with Ernest Hemingway, and Roy McHugh, a sports columnist from *The Pittsburgh Press.* They wrote boxing, and most other sports, as well as anybody ever did it. I thought I was in heaven just to be with two little guys who were giants in the business.

The streets of Detroit were empty this particular evening. There was no one to be seen. Maybe everybody was smarter than the three sports writers who stood on a corner, trying to decide where they might go to catch a bite to eat.

"This town makes Pittsburgh look alive at night," I observed.

"This town," came back Cannon as only he could, "makes Pompeii look alive at night!"

Legendary sportswriter Jimmy Cannon chats with New York Mets' manager Casey Stengel back in mid-60s.

The Bettis Family
Lots of discipline

*"I knew how to stay
out of trouble."*

The Steelers were in the playoffs when I sat down with Jerome Bettis in the players' lounge, just off the clubhouse, to talk to him. This area was normally off-limits to the media, but I had been given permission to sit in the Steelers' inner sanctum where Bettis might be more relaxed. He had just beaten Darren Perry in a chess match at the same table where we sat. Bettis was, indeed, a man for all seasons.

"My father taught me how to play chess when I was little," said Bettis. "When I was with the Rams, there were several guys who liked to play chess. So I got back to playing again. Darren's just learning to play. I hadn't played in a while, but I'm more experienced. I like to play video games, everything competitive. Darren wants a rematch. He's competitive, too. That's what it's all about."

In his youth, Bettis was often told by his parents that sports and games were a good way to keep busy, to stay out of trouble, and he hadn't forgotten that lesson.

"Stay out of trouble" could have been his schoolboy motto. One of his teammates in 1996, Jonathan Hayes, had the same message hammered into him while growing up in South Fayette. It had a familiar ring to it.

Bettis grew up on Aurora Street on the West Side of Detroit. The Bettis family had its own free-standing home.

His father, Johnnie, was an electrical inspector for the city and he taught electrical wiring in adult education classes at night. Jerome's mother, Gladys, worked at a bank, processing checks, when he was growing up.

"Before my junior year in college, she got laid off," said Jerome. "That helped me make my decision to turn pro a year early to help my family.

"I still need two semesters, and I intend to get my degree (in business management). I've gone back to take some classes since I've been playing pro ball. I enjoyed the Notre Dame experience. It taught me a lot, growing up as a person. They gave me a lot of discipline at Notre Dame. They stayed after me pretty good. It was a followup to what my family had stressed. The work was hard. There was no way you could get through it unless you worked hard."

Lou Holtz was his coach at Notre Dame. "I've been back to see Coach Holtz," said Bettis. "He still gets on my case."

Bettis had visited Holtz at Notre Dame in January, 1996, just before winter classes started. The coach greeted him with a challenge.

112

Jerome Bettis was a tailback and wore No. 6 when he starred for Lou Holtz at Notre Dame.

Bettis left Notre Dame after his junior year and was the No. 1 draft pick of the Los Angeles Rams. Draft Day was a family affair. Present were (from left to right) NFL Commissioner Paul Tagliabue, who autographed this photo for Jerome, sister Kimberly, Aunt Gloria or "Auntie Mamma," as she's known, brother John III, Jerome, his mother Gladys and father Johnnie.

"He came in," Holtz recalled to Shelly Anderson of the *Post-Gazette,* "and before he could say anything, I said, 'Jerome, I want to tell you something. There's a guy wearing your jersey that is not doing you any favors. It's not the Jerome Bettis I know, and I know you wouldn't play like that. So it's obviously not you.'

"He said, 'Coach, I came back for two reasons. One, I promised you I'd work on my degree. No. 2, I came back to get my attitude right. When I was at Notre Dame, I left here with a tremendous attitude. Right now, I just want to get my attitude right.'

"He worked out with our players. I visited with him from time to time, and when that trade came through (in April), I was really happy for him," Holtz said.

One of the Steelers' assistant coaches, John Mitchell, had been an assistant coach under Holtz for several years at Arkansas, and liked to share stories about Holtz. Mitchell and Bettis also share a similar enthusiasm and near-reverence when referring to their parents' influence on their lives.

"Yeah, he gave me some stories," Bettis said of Coach Mitchell. "We both share a high regard for Holtz. He was great for me. He helped me as a person and he helped me as a player. Off the field, he nurtured me. He always wanted me to be gracious and humble. He ran a tight ship."

Did Holtz ever come down hard on Bettis?

"I never crossed that line," Bettis said. "I never saw the disciplinarian side. I followed the rules. I never did anything from the start to go outside the rules. Anything you do, you have to respect rules. Rules are a part of life. It was nothing new for me. I had rules to follow as a kid. I learned quickly to follow rules.

"We had basic rules in our home: no fighting with my older brother and sister. I was the youngest of three. There was no turning on the stove after dinner. No company in your room. Visitors were to be in the living room, not your room. Your parents had to know where you were when you left the house. No hats on your head in the house. We had to abide by the rules. You learn to make it part of your everyday behavior.

"With the way kids are being raised, they don't have discipline or manners. When these values are highlighted and promoted, the child understandably follows the lead. In our home, we knew and understood the rules. Plus, I've suffered with asthma since I was a kid, and I've had to be careful about that, too, and make sure I had an inhaler with me at all times. I've had to be responsible.

"My mom was always big on manners. She made sure I opened doors for her and other adults. We always said, 'excuse me' and 'pardon me' and 'may I' and 'please' and 'thank you,' stuff like that. She always said she wanted us to make her proud. And we tried our best to do just that. "My dad was real quiet. He was the disciplinarian. When there were problems, my mother related them to my dad, and he'd get after us.

"I was lucky. I was blessed. My dad was the father to all of the guys in our neighborhood. He'd teach them things, too. He didn't want us standing around on the streets. If they were in our house, he didn't want them standing around, either. He wanted them to sit down, and not to sit on the arm rests on chairs or couches. He kept all the guys in line. What they did at their homes might not be acceptable at our home. He was real clear about that. My friends respected my dad. It was always 'Mr. Bettis this' and 'Mr. Bettis that,' and all the guys admired him. Only three families out of the ten or so on our street had two parents at home."

"I'm comfortable in Detroit."

To hear Jerome Bettis talk about Detroit you would think he grew up not far from the Land of Oz. Wasn't Detroit one of the toughest towns in America? Didn't Detroit's mean streets rival those of New York, Chicago, Philadelphia, Miami and LA?

"It's where I'm from," said Bettis. "It's a city that's greatly misunderstood. A lot of people assume it's the murder capital of this country. Like it has to be a terrible place to live. I see it as home. It's a place where if you give it an opportunity it will surprise you. I can see myself raising my family there.

"I'm comfortable in Detroit. That's home. The city is more receptive to me now. They do things to celebrate me. I'm involved there with PAL (Police Athletic League). I go and see them and give them money. I was involved in PAL as a kid and now they point to me as one of their success stories, a role model. I like to show the kids it's cool to go to school and play sports and to stay out of trouble."

When he signed his new contract with the Steelers, Bettis spoke of buying a bowling alley in Detroit. As a child, Bettis became a bowler because his mother thought it would be a good way to spend his free time on Saturday. "She made us go bowling in the beginning," he recalled, "but I was good at it, right away, and I looked forward to going."

So his older brother and sister and Jerome, in turn, all trudged off crosstown to the Central City Lanes, all 60 lanes.

"My mom would take us every Saturday," recalled Bettis. "I was in a youth league called Coke & Bowl. You got a Coke and a hot dog in addition to bowling as part of the program. I was seven years old when I started. But I was big for my age. I was always a big kid. And I was good at it.

"Nobody else in the neighborhood went bowling, but none of them made fun of me about it. They all understood that was something we did. My parents both bowled."

Bettis went to a private school, Detroit Urban Lutheran, during his elementary school years, and that was important to his parents.

"They did everything they could to give us an edge," he said. "They made sure I didn't have pitfalls that caused a lot of other kids to stumble and fall. My father paid for us to go to private school. I hated it for a long time. It was so restrictive, and we always had homework.

"Every day I wanted to go to the public school. I didn't want the homework. The public school kids never seemed to have homework. They said they did it in school, which was kind of confusing. How can you do homework in school? That makes it schoolwork, not homework. They'd be playing another hour every day after school while I was home doing my homework. I always wanted to be in public school because they never had homework.

"Now I'm thankful they did what they did. When I got to public school for high school I was so far advanced. I graduated with honors from McKenzie High School. I played football the whole time and basketball for one year."

Did he get into any trouble as a kid?

"Not real trouble. I've never been in a situation where that came up. I always thought my actions through before I did them. If I had an irrational thought about doing something I shouldn't do, that was cleared up quickly. If I misbehaved in any manner, my mother always told me why I was getting a whipping. It holds true now. I know right from wrong and watch myself."

What was life like for him when he played for the Rams in Los Angeles?

"When I got out to California that was quite an eye-opener. Here I was 21 and in a fast-moving city. Being from the inner-city, I knew pitfalls and how to get into trouble. So it was easy to stay away from it. I know how to stay out of trouble.

"As a player, you're going to be approached by a lot of people who want your attention, and some of them are bad people. The wrong people, people I was taught to stay away from at an early age. A ballplayer has to be responsible for his own behavior. The guys who get in trouble allow themselves to be in that situation. They have to live with the decisions they make."

Did he see himself as a role model? Some ballplayers say they don't want any part of that, insisting they are not role models.

"That's part of the job," said Bettis. "That's part of being a professional athlete. Whether you like it or not, you're in the public eye. If you do something wrong, you're going to draw the wrong kind of attention to yourself.

"Regardless of whether or not I think I'm a role model, I can't help but be a role model."

Who were his own sports idols as he was growing up in Detroit?

"Walter Ray Williams Jr. and Norm Duke," said Bettis.

I must have looked like I didn't recognize those names. "They're bowlers," Bettis said. "They're big on the pro tour. They're in a profession I love and I'd love to be in. They'd love to be in football. I chat

Jerome Bettis was an outstanding bowler from the beginning, in elementary school and at McKenzie High School. He was often joined at the local lanes in Detroit by, left to right below, his father and mother and brother Johnnie.

Photos from the Bettis family album

with them. I watched bowling on TV as a kid, guys like Marshall Holman, Earl Anthony, Mark Roth and Johnny Petraglia. Chris Schinkel was the announcer. I watched that show religiously.

"I also like Michael Jordan, because of his competitiveness. If he's pitching pennies, he likes to pitch them farther and closer to the wall than anyone else. He's working hard all the time, in every game. You have to respect that.

"Jerry Rice has that same reputation. He doesn't take a play off, even in practice. Emmitt Smith is the same way. All your great competitors are that way.

"One guy in football I idolized was Walter Payton. 'Sweetness' . . . that's what they called him. I wasn't a big baseball fan, so I didn't have any heroes there. I'm getting into the Red Wings more now. I admire anyone who can play on a pro level, those who are willing to pay the price.

"It's important to work out and be ready. You don't want to be in any way, shape or form not at your best because of your own negligence."

"I want to make my family proud of me."

When Steelers' games are on national TV, the cameras often catch the Bettis family in the stands. They stand out because they're obvious in their rooting for Jerome and the Steelers. It probably intrigues fans that Jerome brings his entire family to games, which has to be an expensive undertaking.

In addition to his parents, Jerome's brother, Johnnie, 28, and sister, Kimberly, 31, are usually there.

"I want to be capable of taking care of my family," said Bettis, as if bankrolling them on such trips is no big deal. "If you take away my family I wouldn't be the same ballplayer or person. That's why I take them to road games. They've always been there for me, it's the least I can do.

"They believed in me when no one else believed in me. They were there when I was a freshman in high school. I was a star in their eyes. Back in high school, when I was a knucklehead nobody for two years, they thought I was the greatest.

"When I was at Notre Dame, they came to South Bend. They drove there for every game, and it was a three-hour drive. They went to nearly all the road games, like Michigan State, Purdue, Penn State and Pitt. They'd make those games. They didn't go to our game at USC. But they went to all the home games. They were always there.

"This season they drove to Pittsburgh, and sometimes they'd take the train. They would fly to away games. When I was with the

Rams, they flew out every week. That's the least thing I can do. They were there when they had to pick up the tab. It meant a lot to see them. It still does.

"I look for them at the beginning of every game. When they see me, they always wave. I know they're watching. I want to make them proud.

"Me and my family . . . it means a lot to everybody. They suffer with me. Going to games . . . that's a reward. It means that we all made it. I think about it."

"We were always there to cheer him on."

Kim Bettis, 31 and six years older than her brother Jerome, was attending Wayne County Community College when we spoke in the spring of 1997. She was one of the family members who attended most of Jerome's games and had been to Hawaii at the outset of the year to see her brother perform in the Pro Bowl.

I told Kim I thought most pro football players who were nursing serious injuries the way her brother had at the end of the 1996 season would have begged off from playing in the Pro Bowl game. I felt Jerome struggled to rehabilitate himself in time to play so that he wouldn't disappoint his family and the players he had promised he would take to Hawaii.

"We didn't expect him to play," said Kim. "But he told us he was sending us to Hawaii whether or not he was able to play. He said that was our reward for coming to his games."

Some football fans might think that getting to go to all the Steelers' games, home and away, at the expense of your brother would be a bonus to begin with.

"It's the way we were raised," said Kim. "When we were kids and we went bowling, if one was in a tournament the other was expected to go to cheer. Everyone went. It was an all-for-one and one-for-all sort of thing. It's always been that way. We all went to his high school football games. It's a supportive thing. It's just the way it was. We were always there to cheer him on."

She and Jerome and his older brother, Johnnie, grew up in a disciplined home in the inner-city of Detroit.

"Both my parents were working," recalled Kim. "We had to do housework or homework, and we weren't supposed to have friends in the house when our parents weren't home. Sometimes we'd sneak out, but we knew we were in trouble if we broke the rules. We realized later it was all for our benefit. Some of the kids we grew up with are not doing as well. A lot of them are in jail, some are dead."

I mentioned that Jerome had said friends were permitted in the home if his parents were there, but they better not sit on the arms of the chairs or couches, or be caught standing on the stairway, or something like that. They were expected to sit down, and to sit properly.

"One of my mother's rules was that you have to show people you respect your home. If you don't, they won't."

Like Jerome, Kim loves to go bowling. "All three of us, Johnnie, myself and Jerome, were all brought up as bowlers. My mother wanted to keep us all busy. Jerome was the baby. When my brother and I were away in school, Jerome caught it even worse at home.

"One of his best friends was shot and wounded walking home from school. It was a drive-by shooting and the shot wasn't meant for his friend. If Jerome wasn't at practice he could have been with him. Jerome could have been shot. My parents would take Jerome to and from practice. Rick's OK now, but he could have been killed.

"My mother still worries about him all the time. That never changes. She calls him when he's injured to find out how he's doing. When he gets hit hard, she'll worry.

"We would drive to Pittsburgh, or take the train. It took about five hours either way. Jerome always takes good care of us. He's a nice guy, really a nice guy. We're proud of him. He has remained the same. When he comes home, he's the same Jerome I grew up with. None of it's gone to his head."

"Pittsburgh is someplace special."

No one was happier when Bettis signed a five-year contract to stay with the Steelers — just one day after his 25th birthday — than his family.

"My family was overjoyed, elated," said Bettis. "When I told my parents the other situation had arisen and the other team, there was a lot of negative feedback. My mother was adamant about the fact that she liked Pittsburgh and didn't want me to go. She said if I did, it was OK, but there were reservations in her voice. My father was definitely dead-set against me leaving, and my brother was heartbroken about the thought of me leaving the Steelers. I think he would have suffered the most."

When did it dawn on Bettis just how popular he is in Pittsburgh?

"It's really starting to dawn on me," admitted Bettis. "I was in Detroit and went out to play laser tag. There were about 100 kids there, and nobody said anything to me. I thought to myself, if I was in Pittsburgh I wouldn't have been able to escape one kid without an autograph. I realized Pittsburgh is someplace special in that even the little kids know who I am. That doesn't happen in too many other places."

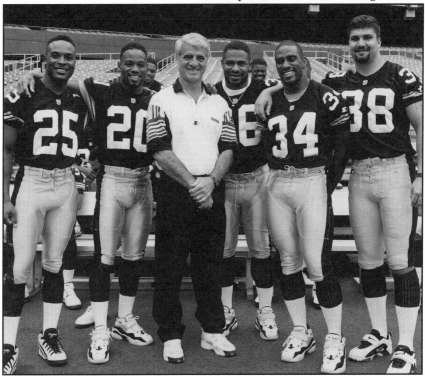

Steelers running backs for 1996 season were (left to right) Fred McAfee, Erric Pegram, coach Dick Hoak, Jerome Bettis, Tim Lester and Jon Witman. Pegram was traded to San Diego in July, 1997.

Jerome Bettis leads the Steelers' pack on sightseeing tour of Tokyo, Japan during late July, 1997 trip there to play pre-season game with San Diego Chargers. Other Steelers leading the parade were (left to right) Greg Lloyd, Bernard Dafney, Oliver Gibson and Ray Seals.

"The Bus" Is Her Baby

By Gladys Bettis

His name is Jerome Bettis, but they've been calling him "The Bus" because he's so big and tough and he runs over people. He's become quite the football player, and we're so proud of him.

I'd never call him "The Bus," though. To me, he'll always be my baby. That's something the fans don't understand. They see him in a completely different light.

I remember him growing up. And he was such a crybaby. But he's so tough now.

Till the time he got to be 12, he just cried about everything. It didn't take much to start him crying. He was so sensitive about everything. He was the baby and I tried to spoil him. He was funny.

When he was in grade school, Jerome used to carry a briefcase with him to and from school. It had been his dad's briefcase before, one of those Samsonite numbers. He always wanted to be like his dad, and do things like his dad did. It was an old briefcase, and it wouldn't stay closed. That's why his dad discarded it.

Jerome would take it and he'd leave the house and as soon as he got out of the house he'd drop the briefcase, and it would pop open and his papers would spill out all over the sidewalk. He'd start to cry. It was like a morning ritual at our house. He and my niece would pick up the papers. Her name was Gloria and they went to school together. My sister and I married brothers, so our families were close.

Jerome wore glasses back then, just like his dad. He wore dress shirts to school, shirts like his dad wore, because it was a private school. He'd always have one of those protective shields for ballpoint pens in the breast pocket of his shirt, just like his dad did. He'd leave his lunch at home. I'd take him and my niece to school before I went to work. He'd end up going to one of our neighbors for lunch. Maybe he liked their lunches better.

Me and Johnnie have been married for 31 years. I came from a large family. I had eight brothers and four sisters, and my mom and dad were there for us. My dad was strict. We grew up in Detroit. I played a lot of baseball myself and I was a big Tigers fan. Back then, I liked Willie Horton. We went to the same school, Northwestern High. I liked Gates Brown and Alan Trammell. I thought my older son, Johnnie III — my husband is Johnnie Jr. — would play baseball. He was quite good at it when he was young. My husband was an electrician for the City of Detroit and I worked at a local bank.

Jerome was a pleasant young child. He was just one of the sweetest young men you'd ever want to meet. He has my niceness about him. That comes from my mom. His dad can be gruff, and he gets a little of that from him, too.

I taught my children how to be gentlemen and a young lady. I also gave them some of the street knowledge I felt they needed. I gave them what I had. I'm a stickler for good manners. I taught them to treat people the way they wanted to be treated, to hold the door open for someone, to say 'thank you' and 'please' and 'pardon me,' and things like that. You can't use those words enough.

I told them that rules are there for a reason. A lot of people in our area didn't make the time to talk to and do with their children what my husband and I thought was necessary. We have three fantastic children.

The biggest problem I feel today is that parents don't have any time for their children.

Jerome is my pride and joy. That's my baby. We back him now the same way we did when he was a child. I told his older brother, Johnnie, that he had to set a good example for Jerome. 'Everything you do, Johnnie, Jerome is going to do. So you have to be a good boy. Johnnie, you are your brother's keeper.' Jerome was always there at his heels. They shared a bedroom and they continue to be the best of friends.

I'm glad we're all able to go to the games to see him play. I can't do anything but go to his games. If he ever got hurt and I wasn't there, I couldn't forgive myself. As soon as we get to the stadium, I start looking around and find the closest way I can get down on the field if I had to be there. I know he'll be looking for his mom.

Before the game starts, he'll start walking behind the bench, and he starts looking for us up in the stands. He has an idea where we are, but sometimes we're not all together. We usually have about five of us there, sometimes as many as eight.

I'm glad he's staying with the Steelers. I told him to be sure to give the Steelers the last chance to sign him. I wanted him to stay there. They treated him so well. They gave him a chance after they downed him in St. Louis. They gave him a chance to show what he's all about. Jerome wanted to stay there, too.

As soon as I sit down in the stands I start praying. I say, 'Lord, it's me again. You know what I'm here for. Please look after him.' I pray every day, at different times during the day. I've been doing it since he was in Little League. I know Jerome is giving his life to this. It's in his heart and soul. I've got to help him. I'm there for him.

You must have faith. If it weren't for faith, I wouldn't be where I am today. God is good. I didn't let Jerome play football when he was young because I wanted him to concentrate more on school and academics. I let him go bowling for his exercise and fun.

You do the best you can in raising kids, but you have to have faith in a higher power to make it all work. I love the Steelers. I have faith in them, too. They've been good for Jerome. We're so happy he's staying in Pittsburgh.

Will Wolford
Veteran of heart-breakers

*"I came to Pittsburgh
to get a Super Bowl ring."*

It was The Big Tease. It was the final play of the American Football Conference championship game at the end of the 1995 season. Indianapolis Colts quarterback Jim Harbaugh had just heaved a "Hail Mary" pass from midfield at Three Rivers Stadium. It was sailing high and then it was coming down in the end zone in the maddening midst of white and blue and black and gold uniformed players. There was a scramble for the elusive ball.

For a fleeting, excruciating instant, it looked like one of the guys in white and blue had caught the ball. There was a hush over Three Rivers Stadium as a disappointing setback, on the final play of the AFC title game in the same end zone for the second year in a row, seemed too real to allow anyone to draw another breath.

A year earlier, quarterback Neil O'Donnell had directed a heroic drive nearly the length of the field in the last three minutes, completing seven consecutive passes, to set up a possible game-winning touchdown for the Steelers, a fourth-and-goal play at the three-yard line. But O'Donnell's final pass took a nosedive and Steelers running back Barry Foster got hit from behind by San Diego linebacker Dennis Gibson as Foster stretched to catch the ball just over the goal line with 1:04 remaining. The pass went incomplete and so did the Steelers' Super Bowl dreams. The Chargers came away with the victory and were headed for Miami and Super Bowl XXIX and the Steelers and their fans were staying home, heartbroken.

"Tough," declared Dan Rooney, the owner and president of the Steelers, to one of his top aides, Joe Gordon, as they stood behind the goalposts at the opposite end of the field.

This time, in the AFC finale between the Colts and Steelers on January 14, 1996, the ball was on the chest of Colts wide receiver Aaron Bailey, then the ball was on his belly as Bailey fell on his back in the end zone turf at the scoreboard end of Three Rivers Stadium. He did not, however, have the ball in his grasp. Steelers defensive back Randy Fuller flung himself at Bailey in a desperate attempt to knock the ball away.

I was standing in the same spot as I had been the year before, just behind the end zone at the opposite end of the field, waiting with many of the media who had come down from the press box to be closer to the clubhouses for post-game interviews. It was difficult from a distance to determine what was going on. We feared the worst. I had been so disappointed the year before. I had been looking forward to going to Miami, where I had started my career as a full-time

George Gojkovich

Will Wolford

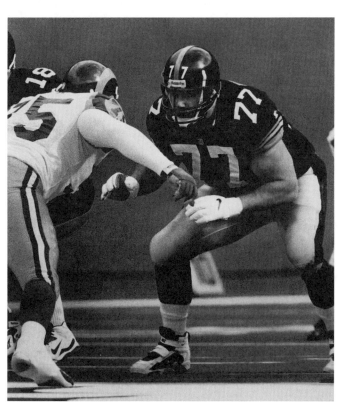

Michael F. Fabus/Pittsburgh Steelers

sportswriter for a daily newspaper, covering the Dolphins back in 1969, and I wanted to go there with the Steelers. Was this going to happen again?

Will Wolford was one of those fooled by his first impression. Wolford was watching Harbaugh's desperate heave from midfield. He was playing left tackle on the offensive line for the Colts that chilly afternoon, pass-blocking for Harbaugh. Like most of the more than 60,000 people in Three Rivers Stadium, Wolford wasn't sure what was happening, but he was hopeful. He watched Harbaugh's final fling flying high through the air, floating up there forever, or so it seemed, like the Goodyear Blimp.

"I saw the whole thing," recalled Wolford two years later. "I thought A.B. (Aaron Bailey) had caught it. I was blocking Chad Brown on that play. The ball got launched, and we all sort of stood there and watched it. I started running toward the end zone. I wanted to get down there to join in the celebration . . . where A.B. was. On my way down there, I saw the official jump in and wave it off. He was doing it with conviction. He wasn't looking around for anyone's help. There was no doubt about it. All our guys were holding up their hands in a touchdown signal, but I knew it was over. I knew we hadn't won the game."

This was not good for a man who already required medication for an irregular heartbeat.

The Steelers had escaped with a 20-16 win and were on their way to Super Bowl XXX in Tempe, Arizona. The Colts returned to Indianapolis heartened by their unexpected playoff run, but wondering what might have been. "It was definitely a woulda, coulda, shoulda kind of game," Wolford said.

Wolford had a sinking feeling. Not only was the game over, not only was the season over, but the way Wolford felt at that mind-blowing moment he thought that, at age 31, his playing career in the National Football League was over as well. His injured shoulders were screaming at him, enough is enough, no more.

"After that game, I was so sore," said Wolford. "After that game, I couldn't imagine ever playing again. We bought a house back home in Louisville. I thought I'd have the time to devote to my family and my horses. I figured it was over. I didn't think anyone would come after me and offer me top dollar."

Life is strange. Now, a year later, he was playing for the Steelers, and he had just completed his first season in Pittsburgh. His presence was a quiet one in the clubhouse, but he stood tall on the playing field.

Wolford was asked if he had played well that day, when he lined up against these same Steelers in the AFC title game. "I wasn't very good," Wolford confessed. "I was too sore to play good. It was that way all season. You were glad you came down to the last play of the season, but there was some sense of relief in knowing you wouldn't have to punish your body anymore.

"Last year (in the AFC championship game at Three Rivers), I was numb. It had been such a great game. But I was numb because I thought it was my last game."

Former pro football player turned TV analyst, Tim Green, has said in his book, *The Dark Side Of The Game*, that many of today's players are not always that disappointed when they lose in the play-offs because they are relieved that the beating on their body will stop, at last. I mentioned this to Bill Cowher, the Steelers' coach, and he just grimaced.

"I don't know anybody who feels that way," he said. "Anybody who has ever been to the Super Bowl would never say that. Just being there is a thrill in itself."

Wolford had been there, three times, in fact, with the Buffalo Bills, but he thought he would get no more chances to go back, that this game at Three Rivers was his last.

It wasn't, however. His agent, the highly-respected Ralph Cindrich, had convinced the Steelers that Wolford would be a prize catch for them as a free agent. Cindrich, who lived in Pittsburgh where he had once performed as a linebacker at the University of Pittsburgh (1969-71) before he turned pro with the Patriots, completed a deal that would solve one of the Steelers' greatest needs, gain Wolford another multi-million dollar contract to extend his career and Cindrich a handsome commission.

Wolford had just completed a three-year contract with the Colts that had made him the best-paid offensive lineman in the game when he signed it.

The Steelers had lost two starting linemen in Leon Searcy and Tom Newberry after their disappointing setback by the Dallas Cowboys in Super Bowl XXX. Searcy had signed a five-year contract with the Jacksonville Jaguars calling for $17 million, gaining him the tag of "highest paid offensive lineman." Newberry had retired after one season with the Steelers. Newberry had left the Rams a year earlier as a free agent to sign a multimillion dollar contract with the Steelers. He had played with nagging injuries most of the year, however, had a hard time staying sound enough to remain in the lineup and decided he didn't need it anymore. Wolford was occupying the dressing stall used by Newberry the year before. Veteran linebacker Jerry Olsavsky had moved during the summer into the dressing stall next to Wolford. "We call him Myron Cope's good friend, Jerry Olsavsky," said Wolford, "because he's always on Myron's post-game show."

That's the way it is today in pro football. Players come and go, usually going where they can make the most money — they have to do what's best for their family, they usually say — and it's different from the days when you could count on having your favorite player play out his career with one club. There were 22 players who played on all four of the Steelers' Super Bowl winners in the '70s. Back then, the Steelers were nearly all Steelers from start to finish.

Distinctions such as "highest paid offensive lineman" don't last long. That's the way it is in the world of professional sports, the world of free agency, the world of uncertainties, the world where royalties are more important than loyalties.

Players like Wolford and Newberry are modern day Hessians, mercenaries, hired soldiers employed to do battle in foreign service. Players seldom see the situation the same way as the fans or the media. It's a business, they tell you. It's simply the way pro sports are structured these days. They give their best effort wherever they work, they insist.

"We blew such a huge, huge opportunity."
— Will Wolford

There is no denying Will Wolford did a wonderful job with the Steelers during the 1996 season. He had an injury-free year and it made a big difference. He moved over from tackle to guard on the left side of the line, a shift he welcomed when he signed with the Steelers. He was flanked by John Jackson and Dermontti Dawson, two of the team's prime-time performers, and fitted in well.

"Playing between those two guys would be at the top of any guard's wish list," said Wolford. "You can't ask for a better situation. These are two great players and two great guys. That's really the most exciting thing of all."

Wolford flourished with the company he was keeping.

"He had a Pro Bowl year," said Steelers offensive line coach Kent Stephenson. "He weighs 300 pounds and he can run. He's just played winning football for us."

Tom Donahoe, director of football operations for the Steelers, shared Stephenson's sentiments. "If you checked the game film," said Donahoe at season's end, "you'd see that Will had a great season. He should have been in the Pro Bowl."

Wolford didn't finish the 1996 season playing in the Pro Bowl or the Super Bowl. It ended in New England, in the second round of the AFC playoffs, when Wolford and the Steelers got lost in the fog that enshrouded Foxboro Stadium.

The game was over almost before it got underway. There had been so much uncertainty coming into the game about who would be physically able to play, about who would end up playing quarterback, and the Steelers who showed up were a pale imitation of themselves. The Steelers trailed 21-0 midway through the second period, and never really appeared capable of a comeback.

It was a shame. So much was at stake. The Jacksonville Jaguars, who had squeaked into the playoffs in the first place, had upset the heavily-favored Broncos in Denver the day before. The door

Will Wolford in his Vanderbilt days

Steelers offensive linemen in 1996 with coach Kent Stephenson were (left to right from front to back row) Jamain Stephens, Brenden Stai, Tom Myslinski, Bernard Dafney, Will Wolford, Jim Sweeney, Dermontti Dawson, Justin Strzelczyk and John Jackson. They were rated one of the NFL's best groups.

was wide open to New Orleans and Super Bowl XXXI. If the Steelers could knock off New England as they were expected to do by the odds-makers, they would have a home game the following week at Three Rivers Stadium against the upstart second-year Jaguars. The Steelers were tough to beat at home.

"Yesterday, I was very disappointed," offered Wolford two days after the 28-3 defeat at New England, before he left town for Louisville to look after his horses and get his new home in shape for his young family. "We win this and we get to come back to Three Rivers. It was a great opportunity. We blew such a huge, huge opportunity.

"I really thought we were going to come back. The only time I felt the game was over was when they came up with that interception in the second half. They started playing 'Whoop, There It Is' real loud through the speakers. That's when I knew we weren't going to come back, that they knew the game was in the bag.

"Looking back, I'm not so sure we had the guns to win the Super Bowl. We had to play the best mistake-free football, and with the mistakes we made against New England that didn't seem possible."

The Steelers didn't have Jerome Bettis at his best; he was hobbled by a groin pull and a sore ankle. Erric Pegram, their other top ballcarrier, was sidelined by an injury. The Steelers were short on receivers, and neither quarterback, Mike Tomczak or Kordell Stewart, had much success. Suddenly, some Steelers' fans conceded that Neil O'Donnell wasn't such a bad quarterback. The defensive unit, which was supposed to be the strong point, gave up big plays right from the beginning and never played with much confidence or intensity. The Patriots went after Rod Woodson on the first play and beat him badly for a big play that set up an easy touchdown.

Bill Cowher and his staff had done a super job most of the season in coping with a siege of serious injuries, constantly patching the holes and playing on, not complaining. Even so, they had lost too many of their best players.

"It finally caught up to us," said Wolford.

Though the Steelers had an up and down season, and were missing too many key players, there was still a great chance to sneak into the Super Bowl.

"This year the race was wide open," said Wolford. "The playoffs have proven it. I started feeling good about our chances."

Who would have been so bold at the outset of the season to predict that two of the final teams in the conference championships would be second-year franchises, the Carolina Panthers and Jacksonville Jaguars? Whenever those teams showed up on the Steelers' schedule that span was often referred to by the media and fans as "the soft part of the schedule." Any student of history would know better.

Wolford forced a smile on that reminder. "The soft parts of everyone's schedule are getting ready to play next week," said

Wolford, "and they're deserving of where they're at. They benefitted from the expansion tag, though that was misleading because of the way those teams were stocked.

"Because they were under-rated, though, teams had a hard time getting fired up for those teams. New England had no trouble getting fired up for the Pittsburgh Steelers. When I was in Buffalo, it was very easy for us to get up for Miami. We were always ready. Rivalries are like that.

"New England is one of those teams that was sick and tired of us doing so well. They had two weeks to get ready and they had us down pat. Everybody's real happy that Dallas got beat, too.

"We were not flat. We caught a team that was, no doubt, on edge and ready. They got us totally out of sync, and they were so much in sync. I've been on the other side of the line and I know what it's like."

"Bill Parcells has been there before, and he'll have New England ready for Jacksonville. He'll drill it into his players' heads to respect the Jacksonville team."

Despite the playoff disappointment, did Wolford find any satisfaction from his one year with the Steelers?

"I enjoyed the year, I enjoyed playing for Bill Cowher," he responded. "He's a straight shooter. I like the way he runs the team, the way he runs his meetings, the way he runs his practice. In my opinion, he got the most out of this team as he could get. We had so many injuries that guys didn't come back from. Our guys went on IR. I think he did a very good job."

Only the day before, Cowher had met for a few minutes with each of his players prior to their departure for the season. The players sat on the floor in the hallway and offered goodbyes. It looked like a college dorm before summer break. Wolford was asked what transpired at the meeting.

"He wanted to know how I felt," Wolford said. "He said he was happy with the way I played and hoped I would come back for next season. He told me to take a little time off and get away from it for a while. After that, he told me to get ready, no one's going to have a better chance of winning it this year. That's why I came to Pittsburgh."

Would Wolford be back? Or would he pull a Tom Newberry and retire?

"I'll be here next year," said Wolford. "I take it one year at a time now. Ever since I first injured my shoulders, it's been that way. They didn't think I could return to play, so I surprised some people. I've always treated football like a temporary situation, which it is.

"Since the surgeries, and in between surgeries, I played in a lot of pain for a few years. I was picking up a lot of money, but it wasn't much fun. Last year, I wasn't hurting for a change. It made a big difference."

If he got nicked, Wolford felt comfortable going to Steelers' trainer John Norwig, who had been the trainer during Wolford's stay at Vanderbilt.

"It's a nice situation here," said Wolford. "It's not easy to go to a new team. I appreciate the Steelers organization, from top to bottom, for making my transition as smooth as possible."

Wolford fit right into the Steelers' offensive scheme and was part of an offensive line that was regarded as one of the league's best. "This line is a good offensive line, but you're probably not as good as everybody thinks you are," offered Wolford. "We're probably not as good as the team that dominated the Colts, or as bad as the team that was whipped by New England."

Wolford was defensive when I suggested he and his fellow free agents were Hessians of sorts.

"Each time my contract ran out and I moved on, I had no regrets," said Wolford. "I saw many of my good friends get let go by teams through the years. It's not like there's a huge amount of loyalty on the part of the owners. They depreciate us like cattle. Personally, I really liked the owner (Ralph Wilson) of the Buffalo Bills, for instance. He's a horseman. Mr. Rooney seems like a nice guy. No one should take it personally; that's the way the business is.

"Indianapolis offered me a deal they knew I wouldn't accept the second time around. When I went there, I was the highest paid offensive lineman in the pro game, by a million a year. I was the highest paid player on the team.

"At the end of three years, I was a restricted free agent. After they signed some other players, they took the tag 'transitional player' off me, and I signed with Pittsburgh the same day. It wasn't hard to leave. After the way our coach, Ted Marchibroda, was treated it made it a lot easier to leave Indianapolis. I don't understand the way he was treated. They made an offer they knew I wouldn't accept. They did the same thing with Marchibroda."

"Remember wide right?"

Will Wolford was relating these stories in the players' lounge, just off the dressing room of the Steelers' complex at Three Rivers Stadium. Team equipment manager Tony Parisi put a football in his lap for his signature. I didn't know at the time that Parisi, a fixture in the football organization for 32 years, would be retiring at the end of the season. Teammate Darren Perry put a chessboard on the table and asked Wolford to sign that as well. "Go home and raise your horses," teammate Curt Botkin urged Wolford. Like it was over, why fret about it?

Neither the setback at New England nor the loss he suffered during the playoffs the year before when he was still playing for the Colts could compare to some of the disappointments Wolford suffered when he was with the Buffalo Bills.

"I mean I did play in the Super Bowl," he said. "Remember wide right?"

That was Super Bowl XXV, when Wolford was with the Bills and teammate Scott Norwood's 47-yard field goal try went wide right with four seconds remaining, allowing the New York Giants to hold on for a 20-19 win. That was brutal. Wolford was with the Bills three of the four times they lost in the Super Bowl.

This should make Wolford, and everyone else, appreciate even more how momentous an achievement it was for the Steelers to win four Super Bowls in six years in the '70s.

"You can never take an opportunity like the playoffs for granted," said Wolford. "I came here because I thought it was my best chance to finally get a Super Bowl ring."

"Running Down A Dream."
— Tom Petty

Wolford likes to listen to Tom Petty tapes as he's driving to and from work. He describes his music preference as country rock. "A lot of his songs are like stories, a lot of his songs have sort of a loner aspect to them."

Some of Wolford's favorites include "Into the Great Wide Open," "Don't Come Around Here," "Running Down a Dream," "Mary Jean's Last Dance" and "Refugee."

Wolford says some of the songs relate to his quest for a Super Bowl ring. "Yeah, it's running down a dream," said Wolford. "Going wherever it seems, doing what you gotta do. . . ."

"I'm at the point of my career when I don't care much about personal goals. I want to win the Super Bowl. I'm at that point where that's all I care about.

"In the NFL, I've had to do a lot of workouts on my own, especially running. I like to run on my own. Do it by myself. I ran track in high school. You are by yourself. No one's going to watch you do it . . . no one knows how hard you're running except you . . . no one knows how hard you're working. I jump rope on my own. Ever since my dad made me do it, I've continued to jump rope. These are things you have to do by yourself. Besides working out by myself, I hate to be alone. I never go to movies or restaurants by myself. I never like to be alone."

I asked Will if he is ever really alone when he's working out, especially when he's jumping rope. In his youth, Will and his brother, Maurice, Jr., had to jump rope for long periods under the watchful and often critical eye of their father, Maurice Sr., or Big Mo, as he was called by his friends.

"No, Big Mo's still there, so is my brother. I learned at a very young age the difference between working hard and not working hard, but I didn't apply it then. But I learned it then."

His dad had some other ideas about football that have stayed with Will.

"My dad once told me even though I may never hate anybody, you have got to hate in football. But it's a controlled hatred. You can't play the game totally out of control. I guess it's like being a boxer; you have that rage."

Will said he would like to go back to school when he's finished with football. This time, he believes he will take it more seriously, and work harder at his studies. He'd like to get into the horse breeding business, and Louisville has an equine major that interests him.

As far as a second career goes, Wolford feels he has to think about it. One of his good friends from his days with the Bills, center Kent Hull, retired at the end of the 1996 season. That got Wolford thinking about life after football.

"I didn't work as hard as I should have the first time around," he said. "I'd like to do it differently this time.

"My cousin Bobby got his act together, when he put his mind to it. His mother told him he'd have to enter military service if he didn't do better at school. Now he's on a cardiology fellowship in Dallas. He went to medical school in St. Louis. We were both lazy, but Bobby turned things around. I think I can do the same. I crammed for every exam in college. You can't remember anything long-term that way."

"Jude is the patron saint of hopeless causes."

Will and his wife, Mary Jude, have two daughters, Grace, born April 27, 1993, and Laren Kay, born April 1, 1995. "I'm lucky I have two girls," said Wolford. "I was just happy they were healthy. No matter how much I push athletics to the girls, it won't be the same. They won't be under as much pressure to excel in sports.

"I've known my wife since she was 15. By the time I was 16 or 17, she was one of my best friends. She went to an all-girls high school and I went to an all-boys Catholic high school."

They first met outside a Bad Company concert, and later at a lake where everyone at their schools went swimming in the summer. They dated through high school and then at Vanderbilt. "I was 'whupped' from the beginning," said Wolford.

Jude was attending law school at the University of Louisville when they got married, during his second year in pro football, and she transferred to the University of Buffalo. When she was in school in Buffalo, she worked in the District Attorney's office and after she graduated she worked in the U.S. Attorney's office. "She always did

Will Wolford's family includes wife Jude and daughters (left to right) Laren Kay and Grace.

well," said Will. "She excelled in front of a crowd, she was a prosecutor for almost two years, and she was good at it."

Jude was the youngest of seven children in a Catholic family. Asked how she got the name Jude, she explained, "Jude is the patron saint of hopeless causes. My mother was 36 years old when she had me." Her parents wanted another child, but thought maybe it was too late. Will was also the youngest of a large Catholic family.

After seven years with the Bills, the Wolfords left Buffalo in favor of Indianapolis. He will never forget the day his first daughter was born because it was the day after he became the best-paid lineman in professional football history.

"The day before our child was born, I signed a contract to go to Indianapolis," he recalled. "Ralph Cindrich came up with a great deal."

Pete Ward, the director of operations for the Colts, flew to Buffalo on April 26, 1993, rode out to Wolford's home in a taxi, and with the taxi's motor and meter running, walked up the sidewalk and rang the doorbell.

"I signed the contract, and right then and there, he handed me a check for $1.2 million as an advance on my signing bonus," Wolford said. "He ran back to the taxi and left."

That afternoon, Wolford took his wife, Jude, to the maternity ward. They dropped off the check at their stockbroker's office on the way to the hospital. He spent his first day as a millionaire watching helplessly as his wife went through a difficult labor. The next day, their daughter, Grace, was born at 7:11 a.m.

"I flew out to Indianapolis the day after for rotator cuff surgery," said Wolford. "They knew I had the problem when they signed the contract. That was a big factor.

"Ralph handled everything. I always had a great relationship with Ralph. I trust Ralph. I let him do his job, and he does it well. Ralph's very good at what he does. He put together one helluva deal. It was a sticky situation, because of my shoulder problem.

"I flunked my physical in Indianapolis. They put a clause in the contract that I had to play at least ten games to get the money we were talking about. I rushed back from shoulder surgery to start in the season opener. But I played in a whole lot of pain. It was my right shoulder. I also had a partially torn rotator cuff on my other shoulder. I had hurt my right shoulder the year before. I was trying to work through it.

"The first salary I made in the league was $150,000. At the time, I thought that was a large sum of money."

Pro athletes often lose sight of the significance of such salaries. To most fans, $150,000 remains a large sum of money.

Louisville
His ol' Kentucky home

"Johnny Unitas was one
of my boyhood heroes."
— Will Wolford

At season's end, William Charles Wolford was going back to Louisville. Pittsburgh was linked to Louisville by the Ohio River, which begins at the site of Three Rivers Stadium where the Allegheny and Monongahela merge and make their way to the Mississippi. When the rivers are high in Pittsburgh, downriver communities such as Wheeling, Cincinnati and Louisville get flooded, as they did in March, 1997, shortly after Wolford went home following his first season with the Steelers. Louisville suffered great damage from the flood, and Wolford had to help his sisters clean up their properties.

As he talked about his hometown, I drifted back to the Louisville I knew as a young man. Louisville brought back a lot of memories. I'd gone there shortly after graduating from the University of Pittsburgh. I was drafted into the U.S. Army and reported to Fort Knox, on the outskirts of Louisville, in the winter of 1964 to begin a 10-week basic training course.

Fort Knox was famous for its U.S. Government gold reserves and for its military tanks. It was so cold that winter of '64-'65, and I learned that there was an Arctic wind that blew through Louisville. I was colder there than I was during a later 10-month service hitch in Alaska.

We never got a weekend pass to check out downtown Louisville during our basic training stint. I had many opportunities to travel to Louisville later on, when I was a sportswriter in Miami and New York for a ten-year period, and covered the American Basketball Association. Louisville was the home of the Kentucky Colonels. They played their home games at Freedom Hall. We stayed across the way at the Executive Inn, and it was one of our favorite stops on the ABA trail. I wrote a column on the ABA and later pro basketball at large over a nine-year period for *The Sporting News*, a nationally-distributed sports tabloid, so I was treated with open arms by nearly everyone in ABA towns like Louisville.

Players, front-office types and owners were eager to get anyone to pay attention to the ABA, and it was a great league to cover. Nearly everyone was cooperative and available to the media.

I remember my wife, Kathie, and I were among those in attendance at a party at the home of John Y. Brown, the owner of Kentucky Fried Chicken and the Colonels, to announce the signing of Artis Gilmore, a much sought-after seven footer from Jacksonville

University. The Browns had several women servants who dressed like Aunt Jemima and I wondered how that struck Gilmore.

Pittsburgh won the first ABA championship at the end of the 1967-68 season. The Pittsburgh Pipers were led by a gifted 6-8 stringbean from Brooklyn named Connie Hawkins, now in the Basketball Hall of Fame. The Pipers departed Pittsburgh after that first season — also the first season of the NHL expansion Pittsburgh Penguins — and moved to Minneapolis. The team returned the following year, without Hawkins who had jumped to the NBA's Phoenix Suns, and was called the Pittsburgh Condors. They lasted two seasons. Their front-office boss, a West Pointer named Mark Binstein, has spent much time in prison since then for fraudulent business activities.

I bumped into Marty Blake, one of pro basketball's enduring pioneers, at the NBA All-Star Game in Cleveland in February of 1997, and Blake harkened back to his days in Pittsburgh with the Condors. Binstein was his boss. Dick Groat was one of Blake's assistants. Blake, who's been the head of the NBA's scouting service ever since his days in Pittsburgh, can laugh about it now.

"It was a crazy experience," he said. "We had some fun, but we definitely didn't make any money."

The Colonels were one of the few class teams in the upstart pro basketball league, and hosted some first-rate all-star games. I remember seeing Muhammad Ali, once known as Cassius Clay and "The Louisville Lip" during his early years as a professional boxer, when he was introduced at halftime of a Colonels' contest. World-rated heavyweight boxer Jimmy Ellis also grew up in Louisville. I would later cover some of their championship bouts when I became the boxing beat writer at *The New York Post*.

Dan Issel, Louie Dampier, Darrel Carrier, Jim "Goose" Ligon, Cincy Powell, Artis Gilmore, Jim O'Brien and Bud Olsen were some of our favorite players. I was interviewing Issel in a hallway outside the Colonels' clubhouse one night during the playoffs when someone pushed a large cream pie into my face, blinding me temporarily and embarrassing me to no end. It wasn't until two years later that I learned that the pie had been pushed into my face by the wife of Colonels' coach Hubie Brown. She didn't care for a column I'd written about her husband. Pushing cream pies into somebody's face was a national craze in the early '70s.

Issel handed me his towel to wipe away the cream that filled my eyes and ears, and I am forever grateful for his kindness. The fans and ABA followers were a special breed, and I was usually treated a lot better than I was that night. I learned a lot about southern hospitality in Louisville.

Names like Issel, Gilmore and Ali all have meaning as well to Wolford, as does Churchill Downs and the Kentucky Derby, Darrell Griffith and Denny Crum and the University of Louisville basketball team. Wolford smiled as we swapped stories about some of those guys.

"My dad didn't talk a lot about himself."
— Will Wolford

I mentioned Johnny Unitas, the great quarterback who grew up in Pittsburgh and played at Louisville. The Steelers selected Unitas in the ninth round of the 1955 college draft, but gave up on him at training camp in favor of Jim Finks, Ted Marchibroda and Vic Eaton. Unitas played sandlot football for $7 a game for a sandlot team in the Bloomfield section of Pittsburgh before getting a chance with the Baltimore Colts in the NFL and the rest is history, as they say. Unitas was my boyhood hero; I wore No. 19 and high top black football shoes the year I played quarterback for the Hazelwood Steelers and tried to imitate all his head movements and throwing motion.

Wolford said Unitas was one of his all-time favorites as well. Will's father, Maurice Sr., had been a lineman at Louisville before and after Unitas, with a four-year hitch in the military service in between.

Wolford's father used to talk about Unitas a lot when Will was growing up. "He was my only football guy that I looked up to," said Wolford. "My dad had autographed pictures from him for my brother and me.

"My dad played pro football one pre-season when he tried out with the Los Angeles Rams," Wolford went on. "My dad didn't talk a lot about himself. He played service ball, too. He went to the University of Louisville (48-49-50) then to military service in the U.S. Navy (51-55) and then came back to the University of Louisville, played his final year in 1955 and finished his work for a degree in 1956.

"My dad's a big guy. My dad knew a lot of people in Louisville. He owned four or five different bars, all very successful. I remember one day we were walking behind Ali. My older brother — we called him Maurice Jr. or Mo Jr. — was a huge fan of Ali. So we were excited to meet him. When we were growing up, if my brother liked something I liked it. My brother kept a scrapbook of the Colonels."

Will and his brother would go to Freedom Hall, which had a seating capacity of nearly 19,000 and remains one of the great basketball arenas in the country. They knew John Decamillis, a towel boy who sat under one of the baskets and wiped up any wet spots on the court, and was able to get them into Freedom Hall for free. Decamillis played against Will in a youth basketball league, as Decamillis played at a rival grade school. "Every year we battled in championship games," said Wolford. "In high school, we became classmates and teammates."

Wolford was a fan of Denny Crum, the coach of the Cardinals of Louisville basketball team, who had gotten his start as an assistant under John Wooden at UCLA and has been elected to the Basketball Hall of Fame.

"I finally met him two years ago, and that was a big thrill," Wolford said of Crum. "I was always a big Denny Crum fan. I idolized Darrell Griffith, one of their star players, 'Dr. Dunk,' they called him. I followed him from his days at Male High School in Louisville."

One of my former sportswriting colleagues, Edgar Allen of *The Nashville Banner,* became the publicist at Churchill Downs, where the Kentucky Derby is held each year. Allen allowed me to tour Churchill Downs, but I've never been there for the Derby, one of the storied events in horse racing's Triple Crown.

"My dad started taking me to the track when I was in eighth grade," said Wolford. "He took me to Keeneland. I remember going there; I thought that was great. I had a relative involved with horses. His name was Ed Kupper. We called him 'Uncle Ed.' He was my dad's first cousin. He owned part of a horse farm, where he raised thoroughbred race horses. It was a brood mare farm, called Lasater Farms.

"My Uncle Ed and my dad were best of friends. I had an idyllic childhood. When I first went to Keeneland, I had no idea about betting. When I was in eighth grade, I knew how to read the racing form. My brother, Maurice Jr., and I would be tagging along with my dad or my uncle. It was fun. I'd have about $10. I'd put $2 to win here and $2 to win there. In high school, I'd have about $20 to play with.

"In high school, I'd go to the track with my friends. To Churchill Downs. I went to Ellis Park in Hendersonville, Kentucky. I never went to Latonia, close to Evansville, but I went to Turfway Park. A lot of my friends from high school went to the track. I started going to the Kentucky Derby at age 15, mainly to party in the infield."

One summer during his college days, Will got a job baling hay on a horse farm, and his love affair with horses intensified. He loved to tend to horses.

He had five horses at Churchill Downs during his first season with the Steelers. They were being looked after by Paul McGee, a St. Xavier High School grad, an old friend and a trainer. "I have two brood mares, three current runners," said Wolford. "I have gone through about ten horses."

Will would have gotten along wonderfully with Steelers owner Art Rooney, who had a horse farm in Maryland, and was a lifelong horse player. There's a tale told that Rooney won the money in a big day at Saratoga to buy his NFL franchise in the first place.

"He was about this high."
— Wolford on Tom Cruise

When Will Wolford was a student at St. Xavier High School, one of the students there at the time was future movie star Tom Cruise, who was Tommy Mapother back then.

Two of Will Wolford's sports heros when he was growing up in Louisville were Muhammad Ali and Johnny Unitas.

"I didn't really know him that well," said Wolford. "When I was in college at Vanderbilt, I went to a party in Louisville and he was there. All the guys hated him because he'd made a couple movies already. And all the girls loved him . . . because he'd made a couple of movies already."

One of Cruise's early movie roles, in "All The Right Moves," was as a high school football player in Johnstown who wanted to get a college scholarship to better his life.

"Can you believe him playing football?" said Wolford. "He was about this high." The 6-5 Wolford extended his hand about waist high to indicate how tall Tom Cruise was. According to movie fact books, Cruise is 5-7. He finished high school in New Jersey.

"When I was growing up, everyone had a basketball hoop in their driveway," said Wolford. "I'd get up and go out and shoot. There were basketball courts in the playgrounds. One had an eight feet high hoop, another was nine feet high, and another ten feet high.

"I was always tall for my age, never heavy. I played guard in basketball when I was growing up. I saw myself as a basketball player. The Kentucky Colonels and University of Louisville basketball were big to me.

"We didn't have a pro football team. I didn't think about football at the time. I played it, though, and ended up being good at it.

"I have three older sisters and one brother. I was the fifth and the baby. I was definitely the baby. I was definitely sheltered. No one ever told me anything.

"I lived in Louisville most of my life, in a couple different homes, and went to a few different schools. We lived in Louisville except for six months in Macon, Georgia, when my father had a business opportunity there. I was in sixth grade at the time, but we moved back to Louisville the same year. For the most part, I went to St. Agnes Grade School and St. Xavier High School. I won 11 letters in high school and was all-state in basketball.

"I started playing football in fourth grade. My older brother was trying out for the fifth and sixth grade team. My dad took me. My dad thought it was a good idea for me to be on the same team even though I was younger than the other kids. The coach said, 'OK, line up at defensive tackle.' I had no idea what he was talking about. My first love was basketball. I knew where the center and forwards and guards ought to be, but I didn't know anything about defensive tackles.

"My dad was definitely more into it than I was. When we were in grade school, he'd give us 50 cents for an assisted tackle, $1 for a solo tackle, $1 for a fumble recovery, $2 for a touchdown. I wasn't nearly as good as my older brother. He was making $15 a game, and I was making about $6.

"My brother matured early. I didn't mature until high school. I'm still maturing. My brother was the best. Everything he did, I did."

Asked if he got along well with his brother in those days, Will paused and responded, "Yes and no. He could be mean. There were not a lot of days in grade school when he didn't beat me up for one reason or another. He was the toughest, strongest kid in high school. He just didn't grow much in his late teens. He was 5-9 in high school and he's still 5-9."

Will has an irregular heart beat. He required hospitalization during his student days at Vanderbilt.

His father suffers from a similar problem and takes medication to control it. Will can't take the same medicine. It slows the beating of the heart, and he has a slow beat to begin with.

"My dad was a football guy."

Maurice Wolford Sr. sounds like an interesting character, to hear Will talk about him. Will said his dad was a lot like Bull Meecham, the U.S. Marine fighter pilot portrayed in *The Great Santini*, a book by Pat Conroy turned into a movie with Robert Duvall as the passionately-driven dad. "Whenever I see that movie, I have to smile," said Will. "I can relate to it a lot. It's so familiar.

"Football was something my dad pushed me into and he used to coach me, individually, though he wasn't ever my real coach, and he worked me out constantly.

"My dad used to work us out . . . he was hard on us. When we were out of school in the summer, he kept us busy. My dad would sleep late after working late in his bar, and when he got up he wasn't always in the best mood, so he was tough to satisfy. He worked us out in the daytime. We'd jump rope for an hour. We'd run two miles or so. He'd take us down to the basketball court and run us through drills our Uncle Ed had shown us.

"We'd do layup drills, lots of fundamental things my Uncle taught us. My dad was a football guy, but he knew we liked basketball so he spent time with us there as well.

"I cleaned my dad's bar from fifth grade on. At one point, he had a bar in Indiana. We'd get up at 5 a.m., and my mother would drive us over and we'd clean the bar before we'd go to school. In high school, I'd clean up after basketball practice.

"My dad's first bar was called The Office Lounge, then it was always Big Mo's Lounge after that. He was well known in Louisville. To me, my dad was a very famous person. Everywhere we went, everyone made a big deal over him. From playing football, he was a big celebrity.

"One time he took us to a pro wrestling match at Convention Center. We went there to see Tojo Yamamoto, Jerry Jarrett, Jackie Fargo and 'Madhouse' Fargo, Jackie's brother.

"We had great seats at ringside. They put a spotlight on my dad, and they announced, 'Maurice 'Big Mo' Wolford is in the audience with his two sons!' I thought, 'Man, Dad is a big deal.' Plus, he was a big man. About 6-4, 365 pounds, he wore a goatee. He definitely stood out in a crowd.

"I remember going to school the next day, and being all pumped up about watching these wrestlers go at it, and I got into about ten fights at school. I was out of control."

Wolford's parents, in a separate conversation, recalled that Will was probably in fifth grade at the time of that incident.

"We had to work out," Will said. "He made sure we had spending money, but in return, he expected us to work out daily. He had to track me down most of the time. My brother would wake up, take his high-protein shake, and do a workout on his own. He couldn't get enough of it.

"I wanted to shoot hoops. My dad would track me down. In fifth grade, it was snowing out, and I was working out with Uncle Ed at St. Leonard's outdoor basketball court. He was working us out. It wasn't easy. Lots of times I'd throw up; Dad made us drink those awful shakes before we'd work out.

"He had us take about 30 vitamin pills. I had a hard time swallowing pills. I'd end up chewing them; they were nasty.

"I knew my regimen was different. I had a cousin my age. His name was Bobby Wolford, or just Bobby. We'd work out with Uncle Ed. I'd call him and ask him if he wanted to join us. Bobby would say, 'No way. Don't even tell your Dad you talked to me.' "

Bobby was 6-5, 205 and Will was 6-5, 235 when they teamed up on the frontline of the St. Xavier High School basketball team. They powered a good team that often drew sellout crowds of 1,300 to the school gym. Decamillis, the towel boy who had once gotten them into the Colonels' games for free, was the team's playmaking guard.

"My dad would sit outside on the steps of our house in his bathrobe. He'd watch us jump rope, count jumps with us, while drinking a cup of coffee. It was serious stuff. I'd get grounded for not working out. I missed parties because I didn't jump rope that day.

"I was a lazy kid, I admit it. It took me a long time to realize what a great work ethic my dad and brother had infused in me. I drove my dad crazy because I didn't share their enthusiasm for working out.

"I was a kid who wasn't that motivated. My brother overtrained one year to the point where he was exhausted. My wife knows how to work hard. In truth, I always did enough to get by.

"I did well in grade school and always tested well on standardized exams, but in college, I was on my own and abused the freedom when I went to Vanderbilt to be an engineer. There were 25 in my class. Most of them were valedictorians at their schools and they had calculus and such before and I was taking it for the first time. I barely passed my classes and I shifted to liberal arts. I did better, but I worked hard enough just to keep myself in school."

Will Wolford is flanked by his parents, Big Mo and Kate, outside Rich Stadium in Buffalo.

Will welcomed cousin Bob Wolford in Buffalo in 1987.

Wolford was a standout offensive lineman at Vanderbilt. He played in the 1985 Senior Bowl and Blue-Gray Classic. Vanderbilt coach George MacIntyre called him "the best offensive lineman in the country." University of Georgia head coach Vince Dooley declared, "No offensive lineman has blocked us better than Will Wolford."

He graduated from Vanderbilt with a degree in sociology. He joined a veteran team in Buffalo. He was a 21-year-old rookie and most of the linemen were over 30. He mentioned Jimmy Richard, Kenny Jones and Joe Devlin. Wolford came in the year after Joe DeLamielleure, one of the Bills' all-time best offensive linemen, had retired. Wolford became the first rookie offensive lineman since Joe D to start every game.

Quarterback Jim Kelly came in the same year, coming to Buffalo after the USFL folded. He had been with the Houston Gamblers. "He was so big, everybody was so excited when he came to Buffalo. He was a big hero before he ever suited up," said Wolford.

"Early on, Jim was a combination Bobby Layne and Joe Namath," recalled Wolford. "He liked to have fun, but he had a lot of talent, and he was a great competitor. He was a great player. It was a shame to see Jim struggling this season.

"During my seven years there, we had one of the best teams in pro football. It's a shame we all didn't win a Super Bowl. At least once. We should have beaten the Giants."

The team that lost to the Giants was one of the best teams ever put together. That's the still talked-about Super Bowl XXV in January, 1991 at Tampa Stadium, when the Bills lost 20-19 when Scott Norwood was wide right on a 47-yard field goal with four seconds left to play. Norwood was never forgiven for that miss by Buffalo fans.

We were talking about how Steelers' fans had taken their frustration out on Mike Tomczak late in the 1996 season, just as they had come down hard on his predecessors at the position through the years.

"It's not personal," said Wolford, "because they don't know him. My wife used to boo Jim Kelly a lot when she was watching the game when we were in Buffalo. Jim heard about it. We were out to dinner with Jim one night, and out of the blue he said, 'So, Jude, I hear you don't like me.' And she said, 'What are you talking about?'

"He said, 'I heard through the grapevine that you were bad-mouthing me in the stands.' She said, 'Jim, whoever told you that is a loser, and doesn't know me. I get worked up over the game and I behave like a typical fan. It's nothing personal.'"

> *"There is no present or future, only the past, happening over and over again."*
> — Eugene O'Neill
> *A Moon For The Misbegotten*

As 2nd grader at St. Agnes

8th grader, Will Wolford is congratulated by football coach George Hayes at awards banquet.

Will takes daughter Grace for a ride in their neighborhood in suburban Indianapolis during his Colts days.

As Xavier High School player in 1979

"I was big on jumping rope."
— Maurice Wolford Sr.

Katie Wolford does not need much prodding to talk about her baby. "He was a real sweet boy," she said. "He'd climb up in my lap and I'd say, 'Will, you're never going to grow up, are you?' And he'd say, 'No, Mom.'

"His brother, Maurice, was more hyper, and more dedicated to training for sports early on. Will was more laidback. But Will played football, ran track and played basketball in high school. They were as different as night and day. But the two of them together were dynamite. They gave us a few scares.

"They started a fire together once behind a chair in our living room, which, thank God, we put out quickly. Another time, Will swallowed some charcoal lighter fluid and we had to have his stomach pumped."

The three sisters were, at the time of this interview, Jackie, age 44; Lisa, 41, and Maureen, 37.

"He got along with the girls very well. He had three older sisters. He followed after Maurice wherever he'd go. Will always liked horses. We took him to the track, to Churchhill Downs."

I asked Will's father, Maurice Sr., about some of the local legends he had known, such as Johnny Unitas and Muhammad Ali, as well as his recollection of Will when he was a young man.

"Johnny came along while I was in the Navy," he said. "He was finished by the time I came back to school. He never had a line in front of him at Louisville. That's why he didn't make more of a mark in college ball.

"Ali was a friend of a fellow who owned a clothing store next door to a bar I owned. He was a friendly fellow and we got a kick out of him.

"Will was always sort of a quiet kid. But we got a call from his teacher about Will's conduct. After he saw that wrestling match he wanted to wrestle all his classmates. He was creating too much commotion. We had to have a talk with him.

"He's done well with horses. He studies the business. He has two good ones. He's been very lucky. You have to get lucky with horses, too."

As for his own brief fling with pro football, Maurice Sr. said he played defensive tackle for three weeks at training camp with rookies for the Los Angeles Rams at their Redlands, California training camp. Bob Waterfield was the quarterback. "I came in late one night, and the coach, Sid Gillman, was upset and told me to go home the next day. I went through Las Vegas, and had a good time. Pro football wasn't such a big deal back then. You didn't get rich playing pro football."

148

"I've been in the bar business just about all the time since then. I was selling Yellow Page advertisements, at first, before I got my own bar. I was invited to go to the Colts' camp in 1956, but I was making too much money to leave. They didn't pay much money to most pro ballplayers in those days; I couldn't afford to go."

It's a good thing Johnny Unitas didn't say no when the Colts called him and offered him a second chance at pro ball.

As for Will, his dad believed it took a while for him to find himself, and take himself seriously as an athlete.

"He kept to himself as a child; he played games by himself. He could amuse himself. I was big on jumping rope and personal conditioning, and kept after both of the boys," said his dad.

Maurice Sr. and his wife went to every Steelers' game in Pittsburgh, except the Monday Night Game with the Kansas City Chiefs on October 7, 1996. It was easier, he said, to get to the games when Will was playing in Indianapolis and, obviously, more difficult when he was playing in Buffalo. They went to three or four games in Buffalo each year. But they have followed him closely throughout his career. Will's brother, Maurice Jr., was selling swimming pool equipment and supplies in Louisville, and that was another reason Will was eager to move back home. He wanted to be with his family again.

Photo from the Wolford family album

Will Wolford oversees his siblings, left to right, Maureen, Maurice Jr., Lisa and Jackie.

"I like Bill Cowher. How can you not like Bill Cowher? He gives everything he has to give to the team. He's involved with the guys. He gets the most out of them. I liked Chuck Noll, too. He was one of my assistants, one of my friends. I like Pittsburgh. I like the Steelers' organization. I've always admired the Rooneys. I like the Pittsburgh fans. I liked having Joe Greene on my staff. I liked having Dan Marino on my team. He's the best quarterback there ever was. Hey, Pittsburgh's OK by me."
— Don Shula, Hall of Fame Coach
Miami Dolphins, Baltimore Colts
in interview with Jim O'Brien,
from Los Angeles, March 28, 1997

Michael F. Fabus/Pittsburgh Steelers

Don Shula shakes hands with Chuck Noll after Dolphins defeated Steelers at Three Rivers Stadium during 1990 season.

"People and times have changed, but the eternal verities will always prevail. Such things as truth, honesty, character and loyalty will never change. I have tried to live my whole life by those words — and it has made me a happy man."
— Paul Brown
Head Football Coach
Cleveland Browns

Tom Donahoe
From ballboy to boss

*"I had a lot of people
help me along the way."*

Even Tom Donahoe has difficulty believing his own story, his successful climb to the top in the Steelers' organization, from ballboy in his youth to front-office boss in his 40s. Worse yet, he is reluctant to share it. It is not his style to speak about himself. He would have made a good monk.

Donahoe is in charge of the football operation of the Steelers. Stylewise, he takes his cue from the club's president and part owner, Dan Rooney, a low-key operator. Donahoe has never sought attention, but his door was always open to those who wished to talk to him.

"It's a little remarkable when you think about it," Donahoe said in the soft tone he favored when asked to consider his own history.

As of 1997, the 50-year-old Donahoe had been with the Steelers' organization for 12 years, the last six as head of the football operation.

Some felt Donahoe didn't get proper credit for his contribution to the Steelers staying power atop the NFL standings.

Mark Malone of ESPN, a former Steelers quarterback, said, "Bill Cowher inherited a decent football team and, as much as people are giving him credit, the unsung hero in all of this is Tom Donahoe in terms of providing Bill with direction and talent. Without that, you can't win football games, period. You have to have talent, you have to have a master plan, and if you don't have an organization behind you that's on top of everything, you're not going to be a very good coach."

In truth, Donahoe wasn't looking for any credit. While he was cooperative and open in a series of interviews over a three-year period, Donahoe declined when asked to provide photographs of himself as a child, posed with his parents perhaps, or with his maternal grandfather, David L. Lawrence, one of the city's political icons.

Donahoe had been a teacher as well as a coach earlier in his career, and I appealed to him on that count, believing he should share his story so that other young people with similar ambitions might stay the course. He had been an English major at Indiana University of Pennsylvania, and could appreciate a good tale, I was hoping. That didn't work, either. He smiled and declined. He even reported me to Dan Rooney as if I had engaged in some subversive activity. That struck me as strange behavior, overdoing the humble bit, protesting too much.

"He's never going to be high profile," said Dan Rooney, "because he doesn't want to be. That's a plus. He's doing the job the way it fits in with our organization."

"I'm not a special person."

Tom Donahoe spoke softly but he carried a big stick with the Steelers since taking over the operation at age 44. With any other team in the National Football League, Donahoe would have been called the general manager. But the Steelers aren't big on titles or salaries for front-office officials. Nevertheless, he and Cowher combined to win 53 regular season games, four division titles and one conference championship in five years.

"I don't enjoy talking about myself," insisted Donahoe. "I have a hard time believing anyone wants to read it. I feel my position is one of just trying to make us better. I'm not a special person."

In truth, Dan Rooney runs the organization. Bill Cowher runs the football team, and usually gets his way when it comes to personnel decisions. It was Cowher, for instance, who pushed for extending Greg Lloyd's contract prior to the 1996 season. It was Cowher who decided it was best to get rid of Bam Morris. Dan Rooney warned him at the time that he better be consistent in dealing with players who get involved in drug problems. Donahoe was not Cowher's boss, even though many reports on the team suggested otherwise. Cowher has the final say on who stays and who goes on the Steelers. Donahoe tried to keep Dan Rooney and Cowher happy, and help steer them to the right decision when they are at loggerheads.

Only Cowher is profiled in any of the team's guides or official publications. Donahoe and Rooney are relegated to two lines in the front-office directory: name and title. It was the same way with Art Rooney when he was alive and listed as the chairman of the board.

His full name is Thomas Donahoe III, but he's listed simply as Tom Donahoe. "People start thinking they're fancy when they use numerals," he explained. "It's like people who use an initial after their first name."

By any name, Donahoe knows where he stands in the Steelers' hierarchy. All three of them are proud, know-it-all, stubborn men, as was Chuck Noll, the former field leader. "I'd like to think I'm the most flexible of the three," said Donahoe, smiling at his disclosure. Like Noll and Art Rooney, Donahoe is a decent man.

As for having or not having a biography in the team's guide book, Donahoe doesn't mix words. "It's not important," he said. "People get too much credit on an individual basis in some of those biographical sketches. We get credit for what the organization does. People here know what I do. A big part of the fun in this job is proving people wrong.

"I always try to do my best. I come in and work as hard as I can and try to get along with people. And respect their opinions. If there's a management style, it's that I think everybody in this organization is important." He has been known to turn down interviews if he finds the writer wants to focus on him as the subject of an article.

"I'd rather have a root canal," declares Donahoe. "I really don't think about that (my role) very much. One of the things I like about

Tom Donahoe directs football operations, but the Steelers are still Dan Rooney's team.

Michael F. Fabus/Pittsburgh Steelers

this organization is that it's very much like our team; it's a lot of unselfish people who don't care who gets credit or who gets their name in the paper. We just want to win."

"He's a high school coach."
— Eric Green

Once upon a time, Donahoe had more modest ambitions than being responsible for the Steelers, one of the premier teams in the NFL. Back in 1987, Donahoe was hopeful of becoming the head football coach at Mt. Lebanon High School, a suburb just six miles south of downtown Pittsburgh. Later on, Donahoe failed in a bid to become the athletic director at Seton-LaSalle High School. Now look at him.

"I was definitely interested," Donahoe said of the Mt. Lebanon post. Indeed, Donahoe would have been happy to be the football coach of his hometown high school ten years earlier.

Now Donahoe had the Steelers to shape and develop. He supervised the scouting staff, oversaw player acquisitions and transactions during the draft, free agent signings and trades, and evaluated pro personnel.

Donahoe joined the Steelers in June of 1986 as a scout for the eastern region of the country. He worked as a scout for Jack Butler's Blesto organization for 14 months before that.

He spent 16 years teaching and coaching high school football and basketball in western Pennsylvania. His 1979 and 1980 Seton LaSalle teams won consecutive WPIAL Class AA football championships with records of 10-2 and 11-1-1. He had a reputation for spending long hours into the night in his office, and for working hard to get scholarships for his players.

Eight years before he was put in charge of the Steelers operation, he was the head football coach at West Allegheny High School, when it had records of 1-7 and 1-9. That should have humbled him, but it certainly didn't hold him back.

After the Steelers didn't resign Eric Green for the 1996 season, the big tight end who had been the team's No. 1 draft choice in 1990, put down the Steelers organization. While doing so, Green dismissed Donahoe as "a high school coach."

That disturbed Donahoe on two levels. First, he felt he had dealt with Green, in good and bad days (and there were plenty of the latter), in a professional manner, and he had attempted to sign him after Green became a free agent. It is sometimes reported that the Steelers got rid of Green, but they did make him an offer to stay. He turned them down to sign a better deal with the Miami Dolphins. Jimmy Johnson dumped Green, and he ended up in Baltimore with the Ravens.

"People are making a big deal about me being a high school coach," said Donahoe, coming to his own defense. "To be honest with you, I'm very proud of it. I look at it as a special part of my experience, a significant part of my education and I don't feel it takes away from what I'm doing now."

Donahoe hasn't forgotten where he came from, and doesn't put on any airs. He can be cool, as frosty as his white hair, as chilling as his glacier-blue eyes, but he can warm up and get comfortable in a hurry, too. He is as willing to come to the Adelphia Cable studios in Bethel Park to do a live show with sportscaster Sean Doherty as he is to be interviewed by the national network superstars.

"Sometimes I have to pinch myself," said Donahoe, with a winning smile. "I started as a ballboy with the Steelers in the mid-60s, and now this . . . I've been a Steelers' fan since I was old enough to walk."

Donahoe did a lot of dirty work to help out at the Steelers' training camp in 1964-66, when the team trained in Rhode Island, and the Steelers included the likes of Bobby Layne, Ernie Stautner and Tom "The Bomb" Tracy. The Steelers shifted their training site to St. Vincent College in Latrobe after that span.

"Roberto Clemente was my idol."

Tom Donahoe is an Irish Catholic who attends church regularly. His faith, family and football are important in his life. It's a profile the Rooneys couldn't resist. It didn't hurt that he was also the grandson of the late David L. Lawrence, the mayor of Pittsburgh from 1945 until 1959 when he resigned to serve one term as governor of Pennsylvania. Lawrence was a close pal of Art Rooney, the founder and principal owner of the Steelers. Lawrence and Rooney were great friends even though Lawrence was a Democrat and Rooney a Republican.

Donahoe looked to the likeness of Pirates Hall of Famer Roberto Clemente on the wall to the left of where he was sitting behind his desk. "Roberto Clemente . . . he's still my hero. He's the only athlete pictured in my office. He was my idol, a tremendous guy from my childhood.

"I remember going to Forbes Field and Pitt Stadium with my grandfather, and getting favorable treatment," said Donahoe. "Someone would drop us off right in front of the ballpark and we never had to stand in line. It was nothing for my grandfather to go to 45 or 50 baseball games a year.

"My grandfather always drew a crowd, and I didn't like it. I don't like people making a fuss.

"Mayor Lawrence . . . he was a great competitor. He was a guy who always put it on the line.

"There are a lot of things you picked up. My grandfather had a great interest in sports. I was always dragged along to sports events, which I liked. David, my brother, went with him to political events.

"Politics didn't interest me. David always had more interest in the political side."

What else did he learn from his grandfather?

"Things that were important were loyalty, respect for different kinds of people. No matter where we were, people walked up to him. Whether we were at the ballpark or having dinner at the P.A.A. He seemed to be at ease with everyone. He was like Mr. Rooney in that regard."

Were they similar men?

"Politically, they were on opposite sides. But it never seemed to get in the way of their friendship. I think my grandfather was influential in getting Mr. Rooney to stay in Pittsburgh when the Steelers weren't drawing well, and other cities were after the franchise. He knew the team was important to the city. He knew sports were important."

On the day Donahoe and I were together, Kevin McClatchy of Sacramento and other out-of-town bidders were seeking ways and means to purchase the Pittsburgh Pirates' franchise. There were hints that the Pirates might pull out of Pittsburgh, that the future of the franchise was in jeopardy.

I asked Donahoe if his grandfather would be spinning in his grave over such developments.

"Probably," said Donahoe.

I recalled that Art Rooney, who loved all sports, once told me that the Pirates were more important than the Steelers to Pittsburgh because they played more games over a longer span. Rooney was quite the baseball player in his youth, named his football team the Pirates when he founded the franchise in 1933, and was a regular at Pirates' games at Three Rivers Stadium.

Lawrence liked the greater frequency of ballgames the Pirates provided as well and, like Rooney, was always looking for action and a crowd. They both liked mixing with people. They were Irish politicians to the core.

"He just had a real love for the city, whether he was in Bloomfield or Shadyside or Brookline," Donahoe said of his grandfather. "He felt Pittsburgh was a special place. He conveyed that to my mom and all the grandchildren.

"He was governor when I was in 7th or 8th grade at St. Bernard's. For a period of time, he was away (in Harrisburg). We'd spend summers in Indiantown Gap, the summer home of the governor. When he was in Pittsburgh, we'd go to our grandparents once a week. It was nothing for me to go to 50 baseball games with him when I was in grade school. My brother David wasn't a big sports fan. He became an attorney. He lives on the same street as (Justin) Strzelczyk in the North Hills.

"My grandfather asked me to go to the games with him. I knew he was an important person, but that didn't enter into my mind much. I liked being with him because he was my grandfather.

"One thing that strikes my mind. I had a newspaper clipping for a long time that was special to me, but it got so dog-eared I had to get rid of it. It called attention to his attitude of never giving up where you were doing something you believed in, no matter the obstacles. I remember the photo caption said 'Mayor Lawrence never gives up.' It showed him raising a clinched fist from behind his desk. He built something special here."

"He made you feel important."
— Donahoe on Art Rooney

I asked Donahoe to reflect on his days as a ballboy with the Steelers. "I had a few favorites. I had a good relationship with Buzz Nutter, a center. Mike Sandusky, a guard. I always had an affinity for offensive linemen. They are special players, special people. They make sacrifices. We had some real characters on that club, guys like Bobby Layne and Ed Brown, and the coach was Buddy Parker. I remember one year at Rhode Island when Parker was the coach.

"I remember Bill Austin at St. Vincent. It was a different world then. I was there for probably about four years. It was a special kind of summer job. I felt *privileged* to be able to do that. I'd been a big Steelers fan and a Pirates fan.

"Some of the other ballboys were Art Rooney II and Mike Burns, the son of Bill Burns, the news anchor at KDKA-TV and close friend of Art Rooney. Both lawyers today. Bill Nunn's son, an actor. Tim Fogarty, the son of bookkeeper Fran Fogarty, who shared an office with Art Rooney when the Steelers offices were at the Roosevelt Hotel, was another. Tim has a sports equipment rehabilitation company. We had a good group of guys. We broke Tony Parisi in as the equipment manager. We'd been ballboys a few years when he joined the team, coming over from the *Hornets*. We had to teach him how to talk; he had that Canadian accent. He'd said 'oot' instead of 'out.' "

The Steelers coach when Donahoe broke in as a ballboy was Buddy Parker. Donahoe also served under Mike Nixon and Bill Austin — returning home when school started to play quarterback at South Catholic. Donahoe did not play football at Indiana University of Pennsylvania, where he gained a bachelor's degree in English, but remained interested in the sport.

What does Donahoe remember best about Art Rooney?

"He was a unique person. I think that anybody who was fortunate to spend time around him came away with something. You had to be a better person. Any time you had a conversation with Mr. Rooney, he made you feel important. He was genuinely interested in

157

Steelers president Dan Rooney salutes stadium crowd after the Steelers Bill Am
defeated Indianapolis Colts to win AFC championship in 1995 playoffs.

you. He was a guy who could have acted like he was a big shot, but never did. I've been involved in the National Football League for quite a while, and I've never heard anybody say anything bad about him."

When I asked him about role models, Donahoe pointed to the photographs of Mayor Lawrence and Roberto Clemente.

"I consider those individuals to be role models. My parents were my role models. If I were more ostentatious, I'd have their pictures in here, too. I feel my parents were really interested in teaching us how to do things. My dad is a very humble guy. He worked for Peoples Gas. I never had too many role models who were sports guys.

"I feel real fortunate that I came from the family environment I came from. They tried to teach you to do the right things. Sometimes I find myself telling my kids the same things they told me. My parents will be married 50 years next year."

"He's a breath of fresh air."
— Mike Ciarochi

Donahoe still doesn't seek the spotlight, but he is often in the center of any controversy stirred up by the Steelers. He is "the trouble guy," as Scott Paulsen put it when Donahoe appeared on WDVE's remote morning radio show at the Steelers' training camp in Latrobe with Paulsen and Jimmy Krenn. Donahoe had come a long way from being a ball boy on the same campus.

Sometimes Donahoe seems so quiet that he can get lost in a crowd. But he more than held his own in light-hearted exchanges with Krenn and Paulsen, professional comics.

"I do a little bit of everything," Donahoe said, in explaining his job to the hard rock deejays, "and a lot of nothing . . . similar to you guys."

That got a laugh and Donahoe looked happy with himself.

One of the writers on the Steelers' beat referred to Donahoe as "a breath of fresh air." He said Donahoe provided more insight and information during difficult contract negotiations than had been the case in the past.

"You know how tough it was to get them to talk about those things," said Mike Ciarochi of the *Uniontown Herald-Standard*. "Tom doesn't get into dollar figures, but he's always accessible and helpful. He'll listen to you, too."

Donahoe said his contract dispute with star running back Barry Foster was one of his earliest big challenges. "I'm old-fashioned, I think you should honor a contract," said Donahoe, "and we can do something for you down the line if you give us a chance."

Donahoe knew he had to be patient with the Pittsburgh Steelers, and that it was a virtue that has paid long-term dividends. "I used to hear from Jerry Lawrence, my cousin who worked with Tim Rooney at Yonkers Raceway, that Art Rooney had a high regard for me early on," said Donahoe.

"Mr. Rooney told Jerry he thought I had a lot of potential, when I was coaching in high school, and said he couldn't understand why the Steelers didn't hire me. I kept in touch with the Rooneys. I always had a lot of respect for Mr. Rooney."

Art Rooney Jr. was the head of the Steelers' scouting department when Donahoe came on board, but later gave way to him in a power struggle. Toward the end of his reign, Noll did not like working with Art Jr.; there was a conflict in styles. Dan Rooney dismissed his brother from the daily operation. It points up Dan's single-mindedness, and how he'll make tough decisions if he feels it's in the best interest of the Steelers. If you can fire your brother you can do anything.

Though his relationship with Donahoe had been strained, Art Jr. gave him his due when discussing him late in 1996. "Tom's relationship with Davey Lawrence definitely helped him get the job as the ballboy for the Steelers," Art Rooney Jr. said, "As far as other things, no. We hired him on what we saw."

Donahoe did not get married until he was 38, and he and his wife, Mary Margaret, have two children, Matthew, 6, and Kaitlin, 4, and they reside in Mt. Lebanon. Donahoe's family lived in Wilkinsburg when he was born, and moved to Castle Shannon for a short time, before settling in Mt. Lebanon. He was one of six children of Tom and Anna Mae Donahoe.

He played football for St. Bernard's in grade school, and was a shooting guard on the South Catholic championship basketball club that was coached by Jerry Conboy and led by star player Hank South. Donahoe credits the late Frank Cipriani, who coached him at St. Bernard's, for being a big influence in his life.

"I think he'd be proud of me," said Donahoe. "I had a lot of people help me along the way. I won't forget that."

Terry Bradshaw on Super Bowls:

"You can't enjoy it when you're playing in it. You can't relax. Every play is a big play. After all our Super Bowl games I had a headache that lasted two days simply because of the stress of the game. I had great games, but never enjoyed them."

Ray Mansfield
Fading into the sunset

"There were times when you thought you could play forever."

A sad note in the news tonight," said Patrice King Brown, beginning the 11 o'clock news at KDKA-TV on Monday, November 4, 1996. "A former Pittsburgh Steeler, Ray Mansfield, has died..."
Two friends had called me on the telephone earlier, while I was watching the National Football League's Monday Night Game between the Denver Broncos and Oakland Raiders, to tell me that Mansfield had died. They didn't know much beyond that, so I turned to KDKA-TV during the game to get the details of what happened.

The timing of the news was intriguing. Monday Night Football had always had special appeal for a player, fan and ham like Mansfield. . .

Patrice King Brown and Bob Pompeani provided few details. Mansfield, one of our all-time favorite Steelers, had died at age 55 of an apparent heart attack while hiking with his son, Jim, and a family friend in the Grand Canyon. His body was flown out of there by helicopter.

James Ray Mansfield was the first football player to die who had been a member of the Steelers of the '70s, the NFL's Team of the Decade. He was one of the pivotal characters in the transformation of the Steelers from being an also-ran to one of the most respected teams in the history of sports. He had been an "Iron Man," so strong, so indomitable, and a stalwart performer for the teams that won Super Bowls in 1974 and 1975. Now the truth was sinking in that he was all too human, that he could die like the rest of us. And it hurt.

The news from Arizona was a reminder that sports is not the real world, but the people who populate it — no matter how great they may be — will grow old, get sick perhaps and die.

Mansfield, who lived in Upper St. Clair and worked in Canonsburg most of his adult life, had two Super Bowl rings and countless battle scars and war stories to show for his 13 seasons with the Steelers and 14 seasons in the NFL. As tough as he was on the field, he was a teddy bear off it, always full of fun.

There was a sense of playfulness about Mansfield that made him a magnet for teammates. He once recalled, "I'm still 12 years old. I'm play-acting as a 51-year-old. I'm somewhere between the Ol' Ranger and Peter Pan and The Lost Boys. I enjoy people. I enjoy life, living it to the fullest."

When I asked him once why he wasn't playing tennis anymore on our local courts, when he was in his late 40s, he shrugged those round shoulders, and said, "It hurts too much. I can't hit the ball without feeling pain. My doctor tells me I have the neck of a 90-year-old man, all splintered and calcified. Too much head-knocking, I guess." Then he smiled, like it was no big deal. Mansfield could force a smile in any situation.

There are surveys by the NFL Players Association which show that a football player's life expectancy is less than the average man. It's not uncommon for former football players to die in their mid-50s and early-60s.

The story of Mansfield's death had a familiar ring to it. I had interviewed Mansfield many times, and had devoted full chapters to him in the first two of my four books about the Steelers, namely *Doing It Right* and *Whatever It Takes.*

I pulled the latter book off the shelf in our family room and began to read Mansfield's chapter at halftime.

We had shared coffee and stories on a snowy Saturday morning at his USC home four years earlier, back in 1992. "I can accept being 51 and looking 51," he said then. "It's how fast those last 15 years went that shakes me. Another 15 years and I'm going to be at retirement age. I hope they don't go as fast.

"I can't imagine slowing down. I never want to be on Social Security. *I want to be out hiking in the Grand Canyon when I'm 70.* I don't want to be out in the park feeding pigeons. I want to be on the other side of the mountain."

And, ironically enough, that's exactly where Mansfield fell dead while hiking. He died of natural causes, according to the National Park Service. At Ray's instructions, his son and traveling companion had gone ahead, leaving him behind. When he didn't show up the next morning, as he said he would, they went back to where they had left him.

It is said he was found in a spot that overlooked the canyon. He had died, it appeared by those who recreated the scene, sitting there, watching the sort of spectacular sunset that had captivated him on his first trip to this wonder of nature. He was just slumped over where he had been sitting.

"He was an adventurer," said former teammate John Banaszak of McMurray, an assistant football coach at Washington & Jefferson College, who once went on a mountain climbing expedition with Mansfield.

Mansfield liked to push the envelope. He had played organized football for 25 years, and never missed a game. He spent his rookie season (1963) with the Philadelphia Eagles before coming to the Steelers for 13 more seasons (1964-1976). He wore No. 56 and played center. He took great pride in being called an ironman. At his death, he still held the team record for most consecutive games played at 182. He often played hurt. Toward the end of the streak, he once put himself into the lineup on special teams without Noll's knowledge, to keep the streak alive.

ay Mansfield and son Jimmy enjoy good cigars before they went off in search of adventure
Grand Canyon National Park.

"I wanted to be out there every play," he once said. "I never wanted to be off the field. There were times, when you thought you could play forever."

"He was the keeper of the memories."
— Rocky Bleier

Ray Mansfield missed football more than most. "I had real withdrawal problems," he once confessed.

After they retired, he and his best friend on the team, Andy Russell, began going on annual challenging expeditions. "It was a rite of passage," as their wives put it. They climbed mountains, went white water rafting and undertook demanding hikes in exotic sites like Nepal and Alaska.

Mansfield, Russell and Rocky Bleier, ironically enough, were part of a Pittsburgh Brewing Company promotion during the 1996 season. Their likenesses appeared on Iron City beer cans, an honor treasured nearly as much as their Super Bowl rings. With that promotional campaign, Mansfield was certified as an official "Iron Man."

Mansfield was a tireless worker as well. He was co-owner with Chuck Puskar of Puskar-Mansfield Associates and executive vice president of Diversified Group Brokerage of Pittsburgh, Inc., in the Southpointe Industrial Park in Canonsburg. He sold insurance, managed investments and helped companies self-insure.

Puskar's three-month-old son, Bryan, died in 1976 of sudden infant death syndrome. Ray had been his godfather. He and Chuck began coordinating a celebrity golf tournament to raise money for SIDS, then Ray got the NFL involved.

"I can't tell you all the things he did for charity in this town," said Puskar. "He had a heart of gold."

A frequent after-dinner speaker, the cigar-chomping Mansfield was a familiar face on the rubber chicken circuit. He could spin a good yarn. He was a fun guy.

He loved to organize Steeler alumni functions, get-togethers, golf outings, fund-raisers, anything to assemble Steelers for a good time and a good cause, a good weekend.

"He was the ol' Ranger for us," said Bleier. "He was the team historian, the keeper of the memories."

Ray's early life was right out of John Steinbeck's book, *The Grapes of Wrath,* so Mansfield felt blessed by the life he led as an adult. His family picked fruit and vegetables in fields in Arizona, California and Washington. Ray had film clips from *The Grapes of Wrath* movie interspersed with family album photos in a striking video family history he and his sister, Shirley, put together.

He was nicknamed "The Ol' Ranger" after the old cowboy who narrated TV's "Death Valley Days" series that was popular when he broke into pro football.

"Life's been good to me," he said. "To me, life was good from the day I was born."

Mansfield's magnificent dream was never realized. "I want to get Chuck Noll to lead us on a hike," he said that Saturday morning in 1992 when I visited his home. "I want him to take us out in the wilderness. We can sleep out. Maybe carry a little whiskey and have a few sips at night. Smoke some cigars. That sort of thing would be so wonderful."

"Ray was a special person."
— Chuck Noll

I was sitting by myself in a seat on the aisle about three-fourths of the way back from the altar at Westminster Presbyterian Church. This was Saturday morning, November 9, 1996, a week after Mansfield had been found dead in the Grand Canyon. This was at a memorial service for Mansfield near his former home in Upper St. Clair.

He was too young too die, only a year older than I was at the time, so it hit home even more. Yet there was some solace from the thought that this was the way he wanted to die. It was eerie, but it seemed as if he had gone to the Grand Canyon to die, like it was part of his game plan.

As I sat there, thinking about Mansfield and the Steelers of the '70s, personal thoughts and such, someone squeezed my right shoulder. I looked back and saw Chuck Noll in the pew behind me. I smiled and acknowledged him. He looked so solemn, so I said hello to him and his wife, Marianne, and to Babe and Joe Gordon, who had come to the church with him. I wanted to talk to them, but thought better of it. It wasn't a good time. Noll was thought to be cold and aloof when he coached the Steelers, and he could be that, for sure, but he was a most decent man, a man of many interests, someone you could talk to about any subject. He lived only a mile from our home for 16 of the 23 years he resided in Upper St. Clair, yet I never felt as close a kinship with him as I did when he squeezed my shoulder at the Mansfield memorial service.

Gordon, who was acknowledged as the best publicist in the National Football League when the Steelers were the best team in pro football, told me later that Noll had driven from his home in Hilton Head, South Carolina, the day before and would be returning there after the funeral service. He came to town strictly for the funeral service.

It had to be a difficult time for Noll. One of his boys, one of the blocks upon which he built the Steelers' dynasty, had died. Too young. Noll had retired from coaching the Steelers after the 1991 season, at age 60, and had been inducted the following year into the Pro Football Hall of Fame. He and Marianne seemed so content with their new life. Retirement suited them well. Everyone who saw Noll in recent years commented on how good he looked. He was proud of what his teams had accomplished in winning four Super Bowls. Mansfield was one of the men who helped get him there. Mansfield had been more than a football player. He was a presence, a personality, and he personified the sort of combativeness and dedication and positive outlook that Noll needed to transform a loser into a winner when he took over the team in 1969. This had to be a sobering experience. The Steelers were 2-11-1 in 1968, Bill Austin's final year, and 1-13 in Noll's first season. During Mansfield's first six seasons with the Steelers, the team's overall record was 19-62-3.

"Ray was a special person," Noll would acknowledge later on, outside the church. "He was a guy who everybody rallied around. He always had a certain amount of levity, but he was a tremendous football player.

"I really remember when we moved into Three Rivers Stadium in 1970 and Ray was one of the guys who remembered what it was like before when we had to practice at South Park Fairgrounds, and we didn't really have a home. He was sitting in the locker room before the first exhibition game and he had a smile from ear to ear. He was just so glad the Steelers finally had a home."

Noll had often scolded me in a light-hearted manner when I approached him during his last days as coach of the club, and encouraged him to reflect on the early years, and how he shaped and formed the Steelers into one of the NFL's finest teams, one of the best over a six-year stretch in the game's history. "Not now, this isn't the time," he'd say. "Maybe someday when I'm in a rocking chair. Can't we wait?" Despite his protests, he would oblige, and he was always a thoughtful, if not especially enthusiastic, interview.

What if I had waited until Mansfield was in a rocking chair? I'd have missed out on Mansfield's reflections and they were both bountiful and meaningful. I was so glad, I thought to myself as I sat in the pew in front of the Nolls and Gordons, that I had sat down with Mansfield on several occasions to get his stories. He was the best story-teller of all the Steelers.

Russell and Bleier both liked to swap stories about the Steelers as well, but they weren't nearly as good at it as Mansfield. They lacked the comic's sense of selection of detail, the order of relating a tale, timing, the punch lines.

And now Mansfield was gone. He would speak no more. How sad, I thought. He was so good at it, he enjoyed it so much. And his stories were the stories of the Steelers.

Alex Haley, who took 12 years to do the research and to write the Pulitzer Prize-winning epic novel, *Roots*, once said, "Every time an old person dies it is like a library being burned down."

How true that was in the case of Mansfield. He was a grand story-teller. That's why he was the focal figure in the outstanding book about the 1973 Steelers called *Three Bricks Shy of a Load*, why he appealed so much to its author, Roy Blount, Jr. This book was

166

With partner Chuck Puskar

Writers Myron Cope and Roy Blount Jr. were special friends.

With Jude Ann Trostle

With pal Andy Russell

With Rocky Bleier

written before the Steelers won any Super Bowls, its timing a matter of good fortune.

And Roy Blount, Jr., was among the many mourners present at Westminster Presbyterian Church that Saturday morning. He was in the company of Ed Kiely, who had preceded Gordon as the Steelers' publicist and had befriended Blount when he was in Pittsburgh to research the book.

"It was like a reunion of the Steelers from that Super Bowl era," Blount told me when we spoke after the service. "He was so full of life. I never thought that he'd be the first to go."

In Blount's book, Mansfield was quoted as saying, "Football's like my father's work because it's hard, grinding work. It grinds you down. It makes for a short life, at least a very uncomfortable life later on."

Blount was the only sportswriter I saw at the service. This was disturbing. Mansfield had been the best friend a sportswriter would want in the clubhouse.

It reminded me of attending a funeral service at a synagogue in Rockville Centre, Long Island, in the late '70s when Milton Gross had died. Gross had been the lead sports columnist for *The New York Post*, where I worked, for over 30 years. He had been a nationally-syndicated columnist, and his stories appeared in newspapers throughout the country. He had championed the causes of the black athletes before it was fashionable. He had profiled the finest of New York's ballplayers. Yet none of them was in attendance at his funeral.

Every sports team and sports entity in the New York area was represented by front-office types, all the public relations men. They mixed at the temple and on the sidewalks outside before and after the service with the sportswriters they served on a daily basis.

It was a lesson to be learned about the relationships between sportswriters and athletes, how it's really just a locker room relationship, nothing more and nothing less, perhaps the way it works best.

The day before, at the Beinhauer Funeral Home on Route 19 in McMurray, I had seen WTAE talk show host Phil Musick, who had covered the club for *The Pittsburgh Press* when Mansfield was on the team, and Bill DiFabio, who had covered the Steelers for 25 years for his Sportscall radio network service. DiFabio was disturbed by the scene, and how much many of the Steelers he had known as ballplayers had changed since he had seen them last. "I can't stand to see these guys get old," he confessed. He cared about them, that's why.

Mansfield was always available to the media. He thrived on the attention. He actually enjoyed going to banquets and being with the fans. He was one of those ballplayers Gordon relied on to represent the Steelers at banquets and public functions, and Gordon felt the loss of an old friend and someone who made his job easier.

"Nobody got more satisfaction out of the first two Super Bowl wins than Ray," said Gordon. "He went through some rough years and had a better appreciation of what it meant to be a champion than some of the guys who came along later.

"I never met a more optimistic person, a more positive guy than Ray Mansfield."

Dan Rooney, the president of the Steelers, had come to the funeral home that same Friday afternoon with his wife, Pat. Rooney wore a black Steelers' windbreaker, and stood out in the crowd though he was slighter in build than most. He did not attend the memorial service at the church. He was in his office that day at Three Rivers Stadium. The Steelers were hosting the Cincinnati Bengals there the following day, and he was taking care of business.

Asked about Mansfield, Rooney described him as "a fun guy and very close to us. He added a lot of humor and spirit to our team."

Rooney's father, Art Rooney, was famous for attending funerals. Usually accompanied by Kiely, he probably attended more funerals and memorial masses and services than any other person in Pittsburgh. He would check the obituary notices each morning, like it was *The Racing Form*, and plan his day around attending funerals. "If he went into a funeral home where there happened to be three people laid out," recalled Kiely, "he'd stop by and offer his regrets to all the families. He was a 100 per cent Irish politician. He shook hands with everybody. He was always surprised when people acknowledged him by name. When we'd leave the funeral home, he'd say to me, 'How do those people know me?'"

I used to duck funerals myself, but Art Rooney taught me why you go, and why it's important to be there when friends or associates have suffered a loss. You're not there to view the deceased, and you don't have to do that if that bothers you.

"I'm fully convinced you can't beat the calendar," said Kiely. "There's no sense in dying your hair or getting a facelift."

As for Mansfield, Keily shook his head and said, "I never figured he'd die the way he died. It got dark, but why somebody didn't go back to look for him, I couldn't figure out. Those things rumbled through my mind."

Sitting across the aisle from us at Westminster Presbyterian Church were Mel Blount and Franco Harris. You would have had to travel to Canton, Ohio to find more Hall of Famers in one building.

Bleier and Russell were there, too. Russell was one of those who offered remarks about his good friend from the pulpit. Mansfield, Bleier and Russell had all separated from their first wives after long marriages about three to four years earlier, almost in a domino-like fashion. Some of those in the church who knew the Mansfields well, and were friends of Janet Mansfield, felt that the eulogies and newspaper obits didn't tell the full story, especially the part about Ray being a great family man. He had been that, especially with the kids, but toward the end of his life he had left his wife for another woman. They felt he had betrayed Janet, who deserved better, in favor of a younger woman.

Those people may have been mollified by a remark interjected by Rev. Robert S. Norris, the pastor at Westminster who delivered the principal eulogy. Norris did not personally know Mansfield, but delivered a well-written, meaningful reflection on his life. He had done his homework more than most clerics on such occasions. "Ray Mansfield was not a Saint," noted Norris early in his talk. "He was a Steeler."

Other former teammates in attendance at the church service were J.T. Thomas and Larry Brown, who had both been so successful in ownership and management positions with a string of Applebee's Restaurants in the Greater Pittsburgh area. Randy Grossman and Mike Wagner, both respected stockbrokers and investment counselors, were there, along with Bryan Hinkle, who was doing some college coaching, and J.R. Wilburn, in from Virginia, and Jim Clack, in from North Carolina. With free agency, and players jumping from one team to another, it's unlikely that many former Steelers will still be residing in the community to come to a funeral when one of the present-day players dies.

I had last seen some of these former Steelers, along with Mansfield, at the Greengate Mall in Greensburg the previous summer at an independently-promoted sports show where Steelers from the '70s were signing autographs. Blount was the only one who didn't look much different from his playing days, save for the salt in his beard. He was still such an impressive figure.

A few weeks after the funeral, Bleier would be in the news. He would declare bankruptcy, which prompted a torrent of sensational and messy stories and fodder for talk shows for several weeks about his divorce and financial problems with his previous wife, Aleta. To protect his four Super Bowl rings from being claimed as assets in the bankruptcy proceedings, Bleier sold, or leased, his Super Bowl jewelry to Herb Conner, an attorney and good friend, for $40,000, with the understanding he could see or borrow them anytime for public outings.

Bleier had been one of the Steelers' most popular players, heralded as a genuine hero in both book and movie, for overcoming disabling wounds suffered in Vietnam to resume his pro football career and to become a starting running back alongside Franco Harris for the Steelers in their best years. Bleier had been a much-sought speaker and commanded a fee of $6,500 per outing to tell his comeback story.

Like Mansfield's death, Bleier's bankruptcy and attending issues revealed that the Steelers weren't invulnerable to the social problems that challenge most people. They were still fighting back.

"There weren't big people and little people to Mr. Rooney. They were just people and he wanted to help everyone. I never saw him say 'no' to anyone in need."
— Mary Regan, Secretary
to the late Art Rooney

"It reminds you of your own mortality."
— Moon Mullins

At the funeral home the day before, I had spotted ex-Steelers such as Russell, Lloyd Voss — he was openly weeping — Gene Breen, Bruce Van Dyke, Jack Ham, Jack Lambert, L.C. Greenwood, Sam Davis, Tunch Ilkin, Paul Martha, Ted Petersen, Moon Mullins and Craig Bingham.

"It reminds you of your own mortality," said Mullins. He admitted he had difficulty sleeping after he heard about his former teammate and friend dying in the Grand Canyon. "I was hoping he wasn't crawling around at the end, hollering for help, groping in the dirt, and no one was there."

Sam Davis looked much different from his playing days. He, too, was a reminder that the Steelers were not supermen. Davis had been beaten up a few years earlier in a strange attack by some tough guys over an unpaid business debt, and suffered permanent head injuries that impaired his memory and communication skills. Several of his teammates said that Davis had been beaten to a pulp with a baseball bat, and been knocked down the steps of his farm house in Gibsonia. It was a story that went largely unreported. Davis had a puffy look to his mottled burnt-orange face, like an old boxer, like Muhammad Ali. Davis was living in a personal care home in McKeesport. His wife was not able to look after him any longer. He was a tragic figure. Yet he was all smiles as he greeted old friends.

Pro sports agent Ralph Cindrich, who had played at Pitt and with the Patriots, Oilers and Broncos, stopped by from nearby Mt. Lebanon to pay his respects. Cindrich wasn't nearly the ballplayer as most of these Steelers, but he had fared better than most of them in the business world. He had gotten rich representing some high profile players in their contract negotiations. Free agency was a boon for all agents.

Bob Milie, also of Mt. Lebanon, the former assistant trainer of the Steelers and at Duquesne University, looking much younger than the 70th birthday he was fast approaching, was talking to Lambert and Ralph Berlin of Bethel Park, the former head trainer. They were all swapping their favorite Mansfield tales. Milie mentioned that Mansfield was not really the first individual from those teams of the '70s to die.

Milie listed team owner Art Rooney, assistant coach Rollie Dotsch and field manager Jackie Hart as ones who were part of that storied stretch who had died earlier. Hart had been a favorite of Lambert. Many thought that Hart had died of a broken heart after he had been fired for failure to show up for work once too often. Jack Splat was standing tall in the middle of the reception area at the funeral home, his hands dug deep into the pockets of his black trench-coat. He looked hollow-cheeked, downright scrawny, but insisted he had lost only ten pounds from his playing weight. Lambert looked like the guy in Budweiser's TV commercial who came to the rescue of drinkers who discovered that their beer was old and stinky and lacked Budweiser's "born" date label.

Mansfield was on view at the funeral home in a business suit, with a fat cigar stuck between the pudgy fingers of his right hand. He was wearing eyeglasses and his Super Bowl rings. He had two more cigars projecting from his breast pocket. He was going out in style.

"How many of us can pick the place where we're going to say goodbye?"
— Joe Greene

Mansfield had explored the Grand Canyon several times. He had first seen it in 1949 when his family was doing migrant work in fields in the area. He knew its challenges well, what it required to get through it. He had not trained for its demands and was not in the kind of physical shape it required to handle the trek, according to Russell, who had accompanied him on earlier expeditions. The two had also accompanied each other in climbing the Himalayas in Nepal, the Rockies in Colorado, and traversing snow-covered woodlands in Alaska.

There had been a history of heart disease in the Mansfield clan. Others in the family had died from heart problems in their 40s and 50s. His sister, Shirley, with whom I had corresponded on earlier books, had died two years earlier. Ray seemed to sense that his biological clock was ticking. He had discussed death with family and friends before embarking on this trip.

Former teammate Joe Greene, a defensive line coach with the Arizona Cardinals, was shocked to learn of Mansfield's passing. "Ray was a good man," said Greene. "He always had a smile on his face and he could make you laugh. He was a joy to be around."

Greene was also intrigued by how and where Mansfield had died. "I keep asking myself, 'Ray, why the Grand Canyon?'" Greene said. "But maybe Ray knew something. How many of us can pick the place where we're going to say goodbye?"

Terry Bradshaw was at his home near Dallas when he heard the news of Mansfield's death.

"I'm still shocked," Bradshaw said in a telephone interview. "The first thing I did was go out and run. You know how you get sometimes when you can go a mile and not even know you are running? I couldn't get Ray out of my mind. He was a big ol' lovable guy. There was always a child in him.

"He had a great personality. He was a very witty guy. He and Andy Russell were the two people when I was drafted by Pittsburgh who always made me feel a part of the family."

172

"He is the first member of our team to die, except for Mr. Rooney. When anybody close to you dies, it makes you think of how mortal we all are."

When I mentioned to Kiely what a thrill it always was simply to stroll the sideline with Art Rooney at practice, something I did at the South Park Fairgrounds when I was in college back in 1963, and at Three Rivers Stadium as late as 1988, and never tired of it. "That's because you were doing something that a lot of great people would have loved to have done," concluded Kiely.

"Ray thought (the Grand Canyon) was the most spiritual place."
— Andy Russell

His business partner and friend, Chuck Puskar, and his good friend and fellow adventurer, Andy Russell, related stories about Mansfield at the funeral service.

"Ray's first client was Steve 'Froggy' Morris," pointed out Puskar from the pulpit. "If he could get a big insurance policy approved for an overworked, overweight bartender, I knew he'd be a big success. I was so impressed.

"He loved movies. Any movie with John Wayne riding into the sunset . . . Ray would love to watch it. He was a real history buff."

In remarks he made prior to the ceremony, Puskar said, "He never ceased to amaze me with his mind. Besides his great love of history and movies and country and western music and '50s music, he was one of the most intelligent guys I ever knew. He was such a gentle, laidback guy that he'd take everybody by surprise with his knowledge.

"For 32 years, I've known Ray Mansfield. I can't even begin to imagine what life's going to be like without him."

Puskar recalled Mansfield at the first Super Bowl in which the Steelers participated. "I remember him at the first one at the first session with the media," Puskar said. "Ray was holding court when the buzzer went off to break things up. He stood up at the table and screamed, 'Where are you guys going? I've still got a lot of stories to tell.' He loved every minute of being there."

Russell related some personal experiences with Mansfield, his best friend from his Steeler days.

"Mansfield felt you should meet every challenge with a smile," related Russell. "You can't smile and be afraid. He'd rather be roasted than praised. He could be tough and gentle, and he loved to put people on.

"When Ray was selling insurance, he had been to visit a prospect several times, and the guy led him on. When the guy didn't come through, Ray kicked a hole in the guy's desk. Then he couldn't get his foot out. When it came to football or the insurance business, he was a warrior."

173

As 5th grader

Mansfield children: (left to right front row) Ray (14), Ted (6), Odie (12), Becky (4) and Gene (20), (second row) Sharon (11), Bill (9) and Shirley (17).

Ray's parents, Owen, at age 22, and Carmel, 21, raised eight children.

Mansfield boys: Odie (5), Ray (7), Bill (2), Gene (13)

In Arizona in 1947

"Grapes of Wrath" family photo (left to right): Gene, Ray, Odie, Shirley, Sharon, Owen and Carmel, holding Bill.

At the same time, Ray could be extremely considerate, extremely compassionate, according to Russell.

"Just ask Mike Reid. When Reid (a former Penn State lineman from Altoona), was playing for the Cincinnati Bengals, he hurt Terry Hanratty, our quarterback, when he hit him extra hard. Before the next snap, Ray asked Mike if he wanted him to blow out his right knee or his left knee the next time they lined up. One way or another, Ray was going to get even.

"At an affair in Nashville, Tennessee, Dick Butkus was there. And Ray hollered out, 'Dick, I owned you!' Everyone there froze, until Ray smiled and embraced Butkus.

"We were at a dinner where Arnold Palmer was honored, and Ray said, 'Frankly, Arnie, I can't see why they get so excited about you. I hear you wear panty hose.' No one was sacred when Ray was roasting them.

"He packed more living into those years. He was like Art Rooney; you enjoyed his company. He was so defensive about Chuck Noll. No one could criticize Noll in his company. He loved the Steelers' family. He was the mentor to so many young men. He taught us all that you have to live for the moment.

"It was fitting that he died in the Grand Canyon. It was a special place for both of us. We often talked about it, how it was like the inside of a Cathedral with all its different-colored layers and crevices. Ray thought it was the most spiritual place he'd ever seen.

"He was my inspiration, he was my friend," said Russell.

For many years, Mansfield had a John Wayne mural in his office, on the wall behind his desk. John Wayne's western movies were Mansfield's favorite fare. His brother, Ted Mansfield, delivered this moving eulogy:

"Among the many things that Ray Mansfield loved were classic movies. As I thought about what to say today, I wondered what Ray would put into a movie script about his life. I do know that all of Ray's stories would end with the hero fading into the sunset.

"His movie would definitely be an adventure. It would open with the birth of a baby boy on a chilly morning in January, 1941 in Bakersfield, California. As the boy grows, he would travel across the land as his father sought work to support a growing family. Ray would make his family *Grapes of Wrath* characters, but without the tragedy the Joad family suffered. Scenes would include Ray and his family shivering in an old pickup truck awaiting enough light to pick asparagus before the kids went off to school. He learned early on the benefits of being a team player.

"Other scenes would include his coaches from junior and senior high school predicting greatness for Ray, not because of his athletic skills, but because of his work ethic, his will to win and his competitive nature. Ray would be shown as a legend in Kennewick, Washington. His friends and teachers would sing his praises as a good friend and a student of life.

175

"The college years at the University of Washington would be a whirlwind of honors and more lessons in life. Our movie hero would fall in love and marry his high school sweetheart, Janet, before moving east to tackle the challenge of professional football. We all know that story.

"As Ray's career moved ahead, a man for all seasons would blossom as father, sports figure, businessman and friend. Those who are touched by Ray Mansfield would feel the special magic he had.

"Special starring roles would be reserved in *The Ray Mansfield Story* for his children: Kathy, Jennifer, Caroline and Jim. New stars of the future would be introduced in this movie, his grandchildren, Taylor Ann and Stone. His parents, Owen and Carmel, his brother, Gene, and sisters, Shirley and Meralene, would be his special advisors. Our movie would show a man working to help others around him through community and business activities. A picture would emerge of a competitor with a heart as big as the great outdoors he loved so much. New challenges would be sought and tackled. His life changes and a new character would be added to his life, Jude.

"Ray Mansfield, our movie hero, would not be cheated out of his grand finale. His zest for life was seldom matched by others, and his big finish won't be either. His stories were heartwarming and leave us with a satisfied, warm feeling. Join me now, if you will, in imagining the script for Ray's final movie scene. Oh, he would have loved it so!

"Imagine deep in the Grand Canyon, sunlight fading, the colors vibrant. The only sound we hear is the river crashing down its course below. Peace has settled upon the land. The Ol' Ranger, weary from his latest battle, pack on his back, sits down to rest and enjoy the scene before him that he loved so much.

"As he slowly closes his eyes, a bugle plays 'Taps' as the words roll across the screen:

Day is done, gone the sun,
From the hills, from the fields,
From the sky,
Rest in peace, soldier brave,
God is nigh.

"Once again, Ray Mansfield steals the show and emerges as the hero. This movie may not win an Academy Award, but all of us who played a part in this epic adventure will never forget."

Ted Mansfield was only one to mention Jude, Ray's girlfriend, with whom he had been living the previous two years, in a home outside Butler.

A eulogy offered by Rev. Robert Norris, who did not personally know Mansfield, captured his spirit so well.

"We gather here this day with sad, yet grateful hearts. Sad because death represents a loss for us," began Norris. "The loss of a relationship. The loss of life as it was remembered, in all its vitality, health and joy. Sad because what was will not, as it was experienced, be repeated and can only be remembered.

"Yet we have grateful hearts that emerge when the memory banks are engaged. And it is these memories of life with Ray Mansfield that sustain you in this time of sorrow and grief.

"In our celebration, we remember Ray's strong yet still gentle nature. We recall Ray's passion for his family and for football, for his teammates and friends and for children in need. We give thanks for the willing and able help he unselfishly offered, for his enthusiastic and ever optimistic spirit, for his humbleness, his wisdom, his fortitude, his kind and gracious words of gratitude and encouragement.

"For years, Ray and Janet would pack up the kids and head to Washington for family reunions."

Norris had previously preached at a church in Houston before coming to Westminster a year earlier. He was born in Bethlehem, Pennsylvania, and wanted all those in attendance to know he was a Steelers' fan from the start. And Mansfield had played with some of those teams that got him hooked on the Steelers.

"Away from the crowds, Ray was a quiet and rather introspective person who really loved to be away and often got away alone for times of solitude and deep reflection," noted Norris.

"Ray would sit and watch from the canyon rim the sunsets and that magnificent southwestern hue of colors that cast one of the most breathtaking sights one on this earth can witness. Perhaps that is why he called the Grand Canyon his 'picture of heaven.' Ray once said he wanted to die in the Grand Canyon.

"Perhaps on Saturday, November 2, one week ago today, God gave that picture to Ray as his last view of his earthly life for the purpose of comparison.

"For you might imagine how, as Ray sat down on that rock on the edge of the canyon at sunset, when the panoramic beauty was so transfixing that what he caught, in that still frame, for just a measurable moment, was a glimpse, just a visual taste right here on earth, of the immeasurable glory that upon waking across the canyon on the other side, that God intends Ray and we might desire to embrace and experience for all eternity."

Kiely: "I don't think it just happens. In my mind, he must have had some kind of indication, something that made him understand. He ought to have checked it out."

Jan Strnisha, the past executive secretary of the Washington-Greene Chapter of the Pennsylvania Sports Hall of Fame, shared a letter in which she offered this tribute to Ray Mansfield upon his death in November of 1996:

"The morning news brought more than a shock when Ray Mansfield's death was announced. The week's elections would affect our immediate futures, but this shook our present. My 40- and 50-year-old friends who, while we did not personally know Ray, cheered

177

his on-the-field success and admired his life's philosophy of living every day to the fullest. We identified with Ray — we worked hard, we officially arrived at middle age and we all chased our dreams. As we reminisced by phone about the Steelers' glory days and Ray's contributions, the first crack in the steel left us missing Ray, missing yesterday and realizing our own mortality. That day the morning news set a tone of reverence and saddens us as we each, in our own quiet way, said, 'Thanks, Ray, and goodbye. We'll miss you.' We needed to talk to each other, we needed to share our feelings and we needed to remember."

"Ray was like a shooting star."
— Andy Russell

Ray Mansfield was missing from the lineup at the Andy Russell Celebrity Classic For Children for the first time in 21 years when the celebrity golf tournament was held May 16, 1997 at The Club at Nevillewood.

This event had raised more than $1.5 million to support Pittsburgh-area children's charities, and was held this time for two principals — the University of Pittsburgh Medical Center and Children's Hospital — and Mansfield had been a mainstay in one of the area's most respected fund-raisers.

Many of Mansfield's former teammates were there, foremost his friend Andy Russell and John Banaszak, Frenchy Fuqua, Gordon Gravelle, L. C. Greenwood, Randy Grossman, Terry Hanratty, Dick Hoak, Frank Lewis, Gerry Mullins, Edmund Nelson, Lynn Swann, J.T. Thomas, Weegie Thompson, Mike Wagner, Dwight White, J. R. Wilburn and their coach, Chuck Noll.

Other Steelers on hand were Matt Bahr, Craig Bingham, Mark Bruener, Barry Foster, Kendall Gammon, Tunch Ilkin, Todd Kalis, Carnell Lake, Rick Strom, coaches Mike Archer, David Culley, Chan Gailey, Tim Lewis, Mike Mularkey, Kent Stephenson, Ron Zook and Kansas City Chiefs coach Marty Schottenheimer and Steelers broadcaster Myron Cope.

Former NFL Hall of Famers, Chuck Bednarik, Bobby Bell, Jim Taylor, and standouts like John David Crow, Bill Fralic, Doug Dieken, Tom Mack, Mark May and Gil Brandt were in the field. Former Pirates Steve Blass, Bob Friend, Dave Giusti, Bill Mazeroski, Jim Rooker, Manny Sanguillen and Penguins Jay Caufield and Dan Quinn were there, too.

No one would have enjoyed their company more than Mansfield who had died in early November, 1996.

Russell offered a tribute to Mansfield in the tournament program:

"Ray was a loyal supporter of this tournament, playing in all 20 years. Ray was a complex man. He was a witty, irreverent, rules-breaking, fun-loving, story-telling, friend-making, very smart (the best at Trivial Pursuit), tough but compassionate guy. He was like a latter day Will Rogers, giving his humorous but accurate perspectives on life.

"He never missed a good cigar or a good story. He proved that everyday occasions were really the stuff of dreams, that life can be exciting without money, or status, or celebrity. None of that really mattered to him.

"Ray and I traveled around the world five times, giving athletic clinics for kids and speeches to all kinds of groups. We also sought out gut-testing journeys in the wilderness, climbing four 14,000-feet mountains in Colorado in one day, and hiking in the Grand Canyon and the Himalayas.

"Ray was like a shooting star. He had shot across our lives and brightened our world. None of us can imagine the energy it took for him to burn so brightly for so many wonderfully rich and exciting miles. We miss you, Ray."

"Ray was invincible."
— Jude Ann Trostle

Anyone attending the memorial service for Ray Mansfield at Westminster Presbyterian Church had to pay close attention to hear about Jude, the woman Ray planned to marry in May of 1997.

His brother, Ted, in delivering a moving eulogy, mentioned all the loved ones in Mansfield's family, and tagged Jude at the end, without explanation. Just Jude.

That was Jude Ann Trostle, a self-employed interior designer from Renfrew, just outside Butler. She and her three children lived in a sprawling farm estate home, called Bonniecroft, and Ray had been living there in what had been the servants quarters for two years.

"He was living in a separate apartment," said Jude.

Mansfield had separated in January, 1994 from his wife, Janet, after 30 years of marriage, but had not yet been divorced when he died. Jude has most of Mansfield's memorabilia, photos, belongings and ashes in her home. Janet remains the beneficiary of his NFL pension. She is now living in Hood River, Oregon.

Jude had been divorced from her husband of 25 years. Their children were Sarah, 20, Katie, 17, and Robbie, 14. She said they all felt left out when none of them was mentioned at the Mansfield funeral.

"Ray loved my children, and my children loved him," said Jude. "Ray's children were all nice and kind to me and my children because they loved their dad so much and they knew how much he loved me and my kids.

Ray Mansfield was always the center of attention at Steelers' reunions such as the one he coordinated on June 10, 1990 at the Melody Tent at Station Square. Steelers on stage (left to right) were Steve Courson, Ted Petersen, Mike Wagner, Mansfield, Bob Kohrs, Rocky Bleier, Jon Kolb, J. T. Thomas, John "Frenchy" Fuqua, John Henry Johnson, Rick Woods and John Reger.

Wedding bells brought the family together on August 5, 1995 at St. Louise de Marillac Catholic Church in Upper St. Clair. The family (from left to right) included the Mansfield's three daughters and son, namely John and Jennifer Garber (holding Taylor Ann), father Ray, Caroline and Jim Lefik, the bride and groom, mother Janet, Kathleen Wolfley and Jim Mansfield.

"I'm Jude, and I felt like I didn't exist. Why? It was very confusing. It was hurtful to my children. They had a lot of questions after the funeral. They felt like they were his children, too."

She said she and Ray planned to get married at Bonniecroft, where Moon Mullins and Joan had married the previous summer. It was the second marriage for Mullins. "Ray's happiest moments were when all of the children were together and he would be grilling his famous 'hockey puck' hamburgers — as his son, Jimmy, called them — with Cleo, his beloved red coon hound relaxing at his feet."

Jude shared some of her feelings in a letter she sent me at my request to clear up matters. She said Ray bought a dappled gray pony and a white pony cart for his two grandchildren — Taylor and Stone — and that he would lead the pony-driven cart through the farm fields of Bonniecroft, the grandchildren giggling in the back.

She said Andy Russell and his friend, Cindy, would come out on weekends. Russell was divorced from his wife, Nancy. "After dinner, Ray and Andy would retire to the front verandah, contentedly puffing long, fat cigars, sipping port and reminiscing, sharing old war stories while bullfrogs croaked their evening vespers," wrote Jude.

"Our life was sweet. Once on a golf trip with Jack Ham, Jack told me, laughingly, that I had turned Ray into a love-sick puppy.

"Ray always said that there could never be a fate so cruel that it would take one of us and leave the other one behind. I believed him because every word that he uttered to me was infallible. But always the brutal knowledge of a (Mansfield) family history of heart problems and early death haunted me.

"I held him in my arms as we wept the night his dear sister, Shirley, died. His big brother, Geno, his hero, died at age 53.

"An unknown, uneasy feeling clung to me that week as Ray and Jimmy eagerly made their plans to hike the Grand Canyon. Even friends asked me why I was brooding over this particular trip when I had never done that before. I couldn't say. After all, Ray and Andy were seasoned hikers. Ray was invincible.

"But I knew in my heart, as he kissed me goodbye, that I would never see him again. Sometimes now when the phone rings, for a split second I know it's him and my heart races. And sometimes when I see Jimmy, I see Ray, and it takes my breath away. The other day, I half-heartedly cleared Ray's garden of winter's shredded debris. I wondered if his roses would bloom this spring."

"Athletics lasts for such a short period of time. It ends for people. But while it lasts, it creates this make-believe world where normal rules don't apply. We build this false atmosphere. When it's over and the harsh reality sets in, that's the real joke we play on people ... Everybody wants to experience that superlative moment, and being an athlete can give you that. It is Camelot for them. But there's even life after it."

— Father of football player
in *Friday Night Lights,*
by H. G. Bissinger

Two Hall of Famers: Steelers' Mel Blount and Pirates' Willie Stargell

Two of Steelers great linebackers: Jack Ham and Andy Russell

Hall of Fame candidate L.C. Greenwood is Pittsburgh businessman.

Dwight White is investment executive in Pittsburgh.

Andy Russell and Mike Wagner are investment brokers.

Joe Gordon greets good friends, Marianne and Chuck Noll, among the many notables at Gordon's "retirement" party at the Grand Concourse Restaurant in May, 1997.

Mel Blount backs up broadcaster Myron Cope at Greensburg appearance.

Two outstanding businessmen: John Stallworth and Larry Brown

Everything's different
Tom Donahoe discusses changes

"Show me the money!"
— Jerry Maguire
Sports agent

D avid Lawrence and Roberto Clemente, whose likenesses share space on the side wall of Tom Donahoe's office, were both looked upon as Pittsburgh paragons of excellence because they were on the scene so long. Clemente was with the Pirates for 18 seasons. Lawrence was the mayor of Pittsburgh for 11 years. Sports fans prefer that their heroes stay in one place. With free agency, many players don't stay around long any more. Just when the fans get to know them, too often the players go elsewhere. And Donahoe believes too many of them make such decisions for the wrong reasons.

"That's my biggest fear about free agency," said Donahoe. "I don't see enough guys going where they have the best chance to succeed as athletes. I'd like to see more guys make a great football decision. Too many of them are saying, 'Who's going to give me the most money and the most guaranteed money?'"

Or as Jerry Maguire, the sports agent played by Tom Cruise in the 1996 movie of the same name, put it, "Show me the money!"

It definitely wasn't Donahoe who nominated the movie for an Oscar.

"You'd like guys to assess the situation, look at all the factors, not just dollars and cents," said Donahoe. "What would be best for me? That's where the role of the agents comes in. That's another thing that frustrates me. Do they really have the players' best interests at heart?

"Our philosophy has changed; it had to. The nature of the game has changed. Even with our involvement in free agency, we do it a little differently from the approach of some other teams.

"Everybody has the same salary cap. It's not like anybody has more money to spend than we do. How are you going to spend that money? That's what you have to ask yourself, what you have to determine.

"Our attitude toward players has changed. We're still trying to get the right type of players. The most important thing is the team. Talent in and of itself is not the only barometer. We had a team here a couple of years ago that was a good team, but the chemistry was terrible.

"Our chemistry the last two years was pretty good. Our players really liked each other and rooted for each other.

"I've been here when it was like the offensive team was one team and the defensive team was one team and the special teams was a team unto itself. That can't work.

"The loyalty factor has been changed by the free agency system. It's not just a matter of loyalty. The economics of the game has changed. The more players who move around the more acceptable it becomes. It's no longer looked upon as a lack of loyalty anymore, not by most players anyhow. Owners and coaches look at things differently these days as well.

"We have a system that can work; it's a workable system. To get the system in place, we should all be playing by the same rules. I get upset because some teams try to do funny things with the cap. Teams try to violate the spirit of that cap."

"How does the guy play the game?"

Donahoe discussed the inner-workings of putting a team together and replacing departing players with prospects obtained in the college draft.

"People have talked about our recent drafts," said Donahoe. "They've been successful. Everybody's on the same page, and everybody has an input. And that's not just lip-service. I think people work harder when you have that kind of working environment.

"I have a chance to sell a player to Tom Modrak or Bill Cowher. We meet in two stages, as soon as we come back from the combine workouts, and then just before we conduct the draft. Coach Cowher sits in on all of it.

"The position coaches do not sit in on the initial meeting. We give them the list we've put together on players or prospects. Then the position coach has the responsibility to look at those players in his area."

What guidelines are the position coaches given for grading or judging players?

"The bottom line on players is how does the guy play the game," said Donahoe. "This isn't rocket science. How does this guy play? Grade it out with film. Coaches love that. There are many variables we consider in our checklist.

"The draft is often over-analyzed. Some of the personnel staffs around the league push it to the limit. They talk to all the draftniks, and the writers, and they have so many opinions. Most of them second-hand opinions.

"The combine workouts serve their purpose, but you have to keep it in its proper perspective. I'm a fan of it from the medical information it provides. The interviews with the players are sometimes worthwhile. But it's often meaningless as far as the numbers go. How high they jump, how fast they can run a 40. Maybe this guy isn't a good player no matter how good his numbers look. On the other hand, maybe a guy doesn't do well in drills or running and jumping, but he can play the game.

"Some guys are workout warriors. One of them gets drafted in the second round, but he's no good because he can't play football. He's good at the combine . . . those are athletic things. Coach Noll had a lot of great qualities, and one of them was assessing talent. And even he made mistakes. But he was more interested in playing speed or playing strength. A guy may not have been good at 40 speed, and he can't bench press, but he can play the game. That's something that's discussed at our meetings."

In short, the task is simpler than some might reckon.

"Bill's been excellent," said Donahoe, when asked about Cowher's contribution to the draft process. He said that he and Cowher sit down for a few days at the end of the season with Tom Modrak and Charles Bailey from the team's pro and college personnel department and discuss the players expected to remain with the team, and what the personnel needs might be in the upcoming college draft.

"Our whole system since Bill came here was we wanted to get everybody on the same page and create the impression, whether it was the draft or the team or a front office decision, that everybody had a significant part to play.

"We make up a list, based on our needs," said Donahoe. He also said some players would become available from other teams after the draft picks were signed, and teams needed to shed high-salaried players to get under the salary cap.

"There are several stages when players become available and sometimes you just have to wait and see who's going to be out there."

No matter how much homework you do, isn't it inevitable that you will make some mistakes in judging talent?

"I learned a long time ago that excuses are for losers. In a sense, all college football players are gambles, because you're projecting them to do things that they have not done. But I feel good about the guys we got, about their toughness, their production and from a character standpoint."

"He's like a Shakespearian figure."
— Doug Miller,
N. Y. Jets

You are never quite sure who's out there, who might be available to fill your needs. Maybe they're sitting on a couch, hoping they can catch your eye, in the lobby of your office complex.

I recalled seeing Carlton Haselrig hanging around the Steelers' offices and lobby right before the 1995 draft. The Steelers were looking for an offensive guard, and few had played the position better than Haselrig had during his five-year stay with the Steelers (1989-93). He had, indeed, played in the Pro Bowl as recently as 1993. He was later released by the team after recurrent chemical dependence, behavioral problems, run-ins with authorities and failures to get back on track after stays at the Gateway Rehabilitation Center in Oakdale, and some similar facilities elsewhere.

Steelers coaches and officials would nod, and sometimes smile at Haselrig, as they passed him in the hallway. Some would even stop and talk to him. Most avoided him, however, because he was looked upon as a lost cause. "Riggy," as his friends called him, was in limbo. Cowher felt he had given him several chances, but Haselrig had disappointed him every time. Haselrig had gone from being a Pro Bowler to being a pariah on the Steelers' scene, a source of embarrassment to management.

Even so, it had to give the Steelers' scouts pause for thought. Hey, we're looking for a guard and this guy's at our doorstep, looking for a job. When I asked the Steelers' scouts if they were thinking that way at all, most smiled and said, of course, there was a temptation, but they thought better of it. Haselrig had worn out his welcome. In fact, the Steelers told him at that time that he was no longer permitted to work out in their facility or on the field at Three Rivers.

Haselrig looked like an old dog that had returned home looking for a bone, but the cupboard was bare. It had been raided too often.

"It's not like we haven't tried," Donahoe said back then, before Haselrig managed to sign and start for the New York Jets. Before long, Haselrig blew that chance as well. He didn't last the full season with the Jets. Dick Haley, who had headed the Steelers' scouting department after Art Rooney Jr. was fired, convinced Jets' management that it was worth it to take a chance on Haselrig. For a while, it looked like a great move. Haselrig was hired at minimum wage, and was starting. He might have been the Jets' best offensive lineman. He dominated people on the line. He had great hands and balance and strength from his wrestling days, and had learned how to play the position during his stay with the Steelers.

I spoke to Haselrig over the telephone on two occasions when he was with the Jets, and he said all the things you'd want to hear. Alcoholics are like that; they lie a lot. They fool themselves. Soon after, Haselrig's troubles with self-control resurfaced again. In time, he had a lot of run-ins with legal authorities. His drug problems persisted.

He has done jail time since his stay with the Jets. It's unlikely any pro team will take a chance on him again. His story was once one of real success, the sort they make movies out of, but it had become a tragedy. Stories surfaced of misbehavior in his Pitt-Johnstown days.

"He's like a Shakespearian character," said Doug Miller, my former neighbor and young friend who had left Upper St. Clair five years earlier to work in the Jets' public relations office, and had been looking after Haselrig. "He has a tragic flaw."

Donahoe didn't have any interest in Haselrig as a player at this stage of the game.

"We won't look at him," Donahoe said back in 1995, "not until he rectifies the problem. There's a guy there, you know, who played as well as anyone in the league. He was headed in the right direction. It's not an easy thing to accept.

"It's affected his family. I don't like to see anyone go through that. Because of his personal situation, I don't even think of the football aspect. I worry about his life.

"Here's a guy who was an NCAA wrestling champion at Pitt-Johnstown, which required tremendous dedication to begin with. And he didn't even play college football. We take him on the 12th round, the last round (in 1989), and four years later he's in the Pro Bowl. It was storybook stuff. You'd think someone could make a movie about that. But the course he's on now . . . I don't think it's going to have a happy ending. Psychologically, how can we help this guy? The lady at Gateway said to me, 'Don't expect miracles.' Believe me, we've tried to help."

I had met and interviewed Dr. Abraham Twerski, the rabbi/psychiatrist at St. Francis Hospital in Bloomfield/Garfield who founded Gateway Rehabilitation Center. I had read several of his books about alcohol and drug addiction and rehabilitation methods , and had written about athletes who had successfully dealt with such problems. One of them was "Sudden Sam" McDowell, once a fire-balling major league pitcher who had been a classmate of mine in our early high school days.

"You have to keep an even keel."

In a lengthy interview with Rick Starr, the sports editor of the *Valley News Dispatch* in Tarentum, and a veteran reporter on the Steelers' scene, Donahoe had some interesting things to say on several subjects in the September 22, 1996 edition:

"Some teams folded up at the first sign of adversity. It's a long season. You have to keep an even keel, because the next challenge is right around the corner."

Responding to a report that the Steelers might be interested in Jeff George, the troubled quarterback of the Atlanta Falcons, Donahoe had this to say: "That would be like Madonna marrying Bob Dole."

Commenting further on how he wanted to spend the Steelers' money for player personnel, he said, "There's so much money involved in the game today. You like to give the money to the right type of people so that they can deal with it and still be motivated enough to play hard. Sometimes that's a concern with young guys. You give them a lot of money, maybe they were from a situation where they never had much. Now they have everything they need and then some. Some people are just not good at handling that ."

"You have to have good chemistry."

Do the Steelers still regard themselves as a special institution in the National Football League, a cut above the rest when it comes to how they operate? It's something they often boasted about in the wake of winning four Super Bowls in the '70s, and even when they were rebuilding in the '80s.

"We think there is something special about being a Steeler," said Donahoe. "Rarely do we have a meeting that someone doesn't stress that the organization is special. Whether you can get that to be the thinking of players today is something we strive for.

"The Hall of Fame did a promotional tape to get people to come to Canton, and there was an excerpt from Jack Lambert's acceptance speech when he was inducted. Lambert made a moving speech. And he said something like 'If I had to do it over again and I could be a professional football player, you better believe I'd be a Pittsburgh Steeler.' We want to find players who want to be here.

"I don't think it's unrealistic to strive to be different, to do it right with the right people. It's not always easy to live by that. You have to find players who have some value. It would be wrong to think you're going to get 53 personalities who are identical. You have to have talent. If you can find 53 players with good morals and good attitudes that would be the ultimate. But it's unrealistic. You have to balance it somehow.

"There is a standard. Over the last couple of years, we've tried to take guys who are good people as well as good football players. We take a chance on some guys who've had a brush with trouble, but we don't want people who are going to stay a troublemaker. No matter how great a player, he becomes a distraction. You have to have good chemistry. You have to have talented players to win, but you can't have talented players who don't get along, who are divisive, who are selfish, out for themselves.

"There's enough pressure in this business, enough excitement, enough different times that you don't have to put pressure on yourself. To think that one player is going to make the complete difference, the idea that you have to have a certain player and will go to any lengths to sign him . . . it always backfires. You have to stay with the idea that it's a team game, and you have to have a foundation of guys who are going to work together and play together and you have to be able to develop your own players."

He has strong support in the Steelers' organization. As Dan Rooney expressed it, "I think that our basic statement of trying to do things right and looking at it from the long-term view is definitely the best."

Pro scout Charles Bailey said, "My personal philosophy is to always get a guy who fits our system, a guy who's happy, a guy who wants to play, a guy who is not just out there for the money. Most of the time I can tell if a guy is sincere about wanting to come to the Steelers. Somewhere along the line, the truth comes out."

191

Donahoe shakes his head at some of the personalities in sports who seem to command the most attention.

"What's Dennis Rodman?" asked Donahoe of the NBA's relentless rebounder and circus sideshow. "Why would you want a guy like that on your basketball team? He's a team player?

"At some point you have to put some of that stuff aside. Sometimes you make concessions because you need players with talent who might make you cringe in other areas. Bill Cowher knows that. He wants the same things we want. You can have some guys on your team who might be bad character guys or eccentrics. I'm not someone who'd advocate everyone should have tattoos and earrings all over your body.

"That's not easy to do. In some cases, sometimes you have to scratch your head and say, 'Is this what we're all about?' That's a tough call. Growing up here, you're always aware of the legacy of Pittsburgh."

Donahoe and Cowher have combined to be successful during a stretch when the team has suffered the loss of many outstanding players, for different reasons, but seem to have been able to make adjustments, and fill the voids and keep on winning.

"You can't replace winning."

Donahoe discussed some disparate subjects relating to the Steelers during our meeting.

Donahoe on the dynamics of the dressing room:

"It's important. You have to pay attention to the chemistry of the team, the way guys get along. Lots of good-natured kidding goes on. They have to care. You can sense it when they do."

On players' responsibilities in public relations:

"I don't like what some players do today. We believe they have a responsibility to help the media. At the same time, there are some people in the media who have abused their privileges.

"We try to convince our players that it's in our and their best interests to accommodate the media. Too many players today take it lightly. There's a difference today in the way players respond to the media. The club has responsibilities today to do a better job in that area. This is our philosophy, not because it's a fashionable thing to do.

"I knew, from a lot of conversations with Mr. Rooney, what the organization expects of the players as far as the community is concerned. He's pleased when they do positive things in the community, when they gave a great message at a school assembly, or something like that. You can't replace winning. We're in the entertainment business, and you're expected to win to be entertaining. But it's a bonus if you can do that and be a good neighbor in the community as well."

Tom Donahoe and the Steelers' leaders encourage players to be nice to the fans, as Darren Perry was during trip to Tokyo, Japan in 1996.

Jerry Olsavsky is Steelers' stalwart when it comes to community activity. Here he helps promote Breakfast With A Steeler outreach program aimed at improving young people's health.

Photos by Michael F. Fabus/Pittsburgh Steelers

Charles "C.J." Johnson
High on life

*"This guy wants to do it
when times are tough."*
— Chan Gailey

C harles Johnson is a source of joy in the Steelers' clubhouse. He has a special spirit, indomitable, uplifting, a mischievous look in his dark luminous eyes, a man-child playfulness in his behavior.
He flitted about the large room, dancing over discarded socks, jock straps, shoulder pads and tape, like the hurdler he was in his high school days. He enjoyed touching base with his friends, especially the other wide receivers, Yancey Thigpen, Ernie Mills and Andre Hastings, and fellow Colorado alumni Chad Brown, Kordell Stewart, Deon Figures and Joel Steed.

No one was better than Johnson at getting the frown off the often-troubled Figures' forehead. Johnson was flanked by Figures and Rod Woodson in the dressing stall lineup at the far corner of the clubhouse. Johnson could crack up the most somber of teammates with his lighthearted antics.

Going into the 1997 season, the 25-year-old Johnson would be missing some of his favorite neighbors, Brown, Mills, Hastings and Figures, as well as Willie Williams and Ray Seals — unrestricted free agents all after the 1996 season — who had left the Steelers for greener (as in the color of money) pastures. Figures might miss Johnson the most. C.J. was his backyard therapist. At the same time, Johnson was losing a support group.

Johnson would surely make new friends. He is one of the friendliest fellows to be found on the Steelers' roster. He's had his ups and downs, health-wise and playing-wise, since he joined the Steelers as their No. 1 draft choice in 1994, but he is usually upbeat and fights his way through the down periods the way he rises above enemy defensive backs to snare a football from their grasping hands.

"What you see is what I am," Johnson said during one of our interviews. "If I'm smiling I'm happy. If I look down or sad, that's how I feel."

This is a young man with a difficult life experience, a comeback story unlike any other in the room. His challenging childhood can best be described as wretched, unfair, often downright horrid, and he almost didn't survive it. His story is a modern day version of Dickens' *Oliver Twist.* As a teenager, Johnson tried to commit suicide. He has only his kid sister and God to thank for saving him for another day and another way of life. This is a kid who could have been lost to the streets.

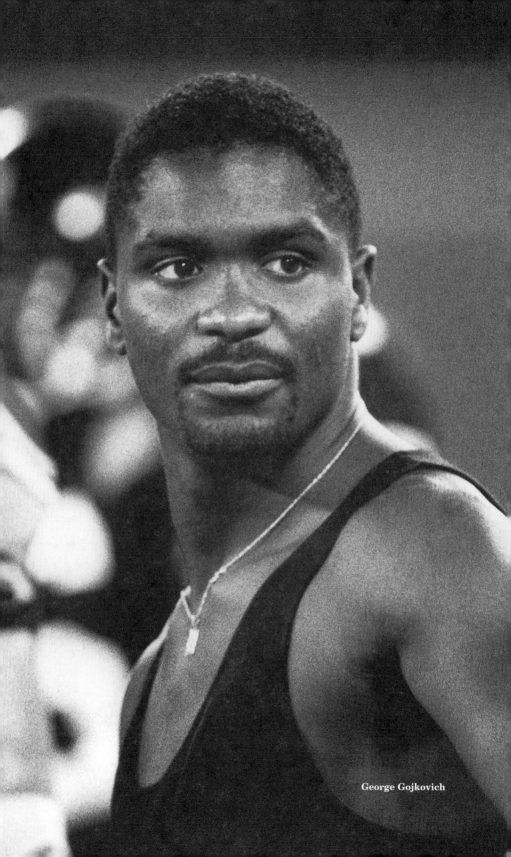

George Gojkovich

Timothy W. Smith of *The New York Times* wrote, "If we were to write the story of Johnson's life, it would be equal parts *Boyz 'n The Hood* and *Horatio Alger.*"

There is a curious mix of individuals in every pro sports club-house. Many of them have emerged from difficult circumstances, and would benefit from periodic professional counseling, or programs that would link them with former ballplayers now functioning in the business world. The NFL likes to think it has addressed this situation, but it gives lip service more than anything to the personal needs of its employees in this regard. Then, too, many players don't take advantage of opportunities that are offered in this respect, sometimes depending too much on their agents for guidance in all areas. Some players are reluctant to come forward and say they are having any mental problems, lest they be branded "nut cases" by the coaches or front-office officials, fearing they might become expendable if there were any questions in that regard. Few teams have qualified individuals looking after the mental health of their players, or assisting them in their preparation for what Chuck Noll used to call their "life's work." By comparison, look how many people they have responsible for the physical well-being of the ballplayers.

In recent years, former Steelers such as Terry Long, Carlton Haselrig, Rocky Bleier, Glen Edwards and Joe Gilliam have gone through personal hell. Terry Hanratty has made a remarkable comeback from a bout with alcoholism. He's one of the lucky ones. Many marriages have fallen apart in the post-football transition to the real world. Many former players have had difficulties in staying the course once they have completed their pro football careers. A young man like Johnson, no matter his cheery exterior, can't be expected to escape his early life's experience without deep emotional scars. These guys need help.

Johnson is to be complimented for coming so far in his personal development, but he may require support beyond the usual rah-rah pep talks from his coaches to maintain his equilibrium.

Johnson had come a long way from wondering where he might be sleeping at night in San Bernardino, California to a condo in Brighton Heights, a neat North Side neighborhood not far from Three Rivers Stadium where he and Figures lived on the same street. "He's always following me," C.J. complained before shoving Figures away from him, and laughing aloud. In truth, it was the other way around. Johnson had been following Figures for several years, from California to Colorado, from Boulder to Pittsburgh and, finally, from Stadium Circle to Brighton Heights.

Johnson's father abandoned the family when C.J. was a mere tot, his mother got hooked on drugs and often left him and his kid sister, Christine, and his older brother, Gary, to fend for themselves. She abandoned them for days at a time. They moved from one house and apartment to another, welfare gypsies. They even lived in Texas for a time. There were nights when C.J. slept under a tree in a park, wondering what could go wrong the next day.

Yet Johnson always seems to have a smile on his handsome face. He's got a gleam in his eyes, especially after he started wearing contact lenses during the 1996 season. He's so positive. How did he manage to get through his childhood with his ego intact? How did he find the light at the end of the tunnel? This is a man who could be angry at the world, unhappy forever about the bad hand that was dealt him in his youth, carrying a lifetime grudge against anyone and everyone who crossed his path. He prefers to think about the people who helped him along the way.

He could be like Greg Lloyd, carrying a large chip on his slender shoulders, but he is more like Levon Kirkland, cheerful, inspirational, helpful. Lloyd could be like that, too, as he is with certain chosen people, as he is when he visits the patients at Children's Hospital. Then Lloyd would really be the leader he likes to fancy himself.

Johnson signs autographs willingly and he answers his fan mail. He chooses to count his blessings. He's so happy and proud of his wife and baby, pleased that he and his mother have worked their way through the cobwebs of the early days, have made peace, and are looking to a brighter future.

Johnson became a father and then a married man over the two-year period from 1996 to 1997. He was married in April, 1997, to Tanisha John, his college sweetheart. That's in reverse order than most people my age used to do things, but this is a new age with new rules, or no rules, the world of free agency in every area. The Penguins' Mario Lemieux did the same thing; he was even married in a church ceremony. Johnson says he wants to make sure his child has a better, more secure life than he had in his youth. Hopefully, he can get things in their proper order from now on, and work as hard at being a husband and father as he did at graduating early from the University of Colorado and becoming an All-American pass receiver and first round draft pick in the pros. Johnson says he will work at his marriage and being a good father, winking and offering his signature smile to affirm his determination to succeed.

Kids must have a gleam in their eyes to get anywhere. I visit and talk to students in elementary and middle schools frequently, and I find all kinds of faces. The kids with the gleam in their eyes and smiles on their face are the best and most attentive students. With some kids, there's no light in the attic, no hope in their eyes, no future unless someone succeeds in turning them around or infusing them with a new spirit somewhere along the way. Many children lack a strong support system at home. There's an African proverb that it takes a village to raise a child. Johnson is evidence of that.

> *"The saddest thing that can befall a soul is when it loses faith in God and woman."*
> — Alexander Smith,
> A Scot poet

"It was like he was on a mission."
— Bill Cowher

Charles Johnson is a speedy, talented pass-catcher, a wide receiver, more like Lynn Swann than John Stallworth, the Steelers' all-time greatest receivers. Johnson has a knack for rising above the crowd and picking the ball out of the air, with all kinds of acrobatic catches to his credit. He can go deep and beat everybody to the ball.

Sunday, September 8, was a special day for Johnson and the Steelers in the team's 1996 home opener at Three Rivers Stadium. The Steelers had suffered a disappointing setback in Jacksonville the week before, and Johnson was still trying to prove that he merited being a No. 1 draft choice in 1994.

Johnson had shown some flashes of greatness the previous two years, but then he'd disappear just as rapidly. His now-you-see-him-now-you-don't act had included injuries, vision problems, a missing ligament in his knee that mystified management and the medics for a spell and a lack of self-confidence, wondering where he stood with the Steelers.

He had 76 catches to his credit over those two seasons and three touchdowns — all scored in his rookie season — and those numbers were not what the Steelers projected when they drafted him. School was still out on whether or not C.J. was the genuine article. He had not established a name for himself in NFL circles.

Against the Baltimore Ravens, the team that was once the Cleveland Browns, Johnson showed the sort of pass-catching acrobatics that his faithful supporters knew he had in him. He made four catches for 66 yards, including a highlight film catch good for 32 yards and a tough high-flying five-yarder good for a touchdown, his first touchdown since Christmas Eve of 1994, as the Steelers ripped the Ravens, 31-17.

"One of Charles' assets is going up vertically and picking the ball out of the air," said quarterback Mike Tomczak, who threw the ball his way, and became a Johnson booster. Better yet, Johnson became a go-to-guy, along with Hastings, when Tomczak was in a tough spot. Johnson, in turn, felt that Tomczak had more confidence in his ability than his predecessor, Neil O'Donnell, who favored other receivers in critical situations.

Thigpen said, "C.J. can focus on the ball while floating through the air. And that takes real concentration."

Coach Bill Cowher became a Johnson believer. "He really stepped it up," said Cowher. "He was given a challenge and he met that challenge. It was like he was on a mission. We gave him some opportunities and he took advantage of every single one."

Johnson and Tomczak clicked again in a big way during the 1996 schedule when the Steelers defeated the Chiefs, 17-7, in a nationally-televised Monday Night Game on October 7 in Kansas City. Tomczak passed for 338 yards and Johnson caught six of them for 125 yards. The Steelers were 4-1 and Johnson was suddenly the team's top receiver. Yancey Thigpen and Ernie Mills, the starting wide receivers in Super Bowl XXX, were both out with injuries. Johnson, who was put on injured reserve with a knee injury during the playoffs the year before, had come back with a vengeance.

For the season, Johnson caught 60 passes for 1,008 yards — only the sixth receiver in Steelers' history to top 1,000 yards. "It's like coming out of the shadows and seeing the sun shining for the first time," Johnson said. "I'm still the same C.J., only a little more mature. I believe in my abilities now."

Johnson turned heads early in his stay with the Steelers. In his first pre-season game in 1994, against the Dolphins in Miami, Johnson caught the eye of Don Shula, who has since been inducted into the Pro Football Hall of Fame in recognition of being the winningest coach in NFL history.

"That kid Johnson showed us a lot tonight," said Shula, who saw his share of outstanding receivers during a 33-year career as a head coach in the NFL. "He's tough and he's not afraid to go after balls over the middle. That's a quality that makes a guy a great receiver."

Johnson already had a big booster in Chan Gailey, who had moved up from wide receivers coach to offensive coordinator in Johnson's first three seasons with the Steelers.

"He's not a prima donna," Gailey said. "He's a tough guy who won't hang around the sideline with every nick and bump and bruise. He wants to be out there playing and that means a lot, especially in these days.

"He's a competitor. He wants to play and he wants to be great. Those are admirable traits. Even though a lot of people have them, they only want them under certain circumstances. They want them when everybody's healthy and everything's nice and rosy. This guy wants to do it when times are tough."

"They gave me love."
— Charles Johnson

Johnson signed a five-year contract in 1994, worth $4.595 million. He received a $1.7 million signing bonus. His contract called for a base salary of $390,000, with annual salaries in subsequent years of $487,000, $585,000, $682,500 and his option year of 1998, $750,000.

What does a kid who once had nothing — not even enough money to buy a Snickers bar or a pillow to lay his head on — do with that kind of money? It's a culture shock that knocks a lot of young athletes off stride, and leads to problems. It's good to see someone like Johnson sharing his good fortune with someone who looked after him along the way.

A month after Johnson was selected on the first round by the Steelers, Johnson drove a thousand miles from Colorado to California on Mother's Day to drop off a 1992 Lexus for his "mother" — Jerry Buckner — who had looked after him during his high school days. Johnson simply handed her the keys, and caught an airplane back to Boulder. It was his way of saying "thank you" for her considerable kindness.

Jerry Buckner was a registered nurse, and the mother of Tonya Buckner, a young woman Johnson had dated, and Doneka Buckner, who played basketball with Johnson in high school. Mrs. Buckner said C.J. cleaned up after himself, not common in her house, when he was staying with her family.

Mrs. Buckner remains one of C.J.'s biggest boosters.

"So many kids use the cop-out that I'm black, I'm from a broken home, I'm from a bad neighborhood, and they do nothing with their lives," said Jerry Buckner. "But Charles took all those things and just inverted them. I don't know how he did it. But he did."

Johnson will never forget the Buckners for being archangels who led him in the right direction.

"They changed my life because they gave me a family," Johnson said. "They gave me security. They gave me love."

Johnson is sometimes reluctant to tell his story because he wants to look forward, not backward. He'll do it if he thinks some young people might benefit from knowing it.

"Looking back doesn't do me any good, because *there's nothing there*," he said. "I'm more interested in what's happening now and what's going to happen in the future."

It sounded like something the writer Gertrude Stein had said about Oakland, California: "There's no there there."

Only now does Johnson see how strange his situation was compared to most other children in this country.

"You don't think about it when you're doing it," he said. "You just do things to survive. I learned what I needed to do along the way. I still love my real mother. I just don't like what she did."

One of the few positive notes I learned about Johnson's childhood was that once upon a time he played the saxophone. How he managed that was a miracle in itself.

"I thought I could be a role model."
— Charles Johnson

Charles Johnson graduated from the University of Colorado the August after his junior season of football — a half-year early. University of Colorado records show that only three of every thousand of its students manage that achievement. Nobody on campus could recall an athlete doing it, let alone an All-America football player who ran track on the side.

"I was driven," Johnson said. "I wasn't going to waste my chance."

He spoke at hundreds of schools during his student days at Colorado, relating his childhood story in the hope that he could help troubled young people. He has done more of the same since he joined the Steelers.

"I thought I could be a role model," Johnson said. "Kids are looking to athletes. I overcame a lot of adversity to get where I am. It was tough, but I still managed to get out of it. It'll prove a point for kids to say, 'Hey, I can do it then, too.'

"Growing up, I thought what I was going through was ordinary. I thought everybody went to sleep at night listening to gunfire. I guess I made it because I kept telling myself I didn't have any problems."

Owing to his upbringing, Johnson remains a man of simple needs. Prior to his rookie season, he slept a few nights in the Steelers' locker room and didn't think it was any big deal. "I don't have a place of my own yet," he explained when equipment manager Tony Parisi found him there one morning on arriving to work.

"I usually don't eat anything at all until night time," Johnson said. "Maybe some junk food during the day, potato chips. That's how it was when I was growing up, because back then it was all I had. And I've got this far, so I figure I've got no reason to change. I would have a pack of cookies and a soda as my breakfast and lunch and be happy."

"He's a strong-minded kid."
— Tom Donahoe

In August, 1985, when C.J. was 13, his mother moved him and his brother, Gary, and sister, Christine, from Port Arthur, Texas, back to San Bernardino, California, C.J.'s birthplace.

Johnson lived in 15 or 16 different places — motel rooms, apartments, houses, welfare hotels — and he never lived in one place longer than five months between the time he was in eighth grade and his junior year in high school. Some nights, Christine would bring him Snickers, his favorite candy bar. Other nights nothing. He and his brother and his sister would go to bed hungry.

"I'd eat here or there, but no serious meals. It got to the point where I convinced myself I didn't have to eat," Johnson recalled.

"To say he had a troubled childhood would be a gross understatement," said Tom Donahoe, the director of football operations for the Steelers, when Johnson was working his way through some early growing pains with the Steelers.

"What he has gone through before has allowed him to understand this part of it," added Donahoe. "He's a pretty strong-minded kid."

"Growing up prepared me for this," Johnson said at the time. "I'm street tough."

Bill Cowher came to appreciate the Charles Johnson story as well.

"I don't think there is anybody around here who can understand the adversities that this young man has gone through already," said Cowher when asked about Johnson. "You talk about people who have things in perspective. He's going to get better. He's a tough kid. He takes some shots and keeps on ticking. A lot of times those types of things make people a lot stronger and make them have a great appreciation for things that other people have taken for granted. He was forced to make some decisions early and he's obviously made all the right ones."

And when he made the wrong decision, he was lucky to have someone who loved him come to his rescue.

Johnson's father fled when C.J. was just two years old. His mother was a junkie, with a cocaine abuse habit. His mother used to go to the blood bank twice a week to sell her blood for $15. It was for drug money. His mother once borrowed $20 or $30 from him. It was money he had saved to buy shoes for a friend's graduation party. His mother used the money to help support her drug habit, and she never paid him back. She had done things like that before.

C.J. dug up some loose change and went to the card store and bought a graduation card for his friend, Johnny Beauregard, and went to Johnny's home. He told Johnny he couldn't go to his graduation party, and gave him a graduation card. He also gave Johnny some other cards he had bought for friends and asked Johnny to hand them out at the party.

Then C.J. went home and he wrote a note to his mother and sister. "Bye, Mom and Christine. I love you."

This was in June of 1989. C.J., age 16, took all the pills — sleeping pills, codeine, etc. — he could find in his mother's purse. He took a sheet of three-holed notebook paper and put that on top of his bed. On the paper he spread the pills into 20 groups of two, aligning them in different sizes and colors, like he was playing a boardgame. He washed down about 40 pills with Coca-Cola in a suicide attempt.

When he woke up, he threw up all over the place. At his side was his 14-year-old sister, Christine, feeding him rice and gravy and 7-Up. He had a headache and a half, but at least he was alive.

"It came to the point where I didn't see any light at all," said Johnson in reflecting on his suicide attempt. "It was all too much for a 16-year-old. All the problems, everything I had to deal with: school, sports, raising my little sister, worrying about where we would live, where we'd sleep. Finally, it all caved in.

"When people heard what I did, they couldn't believe it," he said. "They thought, 'How can someone who always seems so cheerful really be that sad?'"

What advice would Johnson offer to anyone who thinks about committing suicide?

"I'd tell them to talk to a friend, someone they really trust. Don't try to handle it yourself. Kids try to hold things in and everything bottles up inside. Find a person who can help you work through the problem.

"I'm proud to say I failed at that thing. From that day on, I've never failed at anything. What's happened in my life gives me a lot of confidence that I can handle anything that comes my way," Johnson said. "It's given me great strength. It's allowed me to keep my mind clear. I don't let things beat me. I don't like to quit."

"Charles always had a smile on his face."
— Chuck Patterson,
Football Coach,
Cajon High School

After he survived his suicide attempt, Johnson got his act together at Cajon High School in Rialto, California. He had a brutal schedule. He would rise at 6:30 a.m. to catch a city school bus to get to school by 7:45 a.m. After school, there was football, basketball or track practice.

After practice, he worked for the local newspaper, *The Sun*, to earn some spending money, selling subscriptions. Johnson was usually home by 11.

Some nights when he was working at the newspaper, he'd miss the bus. He would sleep under a tree by a library, using his book bag as a pillow, and catch a bus at 5 a.m. to go home and then to school. Johnson was a survivor.

Sometimes he had to interrupt that schedule by searching the downtown area for his mother. The only time he ever missed football practice, according to his Cajon High football coach Chuck Patterson, was to look for his mother.

It was a nightmare situation. Patterson told him: "Charles, you can't do this to yourself. Focus on sports. It's your ticket away from here, nothing else."

During September of his sophomore year in high school, Patterson called Johnson into his office. "I told him, 'The next two years are going to go by real fast,'" Patterson said. " 'Soon enough, you'll be in my office with recruiters, ready to begin a new life that will change all of this. You'll have a new home and a good life with good things.' But it was hard for Charles to understand."

Patterson and others had Johnson to their homes for dinners or for special occasions. By this time, Johnson had moved in with the Buckners. He gave up on his mother, but he kept in touch with his sister, Christine. The Buckners took good care of him. And, during this same span, Johnson gained national attention for his football ability.

Johnson was appreciative to those who came to his rescue during his difficult teen years. "Life was so easy," C. J. recalled of life with the Buckners. "All I had to worry about was school and sports — and keeping my room clean."

Until he got hurt, that is. He suffered a serious injury in his senior year in high school, a lateral ligament in his leg separating from its bone. Doctors warned him that he might not be able to play football again. His leg healed and he was able to play basketball that winter.

That ligament damage, however, would come back to haunt him in his second season with the Steelers. His ligament had been removed, and he would have a lingering problem.

College recruiters were warned by Patterson that this highly-talented kid was coming with a lot of baggage.

"When I first went to recruit him, his coach sat me down and told me the whole story," said Ron Vanderlinden, a former assistant coach at Colorado who had moved on to Northwestern. "I was surprised when I checked his academic records. He was an above-average student who tested well (on the college boards). It didn't add up.

"These types of problems usually produce a very insecure, suspicious young man. But just the opposite was true. Charles just wanted to be loved. I never saw the pain or anguish that Charles felt. He masked it well. He's just as determined and driven. I've never been around anyone quite like him."

During his freshman year on the Boulder, Colorado campus, Johnson sent a letter to Coach Patterson:

Dear Coach,

Don't be surprised about this letter because I would never forget about you. You told me school was always first and that's the way I've decided to approach it. I finished the first semester with three As and one C. I'm not having any problems. I know that should be a surprise and a good feeling considering the hell I went through for four years. I owe you many thanks for helping me get through it. Well, Coach, I guess it's time to go . . .   Love always, Charles

Nothing Johnson did surprised Patterson. "No matter how tough it got," said his high school coach, "Charles always had a smile on his face."

What was it like to go from San Bernardino, California to Boulder, Colorado?

"It was a culture change," Johnson said. "I had to adjust to it. Getting close to teammates. That was the best way to handle it. Colorado had a bad name and bad rap off the field. When anything went wrong a finger was always pointed at football players. People always wanted to test football players. My freshman year we won the national championship. We were a big deal on campus. But everyone wanted to start a fight. We were definitely on alert. Guys would come up from Denver looking for trouble."

Charles Johnson

At UC, he demonstrated a great drive to succeed and a tremendous work ethic. The football team ran the ball more than it passed, but he never complained if he didn't get thrown to as much as he would like. That prepared him for his early years with the Steelers.

He was named the outstanding freshman at Colorado. In practice, he went up against the likes of Deon Figures, Chad Brown and Joel Steed and other future NFL players, so he was in a great developmental environment, and the fellow throwing him the football most of the time was one Kordell Stewart.

Johnson was a happy camper at Colorado. It was no wonder, considering what he had gone through as a child. He enjoyed school, kept busy and wasn't one to go partying at night. It simply wasn't his style. He had three square meals a day, a bed in which to sleep and a family's love.

He excelled in the classroom, earning a 3.0 GPA and obtaining a bachelor's degree in marketing in 3 1/2 years, and was a member of the Academic All-Big 8 conference team.

His other numbers were outstanding as well. Pro scouts were impressed with his time — 4.42 seconds — in the 40 yard sprint. At 6 feet, 190 pounds, he had the size and speed to play pro ball.

He caught 57 passes for 1,149 yards and five touchdowns in 1992, and would have been a high choice had he declared for the draft, but he decided to come back to school in 1993, even though he'd graduated.

"It's an accomplishment," said Johnson. "I don't think anything came close to the feeling I had when I got my degree. That was the highlight of my whole career. It was harder than any catch I ever made, I can tell you that much. But when I put my mind to something, I do it. I have this drive."

He also had a coach who viewed him as more than just a football player when he was at Colorado. His coach, Bill McCartney, left coaching soon after Johnson turned pro to begin a worldwide religious movement called "Promisekeepers," aimed at making men more responsible to their families and more active in their Christian faith.

"You can coach a lifetime and not get someone like Charles," said McCartney.

"He took adversity and turned it into good fortune. It almost cost him his life, but it made him a much stronger person. He just goes hard all the time. He doesn't know any other way. This guy only goes one speed — full speed — in everything he does.

"That's extraordinary in this day and age," continued McCartney. "He had to work for everything, compete in every course. Nothing was easy for him."

Johnson was named the Big Eight Offensive Player of the Year as a senior, the first wide receiver to ever win the award.

*"It could be worse.
I could be dead."*
— Charles Johnson

Johnson would surrender a little more of his story at each meeting. It's no wonder he was a confused kid. His name, his true identity, his home, his sleeping space, whatever, were always up for grabs.

Maybe it's why he doesn't stray far from his comfortable home these days. "I'm not a nightlife guy at all, and that helps," he said.

His mother would abandon him for days. While she regrets what her children experienced, she insists she did the best she could. "My kids are OK," she said. "They were never in a juvenile home, or anything like that. Look, how we had to live hurt him and me both. But I feel Charles came out OK."

He forgave his mother, whom he said had studied to be a Christian missionary at a Houston rehab center.

"Ah, it wasn't so bad," Johnson said of his childhood. "It could be worse. I could be dead."

Johnson grew up believing his dad was dead. He didn't know any different until he went to his grandfather's funeral and his father was there, among the mourners present.

His dad, Charles Stewart, left when Charles was two. Charles didn't see him again until he was 14 — at the family funeral. C.J. adopted the surname of Christine's father because he was the adult male that C.J. knew the best. Yet Johnson can look you straight in the eyes and say:

"It's helped me in everything. It made me more dedicated, more disciplined. I've put my past behind me, and I'm ready to get on with my life. But yeah, I do carry it around with me in the back of my head."

Of all his boyhood bedrooms, Johnson remembers one best: a windowless room that had been built to enclose a water heater and provide storage space. The room, as he recalls, had a twin bed, a 13-inch black and white TV and a bare light bulb hanging from the ceiling. "It was a dump," Johnson said. "Two people couldn't fit in the room at the same time."

It's the room where he tried to kill himself.

"By the time I was 15, my mother forgot all about me. Once I asked her, 'What do you want more, me or your drugs?' She didn't answer. But I forgive her. I love her."

How was he able to rise above the ashes of his childhood? How did he account for his positive disposition?

Johnson looks into your eyes when you ask questions like that. He's not sure he has the answers you seek. Sometimes a sadness enters his eyes, then it gives way to a gleam. Johnson doesn't expect that anyone can truly appreciate his story unless they've lived it. Sometimes he'll shake his head and escape if he doesn't want to go any further.

"It's because of what I've been around, what I'vebeen through," he said. "I try to keep things in perspective. You have to learn how to deal with adversity and with success. I try to stay on a professional level. Try to keep moving forward.

"I think it works both ways. You have to sidestep. It will get hold of you. If you hang on to success it can hurt you, too.

"It kinda reflects. I think it rubs off on others. I'm always smiling. People around here, they ask me if I ever get mad. When you have a positive attitude it makes life better. Andre's like that, too. You don't see him get mad. We enjoy ourselves. When we go to practice we know we have to get work done."

The wide-receivers on the Steelers had become a close-knit group by the 1995 season. "We're a lot closer, it's a tighter group than we were last year," Johnson said. "And I thought we were close last year. We try to fire up one another. We pat each other on the back. We say things to each other, like, 'Put that behind you. Let's go.' And we pat each other on the back when we do something good.

"We want each other to be successful. We do more things together than we did in the past. We watch film more together. On Wednesday or Thursday, we come in after practice and spend more time watching film. Every Thursday night we alternate going to each other's houses. We pick a movie and watch it. It's a special time.

"We were all in town on our own. We're all pretty tight. We mix with each other. Sometimes we watch the Thursday night game on TV, or the movie. We usually get a comedy. We just sit back and laugh. We do things that you can't do at work.

"It's really good for all of us. It really helps. It helps us play better. We bring the best out of each other. We're all trying to do well. We communicate so well."

I asked Johnson about his neighbor, Figures, who had a difficult year in 1995, getting shot in the knee near his hometown during the off-season, losing his starting job at training camp when he couldn't take part in the early rigor of team workouts, and then losing his stepmother, the woman who raised him, when she died during the preseason schedule.

"Deon is a quiet person," Johnson said. "He likes to keep to himself. He doesn't like too much attention. He doesn't want sympathy, either. He wants you to act like nothing happened. He doesn't want anyone to say, 'I'm sorry, Deon. I sympathize with you.' Deon can be funny at times; depends on his mood."

"Track was more exciting than football."

Once upon a time, outstanding athletes used to compete in three or four sports routinely while in high school, and some even managed to do it in college. Some, like Bo Jackson, Deion Sanders and Michael Jordan, have done it as pros.

It's a shame but a lot of high school coaches advise young athletes to concentrate on one sport — better to improve one's chances for a scholarship or a pro contract, they say — and many athletes have abandoned sports at which they would be starters, have some fun, and contribute to the school's sports programs in a larger way.

While Charles Johnson was short-changed in many ways in his youth, he had an abundance of athletic opportunities at Cajon High School and later at the University of Colorado, and he took advantage of them to the hilt.

"In high school, I competed in basketball, track and football," Johnson said. "Football was my No. 1 sport, but I enjoyed track more. It was more relaxing.

"I had a friend, Ladele Jackson, and we ran about the same time in the one hundred. We were both on the football team, good friends. I was the fastest in the quarter mile and I was the best hurdler.

"It was good for my confidence. Track was more exciting than football. More fun. I didn't have the same pressure and stress; you weren't uptight all the time.

"I loved the relay . . . I took the baton with me everywhere I went in high school, and at Colorado. It was my job to have the baton. At Colorado, three of the four guys on the relay team were football players: Ray Carruth, Lamont Warren of the Colts and me. The fourth, Maurice Mitchell, runs professionally. So we had a good mile relay team.

"When we ran outdoors, Lamont didn't have grades and wasn't eligible to compete. We used an alternate, Randy Berkheim, and we still broke the outdoor record.

"I ran track when just about everybody else on the football team was relaxing. If you ran track it was because you loved it.

"I had more free time at school in the spring. Track workouts lasted from 3 to 5. So I had a lot of free time. I used it to study. Some times you do things because you have to do things. I was blessed with things I could do well and enjoy them at the same time. Some people say they used sports to get an education; I meant it. I didn't like to miss class; I really loved school. That was the easy part.

"Sometimes football coaches try to steer you away from serious school subjects. You get advice to take courses just to stay eligible. I didn't see it that way. The football coaches should give you freedom off the field if you show you can handle it. If you give a hundred percent on the field, they shouldn't worry about what you do off the field. I went to my books when I had free time.

Did he have anyone during his high school years that served as an inspiration?

"My older brother, Gary. He was five years older; I really looked up to him," Johnson said. "He ran track, and played football on the playground in the projects. He was always the best athlete in the project. I'd just look at him . . . I never wanted to get hit by him. When he'd go running, he'd hold my hand and pull me along with him. I liked the way he took care of his family."

Johnson wants to go back to school someday and get an MBA. He should speak to John Stallworth about that. Following his 14 seasons with the Steelers, Stallworth went back to school and obtained an MBA, and became the president of an aerospace company in his hometown of Huntsville, Alabama. That is one of the great success stories in Steelers' history.

"He's made big plays all season."
— Chan Gailey

Johnson was only the fourth wide receiver to be taken on the first round of the draft by the Steelers. Other wide receivers who were No. 1 choices were Frank Lewis (1971), Lynn Swann (1974) and Louis Lipps (1984).

"Nothing has set in," Johnson said at the time of the pro draft. "It's all too overwhelming for me to believe."

Going into the 1996 season, Johnson set a personal goal to have a 1,000 yard season as a receiver. He finished with 1,008. "The last 26 yards were harder to get than the first 900," said C.J.

Johnson was second on the team (to Hastings) with 60 receptions and three TDs.

"It was a fine season for that fine young man," said Chan Gailey. "He's got his 1,000. He's made big plays all season. And now he knows he can play with the best of them."

He was the only Pittsburgh receiver with 100-yard games and he had four of them — 125 vs. Kansas City, 155 vs. Houston, 110 vs. Atlanta and 117 vs. Baltimore. His 70-yard reception of a Mike Tomczak pass at Houston was the Steelers' longest completion of the season. He averaged 16.8 yards per catch.

He was only the sixth Steelers receiver to log 1,000 yards receiving in a season, joining elite company such as Thigpen, Stallworth (three times), Buddy Dial (twice), Louis Lipps and Roy Jefferson (twice). For the record, Swann never had a 1,000-yard season.

"C.J. has made big catches all season," said Tomczak. "I put the ball out there, he goes and gets it, time after time. He's a guy I know I can look to in the clutch."

It was a mutual admiration society. "Mike and I have built a relationship that Neil and I didn't have," Johnson said. "Mike has a lot of confidence in me in critical situations. And that means a lot. It makes me try just a little bit harder out there."

Tomczak was told that he would be the backup quarterback going into the 1997 season, and Kordell Stewart and Jim Miller would be competing for the No. 1 position. Johnson had played pitch-and-catch with Stewart during the off-season, both with the Steelers and at Colorado, so he was optimistic that he could click with Kordell or with Miller.

Johnson and Stewart used to hang out together a lot at Colorado. They dreamed of playing in the NFL. "We never dreamed of playing for the same team," Johnson said.

"I'll let my future take care of itself. I just want to help the team reach its expectations. I think I've shown Mike and our quarterbacks and the coaches they can have confidence in me, and that they respect me as a receiver. I don't care what numbers I get as long as we win. That's the bottom line." Johnson hurt his knee the year before and missed the final game, the playoffs and the Super Bowl. "That was the lowest point in my football career," he said.

He dressed for the team photo at Super Bowl XXX, but was unable to play. He had been placed on the injured reserve list.

"Watching the Steelers play in the Super Bowl was one of the hardest things I ever had to endure," Johnson said. "I think I could have played. I should have been out there helping the team."

In an earlier interview with Ed Bouchette of the *Pittsburgh Post-Gazette* at the outset of December, he talked about the excitement he felt as a first-time father. Holding his infant son, Charles Johnson III, Johnson said, "He's still my biggest catch of the season."

Talking proudly of his five-week old son, he related, "I looked at him and I said, 'Look at you; you have no worries in the world. You know you don't have any worries.' I was thinking when I was growing up, you had to worry about everything. It feels great to give him the world."

His mother, who had kicked her drug habit, had visited with her son and his family over the holidays. C. J. said they had been working on their relationship over the previous two years.

"She cooked Thanksgiving dinner for us," Johnson said. "It's the first time I spent Thanksgiving with her for the past nine or ten years. We have a great relationship now."

Steelers officials were pleased that things were turning around for Johnson in a positive sense. "He's such a good person, that's why everybody is so excited for him," said Tom Donahoe.

"They know how important it is to him and how conscientious he is about the game. Generally, when someone has those kind of attributes, you root for them to do well. There are a lot of people, players and coaches, who are happy for him. Really, this whole organization is happy for him. He's a guy who is very respected."

Kordell Stewart said, "Nobody is happier for C.J. than I am. I can't stop myself from running on the field to find him after a big play."

"This book is the truth, my truth."
— James Atlas, Author
The Great Pretender

211

Tim Lester
Leading the way

"If I rush for a hundred yards,
he thinks we rushed for a hundred yards."
— Jerome Bettis

Rainy days and Mondays were particularly challenging for Tim Lester, starting fullback for the Pittsburgh Steelers during the 1996 season. He could count all his bones on those days, as well as a few bumps and bruises. Black and gold may be the colors for the Steelers and the other pro sports teams in Pittsburgh, but black and blue have long been Lester's colors.

"If I'm not hurting somewhere on Monday," allowed Lester, "I know I didn't have a good game."

This was the Monday following the Steelers' hard-fought 30-16 victory over the Houston Oilers, an especially physical contest, much to Lester's liking, on Sunday, September 29, 1996. Lester's right wrist was wrapped in an ice pack. His wrist had been squeezed between a few colliding helmets the day before and it was still smarting.

Lester had been reluctant to shake hands right after the game at Three Rivers Stadium when we approached him, so we patted him on the back instead. That probably hurt him as well.

As a fullback in the Steelers' two-back offense, Lester took a lot of hard licks and delivered a few of his own. A guy can get hurt delivering a block as well as being leveled by one. Lester took great pride in his role as the lead blocker for featured running backs Jerome Bettis and Erric Pegram, and was credited for the outstanding start by both in the 1996 season.

Lester looks at what he does as a job requirement. "I throw my body into people," he said. "It's about being relentless."

Bettis had blasted his way for 115 yards on 29 carries against the Oilers. It was his third straight 100-yard rushing effort, quite an accomplishment, and Bettis was quick, as always, to credit his buddy Lester as well as all of the offensive linemen for his continued success. After a disappointing opening game loss at Jacksonville, the Steelers had come back strong to win three straight games and take over first place in the AFC Central division.

"Timmy T showed the way," said an ebullient Bettis, talking through squinted eyes when he smiled. "He's beautiful. Please write some good stories about Timmy T. The happier he is the happier I'm going to be."

Lester was once nicknamed Timmy L, which seems to make some sense, but Bettis called him Timmy T, because it sounded better to him. Nobody was going to argue with Bettis, a 5-11, 243-pound bulldozer.

Tim and Breanna Lester celebrate holidays in January, 1997, with three-year-old twin daughters, Kendra and Brandi.

Tim's brother, Fred, at left, of the Tampa Bay Buccaneers, visits at NFL game.

Fred and Tim when they were grade school football players

"Our power lies in our capacity to imagine ourselves as other than what we are. Common ground is the higher ground, spiritual and natural, we strive to gain."
— John Wideman,
Pittsburgh-bred author

Bettis had been a happy camper since coming to the Steelers on Draft Day, 1996 from the St. Louis Rams in what turned out to be the steal of the year, and rejoining Lester, his running mate two years earlier when the Rams resided in Los Angeles. Bettis received a lot of national TV and print attention, while Lester often got lost in the shuffle.

Not in the Steelers' clubhouse, however. Everyone from Coach Bill Cowher on down recognized what Lester's efforts meant to the success of the Steelers' offensive game.

If it was Monday, Steelers' trainer John Norwig and his assistant Rick Burkholder knew they were going to be seeing Lester in their work area.

"He has a sprained right wrist," noted Norwig, checking his clipboard which had a list of the casualties from the heated contest with the Oilers, a disliked divisional rival.

"He takes his licks every game," said Norwig. "I've seen Timmy every Monday, and the Tuesday after our Monday game. The way he blocks for Bettis and Pegram, he takes a great deal of punishment. He sells out his body every time out. I like Tim. He's great to work with. He's a good person. And a real pro."

Added Burkholder: "He's not a guy who's looking to be coddled. When he comes in, something's hurting."

So many of the Steelers suffered injuries in the early games of the 1996 season — even punter Josh Miller was sidelined because of a hernia operation — that WTAE's Myron Cope started lugging around a large medical dictionary so he could provide detailed and accurate injury reports to Steelers' fans.

Lester was not sidelined by any of his hurts. He was a real trouper, and didn't want to provide anybody with an opening to take his hard-won starting assignment.

In the Steelers' scheme, Lester seldom carried the ball. Unlike John L. Williams, his predecessor at the position, he didn't get many opportunities to catch passes because he had been giving way on passing downs to Kordell Stewart at one of the slots in four- and five-receiver sets.

Lester did slide out of the backfield away from the flow to nab a 19-yard throw from Mike Tomczak against the Oilers and looked good doing it. Lester expressed a desire to get more opportunities to run and catch the ball, but was quick to tell you he was not complaining. He liked his role, restricted as it might have seemed.

He is 5-9, 227 pounds, on the small side for NFL fullbacks, but Lester is a solid, well-muscled specimen who has good technique and a night club bouncer's enthusiasm for knocking guys out of the way.

Two old scouts watched in admiration from the press box at Three Rivers Stadium as Lester went about his task of burying his helmet into anybody wearing white, blue and red jerseys in an early-season Monday Night contest with the Buffalo Bills. Jack Butler, who had been heading up the Blesto scouting service "for too many years," and Bill Nunn, who was supposed to be retired from the Steelers' personnel department but was still bird-dogging for them, both offered tribute to Lester.

"He's never going to be a great running back," Butler pointed out. "If that's the case, you have to get it in your head (and he tapped his temple to emphasize his point) that you have to block to make yourself valuable.

"The kid from Penn State (Jon Witman) is the same way. He's never going to be a great running back, either. You have to make up your mind if you want to stick around in the NFL you've got to block and be able to catch the ball — that's critical — and be willing to give your all on special teams. There are guys out there who can't do that. Their egos get in the way of them making the team. You also have to be with the right team, a team that uses the two-back offense. Some guys like Emmitt Smith of the Cowboys can do it all — run, catch and block — but he's the exception. He was that way in college, too."

Lester was a 10th round draft pick out of Eastern Kentucky University by the Rams in 1992, and several running backs were among those drafted earlier, so his chances of making the club were thought to be slim and none. The 1996 season was Lester's fifth year in the NFL, and he has hung in there basically on his blocking ability, and his willingness to go all out on special teams.

Bill Nunn talked about John Henry Johnson, a running back who starred in the Canadian Football League, the American Football and the National League, finishing up with some sensational seasons (1960-65) with the Steelers. John Henry was inducted into the Pro Football Hall of Fame in 1987.

John Henry was regarded as the greatest blocking back in Steelers' history, though Nunn thought Rocky Bleier and Merril Hoge were also accomplished blockers as running backs among more contemporary performers. Johnson even played a little linebacker in his storied pro career.

"Now you're talking about one of the great pro football players," said Nunn, nodding his silver-haired head as he does when he gets excited about talking about a player. "I asked John Henry once what was the secret to being a good blocker and he told me, 'You know you're gonna get your butt whipped every time you hit someone, but you still do it.' He was great with the Steelers, and he was at the end of his career when he came here."

It was interesting that Nunn noted that Johnson, a great blocker, had also played a little linebacker. Levon Kirkland, a contemporary linebacking star for the Steelers, had offered this observation about Lester: "He has a defensive player's mentality. He scares me. He's a linebacker playing fullback.

"The first time he came here, he gave an indication of that in our first scrimmage at St. Vincent. We don't like to hit each other. We both go in low, and my shoulder was killing me after our first collision. When he was with the Rams, there was one time when he got me with a good block, and I've never forgotten that. Defensive players don't like to see an offensive player be more aggressive than they are."

Lester needs to learn some Steelers' history. He did not recognize the name of John Henry Johnson, but that hardly makes him unique in the Steelers' clubhouse. It was head-knocking pioneer pros like Johnson, however, who showed the way for guys like Lester. Johnson was one of the few blacks on the ballclub in his day when opportunities were more limited.

Lester never heard of Wally Pipp, either, but he wasn't about to give anybody else a shot at his job. Pipp played first base for the New York Yankees once upon a time and took a day off because he was tired. Lou Gehrig took his place and went on to set an "Iron Man" record for most consecutive starts by a baseball player. Pipp never got his job back.

When Lester looks back for fullbacks he admired, he mentions Matt Suey, a former Penn Stater who played ten seasons (1980-89) with the Chicago Bears and led the way for the great Walter Payton, and Lester also liked Robert Newhouse who played for the Dallas Cowboys (1972-83) and blocked for Tony Dorsett.

Dorsett and Payton both are in the Pro Football Hall of Fame. Maybe that's why Bettis is so happy to have a blocker like Lester leading the way for him in Pittsburgh.

"You can never feel comfortable.
Someone is always trying
to take your job."
— Tim Lester

Hard-working fullbacks and special teams performers like Lester are often overlooked, but Bettis would not let that happen in Pittsburgh. Bettis became an enthusiastic drum-beater for Lester. They hung out together and lived in the same apartment complex in Ross Township, in the suburbs to the north of Pittsburgh where so many of the Steelers and coaches have resided since Interstate 279 was opened a few years back. Tim and Jerome rode to work together. "Jerome drives me in," said Lester, his coal-dark eyes positively glistening as they often do when he's in a jovial mood. "He says he'll drive every day of the week as long as I do the driving on Sunday. He's 'The Bus,' and I'm the 'Bus Driver' on Sunday."

Bettis planned to continue his chauffeuring duties as long as Lester continued to open holes for him and Pegram, and picks up blitzers to keep the Steelers' quarterback intact.

"I told him how important he was every chance I got in Los Angeles, and I do the same thing here," said Bettis. "I envy him, having the attitude that he does. I played fullback in college, so I know what that's like. I can't see myself doing the things he's doing. And that's coming from a true fullback.

"The approach he takes to his job is tremendous. And I wouldn't want to have his job. Everybody wants to be the hero; everybody wants to get the football. His main thing is he wants to do his job. Running the ball is not his thing.

"He likes to get in there and bang with those linebackers. He likes to beat up on linebackers. He tells me that; he takes pride in that. Other people see it as dirty work. He sees it as glamour work. He takes a lot of pride in my accomplishments. If I rush for a hundred yards he thinks *we* rushed for a hundred yards."

Bettis fell into disfavor with the Rams in 1995 and his rushing yardage was halved from his first two years as the leading runner for the Rams in Los Angeles, when he rushed for 1,429 yards and then 1,025 yards. So he was making a comeback with the Steelers and Lester was leading the way.

"I don't take it for granted," observed Bettis. "I know his importance to me and to the team. What he does few people can do. Being only 220, it's even more impressive. He's made quite a personal sacrifice."

Lester was an accomplished athlete in his own right. He was a football and track & field star at Eastern Kentucky He was all-Ohio Valley Conference as a tailback, averaging 5.3 yards on 682 carries for 3,635 yards with 37 touchdowns. He set career highs with 291 yards on 41 carries and three touchdowns in a 29-20 victory over Tennessee Tech in 1990.

"Hey, Timmy will be quick to tell you he can run the football," said Bettis. "He rushed for more yards in college than I did. His appreciation for the game and just being in the NFL may exceed mine. As a tenth round draft pick, he appreciates playing in the NFL more than I do, being a No. 1 draft pick out of Notre Dame.

"I didn't have to struggle just to be on the team. What he had to go through — they drafted two other running backs before him his rookie year — and it took a lot of fight and hard work for him to stick with the team. I'm always telling him what a great job he's doing. I wanted to keep that man happy."

"I never quit on my dream."
— Tim Lester

Lester was an outstanding prep athlete. As a 5-9, 175-pound junior, Lester succeeded Roman Nelson as tailback at Southridge High School in Cutler Ridge. Nelson went to West Virginia. Southridge, one of Florida's top 4A teams, had a reputation for turning out great tailbacks. His mother still has all his first and second place ribbons as a middle distance runner and relay team member at Southridge.

He was quite the college performer as well. He was the top-ranked running back in NCAA Division I-AA, according to *The*

Sporting News, with 1,239 yards as a rookie. He earned first-team all-Ohio Valley Conference honors in 1988.

In his second season, he suffered a knee injury against Delaware State that sidelined him the rest of the season.

Lester made a big comeback early in his football-playing career. He was nearly killed in a motor vehicle collision in the summer of 1987, just before he left home for Eastern Kentucky. His injuries were so severe doctors didn't believe he would be able to play football again.

On this particular day, he was driving to work at a parks and recreation center in Miami and was at an intersection, making a left turn on a green arrow.

That's the last thing he remembers about that day. Everything else he knows from someone telling him about it.

Lester's car was blindsided by a construction truck when its driver ran a red light. Lester's car was totaled. All that was left intact was the seat in which Lester was sitting. He stumbled out of the car, wobbled ten feet and collapsed in the middle of the road.

"I don't even remember the incident," said Lester. "All I remember is making a left turn. And then I went blank. I woke up a week later in a hospital. It was a real knockout punch. I had a third degree concussion. Somehow, they said I got out of the car, and walked for a short distance, then fell over in the street. I don't remember doing it, but that's what they told me."

He was in and out of consciousness for a week, except for an hour or two a day. It took him quite a while to get back to normal. He had to rest. He had lots of migraine headaches. He would get painful jolts to the brain for 10-15 weeks after the accident. It made a pop like a pneumatic drill going rat-a-tat-tat in his head.

"The doctors were saying there was a good chance I might never play football again because of the head injury," said Lester. "They thought I might be bothered by it for a while. I thought I might not play, either. In football, all you have is contact, getting hit in the head. But I never quit on my dream."

After a redshirt year at Eastern Kentucky University, the migraines went away. He played in every game his freshman season, and was outstanding. The next season, however, in the second game, he injured his knee.

This time he was ready to call it quits. He was scheduled to have his knee scoped, and he told his mother, Robbie Lester, that if it turned out that the ligament was torn (it was), he didn't want to play football again. When the doctors did the scope and determined that the anterior cruciate ligament was torn, Lester was out cold. So the doctors asked his mother what to do. Unsure of what to do, she forgot her son's wishes and gave the doctors the go-ahead to proceed with additional surgery.

"If it wasn't for her, I would not be playing today, because I really didn't want to take that chance again. I figured that it was time for me to give up football because so many negative things were happening to me."

Schooldays and family gatherings bring back the best of memories for Tim Lester, who grew up in Miami and starred in many sports.

He returned and played well enough to be drafted by the Rams in the 10th round in 1992. A year later, the Rams drafted Bettis as their No. 1 choice. Bettis went to the Pro Bowl at season's end and paid the way for Lester to come along. Before the start of the 1995 season, however, the Rams cut Lester. This really hurt. The Rams were coming off a 4-12 season and they were saying Lester wasn't good enough to play for them.

"Being released by the Rams was really a low point in my life. Of all the teams in the league, I got released by one of the worst," allowed Lester.

He was set to become a substitute teacher and coach at a Miami high school before the Steelers called. He started one game in 1995 as a backup to John L. Williams and played on special teams.

"You never feel secure."

Because of his approach to playing the game, Lester incurred several concussions during his first five years in the NFL. He had to be cautious in that respect because Merril Hoge, for one, who was now assisting Bill Hillgrove and Myron Cope in the WTAE broadcast booth, had to retire early after suffering a series of concussions with the Bears after his days with the Steelers.

Lester liked all the ballyhoo about his blocking ability that Bettis offers, but was quick to say that it was the offensive line — and the fullback — who were opening the holes.

One of the reasons Lester was so quick to be politically correct was he did not want to do anything to jeopardize his job. Just as free agents will tell you they always feel like free agents, even after ten years in the league, Lester still believes he can't afford to let up for a moment. It took him a while before he moved his family here to the North Hills.

"You never feel secure in this job," he said. "You can never feel comfortable. Someone is always trying to take your job. You never have a home.

"I learned that my rookie year. They had some good backs, and I knew I wasn't going to make it as a tailback. I knew I had to make myself a good blocking back, and a special teams player, and it's kept me in this league five years.

"When the Rams gave up on me, they said I couldn't play special teams. They brought in Ron Wolfley from the Cardinals who was supposed to be good at it. That motivated me.

"When I came to Pittsburgh, I had a good special teams coach in Bobby April. I love being on special teams. I play on the punt, punt return, kickoff and kick return teams. All but the PAT team. When Pittsburgh called me, I felt so lucky. They were the right team, a two-back team. They were the only team that called me. I remember seeing John L. Williams run 30 yards for a touchdown in the playoffs the year before, and I was just dreaming about being in that offense. So I couldn't believe it when they called.

"They've been everything I expected and more. It was great being with a winning team in a town that really cared about football. After coming from a team like the Rams, where we had never won more than five games in a year, it was like going to heaven. Then this year me and Jerome teaming up again. He's playing tailback, but he has a fullback mentality. He loves to run over people.

"Going to the Super Bowl last year was the real icing on the cake. Going to the Super Bowl was a dream come true. Hopefully, we'll go back to the Super Bowl and win this time.

"I love the city. It's a great football city. Every time you go out on the field, you can feel the crowd behind you. You see those people and how crazy they are about their Steelers. When we had that skirmish with the Oilers behind the end zone near the end of the game, the fans wanted to join in the fight. They're unreal.

"I hope I can stay here. I don't even want to carry the ball anymore. I'm like an extra offensive lineman out there. I just want to hit people, and pave the way for our backs to get first downs.

"Me and Jerome have never been with a winner before in the pros, and we'd like to keep that going.

"I feel like I'm still a pretty good runner, and I feel I can catch the ball as well. They've used Kordell Stewart to run the fullback routes on pass plays. I can't complain. As long as he's making the plays and catching the ball and scoring touchdowns.

"But, yes, I remember what it was like to run the ball, and be a big man in the offense, like I did in college. And, in my heart, I know I can do that again if called upon.

"I appreciate where I am today. I earned it. I had to earn it. I had to work hard. Nobody expected me to make the team. At the pro scouting combines, the scouts said I wasn't fast enough to be a tailback and that I wasn't big enough to be a fullback. That motivates me, too.

"This past summer (1996) when I knew John L. wasn't coming back, I knew I'd get the opportunity to play more. I was really looking forward to it. I told the coach all I needed was the opportunity. To be a starter and to make some plays for this team is something special."

He rearranged the ice pack on his right wrist, begged off a handshake, and went to his dressing stall to chill out.

His dressing stall is in an extension of the Steelers' dressing room known as "the ghetto" because it's cramped compared to the regular dressing room and it's occupied mostly by reserves and practice team players. Most of the players in this room are black, and they boast about living in the "ghetto," and have been known to turn out the lights whenever an unsuspecting member of the media strays onto their turf.

When players became starters or frequent performers they were invited to move into the regular room by equipment managers Tony Parisi and Rodgers Freyvogel. Lester declined the invitation.

He didn't want to tempt fate. He had found a home in "the ghetto," and that was good enough for him.

"My twins motivate me more than anything."
— Tim Lester

Lester's wife, Kendra, and their twin daughters, Brandi and Breanna, who turned three years old in 1996, moved from Los Angeles to join him. They are a source of inspiration.

In 1994, during his third season with the Rams, Tim and Kendra, who was six months pregnant at the time, were in Santa Barbara, California when an earthquake struck. It sent Kendra prematurely into labor. The girls were born three months prematurely, both weighing just a bit over a pound. Their chances for survival were 50-50, according to the attending physicians. The girls spent five months in the hospital before Tim and Kendra were able to take them to their home in Orange County.

Brandi had a mild case of cerebral palsy and Breanna initially had eye problems. The twins were in and out of hospitals in their early development, and the Lesters have had more than their share of scares, with pneumonia bouts and problems like that.

"I ask myself all the time, 'Why is this stuff happening to me?' But it makes you grow as a person," allowed Lester. "I've been through so much in my life. I think it's made me a lot stronger person in life now. I can deal with things a lot easier.

"My twins motivate me more than anything. Seeing the struggle that they had, the things they went through just to crawl, and now to walk. I look at them and they were fighters. They had a 50-50 chance to live and they pulled through. After what they went through, I think I can pull through, that I can do anything.

"If the truck accident didn't take me out, I don't think anything else can. I don't know too many people who get hit by a truck and get up and walk away. I felt that if I can deal with that I can deal with anything."

> ## "I've never felt like I 'made it.' I think only fools are totally satisfied. Insecurity is my driving force."
> ### — Comic Alan King

Collectibles
Playing cards put you in the pink

O nce upon a time Jack Butler was a bubble gum card. So were Elbie Nickel, Ernie Stautner and Pat Brady. To me, they were magic figures, more so perhaps because I knew them best only as faces on bubble gum cards, and their actions on the field only as they were re-created by Joe Tucker on the radio and, sometimes, on TV in the days of the Dumont Network.

I saw Stautner play at Forbes Field and Pitt Stadium toward the end of his career, in the late '50s and early '60s, but I never sat in the stands to see the other three play.

Butler, Nickel, Stautner and Brady were the only players named to the Steelers' All-Time team that was selected by the fans as part of the Steelers 50 Seasons Celebration back in 1982.

To some youngsters today, they are all strangers. To me, at the magic 55 mark, they will always be bubble gum cards. Black and white bubble gum cards at that.

To a boy or girl who collects bubble gum cards, though, sports can be an exciting world of faraway fantasies.

The gum wasn't that good. It was so pink with white dust on each slice, and so sweet, and sometimes it was so hard it cracked into a thousand pieces if dropped. It was the cards one craved.

Nearly all the kids collected cards in our neighborhood, except the ones who were more interested in fishing or fooling around with cars, which seemed to be a parlay for the guys who always rejected our offers to play sports.

Did you ever flip cards? You could add to your collection, or lose cards that way. There were lots of ways to do it.

Kids collect cards today and keep them under glass or in a safety deposit box so they don't get dog-eared or bent. Sometimes they never even open the box. Just store it away. So the cards will increase in value. The only attraction today seems to be a monetary one. Doesn't sound like much fun.

We used our cards. We played games with them. We sorted and rearranged them. We knew all the players.

You could play "topsies" where the idea was to flip a card so it would land on the card, or cards, that had already been flipped onto the ground, or floor. If you topped or covered another card, you picked up all the cards as the winner. Then you would flip a new card and continue in a similar manner until someone won again.

Or you could play "matchies" where you had to duplicate what your opponent did — have the card or cards land "heads" or "tails" the same way as the player who preceded you. If your opponent tossed two cards "heads" up or face up, you had to do the same in order to "match" the cards that had been flipped, and you would win if you duplicated what had been done.

You could sail the cards — like a Frisbee — to see whose would land closest to a wall or step, or see who could be the first to land one on a windowsill. A good "pot" of cards could accumulate for the winner in that game.

Or you could play "leansies" to see who could be the first to make a card lean against a wall or step.

Butchie Buffo was the biggest kid on our street, and he was also the best at flipping bubble gum cards. He collected cards, too, mostly mine. His cards always landed first on the windowsill, sticking like flypaper. It was his windowsill. I always suspected he had a homefield advantage. But Butchie bought a motorcycle one day, and my mother told me she never wanted to see me on it. That was one of the few times I ever listened to such an advisory in my life. Butchie was no longer interested in flipping cards, or taking mine.

We had both gotten too old to buy bubble gum cards. So I wrapped mine in rubber bands — we called them gum bands back then — and stored them in a closet. I still collected and swapped sports magazines. I had several tall piles, stacked almost to the ceiling, next to my bed, and loved to look through them from time to time.

I used to cut pictures out of them, change the captions to where it was the kids in the neighborhood — instead of Notre Dame's Terry Brennan, for instance — who were scoring a touchdown in a big game. I'd paste a picture like that on the one-page newspaper I'd post on the front door of my house for everyone in the neighborhood to read as they passed on the sidewalk. I had purchased a toy printing press at age 9.

While I was away in the Army, my mother decided it was time to clean up my bedroom for real. The room was starting to lean toward the nearby Monongahela River. She dumped all the magazines and my bubble gum cards in several trash cans, and the garbagemen hauled them away. I'm glad I wasn't there. The thought of those cards once being carted off by a garbageman depresses me. I see the same cards at trading card shows nowadays, and the prices have escalated considerably. But who knew we'd value such souvenirs some day? Or that they would be worth a lot of money?

Or that the Same Ol' Steelers would become special?

224

Elbie Nickel
One of the magic names

"I didn't make a lot of money, but I had a lot of fun."

E lbie Nickel. The name evokes some magic memories. Elbie Nickel was a splendid end for the Steelers for 11 seasons, from 1947 to 1957. He was among the special Steelers when I started paying attention to them in the mid-'50s. I had his black and white bubble gum card in my collection when I was getting caught up in sports from the time I was ten through my 15th birthday. I kept those cards in the closet of the bedroom I shared with my brother, Danny, in our home in Hazelwood. I had them wrapped with a rubber band, and stored in a shoe box. I'd get them out from time to time and shuffle through them, noting the numbers and info on the back of them. I memorized that stuff. Sports were never more special to me than they were then. There was a mystery about it; it was out there, distant, in a world somehow separate from ours on Sunnyside Street. I read and collected sports magazines, mostly *Sport.* The athletes and the authors were my heroes. The one I liked best was Parry O'Brien, a gold-medal shot putter from Southern California. I would later write for that same magazine and meet some of the writers whose stories I had read as a teenager.

Danny and I delivered the *Pittsburgh Post-Gazette*, the morning newspaper. We would deliver the papers — I remember we had 88 customers one year — and then read the sports section when we got home and had breakfast, before going to school. We knew the Steelers through the stories written by Jack Sell and Al Abrams. They often referred to the Steelers as Rooney U. Sometimes we'd get a copy of *The Pittsburgh Press,* and read stories by Pat Livingston and Chet Smith. We knew the Steelers best from listening to the radio broadcasts of their games. Joe Tucker told us all about them. We never got to Forbes Field to see the Steelers in those days, even though it was less than five miles from our home. Our dad wasn't a sports fan. No one ever gave us tickets. I didn't get to see the Steelers in the flesh until I went to Pitt in 1960. The Steelers played at Forbes Field and Pitt Stadium in the '60s.

Elbie Nickel . . . He was the Steelers leading receiver in 1952 and 1953, with 55 and 62 catches to his credit. His 62 catches were second only to Pete Pihos of the Philadelphia Eagles, who had 63. Pihos is in the Pro Football Hall of Fame. Nickel lives in Chillicothe, Ohio, and that's about the closest he's going to get to the pro football shrine in Canton. Like Jack Butler and perhaps Andy Russell, L.C. Greenwood and Lynn Swann, he performed on the next level.

The only Steelers who ever caught more passes in a season were Roy Jefferson, with 67 in 1969; John Stallworth, with 70 in 1979, and 80 in 1984; and Yancey Thigpen, with a team-record 85 in 1995. Stallworth, in 1981, and Eric Green, in 1993, caught as many with 63. Nickel's numbers were recorded in a 12-game season, Jefferson's in a 14-game season and Stallworth's, Green's and Thigpen's in a 16-game schedule. Nickel's average of 5.16 catches-per-game is better than Stallworth's best of 5.0, Jefferson's 4.78 and just short of Thigpen's 5.31 average. Going into the 1996 season, Nickel's name still appeared several times in the Steelers' record books. Only John Stallworth (537), Louis Lipps (358) and Lynn Swann (336) caught more than Nickel (329). Franco Harris (306) was right behind him.

"That was my biggest thrill ever."
— Elbie Nickel

Nickel remains a big fan of the Steelers. At age 73, he attended a party in Chillicothe two nights before Super Bowl XXX at the home of Bill Lemmon. "My wife and I were born and raised in Latrobe," said Lemmon. "We moved to Chillicothe in 1965 after graduating from college — Grove City for me and IUP for my wife — and we've been here ever since. My basement is a black and gold shrine. I've had a Steelers-decorated Christmas tree for 15 years. The Browns and Bengals fans in the neighborhood have been quite envious. We had 30 staunch Steelers' fans, including Elbie, at our party. That's pretty good for this neck of the country!"

No one in Chillicothe could have been more interested in the outcome of the Steelers' championship contest with the Dallas Cowboys than Elbie Nickel.

Nickel has lived in Chillicothe since 1946, the year before he joined the Steelers. He was a Steelers receiver from 1947-1957, in the days of leather helmets, no face masks and no TV.

He was good enough to be named to the Steelers' All-Time Team, which was picked during the team's 50 Seasons Celebration back in 1982. "That was my biggest thrill ever," said Nickel.

"I had a great time playing for the Steelers. I didn't make a lot of money, but I had a lot of fun."

The basement of Nickel's Chillicothe home has been converted into a veritable shrine of Steelers' memorabilia.

He has lots of photographs on the walls, showing him with such former stars as Terry Bradshaw, Franco Harris, Lynn Swann and Jack Lambert. There are plenty of plaques, game balls, trophies and, of course, one of Myron Cope's official Terrible Towels.

There's a picture of a former racehorse named Elbie Nickel. It belonged to the late Art Rooney. Nickel was one of his favorite players. Nickel's picture remains in the former office of Rooney that

226

has been converted into a library at the Steelers' complex at Three Rivers Stadium, and in the hallway just outside.

"Art Rooney was a super person," said Nickel. "I'll always be a Steeler fan."

He likes to talk about the days when he lined up on the same field as Hall of Famers Frank Gifford, Otto Graham, Chuck Bednarik and Bobby Layne.

"I always had a job," Nickel said in an interview at his home. "It makes you appreciate playing football more, and I had something to fall back on. I knew I couldn't play football the rest of my life. My first job was working for my father who had a business of his own. I worked with him during the off-season and enjoyed it. Being a football player wasn't too important. We didn't get much publicity. But it helped me get started in life."

Nickel has stored up stories he can tell his ever-expanding family about his glory days with the Steelers.

"I can remember the time (in 1954) we beat the Cleveland Browns, 55-27, at Forbes Field in a Saturday night game," noted Nickel. "And another game (1952) in which we beat the New York Giants, 63-7, at Forbes Field. Lynn Chandnois returned the opening kickoff for a touchdown against the Giants. Their quarterback, Charlie Conerly, got hurt early in the game. Tom Landry finished the game at quarterback.

"Their coach, Steve Owen, had a book come out a few weeks before about this special 'umbrella' defense he had concocted. Our game was not good publicity for his book."

One of Nickel's most prized possessions is a game ball from that 1954 victory over the Browns, who went on to win the National Football League title.

It is still fun to flip through the Steelers media guide, or record book, and search for the names of Nickel's teammates on those teams of the late '40s and the '50s. They were mostly mediocre teams, yet the players still hold a special place in the hearts of long-time Steelers' fans. The Steelers posted winning records in only two of Nickel's 11 seasons, but their names bring back a simpler time when sports wasn't the big business it is today.

Nickel came to the Steelers from the University of Cincinnati in 1947 and played one season under the legendary Hall of Fame coach Jock Sutherland, who had made his mark at Pitt. The Steelers had an 8-4 record that year and lost in the playoffs to the Philadelphia Eagles, 21-0. It was the Steelers' only playoff appearance until Chuck Noll's fourth team achieved that in 1972. In 1949, the Steelers were 6-5-1 under Sutherland's successor, John Michelosen. Nickel played four seasons for Michelosen, two under Joe Bach and three under

Walt Kiesling — Bach and Kiesling in their second stints as the Steelers' head coach, unprecedented in NFL history — and his final season under Buddy Parker.

Elbie Nickel. The Steelers seemed to have a lot of players in those days with short, sharp-sounding names. The headline writers at the *Post-Gazette*, *The Press* and *Sun-Telegraph* had to love 'em. The Steelers' stars in those days were Jim Finks, Fran Rogel, Ray Mathews, Lynn Chandnois, Pat Brady, Dale Dodril, Bobby Gage, Bill McPeak, Jerry Nuzum.

For a year or so, Nuzum lived in our neighborhood in Hazelwood, and that was a big deal. I got to know Nuzum when I was covering the Steelers in the early '80s, and he was quite kind to me and my wife.

He once invited us to a dinner he was hosting at the P.A.A. where Kathie and I had an opportunity to dine with some of my boyhood heroes, "Bullet Bill" Dudley and Lynn Chandnois and their wives, Joe Gasparella and Fran Rogel. I saw Nuzum at the Steelers' training camp at St. Vincent in the summer of 1996, and took photos of him telling stories to young students from a Hebrew school. I was saddened to learn of his death from cancer, at age 73, on April 23, 1997. I had been unsuccessful in my attempts to call him at West Penn Hospital to talk to him when I heard he was ailing.

The Steelers of that era also had Gary Glick, John Reger, Tad Weed, Joe Geri, Dean Derby, Dick Alban, Bill Walsh, Leo Nobile, Leo Elter, Lou Ferry. All quick-hitting names.

They had some marvelous names like John Henry Johnson and Ernie Stautner, who are both in the Hall of Fame, along with Stautner's sidekick, Bobby Layne, who came along the year after Nickel retired. In 1955, they had Marion Motley, who'd been a great back with the Cleveland Browns, and also made it to the Hall of Fame.

There was Val Jansante, who was my gym teacher as well as the head football coach during my year-and-a-half stay at Central Catholic High School (1957-58) before I transferred to Taylor Allderdice High School. Jansante was the Steelers' top receiver before Nickel came along. He had played at Duquesne University. It was impressive to have a former Steeler as our high school football coach.

During Nickel's 11 seasons with the Steelers, his teammates included some guys with great nicknames, Jack "Goose" McClairen, Jim "Popcorn" Brandt and Johnny "Zero" Clement.

There were Ted Marchibroda, Willie McClung, Jerry Shipkey, Ed Modzelewski, Chuck Cherundolo, John Schweder, George Tarasovic, Marv Matuszak, Richie McCabe and Frank Varichione.

They drafted Harry Babcock of Georgia in 1952, but let him go to the San Francisco 49ers where he was a terrific end. In 1953, they drafted Lloyd Colteryann, an end from Maryland who grew up in Brentwood, but dealt him to the Baltimore Colts.

There were a few guys who stayed only two or three seasons, but their names will never be forgotten, such as Claude Hipps, Joe Gasparella, Lou Tepe and Ed Kissel.

Nickel was the No. 11 draft choice of the Steelers in the 1947 class. The No. 1 draft choice that year was an end named Hub Bechtol, from the University of Texas. In the 11th round, the Steelers selected a back from Miami of Ohio named Ara Parseghian, but he never reported to camp. He decided he wanted to be a football coach. On the 13th round that year, the Steelers selected Larry Bruno of nearby Geneva College. He also became a coach, and later tutored Joe Willie Namath at Beaver Falls High School.

The Steelers gave up too fast in those days on two quarterbacks named John Unitas and Len Dawson. "That story gets kind of old," noted Nickel.

The Steelers had several big-name collegiate stars come and go, staying a single season before injuries ended their careers, the likes of running backs Johnny Lattner of Notre Dame and Paul Cameron of UCLA, both in 1954; Lowell Perry, an end from Michigan; Jack Scarbath, a quarterback from Maryland and Billy Wells, a back from Michigan State, all in 1956.

The Steelers' scouting system wasn't as sophisticated in those days as it is now, and they often picked players from Pitt. Richie McCabe, a former Steelers' waterboy, was one of them who played several seasons in the mid-50s. Among those who came from Pitt to play for one season with the Steelers were Rudy Andabaker, Nick Bolkovac, John Cenci, Henry Ford, Fred Glatz, Billy Reynolds, Ralph Jelic, John Stock, Bill Priatko and Joe Zombek.

Nickel knew them all, from A to Z.

On the dais at luncheon honoring some of the selections on the Steelers 50 Seasons All-Time Team during the fall of 1983 were (left to right) emcee and author Jim O'Brien, Jack Butler, Art Rooney, Elbie Nickel, Pat Brady and Dan McCann of the sponsoring Pittsburgh Brewing Company.

Ernie Holmes
The Fat Man

"Every time I take a step...
I'm aware that I played football."

I was hardly surprised when I heard that Ernie Holmes had a heart problem, and had been unable to come to Pittsburgh for a well-promoted appearance with former linemates Joe Greene, Dwight White and L.C. Greenwood on April 26, 1997 at Station Square on the city's South Side.

They were to sign limited edition prints showing them in their "Steel Curtain" heyday at the Station Square Gallery. During the previous year, the foursome had several successful signings in the tri-state area, and had hoped to keep the customers and fans coming to cash in on the nostalgia and sports autograph craze.

The show started without Holmes, however, as he was being treated for angina, severe chest pains, at St. Elizabeth's Hospital in Beaumont, Texas, and couldn't keep his date in Pittsburgh. No one needed the money more than Holmes, either, but his health was a continual concern. He had simply gotten too big for his own good. When I saw him 14 months earlier during a previous appearance in Pittsburgh, he looked like a man courting a heart attack. Many poked fun at his huge form, but it was hardly a laughing matter.

Back then, Ernie "Fats" Holmes had quite a view from his room on the 17th floor of the Hilton Hotel. It was a rare winter day in Pittsburgh, with brilliant sunshine illuminating the landscape below. It had been a drab, difficult winter, with more gray days and record precipitation than anyone deserved to endure. Sounded like a good time to hibernate, as Holmes saw it. He admitted he had been lying across his king-sized hotel bed, watching TV, most of this Friday morning, February 16, 1996.

Holmes admitted he spent a great deal of time lying around, relaxing, or "loafing," as his old friend Art Rooney would have put it, at his modest ranch somewhere in southeast Texas, near where he grew up like few other kids in that region near the Louisiana border. Holmes wouldn't disclose his address or his telephone number — he gave me his parents' number; he said they'd know how to get him — as he prefers it that way. He was a lone ranger. Holmes liked his space, and required a great deal of it to get properly comfortable. Who in his right mind was going to argue with "Fats" Holmes?

While Holmes spoke positively, for the most part, about Pittsburgh and Steelers fans, there were some ghosts that remain in the area that still haunted him, and topics he talked about reluctantly, and places he was not eager to revisit. Holmes hoped his worst days were behind him and that he would live long enough to enjoy

Ernie Holmes signs football at Monroeville Expo Mart.

Photos by Jim O'Brien

Ernie Holmes takes time out from signing autographs to be interviewed by KDKA-TV's John Steigerwald, as Dwight White and L. C. Greenwood go on with their business.

better days. He was a changed man, he assured all. It can be fun to be with Ernie Holmes. But his history was such that one worried about him. He had been his own worst enemy. This was a man who spent some time for evaluation at Western Psychiatric Institute.

When I mentioned to a neighbor that I had visited and interviewed Holmes, the neighbor smiled and pretended that he was shooting a rifle at the sky. "Helicopter Holmes!" he cried. "Who could ever forget him firing a rifle at those cops in a helicopter? What ever happened to him?"

Holmes doesn't expect that anyone will ever forget that wild episode. Coincidentally enough, I had driven to Canton, Ohio to talk to a group of Steelers fans at the Stark County Library, not far from the Pro Football Hall of Fame, the night before I visited with Holmes. Naturally, I had thought about Holmes as I headed back and forth on the Ohio Turnpike, knowing I would be seeing him the next day. Back in March of 1973, when he was troubled by the impending breakup of his first marriage, the 24-year-old Holmes had fired a rifle at police officers riding in a helicopter hovering over him on the Ohio Turnpike. The police had been tracking Holmes because he had been behaving in a bizarre manner and they knew he was armed. The Steelers managed somehow to get Holmes out of that difficulty. Dan Rooney and Chuck Noll both went to bat for him. Some insiders say it cost the Steelers a pretty penny to get Holmes out of that jam. It was a sorry episode in the saga of Ernie Holmes.

The eyes of Ernie Holmes were hidden even more than usual as he looked out the window at the Pittsburgh Hilton. They were reduced to mere slits by the glare. It looked like he had twin ear-to-ear smiles running parallel to each other in the folds of his immensely fat face. He looked like the bad guy in one of those James Bond thrillers. The dome of his clean-shaven head was wet with beads of perspiration, as if he had just come through a mist, and it positively gleamed as he surveyed the impressive scene below at the confluence of the Allegheny, Monongahela and Ohio rivers. There were large sheets of soot-stained ice floating in those rivers, as well as a long barge with snow-covered coal. Trains were running in opposite directions on the tracks along the base of Mt. Washington, and the cars were moving up and down the steep hillside at the Monongahela and Duquesne Heights inclines operating across the way. Through the misty windows, it looked like a Nat Youngblood watercolor painting.

There is no scene quite like this in the world. Sometimes when a traveler first wakes up in a strange hotel room they are not sure where they are. But there was no doubt, looking out the window, that Holmes was in Pittsburgh.

"I see the rivers, and the stadium . . . it brings back some memories, some good times, some wacky times. All the memories of football," he offered. "Every time I step down on the ground I'm aware that I played football; I can feel it."

Holmes had not been in Pittsburgh since June of 1985, when he had come back to participate in a Pittsburgh Steelers Alumni golf outing and dinner at the Oakmont Country Club. He had last played football in Pittsburgh in 1977. Ray Mansfield, the mother hen of that alumni group, had made many attempts through the years to get Holmes back to Pittsburgh for one event or another, but had been mostly frustrated in his attempts. Even Steelers officials did not have Holmes' phone number. It was never easy to get hold of Holmes.

Holmes excused himself to go to the bathroom. "With the medication I'm on," he apologized, "I'm going back and forth to the bathroom."

Holmes had been a favorite of the fans during his heyday with the Black and Gold, a fierce, unrelenting defensive tackle. But he had disappeared from the scene, and had become something of a mystery man. Then again, Holmes had mystified friends and foes alike during his controversial playing career. He spooked a lot of people. Even tough guy Jack Lambert kept his distance, not sure what to make of Ernie Holmes. Holmes had gotten into more than his share of trouble. More on that later. Some thought he was simply crazy.

Holmes had come back this time, for a nine-day stay in mid-February, 1996, for a reunion of the front four of the vaunted Steel Curtain defensive unit of the '70s. He and Joe Greene, Dwight White and L. C. Greenwood were back together again for the first time in nearly twenty years. They were to be honored at a charity-related dinner two days hence at the Hilton. The banquet, which was to help celebrate Black History Month, benefitted PACE, a United Way affiliate that raises money to develop social services in western Pennsylvania. It was the start of a series of such appearances by the foursome who found they could make money signing their signatures as a tandem.

Former Steelers such as Andy Russell, Franco Harris, Mel Blount and Rocky Bleier were at the dinner, along with Mansfield and Mike Wagner, and team owner Dan Rooney and some of his staffers. It would be a good time. Back in the '70s, Pittsburgh and the surrounding region were reeling from the downturn in its steel and related manufacturing businesses. Too many mills had closed, people were unemployed, and they turned to the Steelers to escape the harsh reality of their own lives. The rank-and-file looked to the Steelers as a way to feel good about themselves and their hometown. They were a point of pride. People could thump their chests, and claim citizenship in "The City of Champions." It felt good. Two decades later, in the '90s, the large corporations were merging and down-sizing, different words but they also spelled out a loss of jobs and a slow economy, and again the citizens had turned to the Steelers to feel positive about themselves, to get themselves out of the doldrums of a difficult period. Many with jobs still felt insecure in a challenging work environment. Holmes could appreciate their plight. The run to Super Bowl XXX in Tempe, Arizona had been a fun ride. But it was over, the Steelers had come up short in a Super Bowl for the first time in five tries in the team's history. The fans were still in a funk.

"Maybe we could have come up with one for the thumb."
— Ernie Holmes

Holmes had been a much-feared defensive tackle for the Steelers from 1972 to 1977, and contributed to the club's first two Super Bowl championships. Some insiders insist Holmes was the best of the bunch for two of those years.

He came to the team the same year that Chuck Noll took them to the playoffs for the first time — the year of "The Immaculate Reception." Noll felt that Holmes lost his focus somewhere along the line. Holmes had more off-the-field difficulties than Noll or Dan Rooney were willing to suffer, and they finally dispatched him to the Tampa Bay Buccaneers. Holmes had worn out his welcome. Holmes was just too much to handle.

Tampa Bay was a brief stop in his pro career. "I went down there and tried to play ball, but I got caught in another manipulation situation," Holmes said.

Holmes had to notice how good Greene, Greenwood and White were looking these days. Holmes had gotten heavier, tipping the scales at well over 400 pounds — he confessed to getting as high as 600 pounds — and required a walking cane because his legs had long ago given up on transporting his heft without aid. The other three looked trimmer than ever, still big, but not as big as when they were battling in the trenches. White and Greenwood were success stories in business circles, entrepreneurs who mixed well with the business suits in corporate Pittsburgh. White was an investment banker, and Greenwood was running a coal and natural gas marketing company, both in Pittsburgh. Greene had tried some business ventures after retiring from playing with the Steelers, but came back to Pittsburgh to work as an assistant for Noll in his last years as coach of the Steelers, then with Don Shula with the Miami Dolphins. Shula had stepped down as the coach of the Dolphins following the 1995 season, and Joe was out of a job when he visited Pittsburgh the previous weekend. When he came back for the dinner to toast him and his linemates he had landed a new job as the defensive line coach of the Arizona Cardinals. All of them were doing a lot better than Holmes.

Greenwood would laugh that rich bass laugh of his from time to time, White would carry on like he used to in the locker room, back when he was nicknamed "Mad Dog," and argue with his usual outraged vigor on any subject. That wasn't White anymore, but don't we all fall into old roles when reunited with schoolmates at class reunions? Greene just grinned, like an all-knowing village elder, and shared some cigars with White. He spoke softly, thoughtfully, and enjoyed the scene. He wore a black knit jersey, casual all the way. White, Greenwood and Holmes all wore white dress shirts, and Holmes seemed most uncomfortable. His stiff collar was strangling him, making it difficult to breathe. They were under bright lights, and were in the third day of signing their signatures, and Holmes was running out of gas. He was sweating bullets.

They had been brought to the Expo Mart by Sonny Jani, who owned the Blue Eagle Market on Broadway in McKees Rocks and sponsored monthly card shows at hotels throughout the Pittsburgh area. He was bankrolled in this venture by Keith Gary, a defensive lineman for the Steelers in the '80s.

Holmes wore a mustard-colored pin-stripe suit, and a crumpled light-brown hat he called his "sheriff's hat." He hardly looked like a lawman, more like a character in one of August Wilson's plays about life in Pittsburgh's Hill District in the '50s.

His old linemates had welcomed him back with open arms and warm reminiscences of their glory days. They chided him about carrying so much weight, about staying away from them so long, and encouraged him to take better care of himself. They loved him dearly, they assured him, and wanted to see more of him. And they wanted him to take some steps, even if it were painful for him, to see that he would be around if they had another reunion in the next decade. They could see that he was a candidate for a heart attack.

"I hadn't been here in ten years, and it had been 23 years since we'd all been together," said Holmes. "I got out of a hospital to come here. I had a flu, and I started feeling real bad when I was about a mile from my doctor's office. I was going to see him, but I went to the hospital in time to avert congestive heart failure. L.C. got on me about that, and so did Dwight. Dwight had lost his dad to congestive heart failure, and L.C. lost his father this past year. Both were on me about eating so much. So I've been eating organic food — soybeans and stuff like that — and it's working. I've lost ten to fifteen pounds since I've been here. I feel a lot lighter. They're trying to get me thinking about the way I should be living."

That sounded like the same Holmes, and many other people who have problems with their weight. They want to please, and they blow hot and cold on diet and training regimens, but fall back into old self-destructive habits.

"I'm in a physical disability situation, and they're all in great shape," said Holmes. "They look like they could go out and still play.

"I love them all. I miss them much. If I had to do it all over again, maybe I'd have had a better understanding of the situation with the Steelers when I was there. Maybe we could have stayed together longer; maybe we could have come up with one for the thumb."

When Holmes first reported to the Steelers in 1972, he saw some things he didn't like. "I saw old guys sitting in a room, looking at film, and they were laughing at their own sorry play. They saw me in the doorway. 'What are you looking at, Rook?' one of them called out to me. I told them, 'I don't want to play with you guys. You're laughing about losing. I played with good teams; I can't play with you.' Chuck Noll replaced a lot of the guys in that room.

"Joe Greene didn't really know how to play football when he first came to the Steelers. He was just mad at everyone, and beat up on guys. He tried to attack people. We'd bust our butt to hold a team, and he'd do something stupid — kick a guy or punch a guy, or throw a tantrum, and we'd get penalized and they'd have a first down.

"Dwight White was a completely different person than Joe. He reminds me of Cassius Clay (Muhammad Ali), who was a good friend of mine. Dwight was an arrogant sonuvagun. He didn't care if he was running at an elephant. He'd get his point across. He always wanted to put his hands up in your face. That teed off people. That was his strategy, to get his opponents ticked off and out of their game. He'd disrupt you and then run his plays. With him on one side, and Joe on the other, it was a lot of fun.

"The four of us together were something else. I don't think there was ever a team like us, or any who could beat us. We had a sense about where we were, what we did, how we could run plays with just a nod of the head; we just complemented one another. We got on the cover of *Time*. That was quite an achievement. That was quite a compliment.

"*Time* later followed me for a long period when I was helping to coach a high school football team — Choya High School — in Tucson, Arizona. It was quite a challenge. They had to call out the National Guard once, before I got there, because these kids were shooting at each other, and trying to kill each other. There were kids who'd come from Indian and Mexican families as well as some tough black and white kids. I had been coaching a semi-pro team called the L.A. Mustangs when a fellow I knew from the NFL named Ed Brown — he played linebacker for the Browns — asked me to come to Tucson and help him with a tough coaching task.

"The money wasn't much, but the rewards were great," continued Holmes. "This team wasn't supposed to win a game, but we went to the playoffs. They said we were playing 'the Steelers defense.' It wasn't easy to get their attention and respect, though. These were tough kids. One Navajo Indian came on the field the first day of practice and asked me who the hell I was. I told him, 'I'm the baddest ass you ever met and you better get with the program.' One of the other kids told him I was Ernie Holmes and that we had a chance to be a great team. I had that kid run around the field, and do push-ups, for being so smart with me. I told him to do a hundred push-ups. He said he could do only ten. So I told him to give me ten push-ups ten times. It took a while, but he became the best nosetackle in the region."

"He was a problem.
Ernie needed attention."
— Chuck Noll

"Ernie was a guy of excesses," Chuck Noll once related to me during an interview at St. Vincent College in Latrobe. "He couldn't get enough of things. More, more, more. He was that way with food, drink, that way with everything. That way with love. And with hate.

"You never knew which Ernie Holmes you were dealing with that day. He was a problem. Ernie needed attention, and he would do anything to get it, whether it was to balloon to 300 pounds, or to shave his head, or to get into the *Guinness Book of Records*. Attention was important.

"There's a lot of con in him. He was never in touch with reality. George Perles and Dan Rooney and I all spent a lot of time with him. We had a spare couch for Ernie with his name on it. As problem players go, he was one of the larger ones."

Some of his teammates used to complain to Perles about the way Holmes was hitting on them in practice, that he was always going full steam. Holmes had to laugh when I told him what I had heard. "I wanted to be sure everyone was going to play up to their best," he said. "You have to beat yourself and your teammates. When you come off the ball on Sunday, no one was going to play you as hard as what you had experienced in practice that week. I didn't let up on anybody in the line, whether it was Jon Kolb, Sam Davis, Moon Mullins, Ray Mansfield or Mike Webster. I know they got ticked off every so often. That's what makes practice good. That assures you that when they got in the game they didn't have to worry about anybody kicking the crap outta them. It was already out of them. They've already played the game.

"Speaking of Sam Davis, I was sorry to hear about what happened to him. The guys told me some guys really beat him up. I hear he borrowed money from the wrong people, and wasn't able to pay them back. So they paid him back. I hate to hear that."

"I almost died there."
— Art Rooney Sr.

Holmes could see Three Rivers Stadium, where he had once joined Joe Greene, Dwight White and L. C. Greenwood to wreak havoc on the rest of the National Football League.

They had gotten together the previous weekend for a sports card and memorabilia show at the Expo Mart in Monroeville. They had sat together on a raised platform and signed their autographs to anything that was put on the table before them. Tickets were sold for their autographs — each signature on a single item for $15, and $50 for the four, termed the super package.

Holmes has been a holdout from the success that has been enjoyed by the other three since they were last teamed up. Most of his teammates had no idea about the whereabouts of Holmes for much of the previous 20 years. He had not been present at many other similar reunions of the Steelers of the '70s. Anyone who has ever worked on a high school or college reunion committee knows it's always harder to get hold of the alumni who haven't fared so well. They are not eager to come back and play catch-up on their lives.

The view from the window of the Hilton pointed up the damage that remained from floods which had ravaged the area a few weeks earlier, in the midst of the Steelers' exciting playoff run to Super Bowl XXX. It was the worst flood in the city since 1972, if not in the same ballpark as the storied St. Patrick's Day flood of 1936.

The three rivers had all overflowed, causing damage in many low-lying areas. There was still mud and all manner of debris — tree limbs, twisted metal, splintered wood slats, you name it — strewn on the shores. Point Park below had been completely under water during the worst period of the floods. Water had gotten into the Fort Pitt Museum and the basements of many nearby buildings. The wharves were a mess, and cleanup work was still in progress.

Also flooded were some of the parking lots and areas around Three Rivers Stadium, at the base of the statues of Art Rooney, Honus Wagner and Roberto Clemente. Art Rooney, the late owner of the Steelers, always liked to tell a story about how he nearly drowned during flooding in that same area as a teenager. He was riding in a canoe with some of his buddies and it tipped over, and he had a hard time swimming because of the heavy clothes and boots he was wearing.

"I almost died there," Art Rooney used to say. "In those days, before flood controls, if you spit in the Allegheny River, the flood came up. It wasn't anything unusual for us to leave for school by going out a second-floor window in a skiff."

Holmes had to smile when I related Art Rooney's story to him. How Holmes loved that man.

"When I look over at the North Side," offered Holmes, "I think about Mr. Rooney. He was one heckuva guy. There's no one in this entire area who didn't like that man. He was something special. I appreciated all that he did for me.

"Mr. Rooney told me, 'Fats, ol' boy, I'm going to tell you what you're going to do the rest of your life. You're going to deal with kids. You have to work with kids. You have the personality.'

"And he was right. I love the kids. They're the future of this world. And, too often, we let them down. We get caught up in too many things, and forget what's really important in our lives.

Ernie Holmes was waiting for "two for the thumbs." Ernie was always a little different in his thinking.

Ernie Holmes

Photos by George Gojkovich

"I can't get around much anymore."
— Ernie Holmes

"I'm raising red cows, goats and channel catfish at my ranch. It's a nice retreat," said Holmes. "I have a few acres there. My place is surrounded by timber land. My father has a ranch, and he raises cows, too. That's how I grew up. I'm retired now. My legs and body are shot. I've got bad wheels. I can't get around much anymore.

"My legs were gone, as far as football goes, in 1977, my last season with the Steelers. My left knee went out. I couldn't figure out what it was, but the cartilage was gone. Both of my knees are bad from football injuries. But I can still get up on my tractor and get around the place when I need to.

"My father is 73 and he gets around a lot better than I do. He's looking for 19-year-old girls, and I just want to relax and watch things grow, and raise my kids."

Holmes has four sons and a daughter. He said his daughter, Andrea, who was about to turn 19, graduated from a high school in San Diego and was attending Houston Community College with an eye toward going to the University of Houston.

His oldest son, Roderick, 27, graduated from Texas Southern University, and was going for a master's degree in a chemistry/math section.

Sexton, 25, had some problems, according to Holmes, and was serving time in a Texas prison. "I have a hole in my heart over Sexton," said his father. "Before I got back to Texas, the streets got hold of him. I tried to get him turned around. I lost him to the streets. Him and my first wife were always at odds. She did things to him to get back at me. We failed to communicate with him."

Derick, 22, was attending college in New York. Jonathan, 15, said Holmes, "pals around with me."

He spoke of a positive relationship he had maintained with his second wife, Yvonne. "We were married for nine years, and together, off and on, for 15 years. We were friends after the divorce; we're still friends," he said. "She's remarried and has another son." Holmes had no plans to get married again. "Twice is enough," he said. "I'm going to stay with my ranch and the surrounding forest."

Holmes had a hard time holding onto his money when he was playing for the Steelers. He says he was the worst paid player on the team, considering his contribution, and kept going to Dan Rooney for raises. He faults Dan for not being "more accommodating" to him. He feels he deserved better by management. Yet he is never critical of Art Rooney, the club owner. "I went to Dan when I had financial problems, and I could never get any money or caring from the Steelers' front office. It could have been different. I went to see Mr. Rooney just to talk to him; our relationship was not a business one. He was like a father figure to me, maybe more like a grandfather. I lost my grandfather when I was little; he's the one who gave me my nickname — 'Fats' — and I loved him dearly. Mr. Rooney kind of replaced him in my life."

I had always felt the same way. My maternal grandfather and grandmother were both deceased before I was born. My paternal grandfather died when I was an infant, and my grandmother before I turned ten. So I loved to visit Art Rooney in his office, and spend time talking to him, mostly listening to him. He was, indeed, the grandfather I never had. So many Steelers and some fans who were fortunate enough to know Art Rooney on a personal basis express similar sentiments.

"He was a warm man, and that's what drew me close to him," Holmes said. "When I first came here, he'd see me running around the stadium, in the driveway that circles the stadium, and he'd say, 'Fats, we never had a guy who liked to train like you. Be careful, someone might run over you.'"

Holmes talked about how he used to run to and from work from his home in East Liberty.

"I used to run down Penn Avenue," he said. "People would honk their car horns, holler out to me, and wave when they'd see me. I had my own community here; the people loved me. It was especially fun when I'd run through The Strip District on the way to the stadium."

The thought of a big man like Holmes running through The Strip brought several thoughts to mind. "You must have looked like Rocky in the movies when he ran through the outdoor markets in Philadelphia?" I suggested. "Don't compare me to Rocky," responded Holmes.

"If," I came back, "you ran through those streets today, the cops might shoot you."

Holmes said that Robert Wholey, the owner of Wholey's Fish Market, used to holler out to him as he approached his place. "He'd shout at me, 'Hey, Fats, come in and have some breakfast. Eat some oysters and smelts. Stop and eat a couple of fish.' So I'd stop, interrupt my jogging, and join him for breakfast, maybe eat a couple fish."

Ernie never seemed to understand that stopping for a big breakfast like that negated all the good that the long run to work might have accomplished. He once nearly strangled Sam Davis at the Steelers' camp because a liquid protein diet Davis had recommended to him didn't work. Holmes didn't understand that he wasn't supposed to keep eating large pizzas, several cheeseburgers and cheese-covered nachos in addition to the liquid protein diet. That's why he confounded his teammates and coaches alike.

"The older we grow, the more we find ourselves returning to the days when we were young...we find ourselves remembering the one particular house that was our childhood home."
— Frederick Buechner, Author
The Longing For Home

"I was getting sold short."
— Ernie Holmes

Holmes has his side of the story, explanations for everything that went wrong to shorten his pro football career. "When I played ball, just before I retired," he said, "I had some psychological problems and I had some problems because of the medication I was taking for the nervousness I had. I was taking Valium, then Mellaril. I tried some Haldol, and that's too hard on you."

I mentioned to Marshall Goldstein, a pharmacist friend of mine at the Pinebridge Apothecary in Upper St. Clair about the drugs Holmes told me he had been taking. "Valium is a minor anti-psychotic drug, and Mellaril and Haldol are major anti-psychotic drugs," Goldstein said. "They get stored up in your fatty tissues and they stay in your system for a long time. And you want more and more. Some of their side effects are that after someone has taken them they get the shakes, the d.t.s, like some alcoholics get when they go off drinking alcohol. They can wreak havoc on your system. These are definitely drugs you don't want to take for too long."

Holmes said he didn't feel the Steelers paid him what he deserved, and this worked on him. "I was the lowest-paid ballplayer on that team, I think," he said. "It made me feel out of place. I was getting sold short. My coaches in college helped me with my first contract, and they got a substantial cut out of it. I tried to negotiate with Dan Rooney. I never did get an agent. I got married again, and saw a house in Penn Hills I wanted to buy. I asked Dan Rooney to sign for me to get me a mortgage, but he said he wouldn't do it.

"I played for Mr. Rooney and the people of Pittsburgh. Not for the Steelers. I played to make him happy, for what he'd done for me."

One of Holmes' teammates, Lynn Swann, would probably shake his head at how Holmes separated the Steelers and Art Rooney. "Mr. Rooney used to walk around talking to all the players, and patting them on the back, but at the same time he was well aware of how the money was being spent by the Steelers," said Swann. "He was always a tough businessman."

To hear Holmes talk about them, Art Rooney always comes off as the kindly old principal, and Dan Rooney as the vice-principal or prefect in charge of discipline. When I worked in Miami in 1968 and 1969, I got to know Chris and Angelo Dundee, a legendary brother team in boxing circles. Chris was the tight-fisted promoter and his kid brother Angelo the trainer and corner attendant. Chris drove a hard bargain with the boxers in their Fifth Street Gym group, and Angelo would pat them on the back and badmouth his brother as that "cheap so-and-so." Then he and Chris would split the take on their last fight show on Miami Beach. The Dundees were originally from Philadelphia and knew Art Rooney from the days when he and Jack

McGinley sponsored boxing shows in western Pennsylvania. The Dundees and the Rooneys were working the same good guy-bad guy scam with their respective gladiators.

Holmes has selective memories. "I told Dan Rooney in 1974, before our first Super Bowl, 'I appreciate what you've done for me. I'm gonna win a Super Bowl for the Steelers.' And Dan said, 'I don't see how you can win a Super Bowl by yourself.' And I said, 'I'll be a key. I'm going to play beyond my potential.' I was willing to do whatever it took."

Playing with such all-out passion and reckless abandon paid a toll on Holmes. "I came away from football badly bruised," said Holmes. "My calves are highly calcified. I'd wrap them so the swelling would go down. My ankles are shot. I'd play the next game no matter what, while some guys stayed out with smaller injuries to let themselves heal. I suffer now from what I did then."

I asked him about his other problems, the difficulties he encountered during his days with the Steelers. "A lot of things happened, not really my fault," he said. "I had a nervous breakdown. The breakup of my marriage was part of it, and there was a lot of pressure on me. I lost it, no doubt about it. That's when I found out who my real friends were. The people who were helping me the most were Mr. Rooney, and some friends I'd made in Aliquippa, a fellow named Reggie and his family, and there was even a group of policemen who came to help me. I was pretty much shell-shocked, pretty paranoid. I thought people were out to get me."

I told him that two offensive linemen for the Steelers, Terry Long and Carlton Hasselrig, had gotten into similar scrapes with the law, and had cost themselves jobs with the Steelers because of their erratic off-the-field behavior. "I know I'm not the only one it happened to," he said. "I just think the pressure gets to certain people, and they don't deal with it well. I had a hard time coping with stress.

"I come from a smaller town than this. It's different country. Yet I was trying to identify with the people here. There's a pressure that you put on yourself. I was trying to compete and be recognized as one of the best ballplayers. People you least suspect . . . they have other things in mind.

"Mr. Rooney told me to not to go out with people who wanted to give me things. People wanted to take me to dinner, give me things. Mr. Rooney warned me that they always wanted something in return. Don't tell me no secrets, don't tell me no lies. I think I allowed too many people to become a part of my life.

"I was going through some soul-searching. I was wondering whether I wanted to continue to play football. Everything was getting out of hand. I was drinking quite a bit of alcohol. I was experiencing problems from the drugs I was taking.

"Rev. Hollis Halft worked with me very closely. He was our team chaplain and conducted Bible study sessions for us. I was going through some heavy times. My legs were hurting. I was OK in prac-

243

tice, but I didn't have power in my legs in games. Hollis told me there comes a time when you have to walk away from the game, while you can still walk. . .

"I was trying to become a born-again Christian. Life was changing for the big tough gladiator. I had become a baby again. I didn't have those gladiator powers any more. I was in a cocoon; I was in a religious cocoon.

"I told Dan Rooney that I was retiring. I told him I had come to the end of my career. I told him I'd given them everything my body had to give. It was a job and I wasn't able to do it anymore. 'I'm through with the team,' I told him. 'I'd like to get my money and go home.' He said, 'If you leave you'll never play pro football again.' I wanted to leave and start a new life, but he was clearly upset with me.

'What are you going to do?' Dan Rooney asked me.

"I figured I could go back to working for a living again. As a young kid, I hauled logs on my shoulders. They called it pubwood. The logs were five to six feet long. We'd load it on trucks and haul it away. I started out hauling one truckload a day; I ended up hauling five truckloads a day, and I'd make $100 a week. I was a strong boy; my family was a well-built family. I come from large people.

"My father is named Emerson, and my mother is Roxie Elizabeth. She just came from having a dialysis package in her arm. I've been worried about her; I'm going to give her a call. I grew up in a nice house, and she's always treated me like her baby. To your mother, you're always a baby.

"There were eight of us, five boys and three girls. I was next to the oldest. They were wonderful parents; they sacrificed a lot to make a good home for us."

Holmes has no complaints now. "Nobody leads a better life than I do," he said. "When I left here, my life took a turn for the best. When I left here, I began to walk with The Lord.

"In my younger years, I could not describe myself. I did what I had to do to survive. Today, I'm more mellow, more relaxed. I rely and trust in the Lord. I don't go to church that often, but I have a strong relationship with The Lord."

"It was good to see them all again."
— Ernie Holmes

Holmes was asked what it meant to him to get together with his former teammates in the vaunted Steel Curtain. "L.C. and I were pretty tight. I had a relaxed feeling dealing with L.C. We related well. We had similar backgrounds; we had both played at black schools in the Southwest Athletic Conference. He knew some of the things that were familiar to my life. Dwight and Joe were both from

Texas, and that was a common thread.

"It was good to see them all again. There were hugs, lots of hugs. We were like a bunch of old ladies getting together at a convention. We built up a respect for one another through the years. When L.C. saw me, and noted how much I was weighing, he said, 'If George Perles were around, he'd want you weighed, and he'd be all over your ass.' I was up as high as 668 pounds. I'm trying to get down under 400 pounds now. I have been down as low as 386 in recent years."

I asked Holmes if he was just a man of enormous appetites, and he had to smile in acknowledgment. "Mammoth appetite; that's the only word for it," he conceded. "My mother used to cook steaks for breakfast for me; I mean big steaks!

"I used to try and make the ballplayer across from me feel it every time I hit him. Some of the old guys on our team, like John Brown, Lloyd Voss and Ben McGee, told me, 'You can be as tough as you want, but you have to use your body to do what you do. You tear up your own body, too. You'll pay the price down the road.' They didn't lie to me. Every time I move, I can feel it from the top of my head to the bottom of my feet."

Holmes was asked about some of his post-football activities, including a brief fling in motion pictures.

"I got out of movies and came back to Houston," he said. "I bought 40 rental properties, and turned one of them into a half-way house, mostly for people who were trying to rehabilitate themselves from drug addiction, and we had people with mental illness. I didn't make a big deal, but I made a little money and I didn't throw my money away like people thought I did. I just trusted the wrong people from time to time in my life.

"My life is such a mystery and such an onslaught with so many different situations. I'm at peace with myself, at last. You can't expect any more than what you do to yourself."

Fearsome foursome of Steelers early Super Bowl champions were (left to right) Dwight White, Ernie Holmes, Joe Greene and L. C. Greenwood. They were pictured together on cover of *Time* magazine.

Mark Bruener
The good student

"He's been very productive."
— Bill Cowher

Mark Bruener was making the best of a bad situation. He was moving somewhat stiffly through the lobby of the Steelers' office complex at Three Rivers Stadium. There was an ice pack wrapped around his left knee, and it restricted his movement.

This was in early May, 1997 when several Steelers were working out on a voluntary basis at the Stadium, better to prepare themselves for the coming season. Bruener was there twice a day for rehabilitation of a torn left patella tendon, or dislocation of his kneecap. He had worked diligently, which was the way he had customarily approached every challenge, and was said to be ahead of schedule in his healing process. Aren't they always?

The ice pack dripped as Bruener moved about, leaving a tell-tale trail on the black tile floor.

He hurt his knee on November 25, 1996, making a catch in Miami in the 12th game of the 16-game schedule, a nationally-televised Monday night game. It was a 36-yard reception, the longest in his two seasons with the Steelers, ironically enough, when he took a hard hit by Dolphins' safety Shawn Wooden. Bruener's left foot planted in the grass and didn't give at all, something more likely to occur on artificial turf. He was sidelined the remainder of the season and the playoffs. It was one of those personnel losses that weakened the Steelers' arsenal for the stretch run, and undermined them in the big money games, more than most observers realized.

Anybody who asked Bruener how he was doing during his rehabilitation period received the same cheerful reply. "I'm doing great," Bruener would say with his familiar lopsided grin. "I'm coming along fine."

Pressed, Bruener admitted it still pained him. "No one else is feeling the pain I am," said Bruener.

Steelers officials had their fingers crossed that Bruener's bright-faced outlook wasn't merely a mask. They had lost too many starters already in recent seasons to free agency departures and serious injuries and could not afford another critical absence.

Looking to the 1997 season, the Steelers needed Mark Bruener at his best more than ever before.

In 1996, he had only 12 catches to his credit, far short of his own goal, which he had stated the previous July, of 50 to 60 receptions. He had 26 receptions as a rookie.

When anybody asked about Bruener, or suggested he hadn't performed up to expectations, Bill Cowher quickly came to his defense.

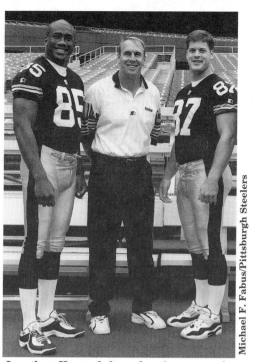

Jonathan Hayes, left, and assistant coach Mike Mularkey, both served as mentors for Mark Bruener in 1996 season.

College sweethearts Traci and Mark Bruener appeared well-matched.

Mark Bruener looks at home in second season at St. Vincent College.

"He's playing very, very well," said Cowher. "He fits in. He's still a big part of our offense. Mark Bruener is a very good football player. He's been very productive.

"If you want to measure a tight end by receptions, you can do that," continued Cowher, "but around here he's measured by how he performs at the point of attack and he's been a big part of the success we've had in the running game."

Seeing Bruener with the ice pack on his knee and by himself made me realize how his circumstances had changed so dramatically since he first joined the Steelers. A familiar sidekick was missing from the scene.

When the Steelers selected Bruener out of the University of Washington as their No. 1 choice in 1995, he couldn't have been coming into a better situation.

The Steelers' starting tight end of the previous seasons, Eric Green, had turned down a series of Steelers' contract offers to sign as a free agent with the Miami Dolphins. The year before, the Steelers had signed Jonathan Hayes, a veteran tight end with the Kansas City Chiefs, as insurance in case Green wasn't available, and Hayes was penciled in as their starter for the 1995 season.

Bruener was lucky to have a classy individual like Hayes to help him make the transition from college to the pros, to serve as his mentor. Hayes, who grew up in nearby Bridgeville and starred in several sports at South Fayette High School, was a good man from a good family, a man of considerable substance, and he took Bruener under his expansive wings. This was a big man with a big heart and a big smile. There was a genuine warmth to his voice and manner. He could make anyone feel comfortable in his company.

Hayes was a team man, and he was smart enough to know the Steelers had drafted Bruener to be their starting tight end. Hayes had no thought of stepping aside and merely turning the assignment over to the newcomer. He had pride in his own performance. No, Bruener would have to earn the job. But Hayes would help him in every way possible to be ready when his turn came.

"There's a reality to the situation," explained Hayes. "Mark was brought in, paid a certain amount of money, and eventually they're going to have to give him an opportunity to start. That's what he's here for. But I'm not going to hand him the job."

The Steelers have always prided themselves on the way the veterans went out of their way to work with and to help rookies or newcomers to the club, even when it could cost them their own job. That was one of the strengths of those wonderful Super Bowl winners of the '70s.

It was fun to watch Bruener and Hayes in their tandem efforts. They arrived early for practice and stayed late, pushing each other to be at their absolute best. They lifted weights together, watched film together, played catch together, ran up the steep hill alongside the practice field at St. Vincent College together. "Where were you on the

248

hill today?" I remember Hayes asking Bruener one day when Bruener passed on the post-practice hill climb to do a TV interview. He playfully scolded Bruener for not pushing himself. "I'll see you tomorrow after practice," added Hayes.

During the season, they dressed in stalls separated only by Andre Hastings in the Steelers' clubhouse. That had to provide Bruener with a certain comfort zone. It wasn't always easy for somebody like Bruener to be at ease in the clubhouse. He was more formal than most of his teammates.

"It's one of the more enlightening places in the world to me," Bruener said, surveying the big room where Steelers were dressing and undressing, and where they often revealed more than their bodies. "So many individuals from different ways of life, so many personalities, so many opinions. There's some competition here, too. Who can get up on the next guy?"

A clubhouse sequence which showed this side of the Steelers' psyche, and also pointed up the differences in the backgrounds and upbringing of some of the players comes to mind.

Running back Erric Pegram was coming out of the showers one day, and strolling naked across the clubhouse. He had a shoulder bag dangling on his hip.

John Jackson, a veteran offensive lineman, hollered out to Pegram, "Hey, Pegram, how come you've always got that bag with you wherever you go?"

"That's because he comes from the projects in West Dallas," I interjected.

"You got that right, brother," replied Pegram. "No one's going to steal my bag."

Then Pegram hollered in the direction of Jackson. "You probably grew up in a better neighborhood than I did," he cried. "Your parents probably stayed together and raised you."

"No, my parents separated," Jackson said.

"When you were two years old?" asked Pegram.

"No, just a few years ago," Jackson said.

"I'm sure you had a better situation than I did," said Pegram.

Hayes and Bruener were both brought up in a two-parent environment. Their parents were a team in their own right, and raised them with love, care and discipline. They were both good examples of how well that can work.

"I'll sleep enough when I die."
— Mark Bruener

Jonathan Hayes and Mark Bruener were both keeping good company, which is essential to any educational process, and they became a mutual admiration society.

Hayes had a good pupil in Bruener. He, too, had come from a strong, supportive family, and had many good qualities that made him an appealing young man. He listened and he learned. He had a great attitude. He welcomed whatever Hayes had to give him. Bruener didn't come in, like some rookies, with a know-it-all attitude. He had proper respect for his elders.

Bruener had good work habits. He prided himself on showing up for work. Bruener boasted that he had never missed a day of practice at Aberdeen High School or at the University of Washington. Hayes had the same kind of commitment.

"I'll sleep enough when I die, I guess," said Bruener in explaining his strong work ethic.

"Every time I'm doing things, I'm making a positive step forward. Even on the practice field, I still make mistakes. I still do a lot of things wrong. Jonathan Hayes helps me correct that. Jonathan is the type of guy who, while he wants to play, wants to help any way he can to help the team win. He made some big catches, too. He's not just out for himself."

It was an odd couple, in some respects, but it was a close-working couple that clicked from the start. It wasn't easy when Hayes had to give up his starting job to Bruener in the sixth game on the schedule. On most pro sports teams, the blacks tend to hang out with blacks, and the whites with whites. Since Hayes was black and Bruener white, their relationship was even more significant, even if it shouldn't be in this day and age. They usually sat together in the dining hall at St. Vincent.

Hayes was remarkable in another respect. He had missed only four games during his 12 years in the NFL, even though he takes several daily insulin shots for diabetes, a condition he learned about as a junior at the University of Iowa.

Hayes, however, would be 35 before the start of the 1997 season, and was making more than $700,000 per year, expensive for a backup tight end, so the Steelers made no attempt to sign him when he became a free agent following his third season with the Steelers. The torch had been officially passed.

A scene comes to mind of Hayes on the day when the Steelers were packing to go home two days after their playoff loss at New England. No one cleared out their dressing stall as earnestly or efficiently as Hayes.

Hayes packed everything, like a man who knew he wasn't coming back. "He did that last year," said Tony Parisi, the team's equipment manager.

"I don't know if there was any message to him doing that or not," said Bruener.

Each player had a one-on-one meeting with Bill Cowher before they left. Players moved about the dressing room, shaking hands, hugging, and exchanging telephone numbers.

250

"The young players are asking everybody for their phone number," said Hayes, with more than a hint of bemusement in his voice. "They'll end up calling maybe one player during the off-season. Once you leave here you leave here. You form very few lasting relationships in pro football. You're lucky if you make a few meaningful ones. That's just the way it is." Hayes dated a lot, but was still single, so he was returning to his ranch and his horses outside of Kansas City.

Within a month, the dressing stall Hayes had occupied for three years had been reassigned to John Farquhar, a tight end who had joined the team during the 1996 season. Hayes hadn't gotten any official word, but his days as a Steeler were over. The Steelers and Bruener would have to go on without him.

Following his rookie season, Bruener married his college sweetheart, Traci Toolen, who had been a cheerleader at the University of Washington. They, too, were an attractive couple.

"She's one of the most supportive people I've been around in my life," said her husband. "Nothing goes by without her knowing."

If Bruener needed somebody to lean on, it would have to be Traci, or the team trainers, John Norwig and Rick Burkholder, with whom he was spending a lot of time.

"I'll miss Jonathan, for sure," said Bruener. "Not having him around will be tough on me. He was definitely a mentor and a friend, someone I could lean on. He really helped me make the adjustment from college to the pros."

"C'mon, you got to get to work."
— Jonathan Hayes

Bruener recognized early how lucky he had been to come to a football team where somebody like Jonathan Hayes would help him fit in and make the most of his ability. Jonathan's aptly-named mother, Joy, was a teacher, so he came by it naturally.

"We were very similar in several ways," said Bruener. "We always had respect for our parents. We couldn't get mad at our moms no matter how much they expressed concern about our well-being, or how much of a fuss they made over us, like we were still little kids or something.

"I don't know how to describe it, how fortunate I've been. I could never dream of coming into such a good situation, having a mentor like Jonathan Hayes. He's kinda like an older brother. He's always looking out for me, making sure I do the right thing. He gets after me. 'C'mon, you got to get to work,' he'll say to me from time to time.

"It's a matter each day of who's going to work the hardest. He's 34, but I couldn't dream about being in that good of shape at his age.

"What Jonathan says to me is of immeasurable value. You can't really put a price on it. He's one of the better teachers out there. He's a team guy. He's not an 'I' guy.

"He sees a young kid like myself come along, trying to learn and trying to get everything down. I think it's just his temperament and personality to help out. I'm a very humble person. I don't talk about myself, nor do I boast about myself, and maybe he likes that.

"Our relationship kinda grew. We'd get in each practice day about 7:45 a.m. and lift weights. We'd razz each other if we were late.

"I've told Jonathan how appreciative I am. I'll say, 'Thank you.' I'll go buy him a beer. But we never really sat down, and discussed it at any length. I really appreciate it, though. I owe him something, that's for sure.

"In the seventh game of my rookie season when I took over as the starter, it was hard on him. It was an uncomfortable time, for a few days anyhow.

"I wasn't sure how he was feeling. There was a little tension. I'm some young punk kid coming in and taking his job. We weren't as easy-going with each other for a few days. The jokes weren't as frequent. The lightheartedness wasn't there. But it only lasted for two days. He was the first to congratulate me when I caught a ball in that game. It was my time to step up, but I can understand where he wasn't in a mood to throw a party for me."

"They know what I'm all about."
— Mark Bruener

Mark Bruener was always thankful for what Jonathan Hayes had given him. He acknowledged how Hayes helped him make the transition from college to the pros. "After you're here for a spell, the relationships become more personal," said Bruener. "Instead of me just knowing them, now they know more about me. There's more communication, more camaraderie.

"I think I've shown enough by now, with my blocking and pass-catching and attitude, that they know what I'm all about. Winning the battle with those players is one of your first challenges when you come to the NFL. To me, if my teammates believe in me, that's the utmost respect I can get. If I have their back, I'll be there supporting them and they'll be there supporting me."

In reflecting on his rookie year, Bruener said, "Being a rookie, you have to earn your way. That's part of the learning process. I felt the same way at Washington in my first year there.

"I remember how strange I felt my first year here when we played at Chicago. I was not in complete awe, but I was certainly impressed with the place. Growing up, you watch games on television from Soldiers Field. I'm out there on the kickoff unit, and I'm thinking to myself, 'I'm in Soldiers Field, what an opportunity.' I mean the Olympic Games were once conducted there.

Going to work at Three Rivers

University of Washington days

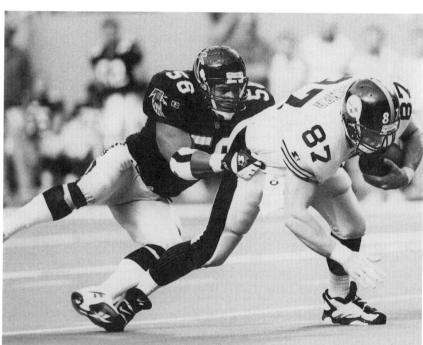

Mark Bruener struggles for extra yards against Falcons in Atlanta.

"You see the old stands. You walk out on the field. It's cold and windy and you can see your breath. A football player lives for games like that. That's bringing it back to the days of the good ol' boys.

"Mike Ditka played there. I met him once at the Hula Bowl. He's an impressive person. I always saw him as one of the first to go out there — excuse my language — and kick the other guy's ass. He set the standard for today's tight ends. In my readings, I know Ditka was a tough guy. I admire people like that."

Since he was a history student of the NFL, how did Bruener react to the news that Cleveland, another of the old franchises, was going to lose its team?

"I think because I'm so new I can't appreciate the rivalry between the Browns and Steelers like some people who've been around here longer," he said "Every day I'm here, though, I see something that shows how much a business it is. That's the bottom line. I'm just slowly gaining that. I can't get overwhelmed by it."

Hayes was not the only veteran who kept after him and made sure he knew what he was supposed to be doing. He also cited Neil O'Donnell, the starting quarterback during his first season with the Steelers, as someone else he admired and respected.

"Neil was constantly talking to me, complimenting me," said Bruener. "He'd tell me about a certain maneuver, 'This is what I'm looking for,' he'd say. He's definitely another person who helped me.

"I think I'm making progress. There's a lot more room to grow. I should have caught two passes in that Bears' game that got away from me. That one down the middle I took a helluva hit, but the good ones catch those. I've seen the film on that one a half dozen times; I cringe each time. It still burns inside me.

"Neil threw to me in overtime and I made the catch to keep the drive going. To me, that was an example of their faith in me. I'll bounce back. We won that game, 37-34, in overtime and it was a significant victory."

As a rookie, Bruener praised the efforts of his position coach, Pat Hodgson. Hodgson and offensive coordinator Ron Erhardt were not rehired after the Super Bowl XXX season.

Under new tight ends coach, Mike Mularkey, Bruener said he learned to use his hands better. Bruener was always better conditioned and more concerned about his diet than, say Eric Green. Bruener cut back on some of his favorite foods. He was not eating as much pizza as he did in college, for instance.

"You have to take care of your body," Bruener said. "Your body is your best asset."

Those were Mularkey's thoughts as well when it came time to being patient about Bruener's comeback efforts during the summer of 1997.

Mularkey played nine seasons as a tight end in the NFL, six with the Minnesota Vikings and three (1989-91) with the Steelers. He felt he might have been able to play longer had he not rushed back on several occasions, in college and in the pros, from knee injuries and surgeries to resume playing.

"He's going to be smarter than I was," Mularkey said about Bruener during the off-season. "He is as stubborn as I was — he's eager to get back on the field — but we are going to take care of him to make sure that is not a factor in his playing below what he did last year."

Bruener knew what Mularkey was warning him about. "I want to do what is right to rehabilitate myself so I can return to play in proper shape and in proper time," he said. "I want to be able to play with my children when I'm 35."

Mularkey became a big Bruener booster in a hurry. "He has played very well in the blocking aspect of the game," said Mularkey, when asked to assess Bruener's abilities. "He worked his tail off to get to that point. He is one of the better ones around. He has come a long way, technique-wise, and with his effort and aggressiveness. He has helped our run game tremendously."

Chan Gailey, the offensive coordinator who had been the wide receivers coach in Bruener's first season, noted the improvement as well. "To me, he is functionally stronger," said Gailey. "He is smarter, his technique is better. I think Mike Mularkey has been very good for Mark."

Bruener had his own ideas about his development, and expressed them this way: "I don't think my effort or intensity has changed at all. The tenacity is still there. I just think I have better hand placement. I feel like I can get my hands inside on any of these defenders — if they are smaller than me or bigger than me — my chances of winning the battles are greater."

I asked him about an apparent touchdown pass from Kordell Stewart which he had dropped while diving in the end zone.

"I didn't sleep after the game," said Stewart. "I'm my own worst critic. If I have one bad play that will stick out in my mind.

"In looking at the film, I would not have been in bounds. But I didn't allow the referee to make a decision on that."

What did he say to Kordell Stewart afterward? "I said, 'I'm sorry.' I've continually replayed that play in my mind.

"I think I've made some great gains. When I first came here, I had some great expectations. I did struggle at first. That's what I want. I want to be somebody who's regarded as a clutch receiver."

> *"Faith is in the heart and hope is in the mind. We have to play with a lot of faith against that team. We can't show any fear against them."*
> — Pat Riley,
> Coach, Miami Heat

"I feel fortunate to have such supportive parents."
— Mark Bruener

The Bruener family is a close-knit one. They have a beachfront home in Westport, Washington, with a view of miles of coastline running along the Pacific Ocean.

It is near Aberdeen, a small logging town about two hours southwest of Seattle, where Mark went to college.

"It's a very simple town, a great place to grow up," said Mark Bruener. "We had about 200 kids in my graduation class. My family still lives there."

Bruener comes from good stock. His parents are German Catholics, the same as former Steelers coach Chuck Noll, and they practiced their religion.

Fred Bruener is a CPA in business for himself. Arlene Bruener raised four children, two boys, two girls. The beach home originally belonged to Arlene's uncle. Fred's mother and Arlene's mother both went to the same high school in Aberdeen. They were married in the same church as their parents. The kids all attended the same grade school, St. Mary's Catholic Grade School, as their father. This is a stable family with deep roots in western Washington.

Mark learned old-fashioned values from his family. A tip-off to his training is that he calls nearly everyone "Sir."

Don't let Mark's polite manner fool you, however. "Don't get in his way," his father advised. "It's almost like Jekyll and Hyde. Off the field, he's laidback and relaxed. On the field, he'll try to knock your block off."

During the summer of 1997, Mark's older brother, Eric, was 28. He had played football at Aberdeen High School and later at Yakima Junior College. He was living in Olympia, just an hour's drive from Westport, married with two children and attending Shoreline Community College while working on the side.

Maria, 27, mother of two, was manager at The Gap and a homemaker. She played volleyball and was a varsity swimmer since 9th grade at Abderdeen. Catherine, who would be 22 in October, was a volleyball player at Washington State.

He said his parents never missed attending any of his games, home or away, at the University of Washington.

"The majority of Washington players are red-shirted their first year, but they decided not to red-shirt me," recalled Bruener. 'You're going to Stanford,' the coaches told me the week of the first game of the season. My parents bought airplane tickets on short notice and they were there. They were so in tune with my life. I saw them every weekend. We made phone calls to each other during the week. They continue to be strong and to be close. I feel fortunate to have such supportive parents."

Mark Bruener wears first pro uniform with friend at vacation retreat.

Newspaper route was first job.

Mark naps on dad's lap.

Mark admires new glove.

"Don't let anyone build any fences around you."
— John Wideman

When he took the 100-question test that the Steelers administer to all prospective draft choices, Bruener scored so amazingly high on the self-motivation part that the coaching staff thought they had found Norman Vincent Peale in pads.

"I'm the type of person that doesn't approach something where I just want to go and get it done," said Bruener. "I'm not satisfied ever with second place. It's kind of my attitude. I set goals for myself. I work as hard as I can to obtain those goals. When I'm satisfied it's when those goals are accomplished. I don't care if it takes a week, a month, a year, two years or five years.

"If I'm not going to get something done right on the first try, I'm going to keep trying and trying and continue to work — a relentless-type attitude. So that way, the mistakes I'm making out there on the practice field I'm always wanting to correct. I'm never satisfied. The day you're satisfied is the day you're not going to succeed. I'm not one of those guys who is not going to show up.

"The day you're satisfied is the day you're not going to succeed. My parents instilled a lot of good values in me. But I felt they gave me a base to build on, and as a person matures they make their own decisions, they choose what path they want to go along.

"Seeds were planted early with my father. He was one of those fathers who would never do things for us, but he'd advise us. 'This is what I did when I was your age. . .' Dad wouldn't coddle his kids. You were expected to clean up after yourself. He wanted us to learn from our mistakes, to accept responsibility for our actions, to be accountable.

"Being from a family of four children, you have to fend for yourself. To get attention, each of us kids found our own personality.

"My parents have always been so supportive of everything we did. My older sister, Maria, played piano, and was on the swimming and basketball teams. My older brother, Eric, was in Little League. My younger sister, Catherine, was in a lot of school activities as well. Our parents were always there, no matter what we were doing, to lend their support."

"I understand the value of a dollar."
— Mark Bruener

Mark Bruener signed a four-year contract with the Steelers worth $3.35 million. He confessed he was frugal in his spending habits, and intended to hold onto his money. The son of a CPA, he knows more about money than most of the players in the clubhouse. He knows not to be in any hurry to spend it.

"My dad knew the value of money and he wanted us to earn our own way," said Bruener. "We had to mow the grass in our yard, we had to wash cars, stuff like that. We learned the value of a buck. Nothing was ever handed to us.

"I feel fortunate. I'm frugal now. I understand the value of a dollar. I am preparing for tomorrow and I don't just live for today.

"In this business, you're rewarded very generously for something you love to do. Not many people make a living doing something they like to do."

At Washington, Bruener drove a 1988 Dodge pickup that had 107,000 miles on it when he was drafted. Some pro candidates manage to get brand new expensive cars during their final year in college, borrowing money or getting it illegally from agents, because of their future prospects.

No, this was a young man with his feet firmly planted on the ground. When he signed, he said, "The only thing I can say is I'm Mark Bruener and I'm going to do the best I can to contribute any way possible. Money is short term. I'm here to play football. I'm a kid who wants to go to work."

When Bruener signed, Tom Donahoe, the director of football operations for the Steelers, couldn't help adding, ". . . and he has no plans to do a rap video."

That was a slam at the team's previous tight end, Eric Green, who had been a catalyst for organizing the players to do a rap video in the midst of the playoffs in 1995, which was regarded as a distraction that helped derail the team's Super Bowl train.

"When you talk to Mark Bruener," added Donahoe, "one of the things that impresses you is he's a winner. He wants to do whatever it takes to be a winner."

Bruener backed away from any comparisons with Green, not wanting to get into any kind of popularity contest. Plus, Bruener knew that when the mood suited him Green was a great tight end on the field for the Steelers. "I just want to be Mark Bruener," said the earnest new man in town.

The Steelers liked the numbers Bruener had put up at Washington — no tight end had caught as many passes (90) in school history. They also liked what people they respected said about him.

Former Washington coach Don James said, "Mark's an outstanding young man, full of character. He's the kind of young man you want your son to be, and your daughter to marry. I also coached a guy named Jack Lambert (at Kent State). There aren't too many guys in Lambert's class as far as toughness or competitiveness goes, but Mark's the same kind of guy. He's a terrific competitor."

Bruener was personally hurt when James quit as coach at Washington. Jim Lambright took over as coach. Lambright said of Bruener: "He's a friend to everyone who knows him. He's one of those special people who makes this job lots of fun."

Washington quarterback Damon Huard said, "He's kind of an old-fashioned football player. Very hard-nosed, very aggressive, very powerful. He's someone you could see playing without a helmet or with one of those old leather headgears."

Lambert liked to play that role, too, holding onto old shoulder pads, old jerseys, pants pads, etc., and one of his proteges, Bryan Hinkle, another Northwest product, had the same habits. At Aberdeen High School, Bruener was a linebacker as well as a tight end, so he's a kindred spirit.

Bruener didn't have any difficulty keeping things in perspective.

"Just because people say you're an All-American and gave you all this praise doesn't mean you have to walk around like you're something special," he said. "I'm not special. I'm Mark Bruener. I'm from Aberdeen, Washington. I'm one player on one team. I don't want to be special."

Mark Bruener signs autographs for students from Hampton Middle School during Steelers' training camp at St. Vincent in Latrobe.

"...in football no one individual can be more important than the team. Sometimes this is a hard lesson for the most talented of athletes to learn. Prima donnas don't often make great football players and it's even more seldom that they make for a successful team."
— Tom Landry
An Autobiography

260

St. Vincent
Summer camp in Latrobe

Photos by Jim O'Brien

Carnell Lake and Greg Lloyd go to work flanked by fans.

Steelers fans have their priorities in order.

Rod Woodson signs one of his No. 26 jerseys for fan.

Levon Kirkland keeps fans happy at St. Vincent.

Eric Ravotti gets held up outside locker room.

Justin Strzelczyk's son and wife, "Little Juggy" and Keana, offer contrasting moods at St. Vincent training camp.

Mark Bruener is interviewed by Norm Vargo of McKeesport *Daily News*.

Carnell Lake meets Jerry Nuzum, who led the Steelers in rushing in 1949, at 1996 summer training camp. Nuzum later had automobile dealerships in Wilkinsburg and Uniontown.

Nuzum shares stories about the oldtime Steelers, surrounded by young Yeshiva students and rabbi on hillside overlooking training field. Nuzum died at age 73 of cancer on April 23, 1997.

Quarterbacks Mike Tomczak and Jim Miller commute from Arthur J. Rooney Hall to dining hall at St. Vincent College.

Mark Bruener and Levon Kirkland show off souvenir jerseys from Japan trip while strolling the campus.

Levon Kirkland
The preacher's son

"I prayed to grow into a
professional football player."

There is a striking similarity to the stories of Levon Kirkland, one of the Steelers' outstanding defensive leaders of the '90s, and L.C. Greenwood, one of the greats of the Steelers' Super Bowl run of the '70s.

They are, indeed, Steelers from two different eras, but there is much about them that offers comparisons and contrasts, and it also provides insight into their well-worn overalls-to-riches stories. They are good role models, testimonials to hard work, resourcefulness and the importance of strong support at home and in school in one's growing years.

Both are Southern-born, deep-voiced individuals, delightful fellows who can spin a good tale, laugh at their own lines, more of a bass chortle really, and they can be downright enchanting.

"How were my stories?" Kirkland asked after our lengthy meeting in the Steelers' clubhouse to discuss his history. Kirkland cared about how he'd done, how he'd come across. It's part of his personality to please people.

Because of his own background and upbringing, Kirkland can't understand, for instance, why fellow linebacker Greg Lloyd gives so many people a difficult time. On the other hand, Kirkland admires Dermontti Dawson because of his ability, dedication and disposition. Dawson is a super nice guy.

Kirkland comes from Lamar, South Carolina and Greenwood was born and bred in Canton, Mississippi and ought to end up with his handsome bust in Canton, Ohio some day, if the voters and gods of George Halas Drive come to their senses.

If Kirkland continues to play the way he has in recent years — he might have been the MVP had the Steelers won Super Bowl XXX — he could be a Hall of Famer himself. He became a Pro Bowler for the first time after the 1996 season.

"I don't care about the attention," Kirkland insisted. "I just want to win."

Kirkland, an inside linebacker who calls defensive signals for the Steelers, was chosen along with Lloyd by their teammates to serve as defensive captains in 1995.

At the end of the 1995 season, Kirkland won the "Chief Award," in honor of Steelers' founder Art Rooney, for his cooperative ways with the pro football beat writers. "I'm glad I was a stand-up guy and answered the questions," he said. He was that way when the team got off to a disappointing 3-4 start, and he was still obliging when the team went on the tear that took them to Super Bowl XXX.

"My approach is when things go bad, I'll be a stand-up guy and answer the questions as honestly as I can. My approach is to be a man about it. If things are going badly for me, I'm not going to whine like a baby about it or start cursing like I've seen some guys do on TV.

"In life, just like in football, there are situations that appear, situations that are tougher than others. You have to deal with them in the same manner. That's how I feel."

Kirkland combined with Lloyd, Chad Brown, Kevin Greene and sometimes Jerry Olsavsky and Eric Ravotti to give the Steelers their best group of linebackers since the days of Andy Russell, Henry Davis, Jack Ham, Jack Lambert, Robin Cole and Loren Toews as the '60s crossed over into the '70s.

Kirkland and Greenwood share a quality to be serious about themselves in battle, but have a rich sense of humor that allows them to laugh at themselves and their surroundings between plays and games. When intense guys like Dwight White and Jack Lambert would be yapping and drooling in the defensive huddles back in the '70s, Greenwood would step back with Mike Wagner or J.T. Thomas and just smile at the scene. Both Kirkland and Greenwood have distinctive laughs that set them apart from the pack. People who meet them often comment on how they can't believe how friendly and warm they are off the field, such a contrast to their on-the-field fiendishness.

They could both cut up in the clubhouse and entertain their teammates with theatrical antics with the best of them. Kirkland can crack up the room mimicking Bill Cowher in one of his intense, in-your-face clubhouse pep talks.

"I like to have fun; I like to cut up," said Kirkland. "People think I'm serious. The only time I'm serious is when I play football."

Kirkland isn't in the same class as Greenwood when it comes to dressing up for a night out on the town, but then Greenwood, along with Frenchy Fuqua, set Hall of Shame standards for their teammates with their colorful wardrobes and accessories that would be hard to beat.

Kirkland is more comfortable in loose-fitting jeans and a flannel shirt, sweater or sweatshirt. He has some handsome duds in the closet of his North Hills pad, but saves them for special occasions. He dresses up well for the Steelers' annual fashion show.

Kirkland has a high forehead and an absolute shine to his ebony skin. There is an absolute glow about him. When he wears wire-rimmed eyeglasses, he has a professorial look about him. Greenwood's beard and goatee have grown white in his middle age years and he's more distinguished looking than ever in his entrepreneurial business efforts. At 6-6, he remains a formidable figure. Kirkland comes in at 6-1, 255 pounds, and surprises a lot of backs and receivers with his speed and agility. He's made some over-the-shoulder downfield interceptions that have drawn envy from wide receivers on both sidelines.

Levon Kirkland points to sky to salute deceased relatives, celebrates interception, and expresses delight at playing inside linebacker for the Pittsburgh Steelers.

Both had busy, demanding fathers and supportive, hard-working, loving mothers. Kirkland's dad is Levern and his mother is Helen. Kirkland's father has three different jobs and tends a large garden in the backyard. From Monday through Friday, he works as a janitor at Levon's old high school. He's a barber on weekends in his own shop and a lay preacher on Sunday. He's a fire and brimstone guy, and the residue of those hot coals still glow in Kirkland's protuberant dark eyes.

Greenwood's father worked in a mill, tended a large vegetable garden on the family's plot, and was also a preacher. L.C.'s father wasn't happy unless his children were busy at their chores. L.C. said he went out for sports so he could escape his father and his limitless work assignments.

Their fathers were disciplinarians — from the old spare-the-rod-and-spoil-the-child school — and Levon and L.C. learned early that it was best to be a good boy, to behave oneself and to take one's school responsibilities and home chores seriously.

Former Steelers such as Mel Blount, Sam Davis, J.T. Thomas and Larry Brown were bred in similar circumstances.

That sort of discipline is often mistaken for child abuse in this day and age, but neither Levon nor L.C. complain about their upbringing. "That's the way they were raised," L.C. said of his parents. "That's the only way they knew how to raise kids. It worked." Kirkland and Greenwood have come to believe they were lucky to be so loved, to have two parents at home demanding something of them and their siblings.

"His character was beyond reproach."
— Tom Donahoe

Kevin Elko, the sports psychologist who tests and evaluates prospects for the Steelers, disclosed that in evaluating Levon Kirkland's personality profile before the 1992 draft he found "a very motivated player with a pretty good moral base who came from a religious background."

Kirkland, a four-year starter at Clemson University who gained some All-America mention, was drafted in 1992 in the second round, after Leon Searcy of Miami. The Steelers were looking for a linebacker because David Little was 33 and Hardy Nickerson was in the last year of his contract.

Kirkland had stayed for his senior year at Clemson even though he was projected as a high draft choice after his junior year. He stayed and helped Clemson claim its first Atlantic Coast Conference championship since 1988.

"Levon is an unselfish team player who loved Clemson University, who gave up a chance to be drafted high and go on to play in the NFL," said Clemson coach Ken Hatfield. "He gambled to come back and be a part of our team."

Kirkland came back because he wanted to finish what he started. "My decision was from the heart," he said.

"I didn't want to leave. I really wasn't ready to leave. I just wanted time. I wanted to leave as a senior. It wasn't the money. The money was going to be there. I thought Clemson had been willing to give me a free education doing something that I love and had even given me the chance to hopefully make some money doing it in the future. They made a commitment to me and I made a commitment to them. If they were going to stick their neck out for me, I needed to go all the way. If I had been injured or had not been a good player, they still would have paid for my education. I owed it to Clemson to stay. And I knew I would never again play in a place quite like Death Valley, which is what they call the football stadium at Clemson. I liked the atmosphere there, and I thought we could have a special year.

"The money didn't seem so important. I've gone without money before and I figured one more year without money before I got into the real world would not mean too much. I thought about it and the cons outweighed the pros as far as I was concerned, so I decided to stay.

"I didn't get recruited that highly for college ball. I probably got the last scholarship Clemson had and somebody else refused that scholarship, so they gave it to me. But I worked real hard and things just started happening for me.

"Besides, I promised my parents I would graduate. They had done so much for me. I thought doing that would make them very proud. For some reason, I wanted to be a senior on the team, whether to be called a senior leader or whatever. I made a commitment to Clemson to stay there and play football as many years as I could, and I was going to keep that."

The Steelers were glad he stayed. He had come to Clemson as a six-foot, 190-pound linebacker who hadn't been heavily recruited. He worked hard in the weight room and built himself up to pro proportions.

"I stayed in the weight room and I hustled," recalled Kirkland. "I think I have a lot of heart. I don't have great talent — I don't run that fast or jump that high, but I do a lot of things well. And it's not over yet; I'm still working at getting better."

He went from the Bible Belt to the Steel Belt without missing a beat.

Searcy and Kirkland were the first two players drafted by Bill Cowher after he became the head coach of the Steelers.

Cowher was committed to the 3-4 defensive alignment and he needed personnel to stop the run. Few teams in the NFL were playing 3-4 — New Orleans, Detroit, Buffalo, Baltimore, Carolina, New England, that's about it — and the Steelers look for certain skills to maintain their strategic schemes.

271

Kirkland is one of the inside linebackers in a defensive scheme that uses four linebackers. With his speed and agility, he can cover tight ends and shifting running backs. This allows the Steelers to do different things on defense. Yet he's big enough and strong enough to stop the running game inside.

Tom Donahoe remembered how impressed he was when Kirkland came in early as a rookie to learn the system, and how he hit the weights right away to get himself prepared for the pros, which showed his strong commitment to wanting to excel.

"You can recognize the players that football is really important to," declared Donahoe, the director of football operations for the Steelers. "Kirkland was very serious on the field, a very disciplined individual. He comes from a very religious and disciplined family. His character was beyond reproach."

Kirkland didn't start any games as a rookie, playing mostly on special teams.

Before the start of the 1993 season, the Steelers traded Nickerson to the Tampa Bay Buccaneers, and Little was waived by Cowher when Kirkland won the starting job at training camp. Kirkland started in 13 of the 16 games in which he played his second year. He finished second to Lloyd with 103 tackles and four forced fumbles, adding one sack and two fumble recoveries, including one for a touchdown.

Chad Brown, a second round draft pick out of Colorado in 1993, moved into a starting job as a rookie soon after Jerry Olsavsky blew out his knee in Cleveland on October 24 of that season.

Kirkland made a game-saving tackle at the goal line on the final play in a 17-14 victory over New England at Three Rivers Stadium in early December.

Kirkland made a big stop, catching Drew Bledsoe of the New England Patriots, in a goal line stand. With 17 seconds remaining, Bledsoe took the snap and tried to dive over the line. Kirkland came across the line at the same time and met Bledsoe in mid-air and didn't allow him to break the plane of the goal line.

In Brown and Kirkland, the Steelers had two of the outstanding young linebackers in the NFL.

Mike Archer, the linebackers coach for the Steelers in 1996, said of Brown and Kirkland, "They have a lot of ability. They have been given something that God gave them that a lot of people don't have. But they also have taken advantage of it in the sense that they are not satisfied with that. They watch the tape, they work, they have great attitudes and they are very coachable. They listen and they see and take it out on the field and they put it to use. That's the thing that sets them apart."

That's why it hurt when the Steelers lost Brown as a free agent to the Seattle Seahawks after the 1996 season.

When Lloyd suffered an injury in the first game of the 1996 season that kept him sidelined the remainder of the year, it kept

With sister Angela

Levon
Kirkland

As high school senior, Levon signed letter-of-intent to attend Clemson.

Levon Kirkland and kids pose for pictures at a meet-the-team event at Clemson University.

Kirkland on the field more often. With Lloyd in the lineup, Kirkland would come out on obvious passing downs in favor of a fifth defensive back. Kirkland showed he could contribute to the pass defense with some highlight film efforts downfield.

"My family is the most important thing in my life right now."

Kirkland grew up in Lamar, South Carolina, a community of 1,300. Lamar is located 60 miles or about an hour's drive east of Columbia, just a stone's-throw off Interstate 20, in an area of the state known as the Pee Dee. It's not much more than a gas stop on the way to the beach.

There's the Egg Scramble Jamboree to look forward to each year, and the townspeople love to watch their high school football team play in the fall. The people of Lamar look at Levon Kirkland as a big kid who put their town on the national map, especially during the pre-Super Bowl hype.

He was one of eight children. Kirkland has something in common with Lloyd and Darren Perry in that respect because they, too, had seven siblings while growing up in the South. "I'm just a small-town boy," said Kirkland.

"My mother has worked at a factory for God knows how long," continued Kirkland. "My father has three jobs. If he can do all those things, seven days a week, I can play this game. I look at him and see what he does. I look at both of my parents and they got most of my brothers and sisters through college. That's amazing.

"I have three brothers and four sisters and my mom and dad work hard. My family is the most important thing in my life right now. We're very close. My mom and dad showed us how to work hard. I believe if I lose everything, I could still go home."

Kirkland has never forgotten where he came from, or who helped him get to where he is today.

When he does something significant in a game, for instance, he points to the sky — a small gesture to memorialize his late grandmother and uncle.

He goes back to Lamar every year and has spoken at his school's athletic banquet.

"He hasn't forgotten his roots," said Don Poole, the athletic director at Lamar High. "He is still one of us."

Kirkland can't see why anyone back home would think he could be otherwise. He knows he's now living a boyhood fantasy.

"I was a strange little boy," recalled Kirkland. "I played by myself all the time. I think I just enjoyed that more because I could pretend whatever I wanted to. Most of the time I would play football by myself, if you can imagine that. I would make up two teams and I would have different names for everybody. The quarterback's name might be J.J. Miller and the wide receiver would be something like Randy Robinson.

"I would be all of them. I would snap the ball, throw the ball, catch the ball. I would even be the announcer.

"I'd say, 'J.J. gets the ball from center, he puts it up, and hits Randy Robinson in the end zone. Touchdown!' Then I would go down there and jump around. Give a high five to the air and scream and yell. My brothers and sisters thought I was crazy, but I always had fun because of my imagination.

"I had three brothers, all older. The next one was five years older. They were always saying, 'Get away from me.' That's another reason why I played by myself so often.

"We had a big front yard. I just threw the ball around, I always had a real big imagination. I pretended I was playing in a big-time game. I'd spin off the trees, go 'Bang!' Provide my own sound effects. I could entertain and amuse myself. I can still do that.

"I could make friends easily, but I also enjoyed times by myself. Let your imagination flow. No one going to make fun of you or laugh at you because no one else is there. I'd come up with a situation, and then make a big play, or an interception. I imagined everything. I imagined being in a big championship game; I was not necessarily in the Super Bowl.

"I always heard my brothers talking about how good they were. I wanted to be even better. I was not an all-state player in high school, or anything like that, so I was a bit of a late bloomer. I still feel like the best is yet to come."

What characteristics did he think he shared with his parents? Listening to Levon share his innermost thoughts gives you great insight into why he's so popular in the clubhouse. He was like a big brother to Brentson Buckner, who came after him at Clemson, and he tried to bring Buckner along as a professional, but failed to keep the bubbly Buckner out of Cowher's doghouse.

"I have the same heart as my dad does," said Kirkland. "He'll help people out, even people who don't deserve it. Always helping. Gentle heart. I'm still striving to be more like him. My mother says, 'You have your father's heart. You're concerned about other people and respect them.'

"Sometimes my brothers and I tell ourselves if we could be half the man our father is. . .

"He had a rough childhood. He raised eight children. My mother is tougher, but she can be light-hearted and funny. He gives. I'm generous like that.

"He was very involved, but not so involved with my playing sports. He knew I enjoyed sports. He was involved with me more as a person.

"I was a very nonchalant kid about school. I didn't have to study hard to get by. I cared more about sports.

"My father didn't finish his education. He went as far as seventh or eighth grade. He felt he always had to work. He felt more responsible. He was concerned about his mother and brothers and sisters. He had a lot of common sense, wise, very successful.

"At first, he worked distributing stuff in trucks, then for a lumber yard. He worked as a janitor at our high school when I was a student there.

"He cut hair on Fridays and Saturdays. On Sunday, he preached. The Church of God, a small church in Lamar.

"As a janitor, he always kept his eye on me. I got to know him better. He'd come down the hall. He had an aura about him that demanded respect. If me and my classmates were cutting up, we'd all stop. 'Mr. Kirkland's coming!' It was the same as seeing the principal in the hallway.

"His look, very serious look, and demeanor would demand that you stand almost at attention when he passed. He was a disciplinarian. He knew we practiced every day, but I still had to ask him every day, 'Daddy, can I go to practice today?' It was the principle of it. My brothers went through the same thing.

"It was tough growing up with him because of the expectations he had for me. He made me respect him. He did let us have our space, but he was so strict. He was so serious; he didn't seem to have much fun. But he told me he enjoyed being a father."

Levon said he was in 11th grade when his dad gave him the best piece of advice he had ever received to that point in his life. He was throwing the football around with his dad in their backyard when his father told him that a determined man can accomplish any goal if he remains focused.

"He told me if a man is determined to do anything, nine times out of ten he will," recalled Kirkland. "He said if this is what you really want to do, you'll have to put your mind into it, you'll have to put your heart into it. It's the best advice I've ever gotten.

"My mom's role was different, she was more relaxed. She said things that were more funny. A funny saying: 'You couldn't hit water if you fell out of a boat.' She was always able to make us laugh.

"She thought I got my toughness from her. She's probably the tougher one. My father had it bad as a kid. She had it rough, too. She had to take care of things. She had a tough life.

"She taught my brother how to play basketball. She was a point guard in high school, she got as far as 11th grade.

"My father . . . he didn't want us fighting at school. He was Christian about everything. My mother would tell us if you get in a fight you better win. I went her way; I didn't want to incur her wrath. She's tall, about 5-9, a big woman. She has a presence about her, too. We didn't ever want to get on her bad side.

Levon Kirkland dresses up pretty good when the mood suits him.

Photos from the Kirkland family album

Family affair: Standing first row (left to right) behind Levon's mother, Helen, are sisters Angela and Barbara, their dad, Levern, sisters Sandra and Kristy. In back row, are brothers Albert, Levon, Levern Jr. and Ernest.

"Now I'm always spoiling her, sending her stuff. To me, that's one of the most important things. People who have made it . . . you share the wealth with the people who got you there.

"I've had to find novel ways to share my wealth with my mother and father. I offered them a new home, but they don't want to move. So they added on to their house. I got her a car my second year. In a way, I tithe to my family. When I get paid they get paid.

"My mother has worked in a factory for a long time, making curtains at a textile company. She wanted to continue to work, but now she's about to retire. I want to make sure their life is comfortable. They don't have to work anymore, but they feel like they have to. My mother and father would be a good book. They're way tougher than I am.

"They took real pride in putting my brothers and sisters through college. My younger sister is going to college next year. My oldest brother didn't go. Another went to the service. Six of eight went to college in South Carolina. They had eight kids; I can't see me having eight kids.

"I'm 27, and I'm still single. When I get married, I want to make sure I'm marrying the right woman, someone I want to be married to for a long, long time. I want to have the kind of bond that my parents have. In my life, I want to have a wife and kids.

"It's just a blessing, growing up the way I did. I didn't appreciate having a father like I had. Being tough and being a preacher. I was lucky to have two parents who love each other and love their kids. That gives you happiness in life."

Like most football players who were churched as children, Kirkland doesn't get to services as much as he'd like. But he does belong to Macedonia Baptist in The Hill. "I go there when I can," he said. "I attend chapel services or Bible study when the guys on the team have something like that. I do a show every Friday morning on 3WS Radio, so I get back in time to come into the middle of the team's Bible study."

"This game is not life or death."
— Levon Kirkland

Levon Kirkland recalls an event that took place after Super Bowl XXX that made a lasting impression.

"Getting baptized was probably the most important thing I could have done," he said. "That probably helped me more than anything I could have done physically. It is kind of like a cleansing of the whole body. It is like changing from one person to another.

"My father kind of kept me under the water a little longer than he had to.

"It's like you really can't lose. You're pretty much on a winning side no matter what, and things are not going to affect you like they did before.

"Accepting Christ into my life helped a lot. I don't know if a lot of people believe it, but it really does. It gives me a little more peace and a little more perspective. It makes you realize this game is not life or death.

"I think a lot of people see Christians as soft people, but you can't be timid out there on a football field, doing what we're doing. And if you're a Christian, you definitely can't be timid in your life.

"I feel we're so blessed. The abilities God gave us. Athletes, in general, don't appreciate what we can do. Sometimes we have a 'higher than thou' attitude. Everyone is not like Levon Kirkland. We're no better than anybody else. Just because you're on TV, and the subject of so many stories in the newspapers doesn't make you more important than anyone else. This disturbs me. We have athletes who are like this. Sometimes we're ungrateful.

"I learned teamwork early. When you have a close family like I had, you learn to work together for a common good. This team is like that; we're a very close team. We have guys who come from other teams, and they say it's better here than where they'd been. Ask them. We feel like rookies are just as accepted as veteran players. We welcome them.

"This is one of the better teams. Not a black-white thing, not a starter, non-starter thing. I feel that we have to be close."

How about the contrast between his on-the-field and off-the-field demeanor? Does it get confusing as to which is the real Levon Kirkland?

"I've always been that way. Always been different on the field," he said. "More aggressive, the mean type. When I was in college, young ladies used to tell me, 'I can't believe you're the same person.' A lot of people would not come up to me. They shied away. When they finally got to know me they'd say, 'You were so aggressive and angry on the field. Once we got to meet you, why you're the nicest guy in the world.' I guess I'm just a softie at heart!

"They said I was an extremely polite and nice gentleman. I liked hearing that. I always wanted to be a classy person off the field. I like to be mean and aggressive on the field. I'm different behind that mask. It's another way of expressing yourself.

"I've been that intense ever since I used to pretend in the backyard. I'm surprised that I've kept that level of intensity for so long, but it's helped me. When I stop giving that level of intensity, that's when I will stop playing. Basically, I'm in my own world when I'm out there. I start getting like that a night or two before the game. It gets even more intense when I start to warm up.

"Greg displays a lot of anger on the field. He's great because he's been around and he trusts what he sees. He plays with an anger. I think I'm a little different; I play with great enthusiasm and I want to

279

hit hard. I think intensity is contagious. I play football with a controlled craziness. If I do what I'm supposed to do and then make the play, I think it's OK to raise my hands up for the fans or just do something crazy. It gets the fans motivated and it gets the team motivated. I feed off that. I don't feel like I have to play with anger. It makes Greg the player he is; it works for him. He must think about something bad that's happened in his life."

Kirkland would miss Buckner, who was traded to Kansas City for a seventh round draft pick in April of 1997, and he would also miss Dick LeBeau, the defensive coordinator, a coach he'd become close to during his stay with the Steelers. LeBeau had left the Steelers when his contract ran out to return to the Cincinnati Bengals in his home state.

"He was always telling us stories," recalled Kirkland. "He's entertaining. You can learn a lot from people who've played the game as well as he did. He knows what you're going through."

"I always feel in my heart that we can win."

No one was more super than Kirkland in Super Bowl XXX. He was credited with ten tackles. Had the Steelers won, many thought Kirkland should have been the MVP. Cornerback Larry Brown of the Dallas Cowboys was honored for intercepting two passes by Steelers' quarterback Neil O'Donnell. Some cynics felt O'Donnell should have been the MVP.

When did Kirkland feel that he was equal to the challenge in that internationally-televised game?

"At some point, maybe the first time I tackled Emmitt Smith," Kirkland came back. "I knew I was going to have a good game. I knew we had to play him well. After I leveled him, I told myself, 'This is going to be a good game.'

"Late in the game, I knew I was playing well. I felt like I was coming into my own.

"Right before the game, one of my teammates, Alvoid Mays, who had played for the Redskins, came to me and said, 'Matt Millen thinks you're a great player.' That meant a lot to me because Millen (who was working the Super Bowl as an analyst for Fox Sports) had been such a great linebacker for the Redskins. He said Millen said, 'Trust your eyes. You're seeing the right thing. Trust yourself.'

"Always had a problem, always downplayed myself. So it was nice to hear positive things from someone I respected. Recognition is starting to come to me. The Pro Bowl selection was the personal highlight of the season for me.

"I've noticed I'm getting a little more publicity and attention, but I just sit in my corner and thank God for the talent he gave me.

"As long as I'm doing my job and my teammates respect me and I play hard and I can look myself in the mirror, that's all I can ask for. If you say to yourself, 'Just play the best you can,' it will work out.

"God gave me the tools and what I build with them is up to me. I have talent, but a lot of guys have talent and don't make it. I have determination, too, but that isn't all it takes sometimes, either. It mostly takes heart. I play football with all my heart. I don't care how far behind we are, I always feel in my heart like we can win.

"I've been blessed by the Lord to play this game. I really have. And I don't want to waste any of that. I'm very fortunate. I've been blessed. What has happened has been a big surprise. I thank God for it because sometimes I think, 'Wow, this is me! Where did all of this come from?' People say that I've been lucky, but I think I've been blessed. And I just want to make the most of what God has given me."

His lifetime habit of talking to himself still works. When he goes home to Lamar, as he does each off-season, it brings it all into focus.

"I really think that I'm still pretty much a country guy. I'm a southern guy from a small town. I don't go back home saying, 'Here I am, Levon Kirkland from the NFL,' or anything like that. I think people for the most part are pleased or whatever, and I really try to keep humble and try to say, hey, I'm pretty much the same guy.

"I'm definitely not satisfied that I've gotten this far," he said. "I think it was just the family that I have, my parents, my brothers and sisters praying for me, the church praying for me. They probably got me through . . . some pitfalls that I could've fell into. I do kinda look at it and say, 'Wow!' It's kinda funny that I was once playing in my backyard, just kind of dreaming of it. And just being persistent, it's here. It's wonderful. It really is."

Levon Kirkland with niece Taylor

Cowher's Coaches
Sam and Marty

"Tomorrow is Monday and life goes on."
— Sam Rutigliano

Bill Cowher was one of Cleveland's Cardiac Kids back in 1980. As a rookie reserve linebacker and special teams demon, Cowher was a member of a Browns team that was branded the Cardiac Kids because they came back to win so many games that appeared to be lost. You had to have a strong heart to be a Browns' fan that year.

The Browns lost the first two games of the 1980 schedule, but bounced back to win the AFC Central title with an 11-5 record and the team's quarterback, Brian Sipe, who masterminded most of those comebacks, was the league's consensus Most Valuable Player.

The Browns' season ended on a sour note, however, as they lost the AFC Championship to the Oakland Raiders, 14-12, and blew a last-minute opportunity to pull out yet another victory. I was at Cleveland Stadium that day, January 4, 1981, reporting the game for *The Pittsburgh Press*, and it was a memorable experience.

Cowher had played on all the special teams that day, and even saw spot duty at linebacker. At the end, he was on the sideline, cheering for the Browns to score once more. Cowher was confident the Browns would win.

"Everyone on our sideline was sure we were going to win," recalled Cowher. "We'd been doing it all year."

I brought up this ballgame in a conversation with Cowher because I learned a lot about one of his coaches, Sam Rutigliano, that frigid afternoon in Cleveland. I wrongly assumed that Cowher was aware of the story of Sam Rutigliano that puts sports, and football playing and coaching, in their proper perspective. As the father of three daughters, Cowher should be able to relate to the lesson learned the hard way by Sam Rutigliano, I was certain. I was wrong. More on that later. . .

"It was an unusual year," said Cowher. "We were labeled the Cardiac Kids. We won so many games late. It was really an exciting year. This was my first year and I thought, 'Boy, if every year is like this. This is going to be something.'"

It was some finish. I'll never forget it. Neither will Cowher, Rutigliano and anybody who rooted for the Browns.

Rutigliano talked to me about it when he was visiting Pittsburgh in 1992 as the head coach of Liberty University to be the featured speaker at Pete Dimperio's Kodak Coaches Clinic at the Green Tree Marriott. We had lunch with Chuck Klausing, one of Western Pennsylvania's most respected football coaches.

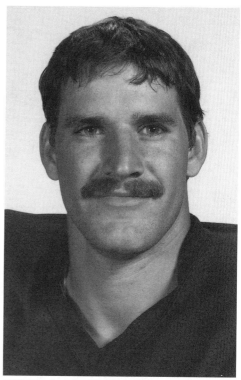

Sam Rutigliano

Bill Cowher in Cleveland days

Photos from Cleveland Browns

Marty Schottenheimer as head coach of Browns

Rutigliano recalled that fateful final drive like it happened the day before:

"We were down to their 13-yard line and it was second down. Brian Sipe threw the ball into the endzone to Ozzie Newsome. He should've thrown it to Dave Logan, who was wide open, or into Lake Erie, which was also wide open.

"We thought we'd try a pass for a touchdown and if we didn't make it we go for the field goal. A field goal was anything but automatic that day because Don Cockcroft had missed three field goal attempts and one extra point. Cockroft told people we never gave him a chance to kick the game-winning field goal, but he doesn't talk about the ones he missed earlier. Sipe told the media it was my call.

"Mike Davis intercepted the pass to Newsome and that was the end of the game for us. That play follows me around like Ralph Branca's homerun pitch to Bobby Thomson. I was in Auckland, New Zealand once and a guy asked me, 'Why did you throw that pass?' I got hot and I said, 'Hey, I didn't throw that pass!' "

Cowher can remember that day as well.

"It was one of the coldest days I've ever experienced as a football player," he said, as we spoke in the Art Rooney Memorial Library in the Steelers' complex at Three Rivers Stadium the week after the 1997 NFL College Draft.

"The windchill factor was minus 35 to 40 degrees during the game," said Cowher, wincing at the memory and squeezing his shoulders as if he were ice fishing on Lake Erie. "The locker room was colder than usual, and it was always really cold or really hot in those locker rooms at Cleveland Stadium. I tried to get near a nice hot pipe in a corner of the room.

"When the game came down to that final drive, I knew we were going to win. All I could think of was that it was a chance to double my salary. I was making $20,000, and I thought we could win the Super Bowl, and get that kind of money."

Both the Raiders and the Browns came away with a $5,000 per player share from the AFC title game. The winner of the Super Bowl got $18,000 that year and the loser got $9,000. I also covered the Super Bowl that year, at the Superdome in New Orleans, and when the Raiders beat the Philadelphia Eagles, 27-10, it only deepened the disappointment in Cleveland. Owner Art Modell died a little more. ("He would have given his liver to win the Super Bowl," Rutigliano once remarked.)

"Back then the playoff money was a real incentive for players because they weren't making the kind of money they're making now," said Cowher.

The payoff was a lot better for Super Bowl XXX when the Steelers' share was $27,000 and the Dallas Cowboys each came away with $42,000, but it was less important because of the huge salaries most players were making these days.

"When I was a rookie, it was still a great motivator," said Cowher. "Anybody who's been to the Super Bowl knows it's not a matter of money. It's a tremendous experience just to be there. But only the winner gets real respect or is remembered in the long run."

As for the way the Raiders ripped the hearts out of the Browns that day in 1981, Cowher says he can still see the final moments clearly.

"We couldn't believe it happened," he said. "I don't think anyone second-guessed Brian Sipe or anyone else. We'd been in that situation so many times before. Who is going to criticize Brian Sipe? He'd won so many games for us all year. We wouldn't have been in the playoffs if it hadn't been for him."

Then again, the same could be said for the Steelers and their quarterback, Neil O'Donnell, for the 1996 season. Yet he was certainly second-guessed, and it began in his own clubhouse right after the game in Tempe, Arizona, and Steelers' fans are still miffed about what O'Donnell did to sabotage the Steelers' Super Bowl hopes with his errant passes.

"When you first get involved in the playoffs, as I did my first couple of years, frankly, you see it as a monetary opportunity," continued Cowher. "When you've been at it for a number of years, you look at the guys with the (Super Bowl) rings on their fingers. They're telling stories about their championship seasons. That becomes a driving force. You can't take those rings from them. Every year we set out to win a championship."

In his first 12 years of coaching in the NFL, Cowher was never associated with a team with a losing record, and in 11 of those years he was with a team that qualified for the playoffs. It's difficult to top that record of achievement. His Steelers had qualified for the playoffs his first five seasons, and won the AFC Central title four times.

While Cowher and so many of his cohorts always talk about the significance of the rings, and how no one can take them away from you, that's not exactly so. That hit home in 1997 when one of Pittsburgh's most popular heroes, Rocky Bleier, declared bankruptcy, and revealed that he had sold (or leased) his four Super Bowl rings to an attorney friend. Bleier was not the first former Steelers' star to sell his rings, either.

"And there goes a dream."
— Brian Sipe

I have different memories of that day in Cleveland from Cowher's. The temperature was, indeed, just one degree and the wind chill factor made it feel like 37 degrees below zero. The wind was blowing off Lake Erie. It was bitter cold. The media mobbed Rutigliano after the game to explain the Browns' strategy at the end.

"Those were all my plays, not Brian Sipe's, at the end," Rutigliano was quick to tell everyone. He didn't mention that he had instructed Sipe not to force anything, or risk an interception if a receiver wasn't wide open, which came to light in later interviews in the locker room.

"One mistake," said Sipe, "and there goes a dream."

As Sipe came to the sideline after the interception, Rutigliano reached for him, and clasped his hands alongside Sipe's helmet and looked straight into his eyes. "I told him I loved him," said Rutigliano.

He let that sink in awhile, and smiled at the sportswriters looking over their notepads, "I say to that other people besides women."

A reporter persisted, and asked Rutigliano if it were the toughest loss of his life.

Rutigliano sighed and shook his head in the negative. "There are moments that you savor, and this won't be one of them," he said. "The only thing that's tough is death. Today is Sunday and tomorrow is Monday and life goes on."

I realized what Rutigliano meant because I had a lengthy interview with him in Hawaii at an NFL Owners Meeting when he disclosed a personal story. His life's experiences have taught him how to keep things such as sports, and football games, in their proper perspective.

The "toughest loss" in his football career came on a New Hampshire highway 18 years earlier when he was an assistant coach with the New England Patriots. Rutigliano and his wife, Barbara, and their 4 1/2 year old daughter, Nancy, were driving home from Montreal. Rutigliano, after a long stretch at the wheel, dozed off for an instant and he lost control of the car. The car went off the road and flipped over. Their daughter went through the rear window of the car and died from head injuries. It's something Rutigliano, understandably, won't ever forget.

Rutigliano is a religious man and his faith has served him in good stead.

"There was a total new outlook in terms of being able to carry on," he said. "It helped keep the problems of my life in order. Over the years I've tried, regardless of my hopes and dreams, to never really get down. After an experience like that, nothing else can get you down."

Some of the reporters were relentless following the AFC title game loss to the Raiders as Rutigliano remained outside the Browns' clubhouse, answering all their questions. Some insisted on re-examining Rutigliano's last-drive strategy. Rutigliano realized he was going over familiar and uncomfortable ground, again and again.

"I know I'm sounding redundant," he apologized, "but so are some of the questions."

He looked around and asked everyone if they'd had enough of his time. Sensing they were semi-satisfied, he said, "Look, I want to thank you. And listen, I hope you all have a happy new year."

Former linebackers Jack Lambert and Bill Cowher compare notes at "meet-the-coach" confab at Three Rivers Stadium in 1992.

Bill Cowher and John Majors meet at Pitt coaches' clinic in 1996.

"He always knew what he was doing."
— Sam Rutigliano
on Bill Cowher

Cowher had never heard the story about how Sam fell asleep at the wheel of his car and how his daughter died in the ensuing accident. I just figured it would have come up during his days in Cleveland, or that Marty Schottenheimer would have said something about it.

Cowher was more greatly influenced by another of our favorite coaches, Schottenheimer, the pride of McDonald, Pa., who was a year behind me at Pitt in the early '60s.

"Bill's into red eyes and sore eyes," said Rutigliano during that luncheon in Green Tree soon after the Steelers had hired Cowher as their coach. "Those young guys are like that. He was the first guy Marty Schottenheimer hired — as special teams coach — when Marty took over for me in Cleveland. Later, he became the secondary coach.

"Bill was one of those special teams guys. He never played regular except maybe one or two games. But he was always ready to play. He always knew what he was doing.

"He wasn't fast, but he could cover those guys who could run 4.4s and 4.5s on the kickoffs, and they couldn't get by him. He covered well. He was originally signed by the Philadelphia Eagles, but they waived him during the pre-season. He came to us the next year. He made the team not on talent, but on dependability. It's hard to believe, at age 34, he's already a head coach in the NFL. He had a meteoric rise.

"If you have a 45-man roster, it's important who you have as the 42nd through 45th guy. Bill wasn't going to be a frontline linebacker, but he was smart and tough. He was a coach's player. He was always ready."

Or as one of my neighbors, former Steelers lineman Craig Wolfley put it, "I played against Cowher. He was one of those gutty guys who kept coming at you. He'd never quit."

Rutigliano was also a fan of Schottenheimer, a former All-East linebacker at Pitt. "I had Marty on my staff for five years in Cleveland," said Rutigliano. "He was a linebacker coach in Detroit when I got him. I've turned out a few guys who've become head coaches."

"You relate to people you've been around."
— Bill Cowher

Rutigliano was such a class act in the NFL. He was one of my favorite coaches, right up there with Bum Phillips of the Houston Oilers. I always thought he was the kind of touchy-feeling football coach Terry Bradshaw would have embraced. He was warm and personable. Bradshaw would have loved Phillips as well.

288

"Players have different perspectives of coaches," said Cowher, when I asked him if he had been influenced in his coaching by Sam's style. "He was the coach and I was a player. My only memories of Sam are good ones.

"Sam was a guy who had a presence about him. He certainly had a lot of good leadership qualities. He had that New York accent, and he loved to tell stories. The players enjoyed playing for the guy. He certainly had a good football mind, and he had an ability to relate to his players. He was a players' coach.

"My three years with him were kind of mixed up. I played in 1980, then I was on the injured reserve list and missed the 1981 season. In my third year, we had the strike. So two of those years, getting hurt and the strike, weren't real good.

"Marty was my position coach, and I was fortunate to play for him. I was fortunate to make the team in the first place. He expects his players to know a lot about what they're supposed to do. He's very detailed in his approach.

"There's no question he had a great impact on me and my coaching approach. You form ideas and philosophies, and you relate to people you've been around. As an assistant, I had been exposed to one head coach — for seven years — before I came here, and that was Marty Schottenheimer. There's no question that the things we do in Pittsburgh are a product of my time with Marty."

Jim O'Brien

Bill Cowher chats with Marty Schottenheimer at 1996 YMCA Scholar-Athlete Dinner at Hilton Hotel where Cowher was honored as Man of the Year.

Photos by Michael F. Fabus/Pittsburgh Steelers

60-Minute Men of Steelers 1995 squad (left to right, front row) are Jim Miller, Fred McAfee, Yancey Thigpen, Mike Tomczak, Kordell Stewart, Erric Pegram; (second row) John Jackson, Tom Newberry, Jonathan Hayes, Bam Morris, Brenden Stai; (third row) Leon Searcy, Ariel Solomon, Justin Strzelczyk, Mark Bruener, Ernie Mills, Steve Avery, John L. Williams, Neil O'Donnell, Dermontti Dawson, Kendall Gammon and James Parrish.

Steelers from the past come out to meet the new coach, Bill Cowher, prior to 1992 season. Sitting up front are Mike Wagner and Ray Mansfield; taking a knee are Pete Rotosky, Bill Hurley, equipment men Tony Parisi and Frankie Sciulli, J. T. Thomas. Standing are Steve Furness, Ted Petersen, Craig Wolfley, Emil Boures, Robin Cole, Craig Bingham, John Banaszak, Bill Cowher, Jack Lambert, equipment man Rodgers Freyvogel, Rocky Bleier, Gerry "Moon" Mullins and Andy Russell.

John Banaszak
One of the few good men

"It was touch and go.
We almost lost him."
— John Luckhardt

id-July was always a time of the year to hope and dream. Once a free agent, always a free agent, so John Banaszak was never sure where he stood with the Steelers when they went to summer training camp at St. Vincent College in Latrobe.

Banaszak had to bust his butt every down, every summer to survive in pro football. He had grown up in Cleveland and his late father had taken him as a young man to root for the Browns and Indians, and being a pro football player was a dream come true for Banaszak. His dad was dead and Cleveland Stadium had been torn down in 1996, but Banaszak was building for the future.

During the glory days of the Steelers, Banaszak was one of several Steelers stars who had not been selected in the NFL college draft, but managed to seize a spot on the roster. Sam Davis, Donnie Shell and Randy Grossman were among the free agents who made the grade. Banaszak had come out of the Marines to make it with the Steelers. He was among the few good men who could make the grade without being a ballyhooed draft choice. His dad had some difficulty, at first, in understanding why his son signed with the arch-enemy Steelers when he had opportunities to join other teams, but in time his dad became the biggest of Steelers fans.

Banaszak and that bunch of free agents who found employment with the Steelers in the '70s became an inspiration for every free agent who has come to camp with the Steelers since then. Banaszak played on three Super Bowl championship teams. Toward the end of his seven seasons (1975-81) with the Steelers, Banaszak worried about losing his job. I remember how Banaszak felt betrayed when he, and later L.C. Greenwood, were both turned loose in the summer of 1982. Nobody is ever ready to get the pink slip in sports or in life. Losing one's job or one's role is difficult to accept.

In July of 1995, 14 years away from his playing days with the Steelers, Banaszak worried about losing something much worse, like one of his legs or, indeed, his very life.

So much for routine surgery.

Banaszak had been plagued throughout his collegiate and pro career by bum knees. His right knee was particularly bothersome. Few pro football players escape without nagging knee problems, and they often haunt them later on.

291

Banaszak had undergone arthroscopic surgery on his right knee at Canonsburg Hospital. The idea was to clean out some of the mush. "It had seen its share of abuse," observed Banaszak.

It was out-patient surgery, and John felt just fine when he returned to his home in nearby McMurray. He felt fine on the Tuesday on which he underwent the operation. He felt fine on Wednesday. On Thursday he felt like he had never felt in his life.

"In an eight hour period, I went from having discomfort to having the most terrible pain," recalled Banaszak. "My leg was in more pain than I'd ever been in my life. I just wanted them to find a way to put an end to that pain.

"It was very serious. It got real spooky. It was an ordeal I never expected."

Doctors at Canonsburg Hospital determined that there had been a mysterious dormant infection in Banaszak's right knee that they traced to knee surgery he had undergone during his days at Eastern Michigan University. The most recent repair procedure, according to their prognosis, released the infection into his blood stream.

With the scare behind him, Banaszak underwent rehabilitation in order to join John Luckhardt's coaching staff when Washington & Jefferson College opened its pre-season training camp on August 21, 1995.

W&J is located about 30 miles south of Three Rivers Stadium, so Banaszak has been able to play and work most of his adult life in his own backyard.

Banaszak was bummed out by the timing of his physical problems because he was preparing for his first year as defensive coordinator of the football team at W&J, where he also coached the baseball team for the first time that same year. Banaszak had helped Luckhardt for several seasons as a volunteer coach before eagerly accepting a full-time offer.

"I told John I wouldn't have asked him to come back to football if I knew it was going to nearly kill him," said the personable Luckhardt during a visit to the Steelers' training camp in Latrobe during the summer of 1995.

"It was touch-and-go," allowed Luckhardt, able to smile about Banaszak's scare a week later. "We almost lost him. They nearly had to take the leg to save him."

The real Banaszak Bunch rallied about him. John's wife, Mary, and their three children, Jay, Carrie and Amye, all provided prayers and support. "It's been a while since Mary worked as a nurse," said a grateful husband, "but she's been the best nurse you could ask for."

Banaszak was still hobbled, moving about his home on crutches, hooked up to i.v. tubes and such when we talked. But he was hopeful, as he's always been in July.

He had remained one of the most popular of former Steelers. He was still a much-in-demand motivational speaker.

The 6-3 Banaszak weighed 245 in his playing days, and about 220 before his ordeal. He was down to nearly 200 pounds.

He looked to Jerry Olsavsky, another Ohioan with the Steelers, for inspiration about a comeback. "Look how Jerry came back from a knee injury that's ended most guys' careers," said Banaszak. "But he still had the desire to buckle up his chin-strap. If you still have that desire, you can do it."

Did Banaszak harbor any such thoughts in recent seasons when he saw the Steelers in action? "I know I'm long past my playing days," he said with a big smile. "People will say, 'John, you still look good.' The truth is I couldn't play a down."

Shortly after he retired, I talked to Banaszak for a book I wrote about the glory days of the Steelers called *Whatever It Takes*. His grandfather and father had both worked in the mills in Cleveland, and he was of Polish descent, which helped boost his popularity in Pittsburgh.

And the fans loved his attitude. He showed the same sort of exuberance about the game before anyone ever heard of Jerome Bettis, and the crowds at Three Rivers Stadium fed off his enthusiasm. "When fans think of me," Banaszak said back then, "I hope they'll feel the same way I felt about my career. I enjoyed every minute of it.

"There's nothing I could look back upon and say I had a bad time or that was a disappointment, or that was work. I enjoyed every single practice, every single meeting, every single camp, every single game. I enjoyed the entire seven years in Pittsburgh as a Steeler."

"We're thankful for what we have."
— John Banaszak

Banaszak will be a Steeler and a Marine forever and, to hear him talk, he intends to remain married to Mary just as long. It's reassuring to hear somebody like Banaszak talk about his wife and family the way he does, and better yet to see him live up to what he's saying.

Banaszak visited the Steelers' offices on Friday, April 18, 1997, the day before the NFL draft activity. He visited with old friends like Joe Gordon and Mary Regan, stopped in to say hello to his old boss, Dan Rooney, and talked for a while with Coach Bill Cowher, who still gets a kick out of spending time with the Steelers of his schoolboy days in Crafton. Then he sat with me at Art Rooney's old desk, now the centerpiece for a library in the team's complex at Three Rivers Stadium.

I had been talking earlier with Tunch Ilkin, the former Steelers' lineman who now is an expert commentator for WPXI-TV, about how so many of his former teammates had become divorced or split from their wives in recent years. There seemed to be an epidemic of failed marriages among the Steelers of the '70s and '80s. Ilkin and Banaszak both consider their marital obligations to be serious ones.

"I'm still very much in love," said Banaszak, who would be married to Mary for 26 of his 47 years by the time his next birthday and

Celebrating graduation in June, 1997 of Amye, at left, from Peters Township High School, are proud father, John Banaszak, mother Mary, brother Jay, and sister Carrie.

W&J coaches John Banaszak and John Luckhardt

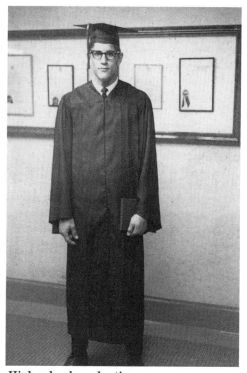

High school graduation

Photos from the Banaszak family album

Grade school days

their anniversary came around in August. "We're best friends. We were high school sweethearts. I was married four days after I turned 21. We're thankful for what we have and where we're at. We've got three great kids, and we enjoy each other.

"We have a tremendously comfortable relationship. All couples get challenged along the way, but we haven't had any mid-life crises or anything like that. I was married before I was a Steeler, back when we couldn't rub two nickels together. She didn't marry me because I was a pro football player."

He said Mary was also working in Washington, Pa., as executive director of Greenbriar Treatment Center, an alcohol and drug rehabilitation center, and their son Jay, 23, a graduate of St. Vincent College, was working with her.

Their daughter, Carrie, 21, was a sophomore student and volleyball player at Washington & Jefferson College, and Amye, 18, was in her senior year at Peters Township High School, with plans to attend Community College of Allegheny County (CCAC) in the fall. So the family remained close and saw a lot of each other.

John's knees still reminded him of all those seasons of football, but he was looking forward to his third year as the baseball coach and defensive coordinator of a nationally-rated football team at W&J.

"This has worked out well," said Banaszak, who had been in industrial sales and had some success in several entrepreneurial activities, before getting back into sports on a full-time basis. "I've always enjoyed my association with sports; it's been a big part of my life. I like working with young people and helping them pursue their personal interests. This is an absolutely tremendous opportunity.

"I get everything I want out of coaching, without carrying a lot of the baggage that goes with big-time sports. I don't feel the same kind of pressure as I might in a different kind of college or pro coaching situation."

We agreed that you determine your success in life by the state of your family. How is the family faring? How are the kids doing? Are they good kids?

"You can't put a price tag on what I have," said Banaszak, looking trim in a W&J red, black and white windbreaker, and, as always, with a lopsided grin on his face. "After what I went through two summers ago, I'm probably more laidback than I'd been before.

"My family and my happiness are paramount in my mind. Healthwise, I'm OK now. My knees bother me, but what's new? Two years ago this July, they could have thrown dirt on me and I'd have never known it.

"So I measure success differently than I did when I was younger. Success and happiness and family go hand in hand, and I am taking full advantage of what I have. I appreciate Mary and the kids more than ever. I wouldn't trade them for anything.

"I love my life a little differently after what I experienced. I've learned to count my blessings."

John Banaszak serves as defensive coordinator at Washington & Jefferson College.

Jim O'Brie

Banaszak speaks to Steelers' defensive back Carnell Lake.

Tim Lewis
Looking back can hurt

*"As a kid, my goal was to get
to the Hall of Fame and
have my number retired."*

Tim Lewis looked into the Steelers' clubhouse and saw a sight that seized his heart. Rod Woodson was clearing out his locker because he felt his days with the Steelers were over, officially or not. Lewis, the defensive backfield coach of the Steelers, was losing one of the game's all-time great cornerbacks. Lewis had realized long before that Woodson's chances of coming back for an 11th season with the Steelers were slim to none, but seeing Woodson packing his bags on a Friday afternoon, May 30, made it hit home.

The Steelers and Lewis had already lost the team's two other top cornerbacks, Willie Williams and Deon Figures, in the free agent market, so this would only add to the challenge for the 1997 season.

In 1995, when Lewis was in his first season as an assistant coach on Bill Cowher's staff, Woodson was injured in the season opener and lost for the remainder of the schedule and the playoffs. That didn't appear to be the best way for Lewis to assume a new job in his first pro coaching assignment. Woodson recovered in time to play in Super Bowl XXX. So Lewis also knows the Steelers can win without Woodson. It just makes it much tougher.

"It's a shame his career here had to come to an end over financial considerations," allowed Lewis, "and that there had to be all the barbs and harsh exchanges and media interpretations about his feelings towards the team and fans. It's unfortunate that he's not leaving under the same circumstances as Mario Lemieux did. I realize Rod isn't retiring now, but he should have been retiring some day as a Steeler.

"Rod Woodson is a great football player. There's no doubt in my mind that he will play great football for someone for another couple of years. I wish it could have been with us. He's a great player and a great team leader. We'll miss him."

When Lewis spotted Woodson removing his personal belongings from his dressing stall, he went over and asked, "What are you doing, Rod?"

"It's obvious I'm not going to be back here," Woodson said.

"We're going to miss you," said Lewis. "I wish you luck and hope things turn out well for you."

Woodson was returning to Purdue University, where he had been an All-American two-way star, to conduct a personal workout the next week. About six NFL teams were to send representatives to

Bill Amatucci

check him out. Woodson wanted to show everyone that he, at age 32, still had what it takes to perform at a high level in somebody's defensive secondary. He was, in a sense, putting himself on an auction block.

It had to be another embarrassing episode in his life. Woodson had made $20 million over ten seasons with the Steelers, but wasn't satisfied with the offers they had made him to continue his career in Pittsburgh. Woodson had sniped at Steelers' management for several months, and it left many with a bad taste in their mouths.

Woodson had been in the news in Pittsburgh the previous week over remarks he had made in an article that appeared in the May 26th issue of *Sports Illustrated*. It created a stir in Pittsburgh because he had blasted some sports fans for being racists.

On the night that Lemieux was playing his final game at the Civic Arena, a picture of Woodson was flashed on the overhead screen, and he was booed.

"That didn't surprise me," Woodson was quoted as saying. "I'm very attuned to racial matters, and anytime a black athlete leaves Pittsburgh and comes back he gets booed. It happened to Barry Bonds and Bobby Bonilla. But when white ballplayers come back — players who left for better deals, just like everyone else — they were cheered. I just wish people would be consistent, but that's the way it is in Pittsburgh."

Woodson drew a lot of flak, and a few defenders, in the media most of the week. By week's end, he was telephoning writers and sports talk show hosts and trying to do some damage control. One of the talk show hosts, Rocco Pendola of WTAE Radio — the Steelers' flagship broadcast station — had urged his listeners to boycott Woodson's All-Star Grille near Station Square.

Woodson said his remarks were misconstrued and taken out of context. He apologized if he had offended anyone. He said he knew that if Neil O'Donnell, for instance, were to return to Pittsburgh to play he, too, would be booed.

"It's a shame it had to end here for him that way," said Lewis. "But I know from personal experience, how my own pro career came and went so fast, how these things can come to an abrupt end. It's the nature of the business."

Lewis had been a Pro Bowl cornerback in two of his first three seasons with the Green Bay Packers, but had to quit the game after nearly having his neck broken in the fourth game of the 1986 season.

"But the Steelers and the game of football will go on without Woodson, just like it went on when I couldn't play anymore. It went on without Franco and without O.J. and without Rockne. No matter how great the individual, the game goes on. The game is bigger than any one guy."

Carnell Lake, another Pro Bowl performer, had filled the void at left cornerback when Woodson was sidelined for the 1995 season. Now he would have to fill the void as the leader of the secondary.

"I was just talking to Carnell the other day and telling him how much I really enjoyed coaching our secondary," said Lewis. "I feel like I've made a lot of progress with these guys in getting their attention and respect.

"When they make mistakes, and we make a lot of mistakes, I just have to nod to them and they acknowledge it, and they've already made the correction. There's a mutual respect. Myron Bell couldn't make it to a workout the other day, and he called in advance to let me know he had a pressing personal problem he had to take care of. Two years ago, he wouldn't have done that. And if I asked him where he'd been, he would have been insulted. When Coach Cowher asked me where Myron Bell was this time, I could tell him. I wasn't in the blind. We have all kinds of personalities, from varying backgrounds, but we're all on the same page."

"I remember those who are dear to me."
— Tim Lewis

They say that if defensive backs are to be successful in the National Football League they need to have a short memory. They need to forget their failures and disappointments because even the best of them are going to get burned now and then. They don't come any better than all-time cornerbacks Mel Blount or Rod Woodson, and both of those legendary Steelers have been humbled by fleet, sure-handed receivers.

Tim Lewis was one of the best defensive backs in the NFL during his playing days (1983-86) with the Green Bay Packers before suffering a career-ending neck injury at age 24. Earlier, he had been a standout in the secondary for the University of Pittsburgh on some of the school's greatest football teams.

As the defensive backfield coach for the Pittsburgh Steelers, Lewis lectured his own charges that a short memory would serve them in good stead.

Lewis was consoling Carnell Lake in the Steelers' lobby one day during the 1995 season a few days after Lake had been burned badly playing cornerback. Lake was out there because Woodson was hurt in the season opener, and Lake was asked by Lewis to move up from his strong safety position to fill the void.

Coincidentally, Mel Blount stopped by that day to say hello to some of the front-office people. Blount came over and gave Lake a big hug. "Hey, brother, if you're out on that corner long enough you're going to get burned," Blount told Lake. "Believe me, I know. I got beaten for three touchdowns one day in Green Bay."

"I was there!" Lewis interjected. "I couldn't believe it. Mel Blount . . . you were my hero, too. But I also remember the Steelers won that game."

301

Lewis remembers stuff like that. Future coaches file that sort of thing to use in their teaching lessons. Lewis also has a long memory when it comes to the men who have disappointed him in his life.

One of them is pictured on a poster that is taped on the door of the spartan cubicle occupied by Lewis in the lineup of offices for the assistant coaches on Bill Cowher's staff at the Steelers' complex beneath Three Rivers Stadium.

It's a poster from a Legends series, dominated by a full-length picture of the University of Pittsburgh's head coach, Johnny Majors.

There's a message in black Magic Marker scrawled under the picture of Majors. It reads: "With a little hard work and determination, someday you might become a legend like me."

It's signed by Johnny Majors. At least that's the way it appears. Lewis laughs about it. The message was written by Mike Archer, another assistant coach with the Steelers.

"It's a joke," said Lewis. "Coach Archer knows that Coach Majors and I didn't see eye-to-eye."

Lewis looks at it, shakes his head and smiles sarcastically. "During the two years I served as his assistant at Pitt," allowed Lewis, "Coach Majors treated me badly. He was always on my case; I couldn't do anything right. He told me flat out that I couldn't coach on a college level. I keep that poster up there as a reminder. It drives me."

Lewis was looking forward to his third season — the 1997 season — as the defensive backfield coach for the Steelers. He was confident he could coach on any level. He was only 35, not much older than Woodson and Carnell Lake.

It's not the first time that men he was counting on had left him in the lurch. When I was interviewing him for this book, at one point I asked him about his father.

"My father doesn't belong in a book," said Lewis, sternly. "My father doesn't deserve to be discussed at all. Let's forget my father."

When Lewis looks back to his days in Quakertown, Pennsylvania, he remembers his mother with great affection, his aunts, uncles and cousins; he was surrounded by many relatives where he grew up. He also remembers many of the coaches who have been a positive influence in his life, and helped him get to where he is today. He's especially fond of Jackie Sherrill, Forrest Gregg and Joe Moore.

Sherrill was his coach at Pitt (1979-82), and gave Lewis his first opportunity to coach as a graduate assistant at Texas A&M in 1987 and 1988. Gregg, who had been his coach in Green Bay, hired Lewis to coach the defensive backs at SMU from 1989-92. Moore recruited Lewis to come to Pitt in the first place, and gave him a lot of personal attention during his student days in Oakland. Moore was a surrogate father to Lewis and some of his teammates.

Lewis thought Pitt made a mistake when Walt Harris, who replaced Majors before the 1997 season, didn't take advantage of an opportunity to hire Moore as his offensive line coach. Moore coached so many future pros at Pitt and Notre Dame, and his charges were fiercely loyal. Lewis thought Moore would be a real plus for Pitt.

Lewis loved his tenure as a student and ballplayer at Pitt, and was eager to return when Majors came back for a second stint and was putting together a staff in 1993. Lewis lobbied for a job at his alma mater, and served there for two years, but it was a frustrating period in his life. Things did not go well at Pitt, the team couldn't win, and Majors made it worse with his critical treatment of Lewis.

When Cowher came calling after Dom Capers left his staff to become the head coach of the Carolina Panthers, Lewis jumped at the opportunity to remain in Pittsburgh and coach in the NFL. Dick LeBeau was moved up from defensive backfield coach to defensive coordinator of the Steelers, and Lewis assumed his former responsibility. Lewis learned a lot from LeBeau and Cowher, who had been a defensive coordinator at Kansas City and a defensive backfield coach in Cleveland. Lewis looked to the future, and wanted to be a head coach on the college or pro level.

Asked if coaching the Steelers in the NFL was a dream come true, Lewis responded, "Oh, God, yes. Oh, God, yes. This is a dream come true for me. You set your sights high as a young football player. I've always been a goal-oriented person. I've always been a football player and a good athlete. And every coach I've ever had always talked about and stressed setting goals, setting goals, setting goals.

"I've always been an achiever. I always set goals and tried to achieve them. I played for Bart Starr. I played for Forrest Gregg. I played for Jackie Sherrill. I played for Foge Fazio. I worked for John Majors. Now I'm working for Bill Cowher. I've been around some really big time winners. I've made notes all along."

"There was always some kind of competition."
— Tim Lewis

Quakertown is 50 miles north of Philadelphia. As a youth, Lewis lived on the outskirts of that community in a trailer. There were three trailers on a plot of ground, and they were all occupied by his family and his relatives. "There was my mother, my aunts, my brothers and sisters, and my grandparents," said Lewis. "Whatever success I've had is probably from having a real strong mother, a strong family situation. I had a strong extended family.

"We all lived within a hundred yards of each other. I was the last of the children, the youngest grandchild. There were 14 boys and 13 girls.

"My mother is one of eight children. Her maiden name was Loretta Roberts. They all have lived on the same piece of property.

They all had families. There were 27 grandchildren. I was the youngest.

"Ours was a very athletic family. There were a lot of family get-togethers. We always played some kind of game. It involved softball or volleyball, horseshoes and badminton. It was how our family picnics and reunions went; there was always some kind of competition.

"I have a memory of things that are really dear to me: the love of my family and the respect of my family, and people I've come in contact with whom I really care about. But, on the football field, I kind of like what Jack Nicklaus said about golf: 'the most important play is the next play.' You should draw lessons from your mistakes, but you can't do anything about them. Forget the last play. Get ready for the next play."

Playing football is a family affair for the Lewis clan and their many cousins. One of Tim's older brothers, Will, played pro football with the Seattle Seahawks and Kansas City Chiefs of the NFL, the Denver Gold and Houston Gamblers of the USFL, the Ottawa Roughriders and Montreal Alouettes of the CFL, and then got into coaching. He was the secondary coach at West Virginia University prior to joining the Atlanta Falcons.

When the Steelers played the Falcons in Atlanta during the 1996 season, their mother had a real dilemma.

"We've both been playing football since we were eight years old, and this is the first time we've been on the same field at the same time," Tim told reporters in advance of the contest.

"I'm excited about it. My whole family will be there. My mom said she will wear a Steelers hat, a scarf that has Atlanta on it, a Steelers shirt and slacks that say Atlanta. So she'll be all dressed up and ready for the affair."

An added feature for the family was that Louis Riddick, a cousin of Tim and Will and a former defensive back at Pitt, was also with the Atlanta Falcons.

Another cousin, Rob Riddick, played running back with the Buffalo Bills for eight or nine years. "The Riddicks were children of my mother's sister," explained Lewis.

Another of their cousins, Richie Roberts, played at Widener in nearby Chester, Pennsylvania, with Billy "White Shoes" Johnson, a member of the all-time NFL team as a kick-returner.

"As a Pop Warner football player," said Lewis, "I'd go watch Widener against Muhlenburg or Moravian; it was Division III football at its finest and I got to see Billy 'White Shoes' Johnson play. He was special."

Richie's brother, David Roberts, played for Widener as well, going up against Wittenburg in the Amos Alonzo Stagg Bowl in 1976. He broke his neck playing football. He's always been a big Steelers' fan.

"When I was hired here," recalled Lewis, "my cousin David called me and said, 'I want tickets for the Super Bowl.'"

There was another cousin who played ball for Wayne Hardin at Temple. The list of Lewis relatives who played football goes on and on. Lewis thinks at least eight of his relatives played college ball.

I pressed Lewis for names and more background on his family. That trailer park or family compound sounded like a unique scene.

"My father died when I was 23 or 24," allowed Lewis. "He was not a good father, not worthy of writing about or talking about.

"I learned about my grandparents when I was growing up. My grandfather was a sharecropper from Virginia, picking different crops at different times of the year, like beans and tomatoes from New Jersey to South Carolina. Picking cotton and tobacco in the south. He ran into a fellow named Clymer, and this man offered him a piece of property in Bucks County. That grandfather was William Henry Roberts, my mother's father.

"He and his sons built a home in the middle of the farm when they got to Pennsylvania. They continued to farm it. Most of the property was a farm. He had four sons and four daughters. The daughters moved off and got married and then they brought their husbands back to the land.

"I had an Aunt Pat, an Aunt Myrtle — she was always Aunt 'Toot'; we never called her Myrtle — and an Aunt Anna. And there were four uncles. They were certainly supportive when I was growing up."

When Tim Lewis was a student at Penn Ridge High School, he remembers everybody talking about Kenny Schroy, who once played there and was then a defensive back with the New York Jets (1977-84). "He was the pride of Quakertown," said Lewis.

Lewis would like to have a family of his own someday, but he's taking his time.

Lewis lives in the North Hills. He was married the month before we spoke, on April 29, to Shawn Cassidy of New Orleans, whom he had known for six years. I saw them strolling together at The Shops at Station Square. They were an attractive couple. Tim Lewis was excited about being Tim Lewis.

"That was the best college football team ever assembled."
— Jackie Sherrill

Tim Lewis was a student-athlete at Pitt from 1979 to 1982, a glorious period when Pitt was in the Top Ten every year, and was rated No. 2 in the nation in 1980 and 1981, behind Georgia and Clemson, respectively, and played in a bowl game each of those two years.

His last game at Pitt was a 7-3 loss to SMU in the Cotton Bowl.

SMU's had its "Pony Backfield" of Eric Dickerson and Craig James, both future NFL stars.

The 1980-81 Pitt teams were ranked the 12th best college football team of all-time by *The Sporting News* in 1987.

The Panthers of that period included Hugh Green, Rickey Jackson, Dan Marino, Mark May, Russ Grimm, Randy McMillan, Sal Sunseri, Jimbo Covert, Carlton Williamson, Bill Maas, Bill Fralic, Jo Jo Heath, Greg Meisner, Bill Neill, Benjie Pryor, Lynn "Pappy" Thomas, Bryan Thomas, Jerry Boyarsky and Rick Trocano. During his stay at Pitt, his teammates also included the likes of Sam Clancy, Rob Fada, Rich Kraynak, Dave Puzzuoli, Ron Sams, Julius Dawkins, Jim Sweeney, Chris Doleman, and Tom Flynn. Just reading those names reminds one of how talent-rich Pitt was during that span, and how far they fell soon after that. As a senior, Lewis had a teammate in the defensive secondary named Roger Kingdom, who went on to win two gold medals in the 110-meter high hurdles in the 1986 and 1990 Olympic Games.

"That was the best college football team ever assembled, talent-wise," said Sherrill, who went from Texas A&M to Mississippi State, and was interested in returning to Pitt in 1993, but was nixed by then Chancellor J. Dennis O'Connor in favor of Majors. "They get a lot better when you sit back and look at what they've done. Never, ever, has a team produced that many great players."

Foge Fazio, then the Panthers' defensive coordinator and Sherrill's successor as head coach, reflected, "I have never seen a college defense like that. It was an attacking defense. They shut people down and took the ball away from them."

Green and Jackson were the defensive ends, Meisner, Neill and Boyarsky were on the defensive line in 1980. The following season, the middle three linemen were Puzzuoli, J.C. Pelusi and Maas.

"The huddles were wild," Sunseri said. "We knew what we had. We knew we had the No. 1 defense in the country. We dominated teams. We knew there was not a tackle in the country faster than Meisner. There was nobody from a technique standpoint better than Neill. There was not a better noseguard than Boyarsky. And when you looked outside, my God, there was Hugh Green on one side, and there was Rickey Jackson on the other.

"What I had to do was clog up the middle and bounce people to the outside to the All-Pros."

All five starters on Pitt's defensive line in 1980 went on to become starters as rookies in the NFL. At center linebacker, Sunseri was a first team All-America and at safety was Carlton Williamson, who would start for the Super Bowl champion San Francisco 49ers in 1981.

The offensive line in 1980 included tackles Jimbo Covert and Mark May, who won the Outland Trophy, and guards Emil Boures, Rob Fada, Ron Sams, Paul Dunn and center Russ Grimm.

"I don't know if Pitt or anybody else will ever have that many great athletes at the same time," said Sherrill of his Pitt team in the early 1980s. "We had a great player at every position on the field, offense and defense. We didn't have a weakness in those years."

"You wanna be a Pitt Panther?"
— Joe Moore

Lewis was a running back and defensive back at Penn Ridge High School in Quakertown. So how did he end up at Pitt?

"Joe Moore came to my high school to recruit me," said Lewis. "There's a story as to how he heard about me in the first place.

"There's a football coach named Mike Pettine, Sr., who is the coach at Central Bucks West in Doylestown, Pennsylvania. He has a record something like 350 wins and 35 losses. His team has been rated among the Top 25 teams in the *USA Today* poll.

"He's as much responsible, after God and my mother, to get me where I am today.

"My high school coach was Wayne Helman, and I love him dearly, but he thought I was biting off more than I could chew when I picked Pitt. But Pettine must have had a higher regard for my potential. He told Moore to take a look at the Lewis kid at Quakertown.

"I got letters from as far away as UCLA, but I had a girlfriend in high school and I didn't want to go too far from home.

"Moore was spending time at Central Bucks, along with every recruiter in the country, because of a kid named Kevin Ward. He was the quarterback at Central Bucks. He and Danny Marino were the two top quarterbacks in the 1979 class. Ward went to Arizona. Mike Pettine recommended me to Joe Moore, and told him to go up and take a look at Tim Lewis.

"We were at basketball practice in our gym, and Joe Moore came through the doors. He was wearing one of those (porkpie) hats like Bear Bryant wore. He was smoking a cigarette. He came out on the floor and said, 'Which one of you's Tim Lewis?' Then he spotted me, and said, 'It must be you; you're the only black kid in here. Come on, let's go talk.' He took me upstairs and he looked at me, and said, 'You wanna be a Pitt Panther?' And I said, 'Yeah, I guess so.' And 20 minutes later, I was signing a letter of intent. That's when you could sign a letter of intent. Today, you just make an oral commitment at that time of the year. I did it in 20 minutes."

Lewis remembers that his basketball coach, Denny Robison, was a little surprised to see one of his players leaving practice to go up in the stands.

"He loves to tell people that story," said Lewis.

"One time, a few years back, Coach Robison asked me, 'Whatever happened to that guy?' And I told him, 'He's the offensive line coach at Notre Dame.' "

Lewis said Moore beat out some good competition to get him. "Tom Coughlin was recruiting me for Syracuse," said Lewis. "He's now the head coach at Jacksonville in the NFL."

Lewis said Moore got a lot of great players from southeastern Pa. and nearby environs. Lewis ran off a list that included John Hendrick, Barry Compton, Bill Neal, Chris Doleman, Randy McMillan, Bill Maas, Burt Grossman and Rich Kraynak.

"I made visits to Syracuse, West Virginia, Temple and Pitt. I was supposed to go to Temple, but I didn't go. I wanted to go to Pitt or Penn State all along. Penn State didn't recruit me; I didn't have good enough grades.

"Dick Anderson of Penn State met me in the hallway one day. He told me my transcript wasn't quite good enough for them.

"Joe Moore wanted me; I knew that from the start. He's an all-timer. Joe called me up into his office one day when I was at Pitt. 'Hey, Timmy, come here.' He liked to say something philosophical from time to time. He said, 'If you had your pick, would you rather die or have a friend die?' I said, 'I guess myself.' He said, 'Nah, if your friend dies you lose a friend. If you die, you lose all your friends.'

"Joe often had me to his home in Mt. Lebanon. His wife, Franny, and 'Hawk,' one of his sons, were like family to me. They had a mutt collie called 'Wilt' because he could jump so high. I felt at home there."

Lewis said he might have come back to Pitt earlier than he did as an assistant coach.

"Mike Gottfried had one of his assistants, Frank DeLorenzo, call me," said Lewis. "DeLorenzo said they might have an opening for a special teams coach. I had an interview with the whole staff. They had me at the blackboard. I didn't know anything about special teams. I had never paid any attention to that. They were trying to recruit my cousin, Louis Riddick. That was their real interest.

"Gottfried asked me to talk to the team before the game with Notre Dame at Pitt Stadium. I did. We won that game, 10-9.

"It was close to the signing date. I had also interviewed with Mellon Bank because I wasn't sure I could get a coaching job. No one at Pitt ever got back to me. Then they called and said I might be a graduate assistant candidate.

"Then Ron Dickerson called me from Penn State. He had been an assistant to Sherrill when I was at Pitt and he had been my backfield coach. 'If Louis comes here, Joe would like to talk to you about a possible job,' Dickerson said.

"I spoke to Coach Sherrill. Jackie wasn't after Riddick. Sherrill asked me, 'What do you plan to do with the rest of your life?' I told him I wanted to be a football coach. So he brought me to Texas A&M as a graduate assistant for the 1987 and 1988 seasons. Jackie truly cared about me. Jackie was the only one from my Pitt days who called me in the hospital in Green Bay after I got hurt."

That reminded me of a personal experience I had with Sherrill. I was covering the Pittsburgh Steelers for *The Pittsburgh Press*, and covered spring football at Pitt for a week or so in 1980.

During spring practice, my younger daughter, Rebecca, had to undergo surgery to remove a bone chip from her neck at Children's Hospital on the Pitt campus. Sherrill sent several of his assistants and players to visit Rebecca, and they brought her a gift, a miniature stuffed bear that was wearing a Pitt jersey.

By the way, Gottfried's staff successfully recruited Louis Riddick and he became a two-time Academic All-America at Pitt in 1989 and 1990.

"This is a sad day for us as it is for Tim."
— Forrest Gregg

Lewis will never forget the night of September 22, 1986. Lewis got hurt on a nationally-televised Monday Night Football Game, playing against Mike Ditka's Chicago Bears team.

Lewis had been the Packers' No. 1 draft choice out of Pitt in 1983. He had played in the Pro Bowl twice in the previous three seasons, and was just coming into his own as a pro cornerback. He had a club record 99-yard interception return in 1984 against the Los Angeles Rams to his credit.

It was the final play of the third quarter during the third game of the season when everything ended for Lewis as far as playing in the NFL.

Willie Gault, a swift wide receiver for the Chicago Bears, snared a short pass and immediately collided with Lewis head-on as both players fell to the Lambeau Field turf upon impact. Gault walked away from the collision, while Lewis lay motionless on the ground.

What had begun as a loud, boisterous applause for the big hit Lewis administered on Gault quickly gave way to a concerned hush as Lewis lay there minutes after he'd made the tackle.

"He caught the ball and ducked, and I came up and tried to get lower than he was," recalled Lewis. "We crunched and it pushed my chin down. You just try to bring him down any way you can, and that's what I was doing."

Lewis had suffered a similar stunning injury two years earlier during an intrasquad scrimmage at training camp, but he knew this was far more serious after 15 minutes passed and he still lay there motionless. There was a fear that he was paralyzed by the hit.

The game was held up while a national audience looked on, wondering whether Lewis was ever going to be able to get up. "I still couldn't find my arms and legs," said Lewis. "So it made me more nervous."

Finally, Lewis was lifted onto a stretcher and wheeled into the Packers locker room for further assessment.

"I was out there for 15 or 20 minutes on national TV," said Lewis. "They shoved that board under my back, cut off the top of my jersey and put those foam pads against the sides of my head to stabilize my head. It was scary stuff."

Eventually, Lewis began to experience some tingling in his arms and legs and slowly began to move again.

Days later, it was discovered that the cornerback had an abnormally narrow spinal cord canal and another bad hit could result in his head snapping back and that could paralyze him forever. The abnormality in his neck ultimately forced Lewis into retirement.

Forrest Gregg, Green Bay's head coach at the time, was saddened by Lewis' injury and retirement. "This is a sad day for us as it is for Tim," said Gregg. "I consider him one of the top football players on this team, and he will be missed by this entire football team."

Lewis said he received about 700 letters during his hospital stay. "For a while, I was completely numb," he said. "I've never been more scared." It hurt for Lewis to listen to the doctors who told him his days as a football player were behind him. He loved playing football, and now they were telling him it was over. It was hard to accept.

"It had happened before, and I was able to play again," recalled Lewis. "So, naturally, I thought that would be the case again. The trauma of being forced to retire was eased by the fact I got into coaching the way I did, but it still wasn't easy.

"It's a love affair, with the conditioning, with the media, with the fans, with the money, with the aggression," Lewis went on. "These guys are aggressive guys by nature, and when you play a sport that allows you to express yourself physically . . . all that, plus there was the fact that I had been doing it since I was 8 years old and all my heroes were football players. When I was a little kid, I wanted to be a football player. I wanted to be Jim Brown. My goal was to get to the Hall of Fame and have my number retired. That will never happen."

Some found a silver lining behind the dark cloud that Lewis and others saw in the sky.

"He should consider himself lucky," a doctor said after the incident. "Had the blow been a little more intense, he conceivably could have received damage to his vertebrae which could have resulted in varying degrees of permanent paralysis."

Lewis conceded that he was lucky. "I've got my arms and I can still move. I think I cherish that more than the dollars and cents that can be made playing professional football."

Author John Wideman on his father:
"He dwelt out there, elsewhere, wherever, and maybe that was the best place for him to remain."

310

"Jackie Sherrill is the father I never had."
— Tim Lewis

Jackie Sherrill had more success than any coach in Pitt football history. He was 9-2-1 in 1977, his first year as successor to Majors following the national championship season. He was 8-4 the following year. Then his teams went 11-1 for three straight seasons against rather demanding schedules.

Yet he departed Pitt on a negative note, and he has never been as heralded as Pop Warner, Jock Sutherland or Johnny Majors among Pitt coaches. He has made several attempts to return, but his sullied reputation always was a stumbling block.

Penn State's Joe Paterno once said he didn't want to retire and leave the world of college football to the Barry Switzers and Jackie Sherrills of the world. That stung.

Sherrill has been successful despite his harsh critics. I asked Lewis why he thought Sherrill was so successful.

"Because he cares," said Lewis. "He's a great recruiter. Very demanding. He cares about his players and that gets across to his players. I love Jackie Sherrill.

"I've gotten into conversations where Coach Sherrill's name has come up, at coaches conventions. There are thousands of high school and college coaches talking in the lobbies. I just let people know up front that I don't want to hear anything negative about Jackie Sherrill.

"During my time at Texas A&M, someone might ask me, 'Where are you now?' And I'd say, 'I'm with Jackie Sherrill.' They'd come back, 'That so-and-so.' And I'd say, 'Uh, uh, hold on. I played for and coached for him. You can't put down Jackie Sherrill to me.'

"He made it fun for the players. He makes you want to go out and practice. He makes it competitive. Gives you just enough fuel to start a fire, but doesn't let it get inflamed. He makes you want to play for your school, your colors, your family.

"He's smart. He challenges you. He'd look you in the eye and say, 'You don't want to win.' You'd say, 'Yes, I do.' And he knew when to ease up and put his arm around you.

"One day in practice, I closed on a pass and should have intercepted it, and I dropped it. Ron Dickerson got all over me. Sherrill started blowing his whistle and he got between me and Dickerson. He told Dickerson, 'Hey, don't tell me you never made a mistake, Ron, or that you never missed a ball in practice! Give him a break! He dropped a pass! It's not the end of the world!'

"I remember that. I'm not glad he jumped on Ron Dickerson. I love him, too, but I remember that he stood up for me when I made a mistake."

Lewis laughed when he considered another Sherrill-Lewis episode during his days at Pitt.

"We were in summer camp at Edinboro," said Lewis. "I didn't stay with a receiver on the other side of the field away from the ball. He was up in the tower. We were in a seven-on-seven pass drill. I didn't know what I was supposed to do. He blew the whistle up on the tower and he started hollering my way. 'Tim Lewis, you don't want to play. You don't want to win a national championship. You've got to run to the ball.' I started hollering back, 'Yes, I do! Yes, I do!' It was like something in a movie."

Lewis knows by now that coaches come in different shapes and sizes and mindsets.

"At Green Bay, I played for Bart Starr and I played for Forrest Gregg, and they were at complete opposite ends as far as their demeanor and approach.

"I played for and coached for Coach Sherrill and I coached for Coach Majors. They will always be 'Coach' to me."

Even though they had parted on bad terms, at least the way Lewis views it, he recognizes that Majors must have been great in his heyday. I asked him why he thought Majors had been so successful, up until his last stint at Pitt.

"He challenges his assistants and his players all the time," said Lewis, even though that was one of the things that put him off about Majors when it got too personal. "He has the ability to squeeze the ability out of everyone he comes in contact with. From the secretaries and support people, across the board. He'll demand the best of you, and if he doesn't think you're giving it to him, you won't stay around very long. He's done it so long. He has a formula and he sticks by it.

"Johnny will look you in the eye. Gottfried wouldn't look you in the eye. When he was talking to me, he was scribbling something on his desk. If I stopped talking, he'd look up, and say, 'Keep talking. I'm listening.'

"I still stutter when I talk to Coach Sherrill on the phone. I'm still intimidated by him. Jackie Sherrill is the father I never had. If I were going to get married, I'd call Coach Sherrill and my mom. If I wanted financial advice, I'd call Coach Sherrill.

"Coach Gregg and I are probably as close or closer than Coach Sherrill myself. I respect him like a father. If I called him, he'd take the call or get back to me in a day. I'd call Coach Gregg right now if I needed to know something.

"He's very demanding. Intimidating. Probably more because of his size. I've never been around anybody in football I didn't like."

I asked Lewis for his opinion of Foge Fazio, who was the defensive coordinator during Tim's days at Pitt, and succeeded Sherrill as the head coach of the Panthers.

"Foge has matured since he's been at Notre Dame and in the NFL," said Lewis. "He'd be a great head coach today.

"I played for Foge as a senior when we lost the Cotton Bowl game to SMU. We had a great team that year and a lot of people think we underachieved. Some blame Foge for that. I regard Foge as one of my good friends in the league."

Tim Lewis is reunited at Montour Heights Country Club with former Pitt coach Foge Fazio who's looking more like singer Tony Bennett every day, at the 16th annual Golf Tournament for Autistic Children by which Fazio and Myron Cope have raised over $500,000. Fazio is now defensive coordinator for the Minnesota Vikings

Jim O'Brien

Coach Jackie Sherrill and Lewis in their Pitt days in Oakland

Coach Joe Moore

The eyes of Lewis light up when anyone mentions Joe Moore. "Joe Moore remains an all-time favorite of mine," said Lewis.

"I went up to Erie a few years ago, where he coached after he left Upper St. Clair, and before he came to Pitt. Joe's still a legend in Erie. He recruited Mark Stepnoski out of Erie Cathedral. Like so many outstanding offensive linemen, Stepnoski wanted to play for Joe Moore. So many great high school linemen came to Pitt, and then Notre Dame, because they knew Joe had a great track record of sending linemen to the pros.

"I went with Alex Kramer (in 1993) when Moore was inducted into the western chapter of the Pennsylvania Sports Hall of Fame. Of all the coaches at Pitt, if you were to ask the players, 'Which of all the assistant coaches do you remember best?' it would be him or Foge. The one that stands out is Joe Moore.

"Off the field, he was like your brother. Just one of the guys. On the field, he was strictly business. He demanded respect. When you saw him work and knew his track record, you knew he was one of the best."

I mentioned Dino Folino, who had been a defensive backfield coach under Fazio at Pitt when I was working there (1983-87) as assistant athletic director for sports information, and Folino later held the same job with George Perles at Michigan State.

"I loved Dino very much," said Lewis. "Ron Dickerson was my position coach and Dino was a grad assistant during my days at Pitt. Dino Folino . . . I love him. He's more than a coach. He's your friend.

"I recommended him to Majors as my replacement. When I told Majors about the possibility of me coming here (to the Steelers), he asked me to think about a replacement. 'If you're going to make a minority hiring, I'd like you to take a look at my brother, Will,' I told Majors. My brother was at Maine at the time. He ended up with West Virginia. 'If you're not going to hire a person who is a minority, then I'd recommend Dino Folino. He's with your friend, George Perles.' Johnny and George are the best of friends. He'd be on the phone with Perles two or three times a week. They ran those Duffy Daugherty Coach of the Year Clinics as partners.

"The creases on Johnny's face turn white — the rest of his face is red — laughing when he talks to George on the telephone."

I called Majors myself to recommend Folino as a defensive backfield coach after Lewis left for the Steelers. "I've already gotten several calls on his behalf," said Majors. "I have to hire a black coach, so I won't be able to hire Dino." I was surprised when Majors told me that.

Majors interviewed Will Lewis, then Teryl Austin, a former Pitt player from Sharon who was serving as an assistant at Wake Forest University. Majors ended up hiring Tony Pierce, who had been the defensive coordinator at Delaware State.

Lewis was concerned about how he would fit in with the Steelers. His boss, Cowher, had been a defensive backfield coach and a defensive coordinator in the NFL, and would be closely scrutinizing what he was doing. Dick LeBeau, the defensive coordinator, had been around the league a long time, as a player and coach, but he couldn't have asked for a better tutor.

My friend Bill Priatko could have assured Lewis that he was going into the best possible situation. Priatko, who played football for Pitt and the Steelers in the '50s, and roots for Pitt alumni like Lewis, had the highest praise to offer about LeBeau, whom he had known since they both went to training camp with the Cleveland Browns in 1959.

"Football and all that it stands for reveals the qualities in men that very few endeavors in life can equal," said Priatko. "You never forget the associations as teammates and their qualities during those times and the ensuing years. Dick LeBeau, as a football player, coach and man, is a pure example of a 'man's man.' Tough, dedicated, intelligent, loyal and a first-class human being."

Lewis introduced himself to his charges, and did his best to ease his way in, without turning off anyone.

"I approached it very carefully," allowed Lewis. "You have to find out what each of your players is like, and learn how to fit in.

"There are things that are more important than x's and o's. You have to be careful not to come on like you have all the answers. Hey, the game will go on with or without you.

"The first thing I had to do was learn the defense myself, before I could teach it to anyone else. I can still demonstrate what I'm talking about, and I think I look like I know how to do it.

"A lot of them don't remember that I played. I think I still look enough like a ballplayer that they can see I've been through this, and I've seen what they've seen. I've covered some of the older receivers round the league.

"Because I was in the NFL, I might be able to make that transition easier. I've gone up against some of the best: James Lofton, Steve Largent, Anthony Carter, Irving Fryar, Cliff Branch and Wesley Walker. I'm not that far away from my playing days not to be able to relate to what they're thinking."

Soon after he was hired by the Steelers, Lewis sat down with Rod Woodson to learn a little bit about him as a person. "One of the things Rod told me was that he didn't need to be coached every play," said Lewis. "He sees himself as an intelligent player, and he knows when he makes a mistake, and he also knows how to correct it. And I really have no problem with that, because that's how I am, too."

Carnell Lake, one of the classiest individuals ever to suit up in a Steelers' uniform, is a fan of Tim Lewis.

"Tim is very easy to work with," said Lake, when I spoke to him on May 28, 1997, when he addressed the 27th Annual YMCA Scholar Athlete Dinner at the Hilton. "He has a great personality, and he knows what he's talking about. He's able to get his points across with all of the defensive backs, and that's not easy.

"It's been a blessing to play here and have coaches like Dom Capers, Dick LeBeau and Tim Lewis looking after me. They're all tremendous coaches. Tim is a perfect suit for my personality. Usually, I have an idea of what I've done wrong on the field. I don't need to be reminded of it. I don't need a coach chewing me out in front of the other players. I appreciate his approach. Defensive backs are the first to know when they've made a mistake."

Bill Amatucci

Tim Lewis learned a lot from Dick LeBeau, Steelers' defensive coordinator, during Tim's first two years as defensive backfield coach.

Gains and losses
Ray, Mossie, Jackie and Big Joey

"They were part of that life,
which is no more."
— Beano Cook

Pittsburgh lost four of its biggest boosters and sports enthusiasts in a two month span during the gray winter that took us from 1996 to 1997. They were Ray Mansfield, Jackie Powell, Mossie Murphy and Joey Diven. They were the stuff of Pittsburgh and books, and I'll miss writing about them.

Everyone who cared about sports in Pittsburgh will miss these guys, real Pittsburgh characters. I'll miss talking to them, interviewing them, arguing with them, getting them to share their stories. They never needed to be nudged much to share their stories. The Pittsburgh sports scene will be poorer for their loss. If they're together somewhere in heaven, we know they're not resting in peace.

They were all larger-than-life Runyonesque characters, at once charming, difficult, enchanting, disarming, good-humored, argumentative, opinionated, bombastic figures who were pillars of the Pittsburgh fun and games community. They shared a love of family and Pittsburgh. They were always boasting about Pittsburgh, especially their particular neighborhood, and its sports teams.

They truly cared about the Steelers, the Pirates, the Penguins, Pitt and Duquesne and Notre Dame — Diven and Murphy thought the Fighting Irish were a Pittsburgh institution as well — and sandlot sports. Diven and Murphy were irascible Irishmen, given to the wearing of the green, and shared a passion for Art Rooney and President John F. Kennedy. Wherever you traveled in Pittsburgh you were likely to bump into these guys. They were like pigeons; they were everywhere. They were men about town, ubiquitous. They were America's guests.

All of them first came to my attention when I was in college, at the University of Pittsburgh, or shortly thereafter. And they held my attention throughout my adult life. They demanded your attention. They'd grab your arm or turn you around to make sure you were listening to them. So they were part of my growing-up process and now they're gone. There is a void.

They were all story-tellers. Any writer worth his or her salt would love these guys, these gremlins, these giants, these often stormy but always soft-hearted hero-worshippers.

"I'm just a sentimental fool," Mansfield said when we spoke at his home for an earlier book. "My dad used to tell us stories when we didn't have a TV. That was our entertainment when I was a kid."

317

Beano Cook introduced me to some of these people. Cook, most recently an ESPN sports commentator, was the sports information director at Pitt in the early '60s, and quite a character himself. I started out writing hometown stories on Pitt athletes at his behest, and we ended up my senior year starting *Pittsburgh Weekly Sports,* an irreverent sports tabloid that got us both into a lot of scrapes.

"These guys form a mosaic of what Pittsburgh and sports used to be all about," commented Cook a few days after the funerals of Murphy and Diven. "They were people who grew up during The Great Depression and knew about World War II, two events that dominated the thinking of their boyhood. They remember when Pittsburgh had three movie theatres in every neighborhood, when each community had its own ethnic identity, when people gathered at neighborhood bars and playgrounds and churches. They were part of that life, which is no more. You don't have that anymore.

"I remember Frank Carver, my boss at Pitt, telling me that you know you're getting old when you go to more funerals than weddings. We're there now. I'm 65, but I'm in no hurry to have people swapping stories about me."

Mansfield was the only one who didn't grow up in Pittsburgh. He came here from Philadelphia in 1964, following his rookie year in the National Football League, which was spent with the Eagles. He played 13 seasons with the Steelers, including the first two Super Bowl-winning seasons. He and his buddies, Andy Russell and Rocky Bleier, were among the few who survived the difficult transition from the woeful Steelers of Bill Austin to the glory days of Chuck Noll. Mansfield remained in Pittsburgh after his playing days and became one of us. He became a successful businessman and a promoter of Steelers' reunions and organized many events that raised funds for charity purposes.

Mansfield was full of fun and full of himself and, like most of the above, was full of something else, as all story-tellers are to a degree. He was a memorable sports figure and will be missed.

Jackie Powell was the goal judge at pro hockey games in Pittsburgh from the Hornets to the Penguins, from Duquesne Gardens to the Civic Arena. For 55 years, from 1936 to 1991, he determined whether or not the puck was in the net. Powell saw more hockey up close in Pittsburgh than any other person in the history of the sport. Who could tell you more inside stories about hockey in Pittsburgh?

He was also a caddy for many years for Jack Sell, a sportswriter for the *Pittsburgh Post-Gazette* who grew up with and was a life-long friend of Steelers owner Art Rooney. Powell accompanied Sell to every sports event Sell covered in Pittsburgh, helping him any way he could to meet the often fierce deadlines of an a.m. newspaper.

As a young man fresh out of Schenley High School, he was helping Sell cover a game between the Steelers and Chicago Bears at Forbes Field. At halftime, Sell dispatched Powell to go to the Bears' locker room to check on the physical condition of Bears' star running back Bronco Nagurski, who had gotten hurt and hobbled off the field.

Powell knocked on the door of the visiting locker room. The door was opened and Powell found himself under the glare of George Halas, the storied owner and coach of the Bears.

"What do you want, Kid?" Halas asked him.

"I'm here for Jack Sell, the sportswriter," said Powell. "How's Bronco? Is he going to play in the second half?"

"Go over there and ask him yourself," Halas shot back, pointing out Nagurski who was sitting in front of a steel locker in the middle of the clubhouse. That sort of thing hasn't happened in pro football in a long time. It was a more innocent era in pro sports.

I was a student sportswriter at Pitt when I first met Powell and Sell, since Sell covered college basketball games in addition to being the Steelers' beatman. After Sell retired and died, Powell still appeared in the press box at Steelers' games regularly. I last saw him at the Steelers' final home game of the 1996 season, a defeat by the San Francisco 49ers, on December 15. I spotted him earlier in the game and went to see him late in the game to exchange greetings, to give him a hug for the holidays. I was told he wasn't feeling well and went home early. He died a few days later.

The visitation was held at McCabe Brothers Funeral Home on Penn Avenue in Bloomfield. A mass was celebrated in his honor at St. Augustine Church in Lawrenceville, just down the street from his home. His wife Fran put Jackie's trademark fedora hat and a copy of my book, *Penguin Profiles*, on display in the casket. The book was opened to the page where the chapter on Jackie appeared.

"I wore a hat even when I had hair," Powell explained in an interview for the Penguins' book. "It was always cold in those hockey rinks, and there was always a draft coming through the tunnel directly behind me at the Civic Arena and at Duquesne Gardens."

Maurice "Mossie" Murphy also lived in Lawrenceville as a young man and graduated from Central Catholic High School and Duquesne University. He was a cheerleader as a student at Duquesne, and loved the campus so much he was there for an extended stay. "The students had a cheer when I was there," said Walt Becker, a classmate of Murphy's. "It went like this: 'Two, four, six, eight . . . when is Mossie going to grad-u-ate?' "

Murphy remained a Duquesne cheerleader the rest of his life. I remember him getting out of his seat at Pitt-Duquesne basketball games at the Pitt Field House and rallying the Duquesne students and fans, exhorting them to root for the Dukes. He made noises like a choo-choo train to get them rolling: "Shoo shoo, rah, rah." He was a great show. Later in life, he learned to love and respect Pitt as well. As Murphy matured, he loved everything about Pittsburgh. He even started a short-lived cheerleading squad for the Steelers in the '60s. He got into the political arena, the biggest sport of them all, and became Pittsburgh's answer to Pierre Salinger.

He got into a spat with Commissioner Robert Cranmer in the parking lot outside WTAE's studios, and was dropped as the station's political commentator. It broke his heart. He loved that role. Some felt he was in a funk over that until he died. He had an intestinal aneurism rupture while he was playing golf at Hilton Head, and fell on the course and bled to death. He was 63 when he died, the same age as my dad when he died. I thought my dad was old; now I know better. Governor Tom Ridge and Mayor Tom Murphy were among those present at his funeral service. Dr. John Murray, the president of Duquesne University, was one of his eulogizers.

I first met Mossie up close at Frankie Gustine's Restaurant in Oakland. After basketball games at the Field House, the coaches of both teams, the sportswriters, and some insiders like Radio Rich, Roundball Liz, Dave Miller and Bucky Pope, who kept the stats and worked at the press table, would gather to gab about the game and world affairs over shots and beers in the backroom of Gustine's. Mossie's wife, Carol, also came to Gustine's on occasion to keep him in check. Murphy would often be there, and he was never a wallflower. He was always raising hell about something. Mossie was always boisterous and loud and lots of fun, unless you disagreed with his point of view. Mossie was Irish, but he waved his hands like an Italian when he talked. Mossie never had a conversation in his life; it was always a debate. He could be gruff, but he had a heart of gold.

Today's sportswriters and media folks wouldn't believe that coaches would actually socialize with them after a sports event. Everything was off the record at those gabfests, but you got to know what was really going on, the coaches came to know you better, and a trust factor was developed. You were better informed and closer to the game and its participants than is possible today, and you knew — or at least you came to know as you got a little older — what to write and what not to write. It was a great education. Coaches like Dudey Moore, Red Manning, Bob Timmons, Carl Peterson, Doggie Julian, Press Maravich, Moe Becker, Paul Birch, Mel Cratsley, Moe Fassinger, Gus Krop and Jerry Conboy (and his wife, Pat) would be there. Coaches weren't as paranoid about the press in those days. When I got to New York in 1969 to work, I was told there used to be similar post-game gatherings at Mama Leone's and Toots Shor's.

"TV and the big money ended all that," commented Beano Cook. "Everybody became a businessman. College sports has become a big business; it wasn't then."

There was also a weekly press conference sponsored by the writers themselves at Gustine's where the coaches and sports information directors from Pitt, Duquesne, Carnegie Tech (now Carnegie Mellon) and later Point Park and Robert Morris would come to discuss their respective team's prospects and everybody paid their own way.

When I was 19 and 20, and not even of legal age to drink, I also frequented a bar-restaurant in Whitehall called Dante's, owned and operated by barkeep Dante Sartorio, where I could keep company with

Mossie Murphy

Mossie was a standup fellow through the years at Duquesne University basketball games, amusing his loyal wife Carol, a constant companion.

"He's an exceedingly noisy and combative fellow."
— Myron Cope
Sports Illustrated
Jan. 28, 1963

As Duquesne student, John Belushi-look alike irked basketball coach Red Manning who screamed, "Get that fat boy outta here!" Murphy matured to acceptable level and was inducted into Duquesne's Sports Hall of Fame by athletic director Brian Colleary.

Photos from the Murphy family album

sportswriters and sportscasters such as Myron Cope, Ed Conway, Tom Bender, Bob Drum and Pat Livingston, who were keeping company with wonderful Steelers such as Bobby Layne, Ernie Stautner, Gary Ballman, Tom "The Bomb" Tracy, Lou Cordileone, etc., and local characters like "Funny Sam." Later on, Bill Nelsen and Jim Bradshaw would drink and kibitz with local media as well. That sort of intermingling hasn't happened in this town, or anywhere else in this country, since that era.

Layne could be difficult, and I didn't care for his company. To me, he was a bully.

Cope once criticized me for not wanting to join him in the backroom with Layne when we were together one night at Dante's.

"He's the Leif Ericson of football!" exclaimed Cope.

"Then you go drink with Leif Ericson," I responded. "I'm staying out here."

One of the writers I came to know and love as a student at Pitt was Ernest Hemingway. I especially enjoyed a book he wrote called *A Moveable Feast*, about his days as a young writer in Paris.

Back in 1950, Hemingway told a friend, "If you are lucky enough to have lived in Paris as a young man, then wherever you go the rest of your life, it stays with you, for Paris is a moveable feast."

I feel the same way about Pittsburgh.

"Get the hell outta here!"
—Joey Diven

The Freyvogel Funeral Home and McCabe Brothers Funeral Home are both impressive white-white mansions in Shadyside, the former on Centre Avenue and the latter on Walnut Street, separated by about ten blocks.

They are rivals of sorts. When I asked one of the attendants at Freyvogel's how I could get from there to McCabe's, he kidded me by saying, "There's no way to get there from here."

I recalled attending services at Freyvogel's for Frankie Gustine, Pete Dimperio and Art McKennan, three other popular sports figures. Myron Cope came into the funeral home just as I was leaving the day Diven was being viewed. Cope used to live nearby in an apartment house when he was a young single sportswriter.

I thought it was a shame that Cope was no longer doing his sports talk show on WTAE Radio because he was one of the few who could properly talk about Diven and Murphy on the air. He knew their stories and had written and related them as well.

I checked on the authenticity of two stories when I saw certain people present at the Diven funeral.

Jack Rafferty was among those who paid their respects. He and two of his brothers, Carey and Mike, were all there. Jack Rafferty has been a career ruffian, with a bark worse than his bite. He was well

Stan "The Man" Musial of Donora and Art Rooney are joined by Joey Diven at sports dinner in Pittsburgh. The Chief always called Joey "Big Shot."

Joey Diven

"I though he was an enter-taining fellow, friendly and a good story-teller."
— Roy McHugh
Pittsburgh Press

Two Oakland guys, Danny Marino and Joey Diven. "Danny turned me into a Pitt fan," said Diven, always a Notre Dame-diehard. Joey's wife, Barbara, loves this picture.

Joey turned up everywhere. Here he's seen with long sideburns (at lower left, in front of Rocky Bleier and behind Art Rooney) in Steelers locker room as team prays after winning Super Bowl IX at Tulane Stadium on January 12, 1975. The Steelers defeated the Minnesota Vikings, 16-6, for the first of their four Super Bowl championships.

into his 60s, but he still spoke out of the corner of his mouth like he was menacing you.

"Is that story true about you and Joey Diven?" I asked.

"What story?" Rafferty snapped back.

"The one about you and the Irish Club?"

"Sorta," said Rafferty.

"What do you mean 'sorta'? Is it or isn't it true?"

"Well, I remember there were 32 steps and they were all hard," replied Rafferty, "if that's the one you mean."

The story goes like this: When he was a young man, with a reputation as a local tough guy, Joey Diven was employed as the doorman or bouncer at the Irish Club in Oakland. It was on the second floor of a building on Oakland Avenue, just off Forbes Avenue, above Pete Coyne's Bar, which had a big green shamrock in its sign. It wasn't fancy. It was just a place to drink on Sunday and after-hours when Coyne's and the Oakland Cafe were closed.

The steps leading up to the Irish Club were steeper than the Monongahela Incline. They were bare hardwood.

Rafferty rapped on the door one evening, seeking entrance to the Irish Club. Opening a peephole, as in the days of speakeasies, Diven demanded, "Show me your membership card!"

"I don't have one," replied Rafferty. "C'mon, Joey, let me in. I'm Irish!"

"Get the hell outta here!" cried Diven.

Rafferty refused to leave and gave some lip to Diven, which wasn't a good idea. After all, Diven was 6-5, 285 in his heyday. Rafferty was about 5-10, 180 back then. Diven opened the door, seized Rafferty, and threw him headfirst down the stairs. Rafferty later related that he counted 32 steps as he hit each of them on the way down to the sidewalk entrance.

Undaunted, Rafferty went back up the stairs. Rafferty rapped on the door once more, even harder than the first time. Diven opened the peephole again and couldn't believe what met his eyes. He told Rafferty to leave, that he was trying his patience, that he was going to hurt him. Rafferty roared in protest. "C'mon, Joey, I'm Irish!" Diven opened the door, grabbed Rafferty and tossed him down the stairs a second time.

Rafferty rose from the floor once more, like a boxer who wouldn't quit until he was counted out, and went back up the stairs. Diven cracked the peephole. "Not again," said Diven.

This time Diven opened the door and stepped back and told Rafferty to come in, saying in a resigned manner, "You've gotta be Irish. Go ahead in."

At Freyvogel's, I also saw Andy "Kid" DePaul, a former pro boxer in Pittsburgh, and a man long associated with the boxing game. He was now the Pennsylvania State Boxing Commissioner, and was being congratulated on being featured in a nostalgic feature story in the *Post-Gazette* the day before.

DePaul had spent a lot of time in Lawrenceville in his lifetime, and he confirmed that a story I had heard about the late Fritzi Zivic from that community was, indeed, true. Zivic, a former world champion, was retired, but some of his younger brothers were still boxing. One of them, I forget which, had a boxing date scheduled somewhere in Ohio with an up-and-coming young fighter. But this Zivic broke his hand a few days before the fight and was unable to box.

But the thrifty Zivic family didn't want to forgo a payday, so Fritzi, even though retired several years, agreed to represent the clan in the fight. When Fritzi showed up in fight gear in the dressing room at the fight site, the manager of the young prospect cried foul.

And Fritzi hadn't even stuck his thumb into the young fighter's eyes yet, as he was wont to do, or hit the kid with a rabbit punch, which he was also wont to do. In short, Fritzi was known as a dirty fighter. "My kid isn't fighting Fritzi Zivic," the manager protested. "He's got a future ahead of him and I don't want him destroyed at this stage of his development."

So they kept talking and negotiating and, finally, Fritzi agreed to carry the young fighter for at least four rounds of a scheduled six-rounder. Fritzi couldn't help himself. He slapped the young fighter around at will; he had too much savvy and skill for the kid. But whenever the kid caught a punch flush on the cheek and his knees buckled, Fritzi would grab him and hold him up, or lean him against the ropes.

As the bell rang to begin the fourth round, Fritzi came out to mid-ring and extended his gloves, and the young fighter, instinctively, shoved both of his gloves out to touch Fritzi's gloves.

Then the young pugilist caught himself. "Hey, this isn't the final round," he shouted as he backed away.

"Yes, it is," offered Fritzi with a mischievous smile. "Believe me, Kid, this is the final round."

Two Lawrenceville loyalists: Mossie Murphy and Jackie Powell both were proud of their Pittsburgh heritage and loved all the local sports teams.

Jim Sweeney
A Pittsburgh guy

"It's a dream come true."

No one on the Steelers was looking forward to the team's trip to Ireland in July of 1997 as much as Jim Sweeney. He had never been to Ireland, but he was a posterboy Irishman, and it would be a special thrill to visit the land of his ancestors.

It would be great to line up in the Steelers black and gold uniform and play football on the ol' sod of the Emerald Isle from whence his ancestors came, even if it was just an exhibition game.

His full name is James Joseph Roger Charles Sweeney. His pale, beefy mug is unmistakably Irish, and he has the deepest voice, if not a brogue. He had gone to St. Catherine's Catholic Grade School in Beechview and Seton-LaSalle High School in Mt. Lebanon, and he had been an altar boy. Faith and begorrah! In Ireland, he'd be Seamus Sweeney. Sounds better, doesn't it?

"My family is from County Cork," said Sweeney, who would turn 35 in August, and was the oldest of the Steelers. His wife, Heather Cumpston, had relatives in Ireland on her mother's side, the Kealtys. Heather, 26, had given birth on May 16 to their second child and first son, a 7 pound 7 ounce baby they named Liam, which is Gaelic for William. "Liam means well-balanced, protector," said Sweeney. Their three-year-old daughter was named Shannon. Get the picture?

Jim said he and Heather had a book with Irish names called *Beyond Shannon and Sean*, which they read to find the perfect names for their children.

Going to Ireland would be yet another perk for Jim Sweeney for signing with the Steelers as a free agent during the team's summer training camp of 1996. It's a shame he didn't join them a year earlier so he could have gone to Super Bowl XXX with them.

When Sweeney was just starting to play football back in the 1970s, the Steelers were always playing in the Super Bowl, or so it seemed anyhow. Sweeney grew up idolizing the likes of Ray Mansfield, Jim Clack and, most of all, Mike Webster. They were all centers for the Steelers. He wanted to grow up to be just like them. His dressing stall in the Steelers' clubhouse, coincidentally, was once occupied by Webster. Sweeney smiles brightly when he tells you that tidbit. He could feel his presence.

For sure, Sweeney can probably still feel the presence of Art Rooney, the founder of the Steelers, who died in August of 1988. Rooney used to like to go around the Steelers' clubhouse and shake hands with his players, exchange pleasantries and make them feel at home. He'd grown up on the North Side, in the First Ward, in Old Allegheny, and never left.

With daughter Shannon

With Justin Strzelczyk on sideline

With hero Mike Webster in 1988

As freshman at Pitt in 1980 with
Coach Jackie Sherrill

Jim Sweeney

Beechview is located at the southern tip of Pittsburgh's city limits, right next to Brookline, before the city gives way to the suburbs of the South Hills. So Sweeney was, indeed, "a Pittsburgh guy," which meant something special to Mr. Rooney. He often said you could tell "a Pittsburgh guy by the warmth of his handshake."

During his senior year at Pitt, Sweeney was invited to Three Rivers Stadium to work out for the Steelers prior to the college draft. The Steelers were interested in drafting him.

The New York Jets beat the Steelers to Sweeney, taking him on the second round of the 1984 draft. Mr. Rooney sent Sweeney a congratulatory letter that same week. That was so typical of Mr. Rooney.

"I still have that letter framed on the wall in my office at home," said Sweeney. "I treasure it. He was a very special man to me." Sweeney recalled Rooney's words in a letter that was hand-written, even though Mr. Rooney had a secretary:

"Dear Jim, I'm a friend of your grandfather. He was a fine man and a top athlete. I hope you will be a superstar. I'm sorry you're not with our team. You will find Leon Hess and Jim Kensil of the Jets good men. I'll be rooting for you. I met your brother Mike at the Stadium. Good Luck. Art Rooney."

Back in the early days of the Steelers, Rooney used to routinely draft players from Pitt and Duquesne. I remember during Dan Marino's senior year at Pitt, Rooney remarked one day in his office, "We've got to find a way to keep that kid in Pittsburgh."

The Steelers passed on Marino, as did most of the teams in the NFL, to draft Gabe Rivera, a defensive tackle from Texas Tech. The rest is history, as they say.

After Mr. Rooney died, Sweeney wore the initials AJR on the back of his helmet while playing for the Jets. The Steelers had special shoulder patches with AJR (Arthur J. Rooney) stitched on them that they wore that season. "I figured I owed him something," said Sweeney at the time.

So Sweeney has a sentimental streak, a good heart, and he's proud of his parents, his family, the schools he attended and represented on the football fields, and he was glad he got the chance to come home to finish his pro football career with the team he loved and rooted for in his youth.

"It's a dream come true," said Sweeney. "I wish I were playing more, but I'm still wearing a uniform that's black and gold. It's nice to live here year round."

When Sweeney was in seventh grade at St. Catherine's, his class was given an assignment to draw a picture of what they wanted to be when they grew up. Sweeney drew a picture of himself in a Steelers' uniform. It showed a Steelers' player sacking a quarterback.

It took Sweeney 21 years to realize his dream, but he did it. He spent 11 of those seasons with the Jets, one with the Seattle Seahawks. He had started every non-strike game of those 12 seasons — 158 straight, beginning with the final two of his rookie season in 1984.

He came to Pittsburgh though he knew he wouldn't be starting. They already had Dermontti Dawson, a Pro Bowl center. But they wanted Sweeney to strengthen their offensive line, as a backup center-guard, as a possible snapper for place-kicking, as a veteran who would contribute in a lot of ways, on and off the field.

He was a favorite of Tom Donahoe, the director of football operations for the Steelers. Donahoe had been his coach during his senior year at Seton-LaSalle High School and theirs was a mutual admiration society.

"Jimmy's a good role model for our young linemen the way he approaches football," said Donahoe.

Sweeney was approaching the 1997 season as a potential starter. I spotted him working out with the offensive linemen on the first day of the team's mini-camp, Monday, June 2, and I knew what was going on in his mind because we had spent two hours together two days earlier discussing his situation.

"I'm going in with the idea that I'm competing for a starting job somewhere in that offensive line," said Sweeney.

He had played every position in the offensive line, even tight end in short yardage situations. During his stay with the New York Jets, he had started 28 games at left tackle, 20 at left guard. During the strike-shortened season of 1987, he had started all 12 games at left tackle.

A dedicated weight-lifter, he could bench press over 500 pounds. He worked with martial arts to help quicken his hand speed, and he liked playing for Bill Cowher.

"I have confidence in my ability," he said. "I don't think Bill would expect anything less from me. If you go into camp with the idea you're going to be a backup you won't make the football team. I can't approach it any other way. That's the way I'm built."

Sweeney is built solidly, the result of a lifetime of passionate workouts in the weight room. Looking to his 14th season in the National Football League, the bull-necked Sweeney stood at 6-4, 295 pounds.

"Walt Harris is a good man."
— Jim Sweeney

Following his first season with the Steelers, Sweeney went to bat for Buddy Morris, who had been the strength coach during his days at Pitt. Walt Harris, the new football coach at Pitt, was looking to make a change in that area.

Morris had lost his position at Pitt during the Mike Gottfried era, and Morris was among the Pitt football alumni who wanted him back. Sweeney weighed 205 when he first showed up at Pitt to work out in the weight room under the direction of Morris, right after

Publicity photo from Pitt sports information office offered imposing lineup of protectors for Heisman Trophy candidate Dan Marino. They included, left to right, Jim Sweeney, Jimbo Covert, Ron Sams, Emil Boures, Terry Quirin, Bill Fralic, Paul Dunn and Rob Fada.

University of Pittsburgh sports information

Sweeney had completed his senior year at Seton-LaSalle. By the time he reported as a freshman for fall practice, Sweeney was up to 224 pounds. He was 265 when he left four years later. Sweeney credited Morris for helping him build himself into being a big-time college football player and a legitimate pro prospect.

Harris had been an offensive backfield coach with the Jets when Sweeney played there, and knew and respected him. Harris hired Morris the same day Sweeney suggested he do that. "Walt called me back that same night and said he had interviewed and hired Buddy," said Sweeney. "Walt said 'Wow!' after meeting Morris. He liked him right away."

Sweeney and Dan Marino, who had been Pitt's quarterback when Sweeney broke in as a starter at Pitt, and some other alumni from that period, including Mark Stepnoski, Sean Gilbert, Ruben Brown, Jerry Olsavsky and Bill Fralic, all donated thousands of dollars to the Pitt football program to purchase more weight room equipment to suit the specifics outlined by Morris.

Sweeney thought Harris was a good coach, a creative football mind, and that he'd help Pitt put some points on the board as they tried to restore the program to its glory days. The key is to stop the other people from scoring.

"I believe in my heart that Pitt will surprise some people," said Sweeney. "They can win. I really like Walt. He's a man of his word. He's not a yeller or screamer type. He'll get along well with the kids. He's a good man; that's his best attribute. If he's a good man, anything is possible."

Sweeney sounded like Art Rooney with that remark.

"You have to take a chance on him."
— Rege O'Neill on young Jim Sweeney

Jim Sweeney was well connected with the college football coaches of Pittsburgh. Pitt's new coach, Walt Harris, had been an assistant coach during Sweeney's stay with the New York Jets. Duquesne University's coach, Greg Gattuso, had been a teammate and friend during their days at Seton-LaSalle. Sweeney had been introduced to Rich Lackner, the coach at Carnegie Mellon University, who grew up and still lived in Mt. Lebanon.

"I was recruited by Pitt in the first place because we had some really outstanding prospects at Seton-LaSalle," said Sweeney. "Greg Gattusso, Glen Strene and Denny Urban were being recruited by practically every college you could think of.

"I didn't play my junior year in high school because the head coach, Frank Cipriani, didn't like my dad. My dad would coach my brother, Mike, and me from the sidelines, and 'Cip' didn't care for that. So the college coaches didn't have a lot to go by.

"Coach Donahoe came in the next year. We went 10-2 that season and won the WPIAL championship. We lost one game by two points and another by one point.

"Rege O'Neill, who was our offensive line coach at Seton-LaSalle, wrote to college coaches and recommended me to them. He said, 'You have to take a chance on him.' " Joe Butler, who lives in Peters Township, gave Sweeney high marks on his Metro Scouting Index reports. Sweeney was looking forward to participating in Butler's Metro Index Football Camp at CMU in the coming weeks.

Sweeney also mentioned that his football coach at St. Catherine's was Dick Frank, who helped get him and Gattuso started off on the right foot. Frank was a tough taskmaster.

Sweeney still likes to take friends past Vanucci Field where he began his playing career with the St. Catherine team. He's always been grateful for Frank's early guidance.

Sweeney doesn't forget old friends. He liked to work out at Gold's Gym in Pleasant Hills, which was operated by Tracy Ruscitto, a friend of his and Heather, and if he needed some physical therapy in the off-season he has visited Joey David at his offices in Mt. Lebanon. David, who resided in Upper St. Clair, was a basketball player at Pitt when Sweeney was playing football there.

Sweeney was living in a not-yet-completed new home in Venetia, a part of Peters Township in Washington County, just past Upper St. Clair and the Allegheny County border line. He was hoping he and Heather could have at least four more children, so he bought a big house to hold them all.

He intended to stay in Pittsburgh when his pro football career was completed. He wanted to play at least 15 or so seasons in the NFL. He wanted to stay around the way Webster (17 seasons) and Mansfield (14) had done. He thought he might like to get into "the wellness" business when he was done playing football.

"I haven't gotten into an off-season job because I feel like football is a full-time job, and whatever I do next will be a full-time job, too. I want to give them my full attention, my full commitment. I wasn't going to get married while I was playing pro football, either, because I think it's a tough life for a family. It's a hard life for a woman to understand. They take a backseat to football."

Then he met Heather, who grew up in the same Brookline community. "Some people think she married me for my money, but I don't think so," said Sweeney, smiling at his remark. "We went to the same high school, only in different decades. I take her everywhere with me. If I can't take her, I don't go. She's my best friend. I take my kids, too. I'm proud of them, and I look better when they're with me."

They were married in Pittsburgh on a Saturday when the city was hit with one of the worst snowstorms ever. It was a memorable event for everyone who attended.

Sweeney was sitting across from me in a booth at King's Family Restaurant on McMurray Road in Upper St. Clair. He knew the place well. His daughter, Shannon, had started taking dance lessons near-by at the Janet Hays & Company Dance Studio, and they stopped at the restaurant afterward for ice cream. My daughters, Sarah and Rebecca, both took dance lessons there when they were young. I knew the routine.

This guy's got quite the appetite. He ate an old-fashioned ham-burger, with all the fillings, French fries drenched with hot brown gravy, a glass of water and a glass of Coke, and washed that down with a milk shake.

It was May 31, 1997. He showed me photo prints he had just picked up showing him and a very pregnant Heather on vacation in the Bahamas, and more recent prints of her and baby Liam and daughter Shannon. He also shared them with a waitress who remem-bered waiting on him and his family.

When I mentioned to Sweeney that so many of the Steelers he had idolized in his youth, Mansfield, Clack, Webster, Moon Mullins, had all split from their original mates, he simply nodded.

"Heather and I were watching something on TV the other day, about how so few people these days were happy in their marriages, and we are determined to make our marriage work. But I don't worry about what happened in the personal lives of those guys I idolized. I don't look at them in that respect," said Sweeney.

"These guys were what I wanted to be when I grew up. I saw the way they worked, the way they played. I know they've had prob-lems. I know they're human and that they'll die. Everybody dies. I'm able to separate their professional lives from their private lives. What those guys have achieved makes them close to my heart. They loved being football players, and they played for a long time. That's what I want to do.

"Webster knocked people down, dusted them off, and then knocked them down again. I still idolize Mike Webster."

"He looks good; he looks like he's been working out."
— Joe Moore

Sweeney shared his thoughts on some of the men he has met in his football life:

• **Tom Donahoe:** "He still makes me nervous. I still have to call him 'Mr. D' or 'Coach D.' There's something about him. He has that aura about him. You have to respect him. He's always been a pro-fessional in his approach. He talked to me earlier in my career, when I was a free agent before with the Jets, about coming to the Steelers. Last season when he called me on the phone, he asked, 'What would it require to get you?' I said, 'The minimum. Coach D., I just want to come here.' I only wanted to play here. We had a home in Seattle, and that didn't make any sense at all."

• **Foge Fazio**: "He recruited me to Pitt. We had several stars on our Seton-LaSalle team that everyone was after, but Foge told me, 'You're the one I really want.' If they had kept him at Pitt he would have become like Bear Bryant. He would've stayed there forever, the way Joe Paterno has done at Penn State. He was a Pitt guy. He got along well with the players, maybe too well. I think some players took advantage of him. When he was the defensive coordinator at Pitt, he was in the huddle with the guys. He could really relate to his players. He'd love to be a player, even today. When he became the head coach, he was thrown into a tough situation. Pitt had been 11-1 in three straight seasons under Jackie Sherrill. Pitt was rated No. 1 in the country in the pre-season in Foge's first season. That was tough to live up to."

• **Joe Moore:** "He's still the best line coach I ever had, and I think we've got a good one here in Kent Stephenson. I have all the admiration and respect in the world for Joe Moore. He's one of the people I love dearly. You always knew where you stood with Joe Moore. I remember him taking the offensive linemen to the Pleasure Bar in Bloomfield, where he grew up, and to some corner bar in Polish Hill. It might have been illegal — some of us were underage — and having a beer or two. But he believed in keeping us close together. He wanted us to be proud to be Pitt linemen.

"We'd always have our own Christmas party at the bowl games. He'd have his wife, Fran, and his kids there, and we were one big family. We were all in it together.

"On the first day the freshmen reported to the Pitt campus, I'm with my mom and dad in the dorm lobby, and Joe came over and sized me up. 'He looks good; he looks like he's been working out,' Joe told my parents. My dad says, 'Yeah, if he gets out of hand, don't be afraid to kick him in the ass.' Joe says, 'I will.' I thought I left my dad at home. I got a new dad, that's all.

"I wasn't afraid to take his criticism. I was very coachable. He could tell me to do anything and I'd do it."

• **Mike Gottfried:** "I received a Wire-Gram from Mike Gottfried right after he was hired as the head football coach at Pitt. He said how proud he was of the way I represented Pitt in the pros, and how he hoped he could call upon me to help him, and how I would always be welcome at Pitt. That same winter, I was working out with some other Pitt football alumni in the weight room at Pitt Stadium, and his assistant, Alex Kramer, came into the weight room and said that Coach Gottfried said we would all have to leave. He said Coach Gottfried said we were taking up machines and equipment that the Pitt kids could be using. But none of his players were there when we were there. That was the last time I worked out there. With Buddy Morris back there, I don't think there should be a problem."

• **Bill Cowher:** "He's a Beechview guy. I remind him now and then he grew up across the valley from where I lived. He lived there till he was eight years old. He's only five years older than I am, but

334

he demands respect. He hasn't hard-balled me, but if you don't do it his way, he won't put up with it. He pays attention to every facet of our football team. He knows what's going on. He should know everything.

"He wants to be involved. I told him I had a great year when we met at the end of the season. He said, 'I hope you're going to come back next year.' I said, 'Hey, Bill, I can't call you Coach. I've known you as Bill too long.' He smiled and said, 'Don't start now.' But I told him I wanted to come back. I like being a Steeler and I like being on his team."

"He's so perfect."
— Boomer Esiason

Boomer Esiason, who quarterbacked the Jets when Sweeney was their center, had this to say about him: "A guy like Sweeney, he's so perfect. I couldn't draw a better picture of a center, a better personality for a center, a better body for a center, a better place to be from."

Jets' publicist, Doug Miller, who came from the same place in Pittsburgh, growing up in our neighborhood in Upper St. Clair, and a Pitt man as well, remains a big fan of Sweeney. Sweeney was involved in so many charity-related fund-raising activities on Long Island during his days with the Jets, and was always willing to make appearances on behalf of the Jets when Miller came calling on him.

"He was the best," said Miller. "He's the captain of my all-time team for community relations. He was great to work with, and my Pitt background meant a lot to him."

Sweeney was active in Special Olympics and Big Brothers, and helped organize a golf outing each summer at the Sharon Country Club to raise funds for the health care of one of the daughters of Buddy Morris, ten-year-old Kara, who needed a liver transplant. Buddy's wife, Karen, who is from Sharon, was a track & field performer at Pitt. To date, they had raised over $40,000 toward the operation she required. Dan Marino makes an appearance every year, and is a big drawing card.

"The ring's the thing."
— Jim Sweeney

Sweeney signed with Pittsburgh in the hope that he could come home and be a part of a Super Bowl championship team. He nearly pulled it off.

With the Steelers in 1996, Sweeney was a member of a division champion for the first time in his NFL career. He was still playing football in January for the first time since he left Pitt.

If the real Steelers had showed up in Foxboro, Massachusetts during the playoffs to go up against the New England Patriots, he might have gotten to the Super Bowl. Another former Pittsburgher and Pitt performer, Curtis Martin, had the best of a foggy afternoon as the Patriots put away the upstart Steelers in a hurry.

Had the Steelers whipped the Patriots, as they were favored to do, they would have had a home game at Three Rivers Stadium the following week against the Jacksonville Jaguars for the AFC championship, and a great chance of going to the Super Bowl for the second year in a row.

Sweeney came within two games of a Super Bowl ring. "The ring's the thing; it's what you play for," said Sweeney as the Steelers prepared for the Patriots. "I know I do.

"My first line coach was Jim Ringo (the former Green Bay Packers All-Pro center who was one of Mike Webster's boyhood heroes). He used to philosophize with me a lot. He used to talk a lot about the ring, and what it means. He was on all those great teams that Vince Lombardi had in the '60s.

"This is a great game, football. It gives you an opportunity to win something and be remembered forever. Fifty years from now, you can be sitting in a crowd of people and someone will look down and see the ring. They'll know without a word that you played in a Super Bowl and won.

"There's nothing like it in the world. A fantastic experience."

Except perhaps a wedding ring or fathering a child, I suggested. That didn't stall Sweeney from making his point.

"It's frustrating to play for so many years as I have and not even have the chance to play in the Super Bowl," said Sweeney. "I've dreamed about it for what seems like forever. Now I'm closer to getting there than I've ever been. I'm excited. This is uncharted territory for me."

So Sweeney was disappointed that the Steelers weren't up to snuff, and never got out of the gate at Foxboro Stadium.

Standing in Three Rivers Stadium at the outset of mini-camp on a humid day in June of 1997, he was excited all over again. "I really like this team," he said. "This is the best team I've been on since I was a senior at Seton-LaSalle. I think we've got a team that could go all the way."

Sweeney said he had remained a Steelers' fan, during all his years in New York and his one-year stay in Seattle.

"My dad used to keep me informed on what was going on here when I was away, telling me how they did, how they played," said Sweeney. "I was always a Steelers fan, except the few times we played them. You can take the kid out of Pittsburgh, but you can't take the Pittsburgh out of the kid."

During his days with the Jets, Sweeney still lived in Pittsburgh during the off-season. "I'm a Pittsburgher, not a New Yorker," he said. "I'd say you have to be born in New York to enjoy it. If you spend a few days there it's OK, but if you spend more than a week there, you're crazy."

One of Sweeney's coaches in New York was Joe Walton, who had been an All-American end during his days at Pitt. Walton, from Beaver Falls and more recently the offensive coordinator of the Steelers in Chuck Noll's last years and the head coach at Robert Morris College, was a big fan of Sweeney.

"He's got guard speed and he's very quick," said Walton during the 1989 season. "But the biggest thing is he's strong enough to move those big nose tackles in the 3-4."

One of Walton's assistants in New York and at Robert Morris was Dan Radakovich, who was also a line coach with the Steelers during some of their Super Bowl seasons. It was Radakovich who retooled Sweeney into being a tackle. Radakovich thought Sweeney would be a tackle forever.

Radakovich compared Sweeney to Jon Kolb, who was an undersized tackle on four Steelers' Super Bowl teams.

"Kolb weighed 205 coming out of Oklahoma State," recalled Radakovich, who grew up in Duquesne and played at Penn State, and was known as "Bad Rad" during his stint with the Steelers.

"Sweeney was bigger, but both had to lift weights to gain strength. Kolb was a little faster, but both ran well. There hasn't been a guard in the NFL as good as Kolb would have been if he had played there. But he was such a good tackle, we never could afford to move him to guard. He never played in the Pro Bowl, but he was an All-Pro," related Radakovich.

Sweeney later switched back to center because it was the position he most desired to play.

"He's a tough guy."
— Jim Sweeney
on his dad

Jim and his brother Mike worked out together as kids under the watchful eyes of their father. In that regard, their stories resembled those of his teammates Will Wolford and Eric Ravotti and their brothers. They all worked equally hard, but one grew up to be big enough for college and pro competition, and the other did not.

"Mike was a year older than me," said Jim. "He was 6-2, about 220, and he went to Thiel. Then he transferred to Westminster. Art Rooney saw to it that he got a tryout with the Steelers in 1984. He had shin splints and he was released. There was nobody tougher than this kid. My brother was such a hard worker.

"When he joined a fraternity, he won the 'Ghoul Award' because he was the one pledge that couldn't be broken. During his initiation or Pledge Week, they wanted him to say that he liked Cleveland better than Pittsburgh, and the Browns better than the Steelers, but he wouldn't give in to that no matter what they did to him. He wouldn't say that."

Sweeney said his father shaped him in every way.

"Most fathers want their sons to be running backs," Sweeney said. "Mine wanted me to be a center."

Sweeney's father, called Jim Sweeney though his real name is Charles James Sweeney, the same as his father, served in Korea as a Marine staff sergeant. He looked the part.

"He was a center in sandlot ball, and in the '40s that was bigger than college football in some cases," said the young Sweeney. "His sandlot team used to play against the team from the penitentiary.

"These were 13- and 14-year-old kids playing against men. They lost a game, 7-6, but he said the only reason they lost was because they didn't have a good place-kicker.

"He told me about a guy getting hit so hard, a patch of hair would fall off the top of his head. After high school, he worked in the steel mills where they made car roofs. He'd have to flip them over. Try doing that for eight hours a day. He's a tough guy. He's 68 years old and I still wouldn't want to mess with him."

Sweeney's dad laughed, but said the prison story was true. "Some of those prisoners in Western Penitentiary had ten years of eligibility. We would go into the prison yards and there were guards up on the wall. One time a scuffle broke out on the sidelines and the guards on the wall were getting ready with their guns."

The Sweeneys' prison stories reminded me of how my boyhood sandlot football team, the Hazelwood Steelers, would occasionally play at the penitentiary at Woods Run or the workhouse in Blawnox, but I never went with them. My theory was that there were plenty of opportunities to go into those places while growing up in Hazelwood, and I had no desire to spend time in either place.

"He tries to be tough, but he's not."
— Jim Sweeney's dad

Sweeney runs out of the huddle to the football, a style he picked up from Mike Webster. He also learned the mechanics of snapping for place-kicks from Webster. During the strike season of 1982, Webster used to work out on his own at Pitt Stadium, and he showed Sweeney some tricks of the trade.

The first long snap Sweeney made in college came on a punt against Temple in 1980 when he was a freshman at Pitt. "It was a 47-yarder," said Sweeney.

The snap went 47 yards, not the punt. Sweeney's snap sailed high over the punter's head and wound up in the end zone, a safety for Temple. Pitt trailed, 2-0, but came back to win, 36-2.

First grader

Jim Sweeney smiles with pride for parents Jim and Shirley, and as child on Easter Sunday, 1966: Mike (6), Kathleen (7) and Jim (5).

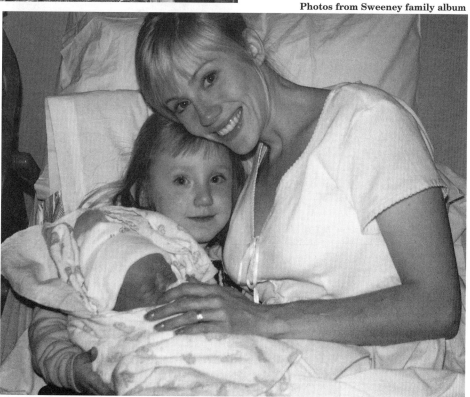

Jim's wife, Heather, and their children, daughter Shannon, and newborn baby Liam.

Like Sweeney, Webster was once pressed into duty for snapping for a punt. He snapped one so far over his punter's head in Cleveland in 1988 that he was never asked to do it again.

As pleasant as he is off the field, Sweeney is a fierce competitor in the trenches. He loves to go one-on-one with a defensive lineman.

"Personally, I just try to put him out of the game," said Sweeney. "You've got to have a little bit of a nasty attitude. You're not out there to hurt him, but you're out there to make him think about you. Sometimes you can just finesse him where he won't get in the play. But then you come back right away and try to drill him.

"I'm one of the last players I know who uses his head a lot, and at the end of a game my head is always bloody. It started in grade school. That's how I can tell if I'm hitting right. I look to see if I'm getting scratches on the front of my helmet. If they're on the back, you're blocking with your head down.

"If my head's bleeding, I know I'm hitting somebody hard. It takes a lot to split your head, but I like it. Your hands follow where your head hits. If you hit with your head, your hands are right in there. You get that good pop, that explosion. Plus, I like it because my head hits where I want to hit him."

Sweeney doesn't want anyone to get the idea he's just a brute. He prides himself on being a thinking man's player. When he was with the Jets, he called signals for the offensive line.

"I have decent strength and decent speed," said Sweeney. "My best asset is that I was blessed with a good mind. I'm not really a school person, but a common-sense person. I remember things that happen and I can pick things up real quickly. I love doing puzzles and I love playing chess. Anything that has to do with thinking, I love."

Sweeney, by the way, returned to Pitt to pick up a bachelor's degree in criminal justice. Sweeney was shy eight credits when he left school for the pros. He came back and took a three-credit course on three different occasions to complete his requirements for his degree.

"I had promised my parents I would get my degree," said Sweeney. "My dad used to say everybody should work in the steel mills for a while, and then they'd be more serious about going to college.

"My father was my real hero, my role model. I may have looked up to Mansfield and Webster, but I always looked to my dad first. He's the epitome of what a man should be. He took care of his wife and he took care of his kids. He was a hard worker. Besides working in the steel mill, he also worked for a printer, J.B. Kreider, near the Market House on the South Side. He took pride in whatever he did. He did some things, he told me, where his pride got the best of him.

"My mother, Shirley, was a nurse at St. Francis Hospital. She took care of Liberace when he was here once. Now she works for the Board of Education in an office in Brookline.

"My parents always taught us to treat others the way we wanted to be treated. They also told us that water seeks its own level.

We knew what that meant. It's not hard to be a good guy. In fact, I think it's more difficult to be a jerk."

Sweeney was always a good kid. He and his brother Mike cared for a mentally handicapped cousin when they were kids by taking him for daily walks. Sweeney became Billy's "Big Brother."

His father remembers that well. "The doggone guy is lovable to a fault," Sweeney's father said. "He used to borrow money off me to give to the kids down the street who needed it. He tries to be tough, but he's not."

During his New York Jets days, Jim Sweeney felt at home working out at Pitt with fellow alumni during the off-season.

"Whatever else history may say about me when I'm gone, I hope it will record that I appealed to your best hopes, not your worst fears . . . And may all of you as Americans never forget your heroic origins, never fail to seek divine guidance, and never, never lose your natural God-given optimism."
— President Ronald Reagan

Eric Ravotti
From Freeport to Happy Valley
...to Mystic Rock

"I have some fans here."

Eric Ravotti was riding a golf cart down the fairway of the 18th hole at the magnificent Mystic Rock course at the Nemacolin Woodlands Resort near Uniontown, and he was enjoying a day in the sunshine. "We are Penn State! We are Penn State!" some fans behind the ropes started hollering. Their familiar chant brought a smile to Ravotti's handsome face.

His was hardly the most familiar face among the celebrities competing in the pro-am golf tournament for the benefit of the Leukemia Society at Joe Hardy's hideaway in Farmington, deep in the Laurel Highlands of southwestern Pennsylvania.

Tiger Woods was playing golf before the public for the first time in the tri-state area, fresh from victories at the Byron Nelson Classic in Irving, Texas, and before that The Masters in Augusta, Georgia, and Tiger-Mania had seized the world. This 21-year-old wunderkind was being celebrated everywhere one looked. Tiger Woods was the reason nearly 30,000 sports fans turned out at Mystic Rock. The promoters said they could have sold out Three Rivers Stadium with Woods as the headliner.

Then, too, Terry Bradshaw, a Fox Sports star who quarterbacked the Steelers to four Super Bowl championships, was one of the celebrity entries who drew a lot of fans and autograph-seekers, so Ravotti relished the enthusiastic response he got from the gallery. They remembered Ravotti from his Penn State days, as well as for his three-year stay with the Steelers. And he wasn't wearing any Steelers or Penn State paraphernalia, either, to help them identify him.

"It was nice to be recognized," said Ravotti. "It made me feel like I have some fans here. Any athlete who tells you he doesn't appreciate recognition is not leveling with you. I subscribe to the Chad Brown theory: 'Anybody who thinks my autograph is worth getting is going to get one.'"

Ravotti also felt good because he had just signed another three-year contract to stay with the Steelers rather than signing elsewhere as a restricted free agent. The enthusiastic crowd at Mystic Rock made him feel he had made the right decision, once again, to stay at home.

Ravotti didn't seek any autographs himself, but he is a celebrity-watcher. He is interested in working in a public relations capacity in industry someday, and he takes notes on the way people like Woods and Bradshaw and even country singing star Garth Brooks interact with their fans and the media.

Born to play football

With kid brother Chad in senior year at Freepor High School

Eric Ravotti

Flanked by sister Chelsie and bride Neva-Lee

th Neva-Lee at St. Vincent's

Eric, Chelsie and Chad suit up.

"I had a chance to meet Terry at a cocktail party the night before we played," recalled Ravotti. "I had never met him before, so it was nice to get to spend a few minutes with him. He was mobbed by many people. He was very nice to people, too. Like most of the athletes I've met who played for those great Steelers teams. Franco Harris is like that, too.

"Those guys who played in Pittsburgh put a lot of time and effort into meeting people. That's nice to see. Terry is still very popular in these parts, no matter what he might think or say to the contrary. They loved him.

"When I see people like Terry Bradshaw, I know he's done some special things in sports that I admire, but I also know that he's just another man, just like me."

He also saw teammate Rod Woodson that same day. Woodson was in the midst of a media flap in Pittsburgh, and getting ready to clear out his dressing stall in the Steelers' clubhouse at Three Rivers Stadium. "He said he'd be all right," said Ravotti. "We're going to miss him."

Ravotti didn't get a chance to meet or talk to Tiger Woods, who didn't arrive until Memorial Day, the day of the pro-am event. "I had my own game to play," said Ravotti in jest. "And Tiger had an entourage of thousands surrounding him, a little bigger than mine.

"It's nice to see a guy like this come along, somebody who's had such an early impact on so many people. He's great for golf; he's great for sports. From all that I've heard and read, he's a special young man. My sense about him is that he's a great person as well as a great golfer."

Some pro athletes and entertainment stars shun the public, and regard fans as pests. So it was reassuring to Ravotti to see country singing mega-star Garth Brooks when both were visiting Penn State during the spring of 1997.

"They don't get much bigger than Garth Brooks," said Ravotti. "He did five shows at Penn State's arena, and he came to football spring practice, wearing Penn State shorts and hat. I had a chance to talk to Garth Brooks and he couldn't have been more of a down-to-earth man. He called everyone 'Sir,' and he was very polite. He took time to meet everyone."

Ravotti was playing at Mystic Rock with a foursome sponsored by Clem Gigliotti, with whom he was working during the off-season in a marketing capacity at Merit Contracting Inc. of Monongahela. "That job goes back to meeting people, and the importance of making good contacts," pointed out Ravotti. "My father-in-law introduced me to Clem, and Clem asked me whether I would like to work for him. That's the kind of work I would like to do when I'm done playing football."

Ravotti is a bright, enterprising young man in addition to being a valued member of the Steelers' strong linebacking corps. He spent

Tiger Woods plays for Joe Hardy at Mystic Rock.

Fearsome fivesome: Former Steelers' quarterback Terry Bradshaw, Mystic Rock and 84 Lumber owner Joe Hardy, touring pros Roger Maltbie and John Daly and country singer Vince Gill were attractions at Nemacolin Woodlands fundraiser for Leukemia Society.

five years at Penn State University, red-shirting his fourth season, and graduated with a degree in labor and industrial relations, and had also taken some graduate courses. His wife, Neva-Lee, was an executive at Kaufmann's Department Store in Downtown Pittsburgh.

Eric and Neva-Lee were living in Wexford, a suburban community just north of Pittsburgh, an easy drive on Rt. 279 to Three Rivers Stadium. "Things are pretty good," he said. "We couldn't ask for more."

He had something in common with Tiger Woods. Their fathers spent a great deal of time grooming them for greatness in sports. While Ravotti remained grateful to his father for what he did to help him get where he is today, he insisted he wouldn't do the same thing when he had his own children.

"I don't want to force football on anybody," said Ravotti. "God willing, when my wife and I have children, I wouldn't show them a football. They'd have to get one from their friends."

"What about Grandpap Ravotti?" I asked.

"Grandpap will be a problem," Ravotti said with a smile. "I'd want my kids to play golf or go bowling. I don't recommend football as a chosen profession. It's a difficult way of life, in college and in the pros. There are a lot of stresses and strains that go with it. No, my kids are never going to see a football from me.

"When my brother Chad and I were young, we wanted to play football. But we didn't know how to go about it. Our dad took an interest in what we were doing. So my dad went out and learned how to help us, and put the time in, so we'd be good at it."

Eric is the godfather of Chad's first child, a girl named Alyssa. Chad is a safety administrator for an insurance company, American General, in Freeport. Their sister, Chelsie, had held several jobs, but had not settled on a career choice. "She hasn't decided what she wants to do yet," said Eric. "She's got a lot of enthusiasm and she'll do fine."

"You're a lot like I was."
— Bill Cowher

Ravotti was looking forward to the 1997 season because he had been assured by Steelers' officials that he would have an opportunity to compete for a starting position as a linebacker. Two of the Steelers' outstanding linebackers, Kevin Greene and Chad Brown, respectively, had left the team as free agents over a two-year span. Greg Lloyd was returning after missing the 1996 season when he suffered a disabling knee injury in the opening game. Ravotti and his buddy, Jerry Olsavsky, enjoyed more playing time as a result. The Steelers had some other talented young linebackers coming back, in Jason Gildon, Earl Holmes, Steve Conley, Donta Jones, and Carlos Emmons, so competition would be keen. To start, Ravotti would probably have to oust Olsavsky or Holmes from an inside linebacker slot.

Ravotti revealed some interesting insights about Greene, Lloyd, Olsavsky, his boss Bill Cowher and the Steelers' front-office during our discussion.

While Olsavsky is a favorite with everyone, some literati had their share of difficult experiences with Greene, Lloyd and Cowher, and questioned whether the Steelers were really something special as teams go in today's pro sports world. Ravotti revealed some personal interaction that gives a different slant on those individuals and the Steelers as an organization.

"Kevin Greene was a big influence on me, right from the start," revealed Ravotti. "My locker was next to his. He set me on the straight and narrow. He showed me how to watch tape, how to really get something useful from it, and really took me under his wing.

"I owe him a real debt of gratitude. Here comes this rookie kid, looking for a job at linebacker, and he didn't have to help me. His attitude was: if you're better than me, then you'll play.

"Jerry O. has been a good friend, and I respect him a lot. Anybody that size (6-1, 220) who can play in the NFL that long merits your respect. He is just a raw football player. He has great instincts for the game. He has a great understanding for the game.

"Greg helps me so much; it's amazing. Greg will answer any question you pose. He'll offer his own insight. He'd be done playing in the pre-season games and he'd stay involved, showing you how to read the offensive sets, talking to you on the sideline.

"He can get quite vociferous. Sometimes it gets to be a bit much. He's a perfectionist. Anything short of that ticks him off. He has his own demons to exorcise. I can put up with it. If you can take constructive criticism you can listen to Lloyd. He knows what he's talking about. He wants to be the best linebacker in pro football, and he wants the Steelers to win the Super Bowl."

So Ravotti recognized that he had a good support system in Pittsburgh, and that the standards were high. It was that way at Penn State.

"Things are pretty good here," he said in assessing his situation with the Steelers. "You realize that when you start thinking about going elsewhere. All indications this spring were I was going to leave Pittsburgh and go somewhere else. Getting an opportunity to be a starter was more important to me than the money. The big thing was starting; the money was secondary. The more I looked into other teams, and met officials from other teams, the more I realized I had something good here that I almost let slip through my fingers.

"They gave me the assurance that I'd get a chance to start here. I love it here. My family is here. All my contacts are here. I don't want to break those ties. I was prepared to do that, though, if I had to.

"I talked to Tom Donahoe, and he felt the Steelers were the right team for me. One of the first things out of their mouths during our discussions was, 'You belong here.' And I said, 'You're right. I do belong here.' So I signed a new contract for three more years. That was nice. I couldn't be happier.

"On Monday, it was exciting and reassuring to have people know who I was when I was at the golf tournament. Some athletes say they hate it, but I have no problem with it."

His experience was similar to when he was a senior at Freeport High School in his hometown, a community 35 miles north of Pittsburgh, and he was visiting glamorous schools such as UCLA and Southern California out West, Tennessee and Georgia Tech down South, and Penn State.

"It turned out I didn't have to go that far from home to be happy and to have my family enjoy my experience, and be a part of it, too," he said.

"There are some intangibles in some schools, and it's the same way with professional teams. Penn State is special; so are the Steelers. I know the Steelers have had a good experience with Penn State guys. When I talked to some of the teams, I came to the realization how well the Steelers are put together. Why do some teams win? Why do some teams lose? The athletes available to them are all about the same.

"It's the intangibles that are different. I don't know how some of these organizations operate. The Steelers are in a class by themselves, from Mr. Rooney to Tom Donahoe to Tom Modrak to Coach Cowher.

"It takes all kinds of guys to coach a football team. Bill Cowher and Dick LeBeau are both different in their approach, for instance, but both are effective. They say that Bill Cowher is a players' coach, but not the same way some people think. You want to play for him, you want to do whatever you can to win for him. You don't want to let him down. You'll play your butt off for him. But he can be hard. He's not trying to win a popularity contest.

"I'm sure it must be tough to coach under Coach Cowher. He wants to be involved in every aspect of the game. He should be. He takes the heat. He gets the credit. He wants to have his hands on everything. He comes into all the meetings, and some coaches don't like that. He's always popping into meetings and giving his two cents worth. I don't see that as a negative. The system is his and he wants to make sure everyone is doing it the way he wants it done. I don't think he's stepping on toes. He's not really a coaches' coach. He's not one of these head coaches who believes in letting the assistants be totally in charge of their specific area.

"He was a linebacker and special teams player during his time as a pro player. So, when we talk, he's always telling me, 'You're a lot like I was.' I guess that's good."

Ravotti was respected because he knew how to play all four linebacker positions, and he could play on all the special teams. Ravotti could read the opposing offenses, and knew what his responsibility was, different at each of those four slots, and what he was supposed to do next.

He credited Greene, Lloyd and Olsavsky for showing the ropes to the young Ravotti. He knew he needed to get even better if he was to break into the starting lineup for good — which was his goal — and make a name for himself with the Steelers.

"You can't be satisfied where you're at," said Ravotti. "You can always get better. As soon as you think you've achieved perfection, you're lying to yourself."

"My brother and I had a great work ethic."
— Eric Ravotti

Ravotti, a 6-3, 247 pound linebacker, hails from Freeport, where he earned *USA Today* All-America, and was a member of the National Honor Society. He was the kind of kid who lent class to any recruiting group. Washington Redskins' quarterback Gus Frerotte played at the same time at Ford City in the same conference.

"I played midget league football for the Freeport Bumblebees. My brother, Chad, who was a year younger, played on a lot of my teams. We were both getting beaten up frequently, by kids who were bigger, faster and stronger. We shared a bedroom and an interest in sports. My dad bought us some sand weights and a bench, which we set up in our bedroom.

"We used them almost every day, benchpressing. That's all we did, at first. We just kept lifting until we couldn't lift anymore. My father didn't know what we were supposed to do. He had no experience himself. We winged it. We kinda figured it out as we went along.

"My father played one year of high school ball, but hurt his back early on in high school, and had to give it up. He went to Freeport High School as well.

"My father saw the pummeling I was taking. I was very discouraged, as most kids are who don't have early success. I liked it more as I played better. As the years progressed, I went from being the weakest to being the strongest.

"It all came from that work in the bedroom. With a lot of help, I had some success by the time I got to high school. My brother and I had a great work ethic. My father instilled that in us.

"My dad put a chart together when I was around 13 or 14. It was a goal path to get me to college and to the NFL. We started out with goals, not only making the team, but becoming a starter. My brother and I took on this challenge together. I grew into a tight end and then a linebacker.

"Chad was a great high school player, but he was only 5-9. If he were a 6-3 kid, he'd probably be where I am today. He had a bad knee, and that height problem. He played a little at Slippery Rock University, and had some success there.

"He helped me a lot, probably more than he helped himself. He was right behind me on that chart. He was pushing me in the weight room. He pushed me in so many ways. If we were running, and I wanted to ease up, he'd push me to go harder. When we lifted weights, he spotted me, and pushed me to use heavier weights or to do more repetitions.

"He lived his sports life through me. I gave him as much credit as I gave myself. Our dad was working with us. My parents were always there. I had a strong support system. My mother is a nurse now, but she wasn't working at the time, so she devoted a lot of time to our activities.

"My dad is a tool and die journeyman. He did manual labor all his life. One summer he found my brother and I a job, lifting railroad ties and building support walls with those railroad ties. We worked some long hot hours. My dad would come to me and say, 'See what the rest of the people are doing to make a living? Do you want to work like this the rest of your life?'

"It only took me one or two days to realize that's not what I wanted to do with the rest of my life.

"At an early age, I know that academics and sports were tied together, and that goal-setting was important.

"My father made up the goals. He found out how to train me. He read books to get the proper information he needed to help me and my brother, Chad.

"I had that support early on. I enjoyed playing football, and other sports. My mother and father were always coming to watch me play. They were supportive when I didn't do well, and praised me when I did well.

"I wanted to play the sport. A lot of my friends just played because their friends played, or because their parents wanted them to play. You have a lot of kids who love the game, and just play it because they love to play. For most of them, there's no chance of going to college with it, or playing pro ball. They deserve a lot of credit.

"In high school, I never really thought I could make a career out of it. I wanted to win a scholarship to go to college. I didn't even follow college or professional ball until I became a senior. Then I started to follow it. I didn't grow up thinking about playing for the Steelers, or in the National Football League.

"The big thing was to get a college education paid for. Anything after that was a bonus. I drew the interest of some college teams. I visited five schools, as most players do. I went to UCLA and USC out in California, Georgia Tech, Penn State and Tennessee.

"Johnny Majors was the coach at Tennessee at the time. He came to my house and sat down and talked with me. So did Joe Paterno. It was really a big deal. Joe came in and had breakfast with us. Joe came to the house and to the school. That's when it hit me.

When he came to schools, when he came walking around, people noticed. They recognized him right away. That made you feel big at school. "At first, I was going to go out West. I was leaning toward UCLA. But there was such a similarity between UCLA and Penn State, I started thinking that my family could see me play if I went to Penn State. I'm definitely happy with my decision. I always felt Penn State was for me, and the chance for my family to be able to drive to the games was the clincher. Penn State was far enough away for me to go to college and escape any distractions, yet close enough that my family could easily come to the games.

"College football is not all just football. You've got to like the place first. For me, Penn State was a 2 1/2 hour drive. I could get home whenever I wished, or if I were needed for something.

"My father and I trained so hard in the off-season. When I got to Penn State, it was easy. I could run and I had the strength to compete. I didn't need a year to develop."

Most freshmen are held out a year, or red-shirted, at Penn State to give them time to get better acclimated academically and athletically, and to mature so they are ready for the challenge of a big-time schedule.

"They tell you up front that might happen," related Ravotti. "They tell you that you'll come in and be evaluated, and we'll go from there. They don't guarantee you that you'll play your first year, or anything else.

"Reggie Givens and I were the ones in my class who played the most the first year."

Ravotti was asked if Happy Valley lived up to its name.

"It was very good at times," he said. "At times it wasn't so great. Some times you wished you weren't there. I think that would have been true wherever I might have gone. But, overall, I'm very glad I went there.

"I have a lot of fans in Freeport at the White Star Bar. I used to go there as a little kid and play bocce with my dad. There are lots of little watering holes there with lots of sports fans. It makes you feel good that they're fans. It's an exciting feeling when you've got fans where you came from. As a child, when I'd go to the White Star Bar with my family, I was being fed all the time. I didn't have a care in the world. So the place brings back some positive memories."

"He's the father away from home."
— Eric Ravotti on Joe Paterno

Penn State is famous for turning out linebackers for the pros. It's been called "Linebacker U." Penn State sent a Hall of Fame linebacker to the Steelers in Jack Ham. Ravotti offered a rave review about Joe Paterno, his coach at Penn State and another man who was a positive influence in his young life.

"Joe just wasn't interested in making you a good football player, but he wanted to prepare you for life, too. I truly believe that now," related Ravotti.

"He'll be on your back if you screw up. He's the father away from home, or just the father figure, especially for the guys who didn't have fathers at home. He's demanding, but he's fair, I can say that.

"He has more stories than anyone. He has certain stories he likes to tell for certain situations. About the fourth or fifth year you know what stories that would be coming out for each situation. But they make sense. They do work.

"He came to my home and to the school on the same day. He came through our school and signed some autographs for anyone who asked for one. Being recruited by Joe Paterno was exciting. You hear about him all the time — the great Coach Paterno; he's a legend. One day you come up in school and you see Coach Paterno walking down the hall, and he's coming to see you.

"Tom Bradley was recruiting me. He and Tom Bradley sat down with me in a room by ourselves, for about 15 to 20 minutes. When the bell rang, they stopped. They didn't want to keep me from class, being a stickler for academics. He received a lot of notoriety during his visit to our school.

"Getting ready for my junior year, that's when I started to think about the possibility of playing pro ball. I had been splitting a position with Rich McKenzie — he played for Cleveland — and we shared it for two or three years. We'd come in the same year. Joe told us he wanted one of us to sit out the next season so he'd have one of us for the following year, when Penn State was going into the Big Ten.

"I thought about it long and hard. I saw the light at the end of the tunnel. I made the decision, and it was mine alone, to stay an extra year. I thought I could graduate early, and take some graduate level courses my fifth year for free. The academic aspect was the deciding point. I thought I could work on my physical ability, and take advantage of that extra year of preparation. Most of the guys who'd come in with me had been red-shirted the first year, so they'd still be there for my fifth year. The only minus was to wait the whole year before I could play again.

"A lot of fourth year seniors have too many distractions, pro evaluations and such, that they don't graduate on time. I knew it could be difficult to come back later and pick up the credits you needed.

"They have rules for football players at Penn State, such as mandatory breakfast attendance for athletes. You have to come to breakfast every morning. They take attendance. Some went back to bed and didn't go to classes, but that was the small minority. Most went to classes. I know a lot of seniors don't go to classes at some schools, but I didn't see that at Penn State. Joe tried to instill in you the realization that it was in your best interest to take care of your school responsibilities. You were reminded, hey, I'm here for an education. You can pick out a handful that took it lightly.

"Joe taught us not only how to set goals, but the best way to achieve them. He taught us respect and how being a better football player would help us to be better academically and better mentally as well."

"I think about missed tackles."
— Eric Ravotti

Eric Ravotti was a reliable performer for the Steelers because he could play all four linebacker positions. He had played on four different special teams. A reserve player who is versatile, responsible and a little hostile can always find work with an NFL team.

Ravotti had to have a strong appeal to a coach like Bill Cowher, who played the same position and was a special teams demon, an over-achiever who always gave his all. Plus, Ravotti was a good guy, someone a coach didn't have to worry about during off-duty hours.

Ravotti was one of those individuals who did whatever it takes to be useful on a football team. "Desperate times call for desperate measures," Ravotti would say with a grin.

He filled in at an outside linebacker position when Greg Lloyd was injured and lost for the season in the opening game of the 1996 schedule. The year before, he got his first start against the Cleveland Browns when Olsavsky and Brown both had ankle injuries. Ravotti had a career-high seven tackles in that game.

"To start, it felt good," said Ravotti. "I started inside the year before, so this was a little different. I'm more suited to play inside, but due to my versatility, they feel confident to play me at any of the four slots.

"Physically, I feel I'm up to doing whatever they want me to do. There are a lot of guys who start who also play special teams. You have to do that sometimes."

Soon after the Steelers started their summer training camp at St. Vincent College in the summer of 1996, rumors that Ravotti was in trouble as far as sticking with the team began to make the rounds.

The Steelers had drafted several terrific athletes at the linebacker position, and Ravotti and Olsavsky were thought to be in jeopardy.

"I was not really concerned," remarked Ravotti. "I didn't put too much faith in what was being said. The coaching staff always made me feel good about my situation. They know what abilities I have. Our coach, Mike Archer, said, 'Don't worry about it. We'll see what the young guys can do.' I didn't play much in the third and fourth preseason games, and that's when people figured my days were numbered.

"The coaches told me they wanted to get a look at the other guys. I knew what I was doing. I have to be challenged, just like Jerry O.

The young guys we've got have great ability, they just have to pick up the system.

"It's always tough watching other people play. Most of the time, it wasn't because I couldn't play. It was a numbers type of thing. It's a little frustrating, but you just keep pluggin'. Good things will happen.

"I really never thought I would be cut because of what I bring to this team," Ravotti continued. "And they knew what kind of player I was so I never had to worry about it. But when they kept ten linebackers that was a shock. It ended up looking like a master stroke when several linebackers were hurt early."

Greg Lloyd was sidelined for the season in the first game, and Jason Gildon and Steven Conley both got hurt at the outset of the season. Ravotti moved to Lloyd's right outside position.

"I know I have the skill to play. The responsibilities at each position are totally different. You have to be pretty good to learn all the positions. You're working in the same defense. I missed a few reads. You need at least two or three days practice at one position to be ready.

"Sometimes there's some hesitation. You have to learn to see what they're doing, and try not to be fooled. You have to remember your responsibility. I feel good about my ability to do that.

"I don't think about tackles. I think about missed tackles. Things start to run together. I had notes on my wrists, regarding strong and weak-side. The picture is the exact opposite in some cases. You learn it from repetition.

"I talk to myself all the time. Coach Archer keeps me alerted to what's going on. My fellow linebackers, like Chad and Jerry and Levon, they trust me. If there's a question, we ask each other. We're all playing the same thing. I have a great supporting cast. The defensive secondary keeps me straight, too."

One of his boosters was Darren Perry, a former Penn State star playing free safety for the Steelers. "Eric did well," said Perry. "Plus, it's nice to have another Penn Stater out there. The thing is the expectations for those players are that they have to step up to that level. They are expected to play at a certain level. If they do, we can go out and have a good, solid defense."

"My own goal is to make it in the NFL."
— Eric Ravotti

Ravotti was excited about his first training camp with the Steelers at St. Vincent College in Latrobe back in the summer of 1994. As hard as it is to believe, considering his early enthusiasm for the sport when he was growing up in Freeport, he had never been to St. Vincent before.

354

"I never got up here as a kid," he explained. "I was always try-ing to work on my own skills, playing in peewee league. Being here is special. It's a long way from everything. It was exciting just to have your name on the back of your jersey. I wasn't used to this: names on the jersey, stripes on the shoulders. It was all foreign to me. At Penn State, they still wore those plain white jerseys without the players' names on the back.

He was the Steelers' second sixth round draft pick in the 1994 draft, and was considered a long shot to make the team. At the Indianapolis combine, where all the pro scouts check out the prospects prior to the draft, he led all linebackers with 30 bench reps at 225 pounds. All that bench pressing back in his bedroom in Freeport was paying dividends. It helped him stick out for the scouts. "My own goal is to make it in the NFL," he said at the time.

"You've got to give 110 percent every day because they're always watching you. I remember thinking that making it happen in Pittsburgh would be the ultimate dream for me and my family."

George Gojkovich

Eric Ravotti recovers fumble in 1996 contest with San Diego Chargers.

"Whatever you have received more than others in health, talents, ability, success, a pleasant childhood or in harmonious conditions of home life, all this you must not take to yourself as a matter of course. In gratitude for your good fortune render some sacrifice of your own life for another life."
— Dr. Albert Schweitzer

It Was A Family Affair

By Guido Ravotti

We are a very close-knit family from a very small one stoplight town, Freeport, Pennsylvania, population 2500 or so. Four counties meet at the bridge in town — Armstrong, Allegheny, Butler and Westmoreland.

Eric's Uncle Bob has been the mayor of Freeport for 19 years, and is still going strong. Eric described it once as a Mayberry-type town, where you'd expect to find Andy Griffith and Ron Howard. Eric went to St. Mary's School and also was an altar boy for the church. He was involved in everything from piano in second grade to all the sports in high school. In senior high, he only competed in track and field and football.

Eric and his brother Chad begged us to let them play football when they were 9 and 10. We were very hesitant about this because of the fear of injuries. Now that we look back, we are still not sure of our decision. Chad had two knee injuries, the last one playing for Slippery Rock University, which put him out of football. And Eric has been injured as well. But life goes on.

Eric was a skinny 12-year-old who used to get tossed around in midget football. He was like a pawn on a chess board. Wherever the other played wanted to put him that's where he landed.

Both his mother and I were very distressed over this, which led to me buying a set of weights at a flea market and getting both boys to lift weights. His brother, Chad, was his best friend and would prove to be his pusher, his motivator and his release valve. In high school, they were both linebackers. You could not talk to either of them before the game. They were so pumped up and ready to go.

They would go out in the yard the day before the game in pads and hit till dark. They both would lift every day in the gym, holidays included. Seeing them both on the same team is a memory we will cherish. Their sister was and still is their biggest cheerleader and fan.

Eric went on to Penn State University and Chad to Slippery Rock. Chad was not as tall as Eric to draw the attention from the big schools.

Eric lettered in his first year as a true freshman and finished as third in Penn State history with sacks.

When he was in junior high ball, we sat down and drew a chart with a goal of playing in the NFL at the top and all the sideroads like grades, not believing in yourself, breaking the law and getting into trouble, slacking off, injuries.

They both knew that to get to the NFL they had to stick to the chart, which included lifting, running hills, jumping hurdles.

His mother would go to the park with him and she would time him on his 40-yard dash. We were always looking for new ways to make him faster. So we got a contraption that was a bunjy cord. One person stayed stationary while the other pulled it as far as it would go, then the stationary one would take off and the cord would pull you faster. If you did this enough times you were supposed to get faster. Well, Eric pulled it and Chad stayed stationary. The cord came off and snapped back faster than anything I have ever seen and hit Chad in the groin and flipped him in the air, and he landed on his back. No injuries. But we still laugh about it. Both brothers still argue about who made the most tackles at a certain high school game.

Everyone sees the finished product on TV. But never the adversity, sweat or tears that goes with it. Eric will agree that to make it you need the confidence and the support of your family and the belief in God to get through the bad times.

In summary, we are most proud that we raised three great kids. The NFL, the good jobs, and nice homes and wonderful wives are all icing on the cake. Eric got his degree in four years at Penn State. He is playing for the Steelers, our hometown team. He has a wonderful wife. The best is that we get to see him reach his goals as he keeps setting new ones.

Eric Ravotti is flanked by his mom and dad, Guido and Sandy, at Penn State's Beaver Stadium during the 1992 season.

From the Ravotti family album

Darren Perry
A policeman's son

"My dad wanted us to take pride in being a Perry."

D arren Perry was one of the most pleasant, positive-thinking, upbeat individuals to be found in the Steelers' clubhouse. He smiled easily, squinting his eyes as he spoke, the same way as one of his neighbors and close friends, Jerome Bettis. He talked easily, about any subject, and was sort of a go-to guy for the media covering the club. When others might be preoccupied, in a bad mood, indifferent, rude, shrugging off inquiries, Perry responded willingly and with good insights. He was thoughtful in every respect. He had time for everyone.

He resided in a friendly neighborhood in the clubhouse, occupying a stall alongside the likes of Bettis, Mike Tomczak, Jim Miller and Carnell Lake, all engaging good guys who treat people with kindness and consideration, the way people ought to be treated. They save their toughness for the football field.

Lead off a profile piece with this sort of fluff, however, and most news editors will be nipping at your heels. "This is too soft," they're apt to scold. "What's the hook? Where's the hard stuff? Where's the story?"

Perry usually disappointed in that regard. While he could be an impact player on the field as a free safety in the Steelers' vaunted defense — rival quarterback Vinny Testaverde could testify to Perry's propensity for picking off passes — he could easily get lost in the clubhouse. Perry was on the small side as Steelers go, at 5-10 or 5-11, and a taut-muscled 195 pounds, and was on the quiet side as well. He was well built, but more like the average citizen in size.

He wasn't the sort to shout across the clubhouse, or to holler just for the hell of it. He wasn't controversial in his comments on the Steelers' state-of-affairs, no matter how well or how bad things might be going. He didn't say the sort of things about the opposition that ended up on bulletin boards in their clubhouses. He got along well with everybody on the ballclub. His smile disarmed most people, even those who thought he did not have a particularly productive year in 1996.

Perry remained positive, bolstered by the lessons he had learned from his parents, teachers and from Joe Paterno and his assistant coaches during his days at Penn State University. Perry provides some insights into those experiences that are edifying.

Perry would often sit on his chair in the Steelers' clubhouse, smiling at his surroundings, bemused by the behavior of his more boisterous, often outlandish teammates. One time I was trying to talk

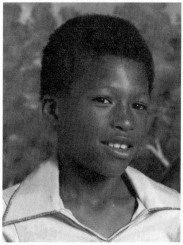

Darren Perry as a child in Chesapeake, Va., and between workouts at St. Vincent's College in Latrobe.

Jim O'Brien

to him, and we both had a hard time concentrating on our own conversation because Carnell Lake and Greg Lloyd were loud and vociferous nearby in a debate about the Bible, of all things. "They can get into it pretty good, huh?" offered Perry with a wink. "Carnell doesn't back down, even though Greg gives you that glare and tries to Bogart everybody."

Perry laughed at his own observation. He was a kid at heart. He loved to play chess with Bettis, and computer games, any kind of competition.

He wasn't into flashy clothes or big cars. "That's a status thing, some guys think if they're professional athletes they have to dress a certain way," he explained. "A lot of that is insecurity, not being at peace with yourself. You have to have exotic things to make you feel good about yourself. There's an irony to that whole situation. That's not me. I know how well off I am now."

It can all be gone so quickly, too. If Perry wanted a reminder of that, on this particular day, all he had to do was look across the room where Delton Hall was visiting with Rod Woodson. Hall won Rookie of the Year honors with the Steelers in 1987, the same year that Woodson, Thomas Everett, Hardy Nickerson, Greg Lloyd and Merril Hoge first joined the team. Now Hall was out of pro football, a man without a team.

Perry had played his college ball at Penn State, and spoke in awe of the positive influence there of his coaches, Joe Paterno, the head man at Happy Valley, and Ron Dickerson, the defensive backfield coach when Perry played there who had moved on to become the head coach at Temple.

Darren was the son of Elnora and Joseph Perry, and a source of great pride to his parents. His dad was a police officer back home in Chesapeake, Virginia, and Darren had often spoken of his dad's discipline and how well-behaved he had been in his youth, staying clear of trouble so he wouldn't disappoint his parents or bring embarrassment to his family. He was raised to respect other people and their possessions.

The Steelers were attracted to players from Penn State, having had many positive experiences with former Nittany Lions. Perry had surprised some critical draftniks who didn't think he was big enough or had the speed necessary to succeed in the secondary in the National Football League. He was a competitor, though; he knew how to play the game. Bigger guys with bigger reputations come to big-time programs such as Penn State's and get lost in the crowd. "When you're a freshman, you're dogmeat," said a former Penn Stater who's impressed with Perry's competitive spirit. "Some guys can't deal with that. Everyone wants to quit and go home at one point during their first season at Penn State."

So Perry was a legitimate success story, a solid citizen, someone who was willing to participate in community projects, especially when they involved kids. He was a good sport. I can recall when Perry appeared at a "Midnight Madness" program in 1994 to tip-off the basketball practice season at the University of Pittsburgh. Perry showed up at the Pitt Field House and promptly donned a Pitt sweatshirt to get into the spirit of things, and participated in a free throw-shooting contest to the delight of the students and fans.

"I'll only wear it here," said Perry, always eager to please everyone. "They wouldn't take too well to it at Penn State."

"I keep thinking about all the people I let down."
— Darren Perry

That's why everyone, especially those who knew him well, were stunned when Darren Perry got himself into a jam with the law during the Christmas season of 1996.

It pointed out how everyone can slip, have a bad day or a bad night, make a mistake, do something stupid, and risk tarnishing their reputation. There's a lesson in there for all of us. Ballplayers, in particular, have to be careful about what they do because any misbehavior will merit headlines in the next day's newspapers and enticing teases on TV. They pay the price for their celebrity status, which is fair enough. It won't be relegated to a single paragraph in the Police Blotter section of the local weekly. The Steelers and their sidekicks had more of their share of scrapes with the law in the early '90s, but no more than the average NFL club.

One day, one hour, one errant walk on the wild side, and someone can spoil everything for themselves, their families and those who care about them. Spending a few weeks observing the doings in the criminal division of the Allegheny County Court House in February, 1997, made me more aware of that than I had ever been before. We must all be ever-vigilant about our behavior and reputation. It's a life-long challenge. The problem is that most people get smarter about such things after they have turned 40.

"If someone steals your Cadillac, you can replace it," a secretary in the Pitt athletic department once told her children, "but if someone steals your reputation you can't replace it."

As a football player, Perry had come a long way, from an eager rookie at St. Vincent's hanging onto the every word of Donnie Shell, a standout Steelers' defensive back from the Steelers' glory days who was there on a minority coaching internship, to duplicating Shell's heroics of intercepting three passes in a game against Testaverde and the Browns at Cleveland Stadium.

Perry had something else in common with Shell. When Shell was with the Steelers, he hoarded his football shoes. Whenever equipment manager Tony Parisi picked up old shoes to distribute to disadvantaged kids in the community, Shell was reluctant to surrender his.

As a child in Columbia, South Carolina, Shell had a hard time getting new shoes.

"It's a small thing," said Perry, "but one of the things that was great about being in college, and more so here, is that you have several pairs of sneakers or football shoes. Growing up, we didn't always have the best of times. We had some tremendously rough times. We'd wear our shoes until they wore out. We never got a pair of sneakers till the rubber was gone off the soles. Your socks would be coming through the bottom of the shoe. I remember when I was in seventh grade, some guy all of a sudden says out loud, 'Your sock's coming through your shoe.' I was so embarrassed. Now I have a Nike deal. I get all the shoes I want. My brothers think it's great. I could never get a new pair of Nikes when I was a kid. I had to beg and plead and cry; I had them for so long."

"I've never been in trouble my whole life."
— Darren Perry

Perry had been a starter at free safety from the first game of his rookie season in 1992, an 8th round draft choice who won the Joe Greene Performance Award as the team's rookie of the year in a vote by the Pittsburgh chapter of the Professional Football Writers Association.

Now Perry was getting negative publicity for a run-in with the police. Considering his reputation, it didn't appear possible, but it was all too true. The same writers who had written rave reviews about him were now bound to write about his misbehavior. Maybe there was a full moon to blame.

It happened in the early morning of December 14, 1996. Perry was arrested by police for a hit-and-run accident in which it was determined that he was driving under the influence of alcohol. According to police reports, Perry was drunk when he was driving his sports utility vehicle. He rear-ended another vehicle on Route 30 in Hempfield, and left the scene. He was caught because a driver behind him (a black man, someone close to the case noted) took off after him, and wrote down his license plate number, which he turned over to local police.

When I heard about what Perry had done, my earlier conversations with him came to mind. He fled the scene, I thought, because he couldn't stand the idea of being caught doing something wrong. The idea of disappointing his dad, his mom, or anybody else he knew for that matter, caused Perry to panic. Drunks often sober up in a hurry when they realize that they have done something wrong. You can better appreciate Perry's personal dilemma if you are familiar with his family, his background, his upbringing.

That doesn't make what he did right. It just helps to understand his situation. They say you don't know a person unless you know their grandparents and where they come from.

Route 30 in Westmoreland County is a road with a history of danger and death, not far from the Steelers' summer training camp at St. Vincent College in Latrobe. Two young Steelers' prospects were involved in an automobile accident on that same stretch in the '70s. One of them died and the other suffered injuries that ended his chances for a professional football career.

I remember Dan Rooney remarking at the time, "That's why auto insurance rates are so high for young drivers."

There was also the tragic story of Gabe Rivera as a reminder of the possible outcome of such shenanigans. Rivera was a promising rookie defensive lineman with the Steelers in 1983, the team's No. 1 draft choice, when he crashed his sportscar into an oncoming car on the city's North Side, not far from Three Rivers Stadium. Rivera was drunk and at fault, according to police reports. He was left a quadraplegic by the accident. The Steelers' fan in the other car — he had Steelers' plates and stickers on his car — came away with minor injuries. Some are luckier than others.

Darren Perry was within two weeks of his 28th birthday when he got into trouble, old enough to know better.

It could have been worse. Perry's incident occurred two weeks after Pittsburgh was mourning the death of Jamil Deen, a 7-year-old Wilkinsburg boy who was struck by a hit-and-run driver in East Liberty.

The media was quick to point out that Perry was a pretty decent individual, whose previous track record was an enviable one. They recognized, however, that there shouldn't be a different set of rules for wealthy football players. The public had come to believe that a jock could get away with murder — can you believe that? — because the public was so forgiving of their misdeeds. Just ask O.J.

As it turned out, Perry drew a suspended sentence, a stern reprimand, and had to pay for auto repair costs and the court costs. He apologized to all concerned, and his previous clean sheet and his contriteness, which was deemed genuine, were taken into consideration. Perry appreciated those who came to his defense, but he was honest enough to own up to his actions. The public tends to be forgiving of those who apologize or are sorry for their sins. No one was more critical of his misdeeds than Perry himself.

"I've never been in trouble in my whole life," Perry told the *Pittsburgh Post-Gazette* soon after. "I keep thinking about all the people I let down. My family, my parents, Bill Cowher, Joe Paterno...

"I run a camp for kids back home. I know they look up to me. The last thing I want to do is let them down. Some players could care less about that, but it really means something to me.

"I know a lot of people are watching to see how I handle this. I want them to know there's great remorse on my part. I'm not just letting go of it. I really am going to make something good come from it. I wish it had never happened, but I'm going to make something positive come from it."

"Don't do anything to embarrass me or your family."
— Joseph Perry

Darren Perry returned each off-season to his boyhood community of Deep Creek in the city of Chesapeake, Virginia, where "everyone knew everyone."

His father, Joseph, was the first black police officer in Chesapeake, according to his son. "There were some things we just didn't do," recalled Darren. "We had to answer to our father."

Keep in mind that Perry offered these thoughts prior to his problems with legal authorities for the Route 30 incident.

"We didn't do things like throwing rocks or join in when friends would break windows, stuff like that. We might be around in the vicinity, but we weren't the ones who were doing it. My dad was very strict. He told us, 'Don't do anything to embarrass me or your family.'

"He never looked at color. To him, it was never a big deal. But he held our family to a higher standard than our neighbors. He took a lot of pride in his work. My mother felt he worked too much. We had a big family, there were eight of us, and he took on extra work to make more money.

"My dad loved his work. He did extra work in security, but it was all police-related. He was always tired when he came home. We didn't do a lot of father-son stuff. We were not out in the yard playing together. There were a lot of us kids and we did it among ourselves. But we knew the rules.

"Growing up, he'd bring the police car home. We lived on the main road. So everybody knew our house. I was a good athlete in high school, and got a lot of attention. 'That's where the Perrys live,' people would say. 'That's where Darren Perry lives.' The car was often in front of our house. We never had to worry about anybody starting anything outside our place. If something went down, people came over looking for my dad to help them out.

"He was always there from a discipline standpoint. He told us to take a lot of pride in our family. 'Your name means something,' he'd often say. It was considered important having people respect you. Not by being the biggest, strongest or toughest. But by your personality and the way you carried yourself.

"My dad wanted us to take pride in being a Perry. 'When they hear that name,' he'd say, 'you want them to say something good. It's not money, that's not the key. When they hear that name, they're going to say something good.'

"He was tough on us, but he was fair. He had a lot of stress on the job. My father could get frustrated at times. But he cared about all of us."

"You're the kind of athlete and person Penn State is looking for."
— Joe Paterno

I talked to Perry about Penn State and Joe Paterno on several occasions. It was a subject dear to his heart, though he confessed it wasn't love at first sight.

Limping about the locker room with a foot injury on one occasion, Perry spoke of his experience at Penn State. In some ways, Joe Paterno and Joe Perry were similar in their approach of dealing with young people.

"While you're there," said Darren Perry, "you don't always appreciate all the things that they did because of what they expect from student-athletes. It takes a while to realize how much you learn that serves you in good stead later on. It's about life.

"You remember the nagging things. Things they're always on your back about. Things having to do with the overall pride of being a Penn State athlete, being different from athletes at some other schools. I hear about what goes on at other programs. People say, 'I can tell you went to Penn State.' We are a little different.

"When I was being recruited, Joe Paterno told me, 'You're the kind of athlete and person Penn State is looking for.' It's the same way with the Steelers. I do know they look for a certain kind of individual. Mr. Rooney likes to keep those guys around.

"I remember Coach Cowher, in his first speech to us when I first got here. He said you should surround yourself with the right people. Hearing that kind of reminded me of what I'd been told so many times at Penn State.

"Besides Penn State, I visited North Carolina at Chapel Hill, Virginia and South Carolina when I was being recruited. Just four schools. North Carolina was my second choice."

I had spent time on all four campuses that Perry had considered, and knew them well. My older daughter, Sarah, selected Virginia over North Carolina for her undergraduate studies in 1992 — the same year Perry signed with the Steelers — so I could appreciate Perry's dilemma when it came time to selecting a school. Perry had his pick of some of this country's most idyllic campuses.

"I had a hard time, at first, at Penn State," said Perry. "The homesick part of it, being red-shirted. Just the whole adjustment. Not being able to go home so easy. It was a four hour drive each way; we just couldn't do that, like some of the Pennsylvania kids could. My roommate, Keith Goganious, was also from the Tidewater area.

"Joe caused a stir when he came down. If I didn't go to Penn State then I think the people would've thought I was crazy. He came to my home and then he came to the school. I think that's how they get you. At home, it's just you and your family and the coach. At school, everyone else gets involved.

"I wasn't as intimidated talking to him on my home turf. I knew of him, sure, but I didn't think of him as a legend. He was somewhat like any other coach. But when he came to the school and our coaches talked to him, and the students saw him, they saw him as the legendary football coach he is. Now he had some allies.

"He told me about what the University could do for me. Joe said, 'If you want to be the best, not only as an athlete but as a student, you can't do better than Penn State.' I can say that now; it's the combination of both. If I just wanted the best in academics, I could have gone to William & Mary, and Virginia and North Carolina. They are outstanding academically, too, and they're not bad sports-wise, either. Joe talked to me about Penn State's graduation rate, which is great, but that doesn't mean a lot to you at that time in your life."

Perry was an all-state quarterback in high school, but he was also a good all-around athlete and he knew he would end up playing a different position at Penn State. He was a leader, too, as captain of the football, basketball and tennis teams at Deep Creek High School in Chesapeake, Virginia.

He played tennis in high school at the urging of one of his coaches to improve his hand-eye coordination which would help him in basketball and in football. He fell in love with the game, and still enjoys playing in the off-season.

"I always prided myself on having soft hands," said Perry. "I thought I was going to be a receiver, back when I was just catching the football with my brother. I always thought I could catch. Even when I went to Penn State, I thought I might play wide receiver, but it never really worked out."

Terry Bradshaw used to say that all defensive backs think they could be wide receivers. "If they could catch the ball," Bradshaw said, "they'd be wide receivers."

Paterno frequently drafted high school quarterbacks and turned them into linebackers, which is why Jim Kelly of East Brady opted for the University of Miami. Perry became Ron Dickerson's pet project as a defensive back at Penn State. Perry had never even played defense during his high school career.

It wasn't easy going at the start. Perry experienced problems in making the transition from high school superstar to squad member at Penn State. In the beginning, Perry had a difficult time understanding why State College was called Happy Valley.

"Maybe I was spoiled by what I had enjoyed and perhaps taken for granted in high school back home," said Perry. "I had always been the best and one of the brightest. I had success and high expectations.

Darren Perry

During Penn State days

Darren participates in many community affairs, such as Joe DeNardo's WTAE Project Bundle Up to provide clothing to disadvantaged citizens.

Darren's college coach, Joe Paterno, is flanked during 1982 season by two Pittsburgh quarterbacks, Mark Malone and Dan Marino, at Curbstone Coaches confab at Allegheny Club.

At Penn State, I felt a little lost. The classroom size threw me. It was difficult for me going out and having to meet people, mixing.

"It was a big campus. They don't know who you are. They don't know you're a scholarship athlete. You're not 6-10, 250 pounds. They don't treat you like a special student. Now I realize that's good, but I didn't back then. Maybe I was selfish, maybe I missed the special treatment. Maybe I wanted to know I was wanted.

"There were problems as far as football was concerned. I was not producing. I was trying to get myself into position to play. Everything was just starting to go good. I was starting to adjust to college life. They expect you to do well in both and I had been having a rough time.

"It all came to a head this one day when I was having a bad day at practice. It was a nice day in early October, but things went badly for me that day, and I overreacted. I felt I wasn't getting a fair shake. Paterno was yelling at me. I felt like I was being picked on. I just walked off the field.

"Joe is very intimidating if you're not doing the right things. If you screw up that intimidation only increases. His expectations of his athletes are just tremendous, maybe too demanding at times. Maybe he expects too much of certain individuals. When he's wearing those dark glasses, you figure he can't see very far. But make a mistake on the other side of the field and Joe will see it, make no doubt about that, and he'll be on you in a flash. It's unreal.

"After I walked off the field that day, I stayed at a friend's house that night rather than in my room. I didn't call home. I didn't want to tell my parents. I didn't want them to think I was a quitter. I tried to sneak into breakfast the next morning, but that didn't work. Coach Dickerson was driving around the campus looking for me, and he found me. We aired out some things. I told him I thought things might be different if I was somewhere else.

"Ron Dickerson talked me into staying. Him and Jim Caldwell; he's the coach who recruited me. They were like father figures to me. They both had great families. I really looked up to those guys.

"They would have you to their homes every so often. Like if you don't have a place to go at Easter, they'll have you to their home, so you have a place that's warm and comfy for the holiday. They'll invite you for dinner. Ron Dickerson is responsible for me being the player that I am. He kinda like molded me. He set the ground work and the mentality I needed to succeed. He told me a long time ago that being a defensive back meant you had to have a lot of pride and a short memory. You'll make mistakes, and no matter how small they are, people will see it.

"Other guys at other positions will make a mistake, or take a play off, but it won't get noticed. But you do that in the defensive backfield and you'll get burned. He taught me everything I know."

Perry pointed to Dickerson as the person at Penn State who straightened him out about his early misconceptions of his role as a student-athlete.

"He definitely talked me out of leaving. He told me my feelings were not unique. He said what I was going through was no different than what the other 29 freshmen who came in the same year were feeling. That it was natural to be a little confused and overwhelmed by what you find at a big college campus after you come out of high school. He said, 'You haven't developed into the person you're going to be. You'll get accustomed to things and you'll mature and you'll be able to handle all of this.' I was lucky to have someone like him on my side. If you don't have someone there to make sure you're doing the right thing after you leave home, someone with a good sense of morals, it's easy to be led away from what you know is right."

How did Paterno treat him after he heard about Perry's departure from the practice field, and his thoughts about returning home?

"I was going to the study hall, and I walked by Paterno. He said, 'Is everything OK?' I told him I had talked to Ron Dickerson earlier in the day. I told him I was just frustrated. He opened up his door. 'Don't hesitate to come in if you are having any problems,' he said."

Things worked out just fine for Perry after his early adjustment problems. He started most of his four varsity seasons during his five year involvement in a big-time program at Penn State. As a senior, he had six interceptions, two for touchdowns, was one of the team captains and earned Football Writers All-America honors.

He had 15 career interceptions, the second best mark in school history, and set a record for return yardage (299) on interceptions, and scored three touchdowns altogether.

During his junior year of 1990, Perry made a big interception to help Penn State beat Notre Dame in a game at South Bend that kept the No. 1 ranked Fighting Irish from winning the national championship.

With less than a minute remaining in the late November game, Perry intercepted a Rick Mirer pass and returned it 20 yards to set up a 34-yard field goal by freshman Craig Fayak of Belle Vernon with four seconds showing on the clock that gave Penn State a 24-20 victory. Both teams finished the regular season with 8-2 records.

Perry remembers what Paterno did and said at the team's year-end awards banquet during his senior year. "I won a big award," said Perry. "When Paterno called my name out, I walked up to the front of the room with my   parents. He told the story about how I almost left school as a freshman.

"Paterno talked about the need to be patient, and about working hard. He looked at me and said, 'See what you've become now!' He surprised me. I thought it was a situation where he'd just talk about good things. But he made his point. He was a big-time philosopher.

"One time Bill Cowher gave us quite a talk, and Jonathan Hayes asked me afterward if Paterno was a good speaker. I told him Paterno wasn't as young or as fiery as Cowher, but that he could make his points effectively. He'd do it his way, the Penn State way.

"Cowher is more personable, more interactive. There's an age difference between the two, and Cowher was a player in the National Football League. So he relates to the players better than Joe, but he doesn't cover as wide an area in his talks. Cowher concentrates more on football. After all, we're not in school anymore."

I asked Perry if he thought about what a difficult time Dickerson, who came from Coraopolis near the Pittsburgh International Airport, must have been experiencing at Temple, where he had been unable to improve the Owls' football program.

"If you said you can't win, Ron Dickerson would be the first person to tell you not to think that way," said Perry. "He wouldn't have taken that Temple job if he didn't think he could turn it around. It must be tougher than he thought."

"He was never boring."
— Darren Perry
on Joe Paterno

Sometimes when Perry is participating in a team meeting with the Steelers he is reminded of his days at Penn State.

"The team meetings are different," said Perry. "There's no comparison. That's what I miss the most about playing football at Penn State. We had these special meetings. Every Tuesday we'd normally have a meeting. Sometimes he'd talk to us two or three times a week. Joe would come in and he'd find a way to motivate you. He'd tell a story or something. He's a tremendous speaker.

"Every so often I've thought about going up there some Tuesday — which is usually our day off — just to sit in on a team meeting. I miss that. He'd talk about what you have to do when things go wrong. He was never boring. You never said, 'Oh, I've heard this before. This is boring.'"

John Mitchell, the Steelers' defensive line coach, offered similar reflections on his days as a player and later an assistant coach under Bear Bryant at Alabama. Mitchell also spent six seasons as an assistant to Lou Holtz at Arkansas, and said he, too, was an inspirational speaker.

"It was like going to church, and listening to a sermon," continued Perry. "I remember Joe telling us about why they had guide rails on highways. How they were like the rules and guidelines we need in our life. How those guide rails become even more important on twisting mountain roads. How some people would drive off the cliff if they weren't there. He compared life to learning how to drive. He said it took a while before you got comfortable, and knew what you were doing.

"And he'd talk about why the younger guys had more rules than the older ones on the team. He talked about how young drivers just don't have the experience to handle certain problems on the road."

370

Paterno's talk should have been ringing in Perry's ears after that early-morning mishap in his utility vehicle out on Route 30 in Hempfield...

"I remember when we were playing football, he'd always tell us to run scared," said Perry. "Stuff like that. His little sayings stay with you.

"You have to keep in mind that he's a coach. He'll still scream and yell at you. When the team loses he'll still tell you you're not very good. The bottom line is that he's still a football coach.

"That makes you realize he's human. He told us not to pay too much attention to our press clippings. No matter how high the praise, he said we weren't perfect, and that you could be humbled in a hurry.

"He taught us what football is all about, and more importantly, he taught us what life was all about. He taught us some lessons that are still relevant to me as a professional football player and as a person.

"He's somewhat taken on the responsibility of being your father away from home. Some guys would say, 'Man, another squad meeting, another lecture from Joe.' But I miss that. Joe was a phenomenal speaker. He could be intimidating.

"He was strong on reminding us about the rules we were expected to live by. We had to have classes in the morning; that was the best way for us not to sleep in. They had a moderator at breakfast. It was mandatory for the football players to be at breakfast. You had to wear a collared shirt, no T-shirts. No hats. If you want to get in his dog house, have a hat on your head inside the building. 'Get it off!' His voice is so squeaky high. 'Get that hat off!' You could have a mustache, but no other facial hair. You were expected to have a clean-shaven face.

"Joe Paterno always told you, 'When you get in front of media you can't let emotions take over. Sometimes you're upset, but you can't let that affect what you say. You have to think about what you're saying.'"

Perry graduated from Penn State in 1992 with a degree in business administration/management. He has attended Old Dominion University during the off-season since he's been with the Steelers, working toward a Master's in Business Administration degree. His wife, Errika, graduated from Penn State with a degree in business logistics.

"We liked the way he played the game."
— Tom Donahoe

Bill Cowher is a big fan of Darren Perry. "He doesn't drop an opportunity when he gets it," said the Steelers' coach when asked about his starting free safety. "The one thing about playing in this league is you get opportunities, and if you want to be a good player, you can't drop them. He doesn't do that."

There was a time when it didn't appear that Perry would have such opportunities. At the end of Perry's career at Penn State, he was thought to be too short and too slow, but Donahoe and Steelers' scouts spoke about his pluses, not his minuses. Donahoe said he could make the play.

On Draft Day in 1992, after the Steelers picked Perry in the eighth round, Cowher commented:

"Perry doesn't have the great speed, which is why a lot of teams were hesitant about him. But when you watch him on the football field, he always makes the plays. He's started for four years at Penn State and he's been productive in a major college program. He's proved himself at that level, and we think he's ready to progress to the next level."

Perry is an instinctive player, something you can't really teach. He became a starter at his first training camp. In 1995, he signed a new contract, a four-year deal worth $5.6 million through 1998.

He became one of the NFL's best pass-stealers, which came as no surprise to Donahoe. "Darren had that same knack in college for coming up with the football," said Donahoe. "Usually when you look at a guy who doesn't have great size, and doesn't have speed, but somehow manages to be around the ball, and makes great plays, often you can trace it to his intelligence and instincts. If you have that, you can make plays.

"Darren didn't test well when he was being evaluated by the pro scouts," said Donahoe. "During the combine and the individual workouts, he didn't really light up people, but that's how you get fooled. If you're just going on measurables, there's a good chance you can err. The bottom line has to be: 'How does the guy play the game?' We liked how he played the game. And he had a great attitude."

Perry was all too aware that he had not impressed too many people at the combine workouts.

"Coach Paterno told me that once I got to training camp, they'd throw all that stuff out the window," said Perry. "In the pros, what matters is what kind of football player you are."

It was unreal how things fell into place for Perry. Thomas Everett was a holdout. Gary Jones tore up his knee at training camp and, lo and behold, Perry became the starting safety. And this was a guy who was the 203rd player picked in the draft.

"He's not under-rated by us," said Dick LeBeau, who had been his backfield coach and then the team's defensive coordinator during his first five seasons with the Steelers. "He's still getting better. He has improved every year. I think his numbers speak for themselves. He's a very stable person, a very intelligent person. He makes a lot of our calls. He's a joy to watch."

Perry was good enough to start in Super Bowl XXX at Tempe, Arizona in January, 1996, when the Steelers took on the Dallas

Cowboys. During Media Day, Perry was sitting in the stands at Sun Devil Stadium, largely ignored, when he was approached by veteran Steelers' beatman and columnist Norm Vargo, the sports editor of *The Daily News* in McKeesport.

Perry told Vargo he was thinking about his junior high days in Virginia. "I grew up a Cowboys fan," offered Perry. "I played quarterback and even wore No. 12, like Roger Staubach. I hated the Steelers because they beat Dallas in all the big games."

Perry's personal philosophy about playing the game is simple enough: "You want to make something happen and make a difference in the ball game.

"It's just a conscious effort to come up with the football and make something happen. I have a knack for doing it, and it's hard to explain. I don't have to set individual goals. Mine are mostly team goals."

He credited LeBeau for his development as a pro. "You study your playbook, you study your opponent, and you get a feel for the game and what teams like to do and who they go to in certain situations," said Perry. "And that will put you around the ball."

"Let's talk about positives."
— Mike Tomczak

I asked Perry what player on the Steelers he admired the most, and he surprised me with his answer.

"Mike Tomczak," he said, nodding toward his next door neighbor's dressing stall. Tomczak wasn't there, either, so he wasn't saying it to get a rise out of his teammate.

"I admire him because of how he handles situations. He always keeps things in perspective. He's seen a lot. Being a quarterback, he's been under scrutiny a lot. He talks about how they love you one moment and damn you the next moment.

"I admire the way he carries himself. Mike is a champion guy. After we lost to Jacksonville in the opener, we came back and beat the Bills at Three Rivers Stadium. Mike called a team meeting that week. 'Let's talk about positives,' he said. 'I think we should have a meeting after something good, rather than after something bad. We never have a team meeting until things go bad.' Everyone was sitting on their chairs around him, and he opened up a lot of people's eyes. He's a real leader. He cares. He wants to be looked upon as a leader. You want to see your quarterback doing that sort of thing. The guys look for that.

"There are a lot of egos in this room. Some players' egos are way out of line. Some of the young guys don't like some of the old players,

373

one of those being Greg (Lloyd). He can be intimidating and hard on you. Some of the young guys resent that. We're all professionals and we all have feelings. Kirk (Levon Kirkland) and I were talking, and we agreed we're not like that. We don't get on the young guys; we try to help them develop. Greg means well; he wants what's best for the team."

Darren Perry (39) and Levon Kirkland (99) combine for tackle against Cincinnati Bengals.

Baldy Regan
Only in America

"I've watched him work his magic."
— Pittsburgh Mayor Tom Murphy

A blue suit should be the staple of every man's wardrobe, according to the gospel of Baldy Regan. Two blue suits are even better, preferably dark blue suits.

At the outset of the '90s, a Pittsburgh men's clothing chain was holding a going-out-of-business sale. They were offering suits for $240 for the first one, and you could get a second one for an additional $10. Or two suits for $250.

This prompted Baldy Regan to get after his pal Paul Tomasovich to go shopping with him.

"We got to get us some suits," said Baldy. "You can't beat the price."

"What do we need with suits?" asked Tomasovich, who usually appeared in casual clothes — a windbreaker over a golf shirt with dark slacks or jeans, nothing fancy — while keeping constant company at sports events and social events throughout the city with Baldy, a pot-bellied fellow who always wore a blazer or suit, white shirt and tie wherever he waddled. The coats were always tight-fitting. The buttons on Baldy's blazers and suits were always under great stress.

Baldy grew up with guys who used to pick up a new trench coat or jacket by picking one off the hanger at a dance hall. It didn't matter that someone else had worn it to the dance.

Baldy had a pudgy pink mug. His complexion had turned from pink to red, and it looked like he was courting a heart attack. He looked like a heavy drinker, but he never drank booze or smoked and seldom swore. But he had an insatiable appetite. For food. For life. He was quick with a fork and a quip and a smile, and boosted everybody's stature as soon as he spotted them.

"Brother, we're getting at that age where a lot of people we know are passing on," Baldy told Tomasovich. "We can wear the one suit to the funerals. We'll keep the other one for our own funeral, so they have something nice to lay us out in. We got to look good, too."

Baldy and Tomasovich were both wearing their blue suits at the Stephen M. Brady Funeral Home on the North Side on September 16-17 in the fall of 1995. Baldy was also wearing a dark tie with small green shamrocks on it. An American flag and a Irish flag were folded and displayed nearby.

Tomasovich was among the mourners in attendance at the funeral of Baldy Regan, 61, who died of a heart attack after checking in at Allegheny General Hospital that Thursday afternoon. Tomasovich and two of Baldy's sons were at his bedside.

"I didn't know what to do," said Tomasovich, a tall, intimidating figure and one of the strongest and nicest men you would ever meet. "I started stuttering. He was so close to his kids. They were so attached to him."

Anybody who ever met Baldy was attached to him. He had a glad hand, and a hearty greeting for everyone. He had the gift for making your day, making you feel like a big deal.

"Thanks for saying hello to me in front of my friends," he'd say. "That makes me look good."

Or when he'd say, "Brother, my mother would be impressed to know I knew a big shot like you."

Stanley "Zundy" Kramer, a Pittsburgh businessman and sports enthusiast, said, "He used to tell me, 'If my mother knew that I knew an important Jew like you she'd spin in her grave.' "

Whenever Baldy would meet a friend who had become a success, he would size him up, compliment him on his attire, and offer his trademark comment: "Only in America!"

Back in the early '60s, there was a popular nationally-syndicated columnist named Harry Golden. He published a newspaper called *The Carolina Israelite.* He loved to write about rags-to-riches success stories. A collection of his stories was published in a best-selling book called *Only In America.* Baldy borrowed that line, and put it to good use the rest of his life.

He was in the Top Ten of the all-time favorites of Art Rooney, the founder of the Steelers. Rooney took a liking to Baldy as a young boy and boosted his cause throughout his life. Baldy was a loyal disciple and helped spread the Gospel of Art Rooney wherever he traveled.

Rooney recommended Regan for a scholarship to Alliance College in Cambridge Springs, Pennsylvania, not far from Erie. Baldy stayed there about a year. Nearly all the students were Polish, but that didn't stop Rooney or Regan from taking advantage of a good opportunity.

Baldy was a high school classmate of Art Rooney Jr. and that is how he managed to get tight with the Rooney family. Baldy was the class president at North Catholic. "He really was a poor Irish kid from the North Side," recalled Art Jr., the second of Art Rooney's five sons, who headed up the Steelers' scouting department during their glory days of the '70s. "He really had a gift of gab."

"I'm ready for The Big Man if he shows up."
— Baldy Regan

Baldy and Tomasovich had been legendary figures on the Pittsburgh sports scene. Both had been fixtures in the press box at Steelers' games through the years, going back to when the Steelers were playing at Pitt Stadium and Forbes Field in the '60s. Baldy had been in charge of running off copies of the play-by-play accounts and statistics

When Irish eyes are smiling: Baldy Regan, former light heavyweight boxing champion Billy Conn, and U.S. Congressman William Coyne.

Jim O'Brien

Mike Tomasovich was Baldy's best buddy.

for many seasons and, in more recent seasons, he and his kids kept the media well-stocked with paper and soft drinks. Paul and his kids helped out as well.

Baldy and Tomasovich traveled the world — to Ireland twice, to Australia, South America, Spain — with kids' basketball teams they recruited and chaperoned. They were America's ambassadors wherever they went. There's a story that's made the rounds that a Pittsburgh dignitary was once dining in a castle in Ireland, and the host asked him, "And would you be knowin' Baldy Regan?"

Regan and Tomasovich made their mark wherever they went. Not bad for two guys who first met in 1952 as opposing players when Baldy was a student at North Catholic High School and Tomasovich was a three-sport standout at Fifth Avenue High School in the Hill District. "Only in America!" Baldy would say.

Baldy's last job, thanks to his friend Mayor Tom Murphy, was as sports director of the Pittsburgh Sports and Festival Federation, at $50,000 a year with offices in the base of Three Rivers Stadium. His task was to bring major sporting events to the city. Word came out after his death that he had landed the prestigious McDonald's All-American High School Basketball Classic for the Civic Arena for 1996. He frequently paid a visit to the Steelers' offices on the other side of the stadium.

In recent seasons, Baldy sat behind the scouts at the far left end of the press box. He played sports as a kid at North Catholic High School, boxed a while, which accounted for his pushed-in nose, and promoted sports events of all kinds. He frequently imported "The King & His Court," a five-man team of softball stars headed by trick-pitcher Eddie "The King" Feigner. Baldy was the promoter and manager of the Steelers basketball team for many years, booking games in the off-season throughout the tri-state area. They helped raise money for many charitable purposes, and the players picked up some extra bucks and had some fun, usually playing against school teachers and police officers at high school gyms.

"He was always friendly with the players," allowed Larry Brown. "He was always after us to play for his basketball team."

Brown was among the former Steelers seen at the church and funeral home, including Franco Harris, Rocky Bleier, Mel Blount, John Brown and Paul Martha. Chuck Noll paid his respects at the funeral home. Brown, a former tackle and tight end, had teamed up with J.T. Thomas to own and operate several Applebee's Restaurants in the Greater Pittsburgh area. Other former Steelers called the team's offices, expressing their sorrow upon learning that Baldy had died.

"Baldy always treated us well," said Brown, looking a lot leaner than when he played so superbly for the Steelers through four Super Bowls. "He was one of the first people to befriend new Steelers. And he was fun to be around. We'll all miss him."

In 1977, Phil Musick, then sports editor of the *Post-Gazette*, wrote that Regan "promotes the way Perry Como sings and Muhammad Ali brags, which is to say effortlessly...He is not necessarily a booking agent, but if you are watching The King & His Court softball team, or a touring basketball team of six-foot red-haired women, or Franco Harris going to the hoop over the prostrate form of Tony Dorsett, it is no worse than even money that Regan did the importing."

He was called Baldy even though he wasn't bald, and he was called "The Mayor of the North Side" and "The Judge," because he was such a booster of his community, and because he was a district justice on the North Side for 20 years. He was once a county detective, and held various political posts. He had friends in the right places. It was known as patronage in political circles. He was a colorful and controversial member of City Council from 1990 to 1992. Baldy was a pretty basic guy who went with his instincts, and this frequently got him into hot water.

He spoke at a sports banquet one night in Carrick when I was on the same dais. He told a funny story that still sticks in my mind. He came from a tough neighborhood on the North Side, and he could poke fun at himself and his hometown. He talked about approaching a cab driver in Carrick and asking him, "Hey, brother, how do I get to the North Side?" And the cabbie came back, "Drink wine, man, lots of wine."

Baldy liked to tell the story of how he came by his nickname as a schoolboy. "My mother figured that if I got all my hair cut off, I would only need one haircut for the summer. People started calling me Baldy. Even the nuns and priests at school called me Baldy. It's become more of a name than a nickname."

He was famous for his annual Christmas party at his district justice offices across the street from Perry High School. "It's the only place where you can mix with bankers and bank robbers in the same room," one of his friends, PR executive Larry Werner, informed me at one of the parties.

One night Baldy stopped the music to make an announcement: "Anyone in here packing heat," he hollered out, "better put your stuff in your cars! We don't want any trouble in here tonight!" Several party-goers suddenly scrambled for the front door.

One night when I was there for the Christmas mixer, Baldy officiated at the marriage of a local couple in the midst of the party. The bride was eight months pregnant and hoping to get married on the sly. "We can handle that," Baldy assured her the day before.

Harold "Mr. Trombone" Betters and his group, popular Pittsburgh musicians — "Rambunctious" — who were also fixtures at Steelers games at Three Rivers Stadium, provided the music at the party and impromptu wedding reception that night. It was a blast. Only in Baldy's North Side...

Betters recalls: "I remember one time he had a black Santa Claus. 'That's for you, Harold,' he told me. 'Only in America.'"

Baldy's best buddy, Tomasovich, always referred to him as "The Judge." Tomasovich, a big guy who calls everyone else "Big Guy," was the Babe Ruth of sandlot softball in this country in the '60s and '70s. They still talk about home runs he hit over distant walls and homes at ballfields around western Pennsylvania. He lived near Magee Field in Greenfield where he hit some of those storied blasts.

Tomasovich had seven daughters. Baldy was the proud father of four sons and two daughters. You have never met more well-mannered, pleasant and polite kids in your life. They are the true legacy of these two legends.

I first met Baldy in 1955 when I was 13 years old. I went with the coaches to purchase uniforms for our sandlot football team, the Hazelwood Steelers, and Baldy was working behind the counter at the Pittsburgh Sports Shop, owned by Joe Goetz, which also provided the Pittsburgh Steelers with their uniforms.

It was only a month before Baldy's burial mass that I bought a new blue suit during a sale at Lazarus in South Hills Village. Already, I had worn it to the funerals of three friends.

I wore it to pay my respects to the family of Jim Madden of Baldwin-Whitehall, a Pitt grad and great fan who, like Baldy, had the ability to put sunshine in the life of those he knew. He died at age 70.

I wore it when Vince Russo, a schoolboy football standout at St. Bernard's Grade School, Mt. Lebanon High School and Virginia Tech, died at age 45 in September, 1995. Russo was such a popular fellow that there was a two hour wait to express condolences to his family at the L. Beinhauer & Son funeral home in Peters Township.

No one had a wake quite like the Irish. Baldy's was right out of Edwin O'Connor's book, *The Last Hurrah*, about the life and times of Frank Skeffington, a fictional but true-to-life mayor of Boston, or *Trinity* by Leon Uris. The Irish pride themselves on their durability, or staying power. They are stubborn, mulish in that respect. Normal visiting hours at funeral homes for Christians are 2 to 4 p.m. and 7 to 9 p.m. The Regan family and friends were scheduled to be present to receive condolences from 2 to 10 p.m. on Saturday and from 10 a.m. to 10 p.m. on Sunday, and both sessions went into overtime. No one complained.

"Baldy was always very upbeat about death," said Tomasovich, who knew Baldy for 33 years. "He used to say, 'I'm ready for The Big Man if he shows up.'"

Tomasovich was asked to explain the magic of Baldy Regan. While Baldy had his faults, just like the rest of us, people were drawn to him. "Everybody has a fear of some type," said Tomasovich. "Baldy didn't want to be disliked by anybody. It tore his heart out when he lost the re-election for City Council. He wanted everyone to like him."

With Mayor Richard Caliguiri

With Governor Bob Casey

At The White House with President George Bush and Steelers' Hall of Famer Franco Harris. Baldy showed up in the darndest places.

"Baldy was a Pittsburgh institution."
— Tom Foerster

"We lost a good friend; it's too bad," said Mary Regan, no relation to Baldy, but a life-long friend. Mary had served as a secretary in the Steelers' front office since 1952 ("I started when I was 13," she added with a smile.) For most of that time, she was the receptionist and personal secretary to Steelers' owner Art Rooney. She was standing outside St. Peter's Church on the North Side, which sits amidst the Aviary, Mercy Providence Hospital, Allegheny Middle School and the Children's Museum. She was waiting for her sister, Joan, and their mother, Mary, a spirited woman at 88, who were crossing Arch Street to attend Baldy's funeral mass.

Mary's sister, Pat, was married to Dan Rooney, the oldest of Art Rooney's five sons and the president of the Steelers. Pat was accompanied to the church by her oldest son, Art II, a Pittsburgh attorney regarded as the heir apparent to his father to oversee the Steelers' operation. Dan was in Miami with the Steelers for a game that day.

Pat and Dan had moved from their long-time home in Mt. Lebanon's posh Virginia Manor section to his boyhood home on the North Side a year earlier. Dan had the home refurbished and added a two-car garage. They were now esteemed members and patrons of St. Peter's parish. Following the mass for Baldy Regan, I overheard a parishioner advising the pastor to put the arm on Dan Rooney to finance the repair of an obtrusive crack in the ceiling of the church.

Baldy Regan grew up in the same neighborhood as the Regan girls, both families in humble circumstances. Many people thought they were related, kissing cousins or something, but they were not. None of them ever forgot where they came from. There were nine in Pat's family living in a two-bedroom house.

St. Peter's was often referred to as "Art Rooney's church." He was its prime benefactor, a role Dan had assumed.

I had been there three times previously, for a memorial service for Richie McCabe, and then, more recently, for the funeral services of Kathleen and Art Rooney, respectively. Art was preceded in death by his wonderful wife, a good sport in her own right. They both drew SRO crowds. "I read where you're rich," Kathleen once chided her husband. "Why don't you toss me a dollar now and then?"

McCabe had a background similar to Baldy Regan. He, too, was a Rooney favorite. McCabe had grown up on the North Side, and played sports at St. Peter's Grade School, North Catholic High School and then Pitt. He was a waterboy for the Steelers as a kid. He was a tough kid, even though he wore glasses and was always thought to be too skinny to play ball on every level in which he ever competed. He went on to play defensive back in both the AFL and NFL, and coached in the NFL before dying of cancer at age 48 while an assistant with the Denver Broncos.

Art Rooney sat near the front of the church, but off to the side, at the services for McCabe and, of course, for his wife Kathleen.

It was a shame Art Rooney missed Baldy Regan's funeral mass. He would have enjoyed it. Any Irishman worth his salt would have. Brendan Behan and Brian Boru and St. Patrick would have enjoyed it. It had all the right touches. For an uneasy half hour, however, it looked like Baldy Regan might miss it as well.

Priests were peeking out from behind pillars at the front of the church, checking to see when the funeral party would arrive. The service was scheduled to begin at 1 p.m., but didn't really get underway until about 28 minutes later.

When Art Rooney died, some suggested he was such a popular Pittsburgh figure and the crowds would be so enormous that the service should be shifted from St. Peter's to St. Paul's Cathedral in Oakland, the bishop's church.

"If they did that," remarked a close friend of Art Rooney familiar with his humble manner, "I don't think Mr. Rooney would show up."

That came to mind as many of those who had come to pay their final respects were growing restless, and looking to the rear of the church to see if a casket was coming through the door and down the aisle.

"Remember when we were kids in Catholic grade school," offered one observer, "and the nuns would scold us about being late for class. They'd say, 'You'll be late for your own funeral.' Well, I'm sure they scolded Baldy more than once with that line."

As an adult, however, Baldy had a reputation for being punctual, a man of his word. "He was a 25-hour-a-day man," remarked Mary Regan, "but he somehow managed to get everything done."

The holdup was caused by heavy traffic outside the church, and the long procession of cars coming from the funeral home, which included Mayor Tom Murphy, a close friend and political ally of Baldy, and many other political dignitaries, including County Commissioners Tom Foerster and Pete Flaherty.

"For 22 years, I've called Baldy a friend and I've watched him work his magic," Mayor Murphy said in a statement his office issued.

"Baldy was a Pittsburgher in the truest and grandest sense, and he was a North Sider. In fact, he was Mr. North Side.

"There was no one in this city who knew more people, both the richest and the poorest, and could talk to them as if they were the most important people in the world. There was no one who touched more kids and created more opportunity for them."

He had what is sometimes referred to as "the common touch." He was a disciple of Art Rooney who often claimed you could tell a Pittsburgher by the warmth of his or her handshake.

Dan Onorato, who beat Baldy out when he sought re-election to City Council, said, "When I hear the name Baldy Regan, I think only one thing — children and youth sports.

"Baldy Regan was a force on the North Side for as long as I can remember. He helped a lot of people, and I think that's how we should remember him."

Tom Foerster goes back even further with Baldy Regan. "I was privileged to be Baldy's first baseball coach in 1950 in the Perry Athletic Association on the North Side. Baldy had a lifelong commitment to sports, from sandlot to professional.

"He leaves a legacy of hundreds and hundreds of children and young adults. He took teens all over the world through his driving determination to succeed.

"But Baldy leaves more than just a legacy in sports — he was a committed public servant as a district justice, city councilman and sheriff's deputy. Baldy was a Pittsburgh institution. People who knew him will miss him, and the people who didn't know him will miss not knowing him. He was a Damon Runyon-like character."

"There are so many stories about Baldy ...that would literally fill this church."
— Father Thomas Ferris

Father Thomas Ferris of St. Cyril of Alexandria Church in the Brighton Heights section of the North Side officiated at the mass for Baldy Regan, a lifelong friend and a former classmate at North Catholic High School. Father Ferris was one of six priests who participated in the service. That's critical on the North Side where people count the number of priests as an indicator of the importance of the departed. "My cousin had more priests at his funeral mass than Art Rooney...," one North Sider was known to have boasted. That's hard to believe since about 50 priests, and three bishops, were present in full regalia at the Rooney mass.

Father Ben Walker, a Benedictine priest, was the pastor at St. Peter's who made his church available for the ceremonies. Baldy had been a member of Nativity Church on Perrysville Avenue, but the funeral mass was held at St. Peter's because of its location and because it could better hold the anticipated large turnout. Father Walker estimated the crowd at about 700 on a weekday afternoon.

"What a blessing it has been for us to have someone like Baldy touch our lives," offered Father Ferris in his remarks to the gathering from the pulpit at the Christian burial service.

"Life has changed for Baldy," continued Father Ferris. "Life changes for all of us who've been touched by him. We become sensitive to the shortness of life. There are so many stories about Baldy — everybody here has one, I'm sure — that would literally fill this church."

Father Ferris reminded me of one of them. His kid brother Denny had been a standout running back at North Catholic High

School and had been recruited by Dave Hart to play football at the University of Pittsburgh in the mid-'60s.

In the summer of 1967, I was escorted by Baldy Regan to visit Denny Ferris at Allegheny General Hospital where he was being treated for a serious eye injury he had incurred on a summer construction job. Baldy had always championed Denny Ferris.

I had returned from a two-year military service stint the year before and had resumed editing and publishing a tabloid newspaper called *Pittsburgh Weekly Sports*, along with Pitt's sports information director Beano Cook. I was married that summer to Kathleen Churchman. She had agreed to give me two years to see if I could make a go of the newspaper. Or else I'd have to get "a real job."

Baldy thought Denny Ferris would be a good story for *PWS*. And he was right. I remember visiting Denny, who had a white patch over his injured eye. He was about to begin his second year at Pitt. He was a good kid, a handsome young man, and he was worried that he would lose the sight in his eye, and wondering whether his football playing days were over. It was one of my favorite stories that appeared in that paper. As it turned out, Denny Ferris had to be red-shirted because of the injury, which affected his peripheral vision. He turned out to be one of the few bright lights in Hart's coaching career at Pitt. Ferris was the Panthers' leading rusher in 1968 and was still in the school's top twenty career rushing record list in 1995. In recent years, Denny has been a regional sales representative for Hart, Schaffner & Marx men's clothing line in Ohio. He had purchased and read copies of the books in my "Pittsburgh Proud" sports series.

Sitting directly in front of me at St. Peter's Church was Harold "Mr. Trombone" Betters, another Pittsburgh institution. He came out of Connellsville — Betters often boasted that it was the same community that produced Heisman Trophy winner John Lujack, Olympic gold medal winner John Woodruff, and Pitt football luminaries, Jimmy Joe Robinson and Dave Hart — to make his mark in music on the Pittsburgh club scene. He was a fixture at the Encore in Shadyside in the '60s. My first date with Kathleen was in the fall of 1966, aboard the Gateway Clipper, following a Steelers' football game at Forbes Field. The party was a promotion of none other than Baldy Regan. The music on the sternwheeler was provided by Betters and his band. They later played at all the Steelers' home games.

When Baldy was buried at the North Side Catholic Cemetery that afternoon, Betters stood on a hillside, about ten yards above the grave site, and played one of Baldy's favorite songs on his trombone. It was "There's A Hush All Over The World." It was some scene. No question about it, Baldy went out in style.

"That's the first time I ever played in a cemetery," said Betters. "Baldy used to tell me he wanted me to play that at his burial. A nun came up to me at the cemetery and told me she'd like me to play 'Bridge Over Troubled Waters' when she dies. I felt good being able to do something like that for Baldy. His wife thanked me.

"We've been good friends for a long time. Baldy booked me several times to play at events at Kiski Prep, and places like that. Baldy was a rare man."

Directly behind me at St. Peter's was Paul Martha, a classmate of mine at Pitt, and an All-America running back his senior season. He was the Steelers' No. 1 draft choice in 1964, played six seasons (1964-69) with them as a defensive back and one more with the Denver Broncos. He became an attorney and headed the front office operation of the Pittsburgh Penguins and the Pittsburgh Maulers for the DeBartolo family. I was at Paul's bachelor party at a club on the North Side when Baldy Regan arrived with a truckful of chocolate cream pies. Baldy passed them around and, of course, people started pelting one another with pies. Martha smiled when I reminded him of the eventful evening. "We had to send out for some more pies," recalled Baldy at a ballgame only a year before his death.

They rounded up the usual suspects for this funeral service. Chuck Klausing, who had an outstanding coaching career on the high school and college level, had retired the year before. He had been the coach at Kiski Prep, where all four of Baldy's sons had gone to school.

"Baldy and his wife, Alice, did a great job in raising those kids, and their two daughters," recalled Klausing.

Jack McGinley, a partner with Art Rooney in founding the Steelers, was present along with his sons, Barney, a judge, and Jack, an attorney. The McGinleys always invite me to join them for a glass of wine when they're having dinner at the Allegheny Club after a Steelers game. "C'mon, Seamus, sit down and relax awhile," one of them will say.

Rip Scherer, the former football coach at North Catholic and Moon Township, had graded opposing football players from a seat in the press box for many years when Art Rooney Jr. ran the operation. He and his kid brother, Dick, a receiver at Pitt (1956-57), were in attendance at the funeral. Jim Lally and George Whitmer from Three Rivers Stadium management were there. So was Jim Boston, who grew up on the North Side and went from being a waterboy to business manager and chief contract negotiator for the Steelers.

Tom O'Malley, a former *Pittsburgh Press* advertising executive and the mayor of Castle Shannon, offered a eulogy. He spoke of how Baldy took such great pride in his Irish ancestry and his Catholic religion, his friendship with Art Rooney — "his personal hero" — and his family. "He never spoke evil of anyone, even his detractors," said O'Malley. "He was always upbeat, saying, 'Hey, brother, how's everything?' Or saying, 'Only in America!' We were all better for knowing Baldy Regan." One of O'Malley's sons, Tom Jr., an associate of former Pirates pitcher Bob Purkey in the insurance business in Bethel Park, had succeeded Baldy in running the stats and play-by-play sheet operation in the Steelers' press box, and in managing and promoting the Steelers basketball team.

Working at Pittsburgh Sports Shop, selling sports equipment in '50s

As Ben Hur in North Catholic stage show

Baldy was always center of attention in North Catholic days

With Steelers' Sam Davis

With Harold "Mr. Trombone" Betters

Mike Kearns came. He and Baldy had been a reliable duet for many years, handling the mimeograph machine in the press boxes of both the Steelers and Pitt football team. Kearns had recently undergone bypass surgery, and his color was not good. But he beamed while reflecting on his friend.

"Baldy and I had our differences, but over the long haul we were good friends and good for each other," he said.

Larry Kuzmanko, the original promoter of the Pittsburgh Marathon, was sitting in the same pew, just to my left.

Mark and Georgia Sauer, the Pirates president then and his wife, the Post-Gazette fashion editor, were present to pay their respects.

I spotted Sean Miller, recently returned to Pitt as an assistant coach to Ralph Willard with the basketball program. As a youngster, Sean teamed up with Patrick Regan in ball-handling drills as halftime and clinic entertainment in promotions offered by Baldy Regan.

There were Don Graham, the basketball coach at North Catholic for over 40 years, and his son, Michael, then the president of Pittsburgh Brewing Co. Baldy's lifelong friend, Dan McCann, who coached football teams on the North Side and at Duquesne University and was an executive sales representative for the Pittsburgh Brewing Company, was there, too. "We lost a great guy," offered McCann.

"Harold, keep those lips wet so you can play at my funeral."
— Baldy Regan's request to Harold Betters

In addition to the usual hymns heard at such services — "Ave Maria" and "How Great Thou Art" and "Amazing Grace" — there were several Irish songs offered by Red Livingston, a native North Sider who had moved to Mt. Washington. One of those was "Four Green Fields." When Livingston sang "Danny Boy," it brought tears from the eyes of many in the church, especially at the end when Livingston substituted "Baldy" for "Danny" in the last two lines. My dad, brother and nephew were all named Danny. And they had all died. So the song was doing a number on me.

It brought tears to the eyes of Carl Kohlman, a former Peabody High School and Duquesne University basketball player who had run the Ozanam Cultural Center's sports activities for many years on Wylie Avenue in the Hill District, one of Baldy's favorite organizations that he thought merited civic support. Baldy took Ozanam basketball teams on international tours. "He was a good man, and you can't say that about too many people," said Kohlman. "Did you see how many black people were present at the funeral service? That tells you something about Baldy Regan."

I asked Baldy's oldest child, Brian, 30, an assistant basketball coach at Slippery Rock University, about the details of his dad's funeral. I had known Brian when he was a graduate assistant to Paul Evans at Pitt and later an assistant to Jarrett Durham at Robert Morris College.

"My mother and I made the arrangements, but my dad had a lot to do with it, too. He had made his wishes known to us through the years," said Brian.

"Dad arranged for Red Livingston to sing at my Uncle Max's funeral, too. We talked to Harold Betters about playing at the cemetery. We thought Dad would want him to play 'When The Saints Go Marching In.' But Harold told us that Dad had told him his favorite song was 'There's A Hush All Over The World.' My Dad used to say, 'Harold, keep those lips wet so you can play at my funeral.'

"He told us of a tradition in the countryside of Ireland about having six people of the same name carrying the body to its final resting place. So we had six Regans carrying him in the coffin.

Paul Tomasovich, Bernie Stein, "Buffalo Ed" Regan and Ronnie Deer were all honorary pallbearers.

"I can't be my dad."
— Brian Regan

Following the burial, there was a buffet meal for the family and friends at Mardi Gras, a restaurant-sports bar just off the Camp Horne Road exit of Rt. 279 in the North Hills.

Among the first arrivals was John McCourt, a native of Ireland, known to the Regans as "Uncle Peachy." He wore a hearing aid, but it didn't seem to do him much good. He heard very little of the conversation. His wife, also Irish, but bred in Scotland, kept repeating everything for him.

"He's my mother's uncle," said Brian Regan. "His brother and he married my grandmother and her sister."

Baldy's six children — Brian, Bridget, Patrick, Moira, Daniel and Sean — were all present.

"I can't be my Dad," said Brian, "and I won't try to be him. But I can be what I am, and what I learned from my parents."

His parents had been separated the past seven or eight years, living at different residences, but it was evident there was still a meaningful bond.

"My dad really planned for us; he and my mother still talked about what they wanted for us," said Brian. "They were still the parents. He still backed her up and she still backed him up. They were apart, but they were still our parents. That was important.

"When I was young, I sometimes questioned why my dad was away so often. He spent so much time with other people and other people's children. Your father's out and about and you wish he were home more. 'Why can't he be home?' we'd ask. As we got older, he took us with him more often. In later years, we all became close. At the funeral, you got to appreciate it more when you see all the people and hear their stories."

From the Regan family album

During political campaign, Baldy and his buddies check out haberdashery in cloak room, from left to right, Tom O'Malley Jr., Bernie Stein and Tom O'Malley Sr., now the mayor of Castle Shannon. Young O'Malley succeeded Baldy in managing the Steelers' off-season basketball team. Stein does security work for Steelers on sidelines at home games.

Baldy Regan, "The Mayor of the North Side," was always organizing sports junkets for young ballplayers.

Tom Modrak
Always the good scout

"His teammates had great
respect for him."
— Chuck Klausing,
IUP Football Coach

Tom Modrak looks more like a former boxer than a former football player. He has the name and the nose for the fight game. His wide nose had a big dent across the bridge, much like those of legendary Pittsburgh pugilists Fritzi Zivic and Billy Conn. Their photographs were still displayed on the walls of the memorial library at Three Rivers Stadium that was once the office of Steelers owner Art Rooney, who befriended them and other sports heroes in his hometown. Modrak smiled at the simile. It wasn't the first time someone told him he looked like a boxer.

You go past Rooney's old office, and keep going to the left, past the lunchroom, until you come to the far end of the Steelers' complex to find Modrak's desk. It's in a relatively small, spartan furnished room. The Steelers' office complex is a no-nonsense affair, a throwback to the days of Civil Defense (CD) bomb shelters. All the tapes and scouting reports on pro and college personnel are stored in surrounding work areas.

This is where the search starts to find future football players as good as Joe Greene, Terry Bradshaw, Franco Harris, Jack Lambert, Jack Ham, Mel Blount — recent Hall of Famers, along with their coach, Chuck Noll — whose photos are all displayed on a wall in the lobby of the team's headquarters. There are some prints of some of those superstars on the walls of the scouting rooms as well, to dress the place up a little.

There was a gleam in the eyes over that battler's nose, as there usually is. The 1997 college draft was behind Modrak, and summer camp was ahead of him. "And we're all tied for first place," said Modrak, looking forward to his 19th season with the Steelers, and his sixth in charge of college scouting.

At 54, he looked like he had arrived at the pinnacle of his profession. This is a man who paid his dues, starting with non-paying positions in the organization, and working his way up through low-paying, always-on-the-road responsibilities. It was easy to root for the likes of Tom Modrak. He and his family made great personal sacrifices as he chased his dream, often living out of a suitcase or rental car, to become a key contributor to the Steelers' successes. As a young man he knew he wanted to be involved in sports somehow, and his persistence paid off. He remembers stopping by the Pirates' office at

Three Rivers Stadium in the early '70s, getting to see Pirates' publicist Bill Guilfoile, a thrill in itself, and expressing an interest in working for one of Pittsburgh's pro sports teams. Now he was doing what he wanted to do. Guilfoile had retired the year before as the associate director of the Baseball Hall of Fame in Cooperstown, New York.

Modrak's scouting career began in 1973 as a part-time scout for the Steelers. He then spent six months as a scout for BLESTO before rejoining the Steelers full-time in 1979. Modrak came back in March, a month before I returned home to Pittsburgh to become the Steelers' beat reporter at *The Pittsburgh Press*. We were the same age, had both grown up in Pittsburgh and gone to city schools, and shared some similar memories of the local sports scene.

We were both lucky to have come to the Steelers in time to be a part of the excitement from the Steelers' fourth Super Bowl success in a six year span in the '70s.

He proudly wore a Super Bowl ring that had four diamond chips in it, one for each of the National Football League championships the Steelers claimed when they were the NFL's Team of the Decade, and Pittsburgh was hailed as "The City of Champions."

"I was so fortunate when I came in," said Modrak. "Now I can see why it's so hard to get to the Super Bowl.

"You're constantly trying to get better. Trying to be better than you were last season. I don't think you can ever sit still and say, 'Geez, it's done.' It doesn't mean we're going to make any dramatic moves, but we'll be trying to get better. Once you think you've arrived, you're going to go backwards."

"There were great people who helped me." — Tom Modrak

Tom Modrak is what Art Rooney would have referred to as "a Pittsburgh guy." He grew up on the city's South Side. His parents were both Ukranian. His father, Bernard, worked at the post office, and his mother, Millie, stayed home. His grandfather was a policeman who directed traffic in front of the *Sun-Telegraph* building in mid-town.

His roots were similar to the Rooneys. He had a grandfather who had a speakeasy on the South Side, and several relatives were "numbers writers" or bookies. "One of my uncles was notorious in that business," said Modrak.

The Modraks moved from the South Side to Oakland, but returned a year later when their house burned down. In Oakland, they attended St. Hyacinth's, right around the corner from the boyhood home of Pirates' home run hero Frank Thomas.

All smiles at pre-draft orientation for media were (left to right) Tom Modrak, Tom Donahoe and Bill Cowher, the three leaders who coordinate the Steelers' choices in the NFL Draft.

Tom Modrak is the fifth player (Braves uniform) from the left in the front row of Pony League All-Star team in Carrick.

Frank's uncle, who kept the original Tumas name from Lithuania, had a hardware store on the South Side. Modrak remembered meeting Thomas there, when Thomas worked at his uncle's store during the off-season. "That was a big deal, too," Modrak said.

Modrak attended St. Casimir's Catholic Grade School. That was when every neighborhood on the South Side had its own schools, elementary and high school, indeed, its own league, the Catholic Class B League. Gus Krop was the coach of the boy's basketball team, and they won several state championships during his stormy reign. Krop was a character, and Modrak remembered Krop going into the crowd to quiet down any dissenters or drum-beaters.

When Modrak finished eighth grade at St. Casimir's, the family was in the bucks, relatively speaking, and the Modraks made the move up the hill to Carrick. "We thought that was the suburbs," remembered Modrak.

Ernie Slessinger was in his first year as head coach of the football team at Carrick High when Modrak made the squad. Al Davic was the assistant football coach and head basketball coach. Modrak also played basketball and went out for track and field. Carrick High did not have a baseball team, so Modrak played baseball for local sandlot teams, from Pony League to Legion ball.

"Athletics was my main interest," said Modrak. "There were great people who helped me. Your goal was to go to college, get a scholarship if you could. I didn't neglect the books. We had a great crew up there, they were very supportive, and everyone was trying to help."

He was at Carrick High from 1956 to 1960. I was graduated from Taylor Allderdice High School, a City League rival, in 1960. I might have been the third-string quarterback that fall for the Dragons, but opted instead to take a job as a copy boy in the classified advertising department at *The Press*. As we spoke in mid-May, 1994, Modrak and I were about the same size — 5-9, 200. My excuse for my sports shortcomings in high school was my size. And speed. And near-sightedness. Modrak just smiled.

"I was always short, but pretty well built, on the thick side," he said. "I always wanted to be a little taller. I should have wished to be a little faster, too. They listed me at 5-10 in the program at IUP and, after a while, I began to believe it.

"At Carrick High, we played down at Philips Park. It was an oil-coated field, like many of the City fields were in those days. When I talk about those fields to people I meet in football they have a hard time believing me.

"After a game, it was impossible to get the black out of your uniform, and you had a smell about you for a few days. When it rained, there'd be rainbow slicks on the sidelines. If you hit one of those you were suddenly surfing. You could go right on your butt, or worse. Most of the City school fields had that same pitch-black oil coating. Many of those fields were only 80 or 90 yards long, and the endzones and sidelines were up against fences in some spots. You had to be careful where you ran, or you could get hurt.

"I remember Langley had thick grass. It was a great feeling to play there. We also competed for a Triadic championship each year in the pre-City League games, our exhibition schedule, with neighboring schools in Brentwood and Baldwin. They had nice grass fields, too, nice, well-manicured fields, so we were kind of envious. We thought those kids were rich, and had it made."

We lived about the same distance from Forbes Field, though we approached it from different sides of town. "I climbed over the wall at Forbes Field, and hid out until it was time for the game to begin," remembered Modrak. "We could leave our neighborhood on the South Side, and get to Forbes Field after school by the seventh inning when they opened the outfield gates, and let you in free. We'd walk across the Brady Street Bridge, and up Forbes. We always stopped at Isaly's main store on the Boulevard of the Allies in Oakland and got an ice cream cone — remember the skyscraper cones? — on the way home."

It all sounded so familiar, as did his reminiscences about players on the Pittsburgh sports scene during his early teens. "I remember seeing Ted Marchibroda throwing a touchdown pass," Modrak said. "I remember Russ Craft intercepting a pass and running down the sideline. It's funny how certain plays stick out in your mind."

Those sequences come from the mid-50s. This prompted me to tell Modrak how I had recently overheard a conversation at a sports card show where a man was looking for a Lynn Chandnois card, the only one missing from his 1956 series of Steelers players. It was obvious the man knew nothing about Chandnois. To him, Chandnois was just a bubble gum card. "I remember seeing Lynn Chandnois downtown one day. He was wearing a camelhair coat, and he had such a presence about him. You knew he was special," said Modrak.

"That's funny you remember Chandnois wearing a camelhair coat," I told Modrak. "I remember when I was about 14, I went to a Pitt basketball game at the Pitt Field House. And I saw Si Green and Dick Ricketts, two of the great basketball players from Duquesne University, at the game. They were both wearing camelhair coats, and they looked so tall, so classy, so majestic to me."

Modrak's eyes lit up. "I remember Si Green and his special jumping socks at Duquesne," said Modrak, "and how he'd bank the ball in high off the boards."

Steelers President Dan Rooney talking about Bill Cowher after giving him a contract extension:

"He's really one of us. That's the best thing I can say. He's like one of the family. He has the same values. He's a Pittsburgher. He thinks like we do. He's a good person and a good family man. And he's a successful football coach, which helps."

"We spent our honeymoon
with 100,000 people."
— Tom Modrak

Modrak matriculated to Indiana University of Pennsylvania, which fielded an NCAA Division II football team in Indiana, Pennsylvania. It is best known as the hometown of Academy Award-winning movie legend Jimmy Stewart and the self-proclaimed "Christmas tree capital of the world." His coach at IUP was Chuck Klausing, a legend in both high school and college ranks.

"Tom was a very good linebacker and a tough guy," recalled Klausing, who retired after the 1994 season following a short but mostly satisfying stint at Kiski Prep in Saltsburg that concluded a distinguished career in coaching. "He was a smart football player and gave us great leadership as a captain. His teammates had great respect for him and followed him very well. When he became a coach, he gave us a very good apprenticeship and carried over the things he had done as a captain."

During the summer months when he was in college, Modrak worked at the Jones & Laughlin Steel Works on the South Side.

"We did laborer's work, whatever they could find for a college student to do. I shoveled on top of blast furnaces and under blast furnaces. We did the dirty work. I knew that's not what I wanted to do the rest of my life."

Modrak earned his bachelor's degree in geology in 1965. He was named to IUP's all-'60s football team, and stayed on as a graduate assistant coach under Klausing. He went to West Point, getting a good recommendation with Paul Dietzel from Klausing, who had previously served as an assistant coach at Army. Dietzel departed Army for South Carolina before Modrak arrived, and was succeeded by Tom Cahill. Cahill's coaching staff included the likes of Bill Parcells, Ken Hatfield and Bob Mischak, who all went on to become successful coaches in the National Football League.

"Sandy and I got married on Thanksgiving when I was at Army," said Modrak. "The next day we're in Philadelphia for the Army-Navy football game. We always said we spent our honeymoon with 100,000 people."

From Army, Modrak moved on to Utah and Harvard. "When our staff was let go at Harvard, we had to decide where we wanted to go next," said Modrak.

I asked Modrak if Ralph Jelic was on that same coaching staff at Harvard. Jelic was a former Pitt and Steelers' player who grew up in Brookline and resided in Mt. Lebanon, and had given up college football for the sales world. He was someone I'd gotten to know, and I knew he'd been at Harvard once upon a time. . .

"Yes, he was," said Modrak, seemingly surprised that I'd made the connection. "He was a good defensive coach, and he was a good friend. I didn't know what we were going to do next. I was frustrated. I was married, with one daughter born at West Point, another at Harvard. They were young girls. I'm sending out resumes, for jobs like dean of students. I'm not sure what to do.

"I remember one night at ten o'clock, my wife and I were talking about our dilemma: where do we want to live? We both agreed on Pittsburgh. I always liked Pittsburgh. We packed our car and came back to Pittsburgh. We struggled for a while. Then I got a job.

"Ralph Jelic helped me get involved with a summer film program with the Steelers. He was on an airplane talking with Tim Rooney, who was with the Steelers scouting department at the time. Ralph recommended me to Rooney. It was a part-time deal at your own convenience. You came in during the summer and broke down film and evaluated guys.

"I got a job at Penn State's McKeesport campus. I was running a continuing education program. I was doing programs for companies, management training, special seminars. I took a job with the Steelers on the side. Tim kept me on the next year. Chuck Connors had worked with me for a while. He went with the Miami Dolphins and he talked Don Shula into interviewing me. I went down and met Joe Robbie, their owner, and I was real excited. But I didn't want to leave Pittsburgh. I wasn't ready to go.

"Jack Butler took me with the BLESTO scouting service for awhile. I had 8 1/2 years at Penn State to my credit, and I needed ten years to be vested in their pension program. That seemed pretty important at the time. My wife was great. 'You do what you want,' she said. 'If you want to get back into football full-time, that's fine with me.' "

In the meantime, doing moonlighting studies on his own, Modrak managed to earn his master's degree in physical education from West Virginia University in 1972. In 1973, he joined the Steelers as a part-time scout. In 1979, he had an offer to become a full-time scout with the Steelers. In 1987, he was named director of pro scouting.

"It meant traveling a great deal," Modrak said of his full-time position in the Steelers' scouting department. "The opening came when Tim Rooney went to Detroit. They knew me here. That's when I got the full-time job. The kids were great. They gave me quality time, rather than the other way around. They never gave me a rough time."

The Modraks were living in Pleasant Hills, a suburb to the south of Pittsburgh, between West Mifflin and South Park.

He and his wife Sandy had two daughters, Stephanie and Erin, who were 28 and 25, respectively, in 1997.

"Erin is the real sports fan, she knows the names and numbers, and she went to Penn State," said Modrak. "Stephanie went to IUP. Both were on the track and field team at Thomas Jefferson. They were both on the school's 4 x 100 state relay championship team. They had a great anchor; she smoked them all," said Modrak.

Modrak can rattle off the heights, weights, 40-yard sprint times, vertical jump measurements, and so forth, of college football prospects throughout the land, but he had to pause on several occasions to come up with facts and figures relating to his family. "I was oblivious to a lot of things; I still am," he said.

"My family has flourished, however. My girls are great on their own. Stephanie opened up a dress store, a women's formal sales and rental shop, in Indiana, Pa., where she went to college. She didn't have the usual background or education, but she had some ideas about what she wanted to do. It's successful.

"Erin works at City Club in Downtown. She's into physical fitness. And Sandy is at the Bradford Business School. She's the director of student services, funding, grants, placement, and her office is in Downtown Pittsburgh.

"I met my wife when I was at IUP. She was teaching in the physical education department. We played racquetball and got to know one another. She asked me to teach a class in Introduction to Football for students. I was a graduate coach at the time, my first year out of IUP. We were introduced by Owen Dougherty, who was on the phys ed staff. Now Stephanie is married to David Dougherty, the son of Owen Dougherty. Quite a coincidence, huh?

"The support from my family is major. My wife and I have a joke. We're never around each other long enough to get mad at each other."

"This is a team approach."
— Tom Modrak

Modrak served as a pro personnel scout under Chuck Noll. Noll preferred homegrown players, and seldom traded players.

Modrak served as advance scout, checking out future opponents, but the files on other team's players were seldom put to use.

When Modrak joined the Steelers scouting department, it was headed by Art Rooney Jr., the second son of the Steelers' founder, and Bill Nunn Jr. and Dick Haley. Rooney was released in an infamous firing by his brother Dan. Nunn retired shortly thereafter. Haley stayed on, but left shortly after Tom Donahoe was promoted to head up the team's football operation. Haley had been with the Steelers for 21 years, but left to take a similar position with the New York Jets. Haley and Donahoe had been critical of Noll in his last years for not providing more opportunities for young prospects they felt merited more playing time.

Modrak ducked any questions relating to such history, or to the success or failures in past draft classes. "Hindsight is 20/20, as they say," Modrak remarked. "We've made some mistakes; we took guys we shouldn't have taken.

"I think we've been successful more so lately because we've changed our approach. This is a team approach. Tom Donahoe and

Bill Cowher and Dan Rooney and our assistant coaches and scouts are involved in this, too. And I don't want to cast a bad light on anything that was done when Chuck Noll was the coach, either. They had some great draft classes, classes that would be tough to equal at any time."

Cowher and Donahoe have stressed that decisions will be made by committee, not by individuals, and Modrak has no problems with that. They poll their information, swap thoughts, rank players, and then they draft them.

"We sit down collectively, and we talk about people, try to rank them, adjust them some, talk about their character, and try to come up where that player would be interesting to the Pittsburgh Steelers, and where we would take them. It's a collective decision."

I asked Modrak about Dan Rooney's role in the draft process. Does he challenge everyone to defend their positions about players — "Are you sure he's as good as you say?" — or ask questions about possible picks?

"His presence is always there. You take a guy, though, and he's supportive. He's not into second-guessing. He may ask questions, and he might say something later on like, 'He's not quite as good as you thought he'd be,' but never in a mean-spirited way.

"He's there. He wants you to do what you have to do to get the job done. If that means more travel, then make the reservation, and go for it. He's interested in the character of the players, and the intangibles. He says that should never be overlooked."

Dan Rooney often says the Steelers are special, that they don't necessarily do what other NFL teams do. He likes to talk about "doing it right" with "good people."

I asked Modrak if Rooney's standards put restrictions on the scouting department.

"It's important here to get good people," said Modrak. "It's rubbed off. It's magnified here. They want good people. That doesn't mean we're always right. But that's our philosophy.

"You don't want everyone being alike. It's not a robotic thing. But you want guys all pulling in the same direction. You have 53 different personalities, but you want all those guys interested in winning. You don't want a guy who's pulling other guys down."

I asked Modrak what they do when they are checking out a candidate and come across some negative information about his history.

"If a flag goes up, we try to find out more about that prospect," said Modrak. "We talk to a lot of people. If it's an isolated incident, and we don't think it's an ongoing problem, we'll draft him. If that flag is big enough and red enough, we may grade him, but not take him. If it's a major problem, we'll put a character dot next to their name on our list.

"I came on full-time with the Steelers when the team was at its all-time best. The first thing I can remember, and it epitomizes the team concept of that group, was something I saw at my first camp at St. Vincent's. I kept seeing stars staying after the regular practice session and working with young guys on their techniques. I remember thinking 'these guys are trying to beat them out of their jobs and yet they are helping them to get better.' They were confident in their own ability, but they wanted to bring along the next generation. I think that was so important to our success."

Modrak attracted attention from the Jacksonville Jaguars and Chicago Bears during the 1995 and 1996 seasons, but was satisfied to stay with the Steelers.

"This is my home," said Modrak, "and I'm happy here."

From the Modrak family album

Tom Modrak and his family: daughters Stephanie and Erin and his wife Sandy.

400

Joel Steed
The quiet man

"He gives you an honest day's work."
— John Mitchell,
Defensive Line Coach

Joel Steed is one of the sturdiest and strongest of the Steelers, at 6-2, 300 and some pounds. Yet he manages to get lost in the locker room at Three Rivers Stadium, no easy feat. He is the strong, silent type. He doesn't seek the spotlight, and he speaks softly, though thoughtfully, when asked about anything. He pauses and considers every question before attempting an answer. Sometimes a smile suffices.

He's a big teddy bear of a man, warm, gracious, garrulous, a welcoming smile and glint in his dark eyes; he'd probably be great company on a fishing trip. His dressing stall is the last of three just to the left as one enters the Steelers' clubhouse, and is next to the entrance to the players' bathroom and showers.

Steed seldom gets much ink or TV time, though he is regarded as an outstanding nose tackle. He's not a flamboyant character and he's careful about what he says — which doesn't make for punchy soundbites — so he's virtually ignored. "That's okay," said Steed, "I don't usually have much to say anyway."

The most attention that's come his way was midway through the 1995 season and he could have done without it. It was embarrassing. He was suspended for four games because he tested positive for anabolic steroids, insisting he unwittingly ingested pills that contained illegal performance-enhancing drugs. Steed said he took an over-the-counter dietary supplement and did not know anything in it was prohibited. The Steelers were short-handed on the defensive line and had lost four of their last five games to post a 3-4 record, and could hardly afford to lose another starter. The Steelers won those four games with Steed on the sidelines, and eight in a row to qualify for the playoffs.

The report rated the headline on the sports pages of the *Pittsburgh Post-Gazette*, along with photos and offenses of previous Steelers who had gotten into trouble over the NFL substance policy: Terry Long, Tim Worley, Eric Green and Carlton Haselrig. It was the sort of negative publicity the Steelers and any pro team dread.

Steed was scared. He thought his days with the Steelers were over. He fully expected the team to get rid of him.

Instead Steelers' president Dan Rooney came to his defense. "I think Joel Steed is as fine an individual as we have, but I think he didn't know what he was doing," said Rooney, the Steelers' straight-arrow boss. "I think he made a mistake and didn't know what he was taking (steroids), but he's responsible. I'm not trying to lessen his responsibility."

John Mitchell, the defensive line coach of the Steelers, supported Steed as well, believing him to be a good man who had made a mistake.

"He's what I call a great pro player," said Mitchell. "He knows what he has to do. He gives you an honest day's work. He'll work hard every day.

"He was very embarrassed by the incident when he was suspended for four games for steroid use. When he came back, he apologized to me first. He said, 'I know the Steelers are going to cut me. I'll clear out my locker.' I told him to hold on. 'You made a bad decision, and you paid for it. I hope you learned from it.' "

Steed had served as a Steelers' representative in several community fund-raising activities, and feared this would lessen his attractiveness or effectiveness in that regard in the local business community. It was also embarrassing for his wife, D'Angela, who had received a law degree from Duquesne University and was working at Reed Smith Shaw & McClay, the city's foremost law firm. She has since left the firm and returned home to Atlanta.

His steroids episode apparently had nothing to do with his wife moving to Atlanta. She simply wanted to return home. Reflecting on that difficult episode, Steed said, "It was hard, definitely, but with the support of my wife, family and friends, people who counted, I wasn't facing it alone.

"It was definitely a drain," said Steed, 26 at the time. "It was a boneheaded mistake on my part. But my family members stood by me. All the people important to me, who know me, understood it was really a mistake. I did the time, I'm back, and I'm ready to move on with my career. "A lot of people have a different way of coping with things. We all come from different backgrounds and environments. It was very scary. I wouldn't put anybody through that. You also find out who your true friends are. Coach Mitchell comes to mind, definitely. I'm not trying to suck up or anything, but he brings a lot of experience to this, a lot of things he tries to share with me. He told me, 'It won't kill you, it'll make you stronger.' "

Mitchell was definitely among those who lined up behind him. "He's a good person," said Mitchell. "He has a great wife, a beautiful woman, and they're both good people. He's very sensitive, and I have to be careful what I say to him in front of others. He doesn't handle public criticism well. Everyone is different."

Steed is living proof of that. His next-door neighbor in the Steelers' clubhouse is Levon Kirkland, who often draws a media crowd because he's an outstanding player who is comfortable in interviews, has a lot of ham in him, and has lots of fun in the give-and-take of interviews. Kirkland gets crazy once in a while, and entertains teammates with his antics, especially imitations of Bill Cowher's vociferous

Joel Steed outside Three
Rivers Stadium by Susan
Wagner's statue of Pirates'
Hall of Famer Roberto
Clemente.

Joel Steed

Photos by Jim O'Brien

pep talks. All in good fun. Kirkland has been recognized by the Pittsburgh Chapter of the Pro Football Writers as one of the most cooperative and accommodating of the Steelers when it comes to media relations.

Kirkland was chosen to play in the Pro Bowl after the 1996 season. It was the first time he was so honored. Steed was still waiting for the call, but Mitchell and Kirkland have boosted his candidacy with great conviction.

"Joel is our 'Quiet Man' in the middle," said Kirkland, before the Pro Bowl selections were made. "But don't let that fool you. Joel's got a fire burning inside him that won't quit; he's got a desire to be the best. A quiet rage in the middle of a knockdown, drag-'em-out war every weekend. He deserves to be in the Pro Bowl. Wouldn't it be great if Joel and I both go? He's been overlooked too long."

Said Mitchell in October of 1996: "I think he's even better than he was last season. And I felt Joel should have made the Pro Bowl last year. He's vastly underrated."

Steed doesn't feel sorry for himself in any respect. "Yes, going to the Pro Bowl is one of my goals," said Steed, almost reluctantly. "But that's not up to me . . . it's up to me to convince my peers I'm worthy of going to Hawaii."

Kirkland has suggested to Steed that maybe he has to do a post-sack dance or something to call attention to himself but Steed resists, thankfully. It's simply not his style.

"It was like being in a dream."
— Joel Steed

Steed, for sure, is a thinking man, though his brush with NFL officials over his steroid usage might suggest otherwise. Since his childhood, he has enjoyed a good book, a good story and, given a chance, he can tell a good story himself.

Joel Steed has simple tastes. Consider this Steed sampling: His favorite food is collard greens. As a kid, Steed idolized Mike Singletary, the outstanding linebacker for the Chicago Bears. His favorite football moment: "Winning the national championship at Colorado in 1990." Steed majored in sociology and black studies at Colorado. The person he admires the most is his mother.

It takes a while and patience and persistence are a must for the visitor seeking Steed's attention and thoughts.

Consider what he offered during an interview on January 9, 1995, two days after the Steelers had defeated the arch-rival Cleveland Browns in the first game of the playoffs, the third time the Steelers had beaten the Browns that season.

Three Rivers Stadium overflowed with boisterous fans, and the buildup for the ballgame had been unbelievable, more so than the playoffs of succeeding seasons. It was an exciting time in Pittsburgh.

The Browns always brought out the best and the worst in the Steelers and their fans.

"It was an atmosphere full of energy, real charged," said Steed. "You could feel it from the fans. It's a cliche, but it was like being in a dream. You got into a euphoric state. It was like you were in the clouds. It was a different feeling, for sure.

"You try to feel out the opposition, see how the game was turning. There was a period of time when everything was just clicking."

Sitting on a three-legged stool, eye-to-eye with Steed, I was reminded of Ernie Terrell, a high-ranking heavyweight boxer during the Sonny Liston-Muhammad Ali-Joe Frazier-Jimmy Ellis era. Steed resembles Ernie Terrell in appearance and demeanor. We talked about boxers, and how Muhammad Ali appeared frightened before he entered the ring. Steed could relate to that. Fear of failure is a great motivator in sports. One of sports' ill-begotten theories is that it's hard to beat a team a third time in the same season, so the Steelers were serious and concerned as they approached their battle with the Browns.

"You start listening to what people are saying," said Steed, "and it can get you in trouble. Like we can't beat them three times in a row. And you wonder whether there's any truth to it.

"It's different in football vs. boxing or tennis or individual sports, where you have a firmer control over the game because it's one on one."

Any game played in January in Pittsburgh, or Cleveland, always offers extra challenges.

"It's still cold, you feel brittle," said Steed. "You just have to keep playing through it. During the flow of the game you get hot and cold. Your muscles tighten up again when you go to the sideline.

"We beat the Browns a third time and we beat them good, 29-9. Our offensive line was totally dominating, definitely."

Steed says "definitely" a lot, the way some people say "like" and "you know" to keep going and to hold your attention.

"I can say this now," Steed went on. "After three victories, the offensive line really dominated. It made our job easier. Definitely. We just went out there and held the fort. The points were just coming and it made our job easier. For a moment, I felt sorry for the Browns, but very briefly."

"I rooted for the Steelers."
— Joel Steed

Joel Edward Steed was born on February 17, 1969, in Frankfurt, Germany where his father, Billy Steed, was stationed in the U.S. military service, and Joel spent most of his youth in Denver. Billy is retired and still lives in Colorado.

"Growing up, I was a fan of the Denver Broncos," said Steed, 28 going into the 1997 season. "But when it came to Super Bowl time I was for the Steelers.

"I'm sure everybody recalls the Steelers of the '70s. I remember them when I was sitting in front of the TV set. I was always for the Steelers because my cousin, Harold, always liked the Cowboys. Cousin Harold liked the Oakland Raiders and the Dallas Cowboys, so naturally I went with the other side.

"I rooted for the Steelers. I liked them because they were the underdogs or bad guys, compared to the Cowboys. The Cowboys were 'America's Team.' It just seemed like the Cowboys were more flash and the Steelers were more hard workers, just get the job done.

"In Denver, it was just my mom and my two sisters and me. My mother . . . she had to deal with me and my two sisters. The things she had to deal with when we were growing up had to be challenging. She did all she could to keep us going.

"She grew up in a number of places, like Van Buren, Arkansas and Detroit, Michigan. From what I understand, she married my father and they moved all over the country.

"Coming up back then for African-Americans was difficult, especially in a place like Van Buren, Arkansas. They ran into a lot of tough situations. The reality of Jim Crow laws and second-class citizenship was evident in Arkansas. It wasn't always easy to get a good job. That's why my dad went into and stayed in the military service."

His dad was a master sergeant in the Army. Sergeant Steed received two purple hearts. He was wounded in action in Vietnam trying to protect people.

"I was like six years old when he left," recalled Joel. "He was definitely involved in a certain sense with me. He would call, send packages. When I was in high school, he returned, and he lived in Colorado Springs, about an hour away from Denver. He was involved in my life.

"It's a little hard to keep track of the men in my life," said Steed with a smile. "First, there was my mother, Barbara, and my dad, Billy. Then came my stepdad, David Chiles. He died of cancer of the kidneys (in 1982) when I was a teenager. She remarried and her third husband passed away (from asthma and emphysema in 1994) my first year in the National Football League. His name was Raymond Bobbitt."

Steed is proud of his wife, D'Angela, the attorney. "I got lucky; I threw sevens," he said with pride of his wife of four years.

"I met her when I was in college. We met in Houston, where she was spending her Thanksgiving break during her student days at Spelman College in Atlanta.

"She's been working for a top law firm in Pittsburgh. I drop her off and go over to pick her up after work. She's a morning person. She gets up at six o'clock. I'm an evening person. I can stay up till 3 or 4 in the morning."

He has a daughter in Denver from his college days at Colorado.

As 2nd grader

College days at Colorado

As 5th grader

Photos from the Steed family album

Joel Steed stands behind his mother, Barbara, and family (from left to right) grandmother Martha Johnson, sisters Leandia and Terri, and his niece, Rachel, at her graduation ceremony in May, 1996. Joel's daughter, Traicee, is in foreground.

Her name is Traciee, and she was 4 as we spoke. He said his mother worked at the post office in Denver, and that she and his sisters all kept an eye on his daughter, who lived with her mother. He believes he's been involved in his daughter's life, if on a long-distance basis.

"I go out during the off-season to spend time with my daughter," said Steed. "She comes up to Pittsburgh once in a while during the season to see me. She came here on Thanksgiving with my mother and sister. She's accepted my wife; she knows her as Dee."

"He has the heart."
— Dermontti Dawson

Playing nose tackle takes dedication, discipline and attention to detail, and a lot of sacrifice. It can be a thankless task. There are magic moments when a nose tackle like Steed seizes everyone's attention. Steed savors moments like the time he hit Lorenzo White for a 4-yard loss in the first quarter of a game with the Houston Oilers on Monday Night Football. He was lining up opposite Bruce Matthews, a 12-year center who was a regular in the Pro Bowl, and he beat him before a national television audience, and had Frank and Al and Dan extolling his virtues.

"Hey, it's prime time, time to get after it," Steed said of Monday Night Football.

He was a third round draft choice in 1992, one of those picks that makes Tom Modrak, the Steelers' college personnel coordinator, feel good about the Steelers' scouting system.

"In a 3-4 defense, you must have a nose tackle who can take people on and control the inside," said Modrak. "Joel's a strong guy who plays with leverage and has a good feel for where the ball is. That made us stronger on the inside."

Steed has a size 40 waist. Gerry Dulac of the *Post-Gazette* described Steed as a "six-foot-three, 300-pound waterbed of a body."

Steed didn't look so good, at first, because he was going up against Dermontti Dawson every day in workouts.

At the same time, it has to help to improve oneself by lining up against a Pro Bowl performer regularly. "I was going up against the league's best center," said Steed. "It was hard, coping with all kinds of things. But D's the best in a lot of ways. He's a great person to boot."

Dawson said, "You don't find many nose tackles who can explode off the ball like him. He's a load in the middle, believe me. He has the heart."

As a rookie, Steed began training camp by getting into a fight with Carlton Haselrig, a former collegiate wrestling champion. Steed was beaten out that season by free agent Garry Howe, another Colorado product.

At one point it was thought the Steelers had drafted another defensive lineman who was a stiff. He was called "Pigpen" after the character in the cartoon "Peanuts," because his uniform was so soiled. "The pace is much faster than in college," said Steed, explaining his slow start.

His teammates now appreciate his play. Levon Kirkland, who plays behind Steed, said, "Joel keeps me clean." Steed keeps blockers from getting at Kirkland, and frees him to make tackles.

Steed was a three-year starter at nose tackle at Colorado, though he got off to a bad start there, and he also had a life-threatening scare that was far worse than his steroids scare with the Steelers.

His coach at Colorado recalls those early days.

"When Joel Steed first came in here, he stayed about a month and then went home," said Bill McCartney. "We got in touch with his mother and she was inclined to side with him. Basically, he was in over his head at the time, and we encouraged her that it was just something he had to work his way through. From that time forward, he just matured and developed and established himself as a real strong run-support guy."

"I had a difficult time adjusting to the University of Colorado," said Joel. "My dad, who was in the military for 25 years, wanted me to go to West Point, but I didn't want to do that, or go that far from home. Soon after I got to Colorado, I told Ol' Bill (Coach Bill McCartney), 'I'm not really up to this.' I thought I could, but I had doubts when I got there. I thought, 'Hey, I'll go into the Army.' My mom told me to get back to school."

During his college career, Steed was named the Big Eight's Defensive Player of the Week when he had 11 tackles (seven solo) and 1 1/2 sacks in helping Colorado defeat Nebraska, 27-12, during his junior year.

When he was recruited from Hinkley High School in Denver to CU in 1986, Steed was just another player with potential. As a sophomore, he was honorable mention All-America in *The Sporting News*. As a junior, he was on a national championship team. As a senior, he was a consensus All-Big Eight selection as well as being named to many magazines' All-America squads. He was a finalist for the Lombardi Trophy as one of the top linemen in the country.

Steed ran into another scare at Colorado when a bizarre illness was making the rounds on the campus.

Steed was struck by a mysterious illness shortly after spring break and just prior to the start of spring football practice in 1991, going into his senior season and his fifth year at Colorado. He developed flu-like symptoms, and lost 30 to 35 pounds, his weight dropping to 240 pounds. Frankly, it scared him, and with good reason. As a redshirt freshman, Steed was at Colorado when quarterback Sal Aunese died of a stomach tumor, then offensive tackle Vincent Smith developed meningitis and almost died.

"I thought I was next," said Steed.

The virus lasted nearly four weeks and Steed missed all of spring practice. He eventually regained his weight and went on to become a first team All-America his final season.

"I got a scare. I was sick and started to develop little white spots on the back of my throat. I went to the team doctor and University doctors. They didn't know what was going on. I lost a tremendous amount of weight. I was only eating oatmeal; it was the only thing I could swallow. I was taking antibiotics.

"They really didn't know what was wrong with me. I was on display for a lot of doctors. They were trying to figure out what was wrong. Was it a virus or what?

"You're fighting the unknown. To get sick like that is really scary. I thought it was something fatal. I thought, not only football-wise, but life-wise, that I wouldn't be able to go ahead and get past that. That impacted my life. It put my life in the proper perspective."

Steed was bedridden for the better part of 3 1/2 weeks and unable to eat and drink much because of a bad sore throat.

"I had a cyst or something in my throat. I had four or five blood tests — I got poked a lot," said Steed. "They couldn't figure it out. And they kept switching antibiotics. They must've tried three or four different antibiotics."

Some symptoms hinted at viral mononucleosis, but tests could not confirm that diagnosis. Eventually, the symptoms disappeared and he regained his weight and strength.

As a senior in college, he won the "Hang Tough" Award that went "to the 1991 senior who has shown the greatest courage and fighting heart."

Steed sounded like every coach he's come across in his life when he said, "You've got to stay focused. There's going to be a lot of adversity all the time. You just have to keep playing."

His mother had given him the guidance to get through those tough times: "She's been a great motivator," said Steed. "When you would get down and didn't feel like you could do something, she'd always tell you it's been done before, so you can do it."

Steed likes to address the importance of his family in his development. "If everything else fails, you always have your family," he said. "They were there before you were even a Steeler, before you made it anyplace.

"Basically, everything I have I owe to my mother. My mother is the one who stuck by me through thick and thin, and she's always been there. She's the love of my heart and everything I was doing out there I was doing for my mother."

"I have always drawn support from my family. I feel sorry for people who don't have that kind of benefit. Broken homes and such. My dad was a military guy — he spent 25 years in the service — and when I was real young we moved around a lot. When my mom and my dad split up, I was about six. My step-father died of cancer, kidney cancer, when I was 14. That hurt. That was a hard time in our lives."

"You have to be strong up the middle."
— Bill Cowher

"Football is a lot like baseball," said Bill Cowher. "You have to be strong up the middle." With Steed and linebackers like Levon Kirkland behind him, the Steelers are strong up the middle.

Gary Dunn was the Steelers' first nose tackle after Joe Greene. Steed was the first pure nose tackle since Gabe Rivera's auto accident ended his career during Rivera's rookie season of 1983.

Gerald Williams, the Steelers' nose tackle when Steed came in as a rookie in 1992, was one of his mentors.

"He told me to just be patient, my time would come," said Steed.

Cowher really changed the defensive line in a hurry. Williams was the only holdover from the Noll era.

Three weeks before the draft, the Browns sent Nick Saban to Colorado to put Steed through an hour and a half workout. The Steelers did not work him out individually. Tom Donahoe liked what he saw of Steed in the Peach Bowl vs. Kentucky on New Year's Day. He went higher than he was projected by draft analysts Mel Kiper and Joel Buschbaum. They had Steed going from the sixth to ninth rounds.

Steed watched the draft with his mother and stepfather. Steed thought for sure he would be drafted by the Browns.

The Steelers drafted him third, after Leon Searcy and Levon Kirkland. On April 7, 1992, when he was drafted, Steed told the Pittsburgh media in a telephone press conference, "It's a thrill just to be in that type of setting that has produced players like Joe Greene."

"You realize you're part of something special."
— Joel Steed

Joel Steed and I spoke again at length on January 19, 1996, just before Super Bowl XXX. We talked about the Steelers tradition and about those teams of the '70s that had won four Super Bowl championships. Steed was one of the Steelers who liked checking out the lobby of the Steelers' complex at Three Rivers Stadium, seeing the four silver Lombardi Trophies, the team photographs of the four championship teams, the photos of all the Steelers who have been inducted into the Pro Football Hall of Fame.

"It can't really sink in until I'm done," said Steed. "Occasionally when I go back there (the lobby), I look at the Super Bowl trophies, and the pictures of the people who have been involved, and you realize you're a part of something special, a tradition. You know that guys like Joe Greene once played in the middle of the Steelers' line. They don't come any better. It's hard to play up to that standard.

411

"I remember The Steel Curtain, Franco Harris, Terry Bradshaw, Mike Webster, the whole offensive line, Lynn Swann, John Stallworth and L.C. Greenwood. Just a number of names. I remember those guys, what a great team they had."

How does he react when some of the great players from the past appear from time to time in the Steelers locker room?

"You're excited, in a sense, but you don't want to show it," said Steed. "People try to be macho. No one wants to admit it, that they're excited about seeing those guys. You were rooting for Franco Harris when he caught the Immaculate Pass. But, sure, the kid comes out. You can only respect and admire what they've done. He's (Franco) really put together. For a brief moment, I spoke to him.

"But I was a Broncos fan, foremost, as a kid. I grew up with Craig Morton and Haven Moses and Tom Jackson. Those are the guys I really rooted for. I couldn't afford tickets, but I snuck in there one time. I remember them playing in the Super Bowl, and how disappointed I was when they always lost the big game.

"To reach the pinnacle in your profession and to be regarded as the world's best in your sport — just thinking about what it will be like — is an exciting challenge. You don't want to fall short of that, the way our team in Denver always did.

"It's great. It's a great opportunity. Despite what anybody thinks, we have an opportunity. The question is: What are we going to do with it? Today is the future."

"It will always be a game to me."
— Joel Steed

Steed said he felt comfortable in the clubhouse, surrounded by similarly ambitious ballplayers. "We've all been playing football since Day One," he said.

"We fling a lot of stuff around here. Some people always think they're right, whether we're discussing religion or politics. No matter what you say or do, some people just aren't going to like you. You may not get along with everybody, but you still have to play together as a team."

Steed had something in common with Brentson Buckner, who lined up next to him on the Steelers' three-man defensive line. Some of us were too small to be effective as football players in our youth, but these guys had the opposite problem — they were too big and weren't allowed on their local age-group teams.

"It was the same way in junior high," said Steed. "I had to play with the high school players. I wasn't allowed to play with the guys my age."

Were you always the biggest kid in your neighborhood?

"I was the roundest. We had a couple other big guys. People don't know this, but I looked at football as something to do to keep

412

busy. I enjoy the game for what it is. It will always be a game to me. I take it seriously as a business, but it's still just a game.

"I've always had other interests. I've got business interests . . . entertainment interests." He said he loved to read books, and that he had four or five shelves of books at his condo in Deutschtown Square, a newly-constructed community of townhouses on the North Side, a block away from the Park House on East Street. He said he liked to go Downtown and browse through the Barnes & Noble Book Store on Smithfield Street.

"Ever since high school, I love reading," said Steed. "It's like lifting. You lift weights to build up your muscles and your strength. If you're not working your mind, you're not growing. You have to exercise your brain, too."

I told him something that Alex English had once told me. English, who had starred as a basketball player at the University of South Carolina and with the Denver Nuggets and had just been voted into the Basketball Hall of Fame, said he didn't have much money or travel opportunities as a kid, so he went to the library where he could read books and be anywhere in the world he wanted to go. From a book like *The Wizard of Oz*, one learns that imagination can take you anywhere, even over the rainbow.

"That's true," said Steed. "My favorite book was *Grapes of Wrath*, by John Steinbeck. It affected how I felt about the Midwest and what went on at that time, during the Depression, especially what went on in places like Oklahoma, and how everybody thought California was the Garden of Eden.

"I remember the influence of my teachers growing up. One particular teacher, in third grade, really emphasized English and literature. It wasn't easy wanting to read at that age. Reading a book was definitely not a top priority in my school. During recess, everyone wanted to play tag football or something like that. Nobody talked about books.

"The teacher who got me inspired, she really boosted my self-esteem. I remember being involved in a lot of busing when I was in school. Coming from inner-city to a suburban school was challenging. I was a different student; there were not many African-American students in the school.

"This teacher put me in a higher level reading group, a gifted group. I wondered 'What am I doing here?' Of course, sometimes I have the same feeling right here.

"I don't know what to make of our clubhouse," continued Steed. "You're in here and sometimes you don't think you're in here at all. They can swing. I just try to mix in. Lot of egos in here. Lot of people want to lead. Greg (Lloyd) comes to mind. He's an ardent blue collar worker. Once in a while, he takes a practice off, but he really puts out on game day. He's a voice in this locker room, definitely.

"He gets after all of us on the field, too. You don't really need to hear that sometimes. The coaches are making adjustments. You're trying to hear them. Greg's a tough guy, a really down-to-earth guy, and I believe he means well.

"It can get distracting, though. In this business, you can really lose your mind. I'm kind of a reserved person. It's easy for me to sit back and just listen. Other times, I can get into the conversation."

It was easy to talk to Levon Kirkland. Steed's neighbor two years before had been Jerry Olsavsky. He was a neighbor when Olsavsky made his comeback from a career-threatening knee injury, and he came to admire the man.

"Definitely, when he came back," said Steed. "For him to do that took a lot of courage. I remember coming in during the off-season and Jerry was working out. I couldn't believe it. He'd have ice on his knee and he'd never stop. He'd scream sometimes when he'd extend his leg against pressure in the weight room."

Just as he found it difficult to pursue his own personal interests in grade school, like reading books, Steed said he sometimes felt like an outsider in the Steelers' clubhouse as well.

"Lot of times, if you're not involved in certain cliques, just like society, you can find yourself on the outside. There are certain people you find comfortable. I'm closest to Levon Kirkland; he's my roommate on the road.

"We talk about a lot of things. We can talk about intellectual-type things, things substantive. Even though Kirk is not married, we have a lot in common in our approach to things.

"Most of the guys talk about women and cars and clothes, going out. There's nothing wrong with that. That's not what I want to talk about all the time, that's all."

Asked if he felt he belonged in the Steelers' clubhouse, Steed said: "That passes through everybody's mind. You'd be surprised who's asked me that. It can be an overwhelming situation. Look at the numbers. It's like the lottery. You beat the lottery. You have to come in here with a very thick skin."

Steed appreciated that he had worked under people like Dick LeBeau, the team's defensive coordinator, and John Mitchell, the defensive line coach.

"They have a good attitude," said Steed. "With LeBeau, he's not a yeller or screamer, but he'll let you know what's on his mind. He's played, and he knows what really motivates guys. He can tell you when you mess up. He can use some colorful words, but he's not offensive. "Here's my attitude toward all this: Just tell me what I'm doing wrong and I can correct it. Just man to man.

"I do a lot of listening in this locker room. Just things that go on. The scene here is really a reflection of the guys. Gerald Williams was great for me. We had an understanding. He was a seasoned veteran. He knew what was going on. He helped me, even though I was after his job. You never know how you really stand in pro football. It's a cutthroat business. Players come and go. That's the nature of the business."

414

Laughing eyes and quick smile

By Barbara Chiles-Bobbitt

On February 17, 1969 in Frankfurt, Germany a beautiful 9 pound baby boy came into the lives of me and my husband, Sgt. Billy Steed. His name . . . Joel Edward Steed. His laughing eyes and quick smile that displayed dimples that "were to die for" made him a joyful and pleasurable addition to this family. Love was always displayed in his life.

Joel grew up in the Denver, Colorado area where he played Little League Football with Skyland Recreation Center. His team won the championship in their league. He did not play football again until he went to Hinkley High School in suburban Aurora. Along the way, he attended Ash Grove Kindergarten, Elkhart Elementary School and East Middle School.

There is a quiet side to Joel that will not be apparent on the football field. He learned to play the trumpet in middle school and was a member of the band. Also at this time, his writing ability was displayed by winning an award for composing a poem. He was the only student to be recognized and given an award by the Mayor of Aurora for his grade level of the Aurora Public School District.

One of his teachers stated, "Joel could always make his career in politics because he has a great imagination and he can put it into words so well." Joel was a good student and excelled in journalism and literature.

Joel has always been a special person in our household. With the death of his step-father in 1982, Joel rose to the occasion, not being head of our household, but maturing and establishing goals and dreams. Joel's father was still in the military overseas. From the time he was old enough to work, Joel has held several jobs. These were during the summer and after football practice. He worked at the Around The Corner Restaurant and in the paint department at Sears.

Joel is a member of Union Baptist Church in Denver. He sang in the youth choir (for a short time) and was involved in the church youth programs.

Many people touched Joel's life during his years in Denver. And a few contributed to his success. His grandmother, his sisters and I gave a lot and prayed a lot. During his years in football, lacrosse, awards, dinners, plays and recitals, there was always someone sitting in the audience, swelling with pride regarding his accomplishments.

He was the Defensive MVP three of his four years at Hinkley High School, and played in several All-Star games. At the University of Colorado, he was named Defensive Player of the Week four times, and was a Walter Camp Foundation All-American.

I have always supported Joel in everything he has accomplished or attempted, by prayer, love, words of encouragement, words of wisdom and more prayer. Joel is a gifted young man with a beautiful personality. He'll always be loved and be special with me.

Now he is special to someone else, his wife, D'Angela Proctor Steed. They met during the Christmas break before an all-star game in 1991. They were married September 15, 1993. D'Angela is a graduate of Spelman College in Atlanta, and received her law degree at Duquesne University in Pittsburgh. Joel has a daughter, Traicee Elaine Steed. He cares about his family the way his family always cared about him.

From the Steed family album

Joel Steed and his college roommate flank Joel's mother during Colorado schooldays.

416

Return to Fort Valley
Lloyd says goodbye to "Mom"

"She never complained."
— Greg Lloyd

George Gojkovich

It was late June, 1997, and the Steelers coaches were on vacation, and there was little football-related activity at Three Rivers Stadium. Things would pick up again after the July 4th holiday.

That's when Greg Lloyd left Pittsburgh to return to his boyhood home of Fort Valley, Georgia. His Aunt Bertha Mae, who had raised him and who he considered his mom most of his life, had died from the ravages of diabetes.

She had to have a leg amputated earlier and had been suffering. "But she never complained," Lloyd allowed in a conversation with a friend upon returning to Pittsburgh following her funeral.

"A lot of my relatives were there," Lloyd told his friend. "They all wanted something from me. It was want, want, want. I had to get out of there."

Lloyd was born in Miami, but his mother left him and his four brothers and four sisters at her sister's home in Fort Valley. Lloyd was two at the time, the youngest of her nine children. He never knew his father.

"My Aunt Bertha, she taught us discipline," Lloyd once said when he was speaking to sportswriters. "We had to go home when the lights came on. The worst thing you could do was lie to her. She was direct and honest and I learned that from her. I studied hard in school. I was in the church. I was a Boy Scout, imagine that, me a Boy Scout.

"When I was nine or ten, I was playing in the front yard one day and someone just drove up and said, "Hello, I'm your mother.' How do you drop off a two-year-old and then just show up years later? My dad, I have never met him. In both situations, I have had to overcome the bitterness, and I'm still working on that.

"I love my aunt more than she will ever know even though I have told her that. But the love from your mom, your own parents, is something that, really, you can't replace."

The absence of his parents in his young life may have contributed to Lloyd's standoffish posturing. He's friendly with few of his fellow workers in the Steelers' organization.

It's unlikely that many of them even knew his grief when he lost his aunt in June, and how difficult the trip was to and from Fort Valley. He could have used a few good friends.

Joe Zombek
"The greatest Steeler there ever was"

"It was an honor
to have been a Steeler."

Joe Zombek was lying flat on his back in Bed 2 of Room 604 at Allegheny General Hospital on the North Side of Pittsburgh. His back did not bother him as much, he said, if he lay that way. His back had bothered him most of his adult life.

Zombek had a room with a great view of West Park and the downtown Pittsburgh skyline, yet he seldom looked out the wall-length window to his right. He was watching the overhead television when he was not dozing off, catching the final days of the O.J. Simpson Trial, some soaps, talk shows and, better yet, all the college and pro football games he could find with his bedside channel selector.

Of O.J., Zombek said, "I think he's guilty. Killing a woman . . . killing her friend . . . it's really, really bad.

"I met O.J. once. In Buffalo. Had a handshake. He said, 'How do you do, Sir?' That's it. Like a guy going through a reception line. He'd never remember it. Why should he? I remember it because he was O.J. Simpson."

Whereas O.J. was a college and pro star of the greatest magnitude, a quintessential celebrity, Zombek was just a guy who had played football at the University of Pittsburgh and for one full season with the Steelers before starting a successful business career.

Zombek's name was near the bottom of both teams' alumni lists because his last name began with the letter Z. He had more than the 15 minutes of fame that pop artist Andy Warhol said we would all enjoy, and he was grateful. He was a throwback to another era. His story provides insights into a different time, and a better understanding of some events relating to Pitt and the Steelers and the coal towns that turned out some hardrock football players. Somewhere in between there's also quite a love story.

He enjoyed talking about football, but he was both puzzled and dismayed that he was back in the hospital again. How the mighty had fallen.

"I'll never get used to this," he said softly.

He had taken Percodan and had a morphine patch just above his left hip, and an i.v. above his right breast. All pain-killers. The drugs caused him to drift in and out of sleep. Sometimes he would be talking and his eyelids would just lower themselves, like windowblinds. Then his eyes would pop open, and he would try to continue the conversation. "Where was I?" he'd ask.

Glenda and Joe were together till the end.

Joe Zombek is flanked by friends, author Jim O'Brien and Foge Fazio, at a 1984 Pitt football outing at Joe's country club in McDonald, Pa.

"When you live in a world that is mediocre, good is going to take you a long way."
— Alan King's father

"This has knocked the hell out of my sails," he said. "I can hardly walk. My feet went numb. Everything went wrong. And the pills make things go wrong. I've got to get straightened out. I'll be OK."

September was moving into October of 1995 when I visited Joe Zombek three times in a four-day span. I had been to see him a month earlier during another stay at Allegheny General Hospital. That time he was in Bed 2, Room 630.

He was in the oncology unit both times. "That's not a 'good news' section of the hospital," as one of his friends put it. How well I know. My wife, Kathie, a medical social worker, had been serving in that department for three and a half years, and had assisted Zombek and his family before. She often visited former patients at personal care homes. She started each day by checking the obituary notices in the newspaper to see if any of her patients had died. She went to too many funerals. "You get close to certain people," she'd say. Kathie was in the process of arranging for Zombek to be transferred to the Harmarville Rehabilitation Center. "You better bring some big guys to get him into the ambulance," she advised whomever she spoke to in arranging his transportation. "He's a big fellow."

Zombek was nursing several ailments — he had diabetes, back problems, sleeping problems, he had suffered congestive heart failure two years earlier, and a broken pelvis — but his biggest concern was the cancer that was spreading throughout his system. His legs had gone numb on him. His wife, Glenda, and the nurses were looking after him, and trying their best to keep him clean and comfortable. Glenda was the good wife, the good nurse, all in one. I reminded her that Glinda (spelled differently) was the beautiful Good Witch of the North in *The Wizard of Oz*.

"She looks after me hand and foot," Joe acknowledged. Glenda had learned to be patient early in their relationship. Joe was lucky to have her at his side. Joe and Glenda had more questions than answers about his condition. He would require several weeks of rehabilitation to get back on his feet again, they were told. They felt he was up to it.

I wondered what some of the current Steelers might have thought if they had seen Zombek flat on his back. He had been a Steeler, he had always been one of the biggest and strongest guys on the block. Now he was like a baby, back at the beginning, needing his wife to take care of him. Humbling stuff.

"Why am I here?" Joe said he had asked himself more than once. "What's going to happen? What did I do wrong?"

Zombek had always been a good guy, a fun guy. Zombek had always been a big man. During his playing days, he weighed about 220 pounds. Now he weighed 275. His face and chest and stomach were all bloated from the steroids he was given as part of his treatment. His color was different, from the radiation treatments he had endured. A burnt orange crayon from my coloring days came to mind,

420

the sort I had used to color American Indians. The radiation treatments had ruined some of his internal plumbing, according to Glenda. There was talk about more chemotherapy treatments.

He was always clean-shaven and his hair was always combed just so whenever I was there. He was always able to smile. The doctors would sound ominous when they discussed his condition at bedside, but Zombek remained upbeat and optimistic. He had overcome a lot of adversity in his life; he was a tough guy and took pride in that appellation. He had learned how to battle back in the 1950s as a high school player when he was one of the biggest kids in Carnegie and starred at Scott Township High School, then as a starting end at the University of Pittsburgh — he was a three-year (1951-53) letterwinner — and during his one full season with the Steelers in 1954. Along the way, he had gotten into more than his share of scuffles.

Atop a table at the foot of his bed was a large floral bouquet, husky yellow-gold mums with baby's-breath about them, with a black and gold ribbon, and an inflated miniature Steelers helmet topping it off. There was a white card from his sister, Antoinette, and her husband, George Jucha. It read: "To the greatest Steeler there ever was . . . Love, Anty and George."

Joe Zombek had played only one season with the Steelers, mind you, and stood on the sideline with a wrecked knee for a second season before giving up the ghost. To his sister and brother-in-law, however, he was still the greatest.

All his life he was remembered for playing at Pitt and with the Steelers. He was still a Steeler.

"Art Rooney would have tossed us in the river."
— Joe Zombek

On Sunday, October 1, 1995, the North Side was already starting to fill up with fans who would be rooting for the Steelers in a 4 o'clock contest with the San Diego Chargers. It was a rematch of the AFC championship contest that brought an abrupt halt to the Steelers' season in January, just three yards shy of a Super Bowl berth.

The Steelers had looked bad in dropping their last two games after winning their first two games of the 1995 schedule. They needed a win, and it didn't matter who it came against. They needed to beat somebody. Anybody. Revenge for what happened in the playoffs wasn't possible. In boxing parlance, this rematch with the Chargers was a non-title bout.

Zombek was lying on his back. He did not have a pillow under his head. He had a hair brush in his left hand. He would brush the hair back on his head, then he would use the brush to scratch himself, brushing the skin on his elbow or chest or stomach. There were some tubes attached above his right breast.

He was such an enormous man, yet there was a strange and appealing little boy look about him. His hair was combed so neatly. Like a choir boy. Like a Hummel statue. Zombek did his best to keep smiling, to be upbeat, but one could only imagine the fears and concerns he kept to himself.

As if matters were not confusing enough, his uncle, Stanley Zombek, had checked into the same unit at the hospital. He was on the other side of the oncology treatment department. He, too, had cancer. It ran in the family. Joe's sister, Alberta Raffaele, had died at age 32 of cancer. Joe said his back problems — something to do with his third, fourth and fifth lumbars — was a hereditary problem as well.

He was watching the Washington Redskins playing the Dallas Cowboys on the TV overhead. Zombek had once done battle with the Redskins.

The Redskins were one of the original franchises in the National Football League. "The Redskins were one of our rivals," Zombek said. During that 1954 season Zombek had been with the Steelers, the team won four of its first five games under Coach Walt Kiesling. Then they lost six of the remaining seven games, including one against the Redskins. That would prompt their fans to bring out the S.O.S. signs, short for Same Old Steelers.

Gus Frerotte (fur-ROT), a Ford City High School graduate who later married the coach's daughter, a nurse who graduated from Pitt, was quarterbacking the Redskins. When Frerotte threw a five-yard touchdown pass to Terry Allen just before halftime a celebration ensued in the end zone.

"Lookit 'em!" cried Zombek. "Bumping each other, knocking each other with their helmets, jumping up and down, dancing . . . Damn, I hate that stuff. If we'd have carried on like that, Art Rooney would have tossed us in the river."

"I wonder what it would be like to be at a school that hardly ever won."
— Mike Hagan
Steelers controller

It was an idyllic autumn afternoon, with temperatures near 80 degrees. There were more people than usual in West Park, one of Pittsburgh's best-kept secrets. That made it safer for everyone. The park is a real oasis, like New York's Central Park, but workers at Allegheny General Hospital and Mercy Providence are warned to walk through it with caution and, better yet, in the company of others.

I had been dropped off at AGH on Friday by Jack McGinley, Jr., a Pittsburgh attorney and the son of Jack McGinley, a Pittsburgh beer distributor who owned a minority interest in the Steelers since their birth in 1933. Young McGinley had stopped by the Steelers' office for a visit, and had to get back to town for a court date.

On Sunday, I was dropped off by Mike Hagan, the Steelers' controller in 1994 and 1995. I had first gotten to know Hagan when he served as assistant to the president and then acting president of North Side Bank. Art Rooney II was on that bank's board of directors and had recommended Mike to his father when he was in the market for a controller. We often saw each other at sports events at Upper St. Clair High School where our children had gone to school. We had traveled together that Friday night to Canonsburg to see the USC football team beat Canon-McMillan, 49-0. It was the 50th straight conference win for the Panthers, who had the best high school record in western Pennsylvania over a ten-year period under Coach Jim Render. "I wonder what it would be like to be at a school that hardly ever won," Hagan had wondered aloud as we sat in the stands on a perfect Friday night for high school football. Mike would later return to the banking business as the president of the Iron & Glass Bank on Carson Street in the city's South Side.

One of his daughters, Christine, was in the USC marching band. His older daughter, Jennifer, had been in the band a few years earlier and was now a student at the University of Notre Dame. On Saturday night, Hagan had attended a band competition at North Allegheny High School. Hagan was one of those guys who enjoyed sports on every level. I returned to Three Rivers Stadium each day by walking through West Park, and stopped both times to see Stella and Gus Karalis, who succeeded his Greek parents in operating an orange pushcart from which he dispensed "Pittsburgh's best iceballs," peanuts and buttered popcorn. On one of those days, Gus gave me frayed and well-worn copies of special supplements of the *Pittsburgh Post-Gazette* from the summer of 1970, devoted to the opening of Three Rivers Stadium. "They say all the same things in these articles that they're saying about what's needed now in a new stadium," said Gus with his trademark grin. On another visit during that same weekend stretch, Gus gave me a beautiful black and white photograph of the Hope-Harvey football team that played at Exposition Park, on the same site as Three Rivers Stadium, back in the early '30s. Gus identified all the local landmarks in the background. Those buildings were all long gone from the landscape. They were the kinds of buildings that once surrounded Forbes Field, and they would provide the kind of neighborhood sorely needed around the sterile surroundings of Three Rivers Stadium.

The Hope-Harvey sandlot or semi-pro team was sponsored by and managed by Art Rooney, and was the predecessor to his National Football League franchise, first known as the Pittsburgh Pirates, which came into being in 1933. Gus was giving me a piece of Pittsburgh sports history. It was as welcomed as a banana-blueberry flavored ice ball.

I came upon a touch football game in the park. One side was wearing green slipover jerseys, the other yellow slipover jerseys. It was football in its purest sense.

There were parents pushing their children on swings, or watching them climb monkeybars. There were ducks in the pond, couples sitting on benches, and the city's skyscrapers peeking over the trees that were changing colors, changing to their autumn attire. It was a scene seldom seen in photographs or paintings of Pittsburgh. The park was so serene, so peaceful, until a Conrail train came rumbling through on one of four tracks that run under bridges. Its harsh hoot-hoot sounded its passing.

There were bedraggled men sleeping on some of the benches, winos and such stretched out on the grass, using the emerged roots of trees for pillows. The Light of Life Rescue Mission for homeless people was located just across North Avenue from West Park. The Steelers' players participate in fund-raisers and other activities that benefit the homeless at that facility. It was a city park at its best and worst. The sun shone warmly on my face and I felt fortunate to be walking to Three Rivers Stadium to see a football game.

"There was a time in my life when I never took an aspirin."
— Joe Zombek

Zombek talked about his condition and how he was coping with all his problems. He spoke of spending some time at the D. T. Watson Rehabilitation Hospital in Sewickley after his legs had gone numb at his home.

"My legs were coming along real good," said Zombek. "All at once they started feeling funny. I got up at three in the morning and went to the family room and read the paper. I couldn't sleep. When I went to get up I didn't have any strength in my legs. I hollered out to Glenda to come and help me. 'I can't move!' I told her."

Now he was at Allegheny General Hospital. He had undergone some sleep study tests during prior hospitalization. He still couldn't sleep well. "I eat good; my appetite has never been a problem," he said, proudly, patting himself on his ample stomach. "I used to like my beer, but I don't drink anymore."

He bought a Milky Way when a man came through the rooms with a snack cart. "I shouldn't be doing this," said Zombek. "But I love them."

He chewed on the candy bar like a kid in a grade school class-room trying to get rid of the evidence before the nun returned to the room.

"I'll be OK," Zombek promised. "There was a time in my life when I never took an aspirin. I don't know what dope smells like. Now I'm taking all these pain-killers and they affect your alertness."

He mentioned that he heard that Baldy Regan had died. Regan had been an institution on the North Side and had been associated with sports and the Steelers all his life. "He always came over and patted you on the back," Zombek said of Regan. "He was just 61. I'm 62."

"He always treated me like a son."
— Joe Zombek on Art Rooney

Talking with Zombek was like traveling in a time machine back to another era in Pitt and Steelers' history. He brought up some magic names and places that sparked warm memories.

When Zombek was playing at Pitt, he befriended Richie McCabe, who had come to Pitt from North Catholic High School. McCabe had played high school ball for the Trojans with Dan Rooney, and had helped out as a water boy with the Steelers for years. Zombek remembered McCabe taking him to watch the Steelers practice and play at Forbes Field.

John Michelosen was the coach of the Steelers during Zombek's first two seasons at Pitt. Then Joe Bach came back to coach the Steelers, and Michelosen moved across the street to serve as an assistant to Red Dawson and Tom Hamilton at his alma mater. He would become the head coach in 1955. Michelosen had originally gone to the Steelers as an assistant to his college coach, Jock Sutherland, and later succeeded him as head coach.

Under Michelosen, the Steelers were the last team in the NFL to employ the single-wing offense.

"When I went to the Steelers, Michelosen came to coach at Pitt," said Zombek. "Richie McCabe and Lou Cimarolli were both buddies of mine at Pitt. Richie was a helluva guy. First off, he didn't like girls back then. He was very studious, so he was a good influence on me. He knew his football. He loved sports. He was skinny, but he was a good athlete. He was fast and real hard-nosed.

"He was very close with Art Rooney. If Art Rooney was going to the race track, he'd take Richie with him sometimes. Richie would run to the betting windows for him. That's how I first met Art Rooney. He knew me extra well because of Richie McCabe. He always treated me like a son. He was just a nice man. He'd take me and Richie out to lunch or to the track. Years later, he'd never pass you up. He'd always stop to shake hands and say hello.

"As a Steelers' alumnus, I was invited to a dinner and the unveiling ceremonies for Art Rooney's statue (October 6-7, 1990). I sat only a table away from Dan Rooney. I got to see a lot of my former teammates. It was special.

"My first year with the Steelers, I was paid $8,500. The second season I was paid even though I was unable to play. They let you hang around, in case they needed you to do something at practice. I had torn cartilage. Today it could be arthroscopic surgery, and you'd be back just like that."

Back in those days, the players and the assistant coaches all had to find jobs during the off-season. They needed the money and the coaches had not yet turned football into a year-round endeavor.

Zombek worked in sales at Jessop Steel Corporation in Washington, Pennsylvania. Other football players like Lynn Chandnois and Joe Marconi worked there, and Zombek said he helped the Pirates' Dick Groat get a job there.

"I worked on a commission basis and I sold the hell out of that steel," said Zombek, beaming. "I did very very well. I became a salesman in the steel industry because I had played ball for the Steelers, and it was a door-opener for me throughout my career."

Zombek had his favorites on the Steelers, like Chandnois and McCabe, Fran Rogel, Ray Mathews, Ernie Stautner, Dale Dodril, Jack Butler, Elbie Nickel, Bill McPeak, Bill Walsh, John Schweder, Lou Tepe, Pat Brady, John Reger.

He said he had visited with Mathews the past year at a bar-restaurant, My Brothers Place, that Mathews owned about a mile north of the Grove City Factory Shops. Mathews, who came from McKeesport and Clemson, remained in the Steelers' record book. Back on October 17, 1954, Mathews scored four touchdowns against the Browns. He and Roy Jefferson hold the team record for most touchdowns scored in a game.

Zombek said the Steelers played their home games at Forbes Field and practiced at the Fair Grounds in South Park and had their training camp at St. Bonaventure University in Olean, New York. Art Rooney's brother, Father Silas Rooney, was the athletic director at St. Bonaventure.

Jim Finks was the starting quarterback and Ted Marchibroda was the backup quarterback in 1954. John Lattner of Notre Dame was the No. 1 draft choice that year. The Steelers selected another well-known running back on the eighth round, Paul Cameron of UCLA. Lattner and Cameron stayed only one season with the Steelers. Lattner also suffered a career-ending knee injury. Zombek was a ninth round draft choice and Cimarolli was an eleventh round draft choice.

Zombek was at the team's training camp the next year when the Steelers selected Vic Eaton, an eleventh round draft choice out of Missouri, over Johnny Unitas, a ninth round draft choice out of Louisville, as their No. 3 quarterback.

"Unitas didn't even get a chance," said Zombek.

Unitas, who grew up in Pittsburgh and played at St. Justin's High School in the City Catholic League at the same time as Dan

Rooney, played for a sandlot team in the Bloomfield section of the city before getting signed late in the season by the Baltimore Colts. The rest is history, as they say. Unitas was later tabbed "the greatest quarterback in pro football history," and was honored in the Pro Football Hall of Fame.

Zombek got to play one more season with the Steelers than did Unitas, and he made the most of it.

"I did the job they wanted me to do," said Zombek. "There were a couple of games where I was exceptional. I had my big moments. I was the smallest defensive end in professional football. Len Ford of the Browns stood next to me once and I looked up at him and I looked like a little kid. Bill McPeak (another Pitt guy from New Castle), played the other end that year."

Zombek remembered vividly how his pro football career came to an end. "I tackled Buddy Young, the little running back for the Baltimore Colts, along the sideline," he said. "In those days, if the whistle didn't blow you could get up and run. I tackled him, and he got up. I tried to get up and get him, and I got hit blindside and was knocked out of bounds. I knew my right knee was gone; it was like he broke a two by four over it. The game was almost over. They carried me off the field."

He showed me his right knee. There were stitch marks on both sides. It looked like an old deflated football. "I had a knee replacement a few years back; it's been good," said Zombek. "When I got hurt, they wanted to let the swelling go down before they operated on me. They waited until after Christmas, and they removed the cartilage. I was operated on at Mercy Hospital; that was always Art Rooney's favorite hospital. The family had its own private suite there. Somebody in their family was always using it when they had babies; a lot of Rooney babies were born there. I went to work on a construction job that summer. I was a hod carrier; I wanted to build up my leg strength again. I went back with the Steelers the next season. I wore a knee brace, but I couldn't play. That was it.

"When I left, I paid off my mother's mortgage and cleaned up my father's debts. I had worked on a farm since my senior year in college, and bought the farm land — 127 acres — and I raised beef. I bought up some other farms. I kept improving farms and reselling them in parcels. I had rental property in Mt. Lebanon and Carnegie. I ended up with a half million cash. One of my customers talked me into building a golf course. I borrowed another million to do it. I paid it all off, and I'm fully insured. I have $500,000 term and $500,000 paid-up life insurance. So I did all right, all things considered. We don't need anything; we're loaded. We have everything we need. We live good, but not wild. We go where we want to go.

"It was an honor to have been a Steeler, even if you only played one year. A lot of fellas only played one year. A lot more never played at all. It's like a brick in the wall, but it's important to the wall."

Zombek's golf course was called Cherry Hills Country Club, which he operated for 26 years, selling it in 1987. Pitt coaches came there often to play golf or to dine, and Zombek took good care of them.

His son, Joe, played football at Fort Cherry High School in McDonald. One of his teammates was Marvin Lewis, the linebackers coach of the Steelers during the 1994 and 1995 seasons before moving on to Baltimore as defensive coordinator for the Ravens. As teenagers, Joe's son and Lewis went to a football camp with Bill Cowher, who became the Steelers' head coach. He was also close to Marty Schottenheimer, who had come out of McDonald to play at Pitt, and was the coach of the Kansas City Chiefs.

"If he's here, I'm here."
— Glenda Zombek

Glenda Zombek was a woman of real substance. Joe was lucky to have her. She was rooting for her husband to beat the odds. "If Joe has a good attitude, he'll beat this," she said.

She spent a great deal of time at the hospital, and when I questioned her about that, she responded, "If he's here, I'm here. I can't imagine being out having a good time when he's in here."

She was Glenda Barger of Steubenville, and she was a receptionist at Weirton Steel when Joe would make sales calls there.

Glenda had never been married, and Joe was divorced from his first wife, Charlotte Nichols, when he and Glenda began dating. But his first wife came back and convinced Joe that they should get back together again. "She thought the kids needed us to be together," said Zombek. They had four children, Patricia, Jody, Marguerete and Joe Jr. So they were remarried. "It didn't work out, so we split up again."

Glenda came back and she and Joe were married in 1991. She had been living in Steubenville with her mother. Her mother was 88 and in relatively good health. Joe was glad Glenda had been so patient with him.

"She waits on me hand and foot," he said. "I'm so lucky to have her."

If Joe sounded like he came from the old school, he did, indeed. He grew up in Carnegie, and had an early introduction to hard work, football and sports activity.

Pirates Hall of Famer Honus Wagner was living in Carnegie in those days. Did Zombek ever see Honus Wagner?

"I knew where his store was," said Zombek. "I seen him from a distance, about a half-block away. I wasn't a glamour boy, I was a bad boy on a corner. I was a bad kid; I'm not condemning myself. I wasn't bad in the sense that kids are bad today — like in gangs. I was just mischievous."

He was able to channel his aggressive tendencies into playing football.

"They'd come to our house, and they'd want my brother to play," said Zombek. "He was a helluva ballplayer. His name was Al, as in Alfred; he was a tough guy. He was the type of ballplayer that if he'd break loose down the field, he'd look for someone to run over. He was just hard. A rock. He was something else."

"He was different," interjected Glenda.

"We'd play against Heidelberg, Bridgeville, South Fayette, Mt. Lebanon, teams like that," Joe continued. "Everyone around had a team. There was a place called Irish Town in Carnegie. Those were the kids from St. Luke's. They were tough kids. I grew up in East Carnegie and played at Scott Township, starting with my freshman year. At Scott, we had a terrific team. Every year we might lose about one game and that was it. We were always in some sort of playoff. There were schools in Carnegie, Crafton and Bridgeville, but those schools are not in existence anymore."

He remembered how the lights over the football field at Clark High School on Main Street would light up the sky on Friday nights.

"That was big time," said Zombek. "It was like running for President of the U.S. It was big time. Guys in the town would bet on the games. Everybody was talking about the game. You're like the big hero. Everyone looked up to you like you were a god. You walked around the school on game day like a big hero. Even though you hadn't played yet."

Zombek's parents, Joseph and Josephine, were of Polish descent. Zombek's dad worked at Universal Cyclops. He was a molder in the mill in Bridgeville for 40 years.

Joe was always an enthusiastic worker. At 13, he landed a job washing dishes at Mercy Hospital.

During Joe's senior year in high school, his father got sick, and the family had no insurance. Joe was 6-2, 185 and had attracted attention from a lot of schools, including Maryland, Navy and Notre Dame.

"I was all set to go to Annapolis," said Zombek. "But when my father got sick I had to go to Pitt. That way, I could work and help support the family." His brother, Alfred, had already entered the military service.

Zombek was at Pitt from 1951-1953. "Playing at Pitt was special. What was it like? It was like going to church. You were real solemn. Everything meant something.

"I was recruited there by John Chickerneo and Steve Petro. Chickerneo left during spring drills my first year. We had three different head coaches during the four years I was at Pitt: Len Casanova, Red Dawson and Tom Hamilton. Hamilton was also the athletic director. He was special. He had been an admiral in the Navy. He had a military manner about him, a look. You worshipped him like a god. He was always serious. It was the way he walked, the way he approached you. When he shook your hand you knew it.

"We stayed at Ellsworth Center in Shadyside. It had been an academy at one time. There were about 30 or 40 rooms there. There were three different levels; I was up in the attic. We had a school bus, shuttle, that took us back and forth to and from our classes. It came by every hour.

"There was a football field behind Ellsworth Center and that's where we practiced.

"I worked all night in the steel mill, Universal Cyclops, where my dad had worked. I worked the 11-to-7 shift. They called that overnight shift the 'graveyard shift.' I had a piecework job. As long as you got the job done, that's all they cared about. So if you hustled and got your work done, you might be able to study and sleep a little bit. I'd get a shower in the morning and then head off to Pitt. I supported my whole family that way."

I mentioned to Zombek that some of his Pitt teammates and classmates remember shaking him or bumping him to keep him awake at early-morning classes. He just smiled when he heard that.

"Oakland was different then," said Zombek. "Pitt was a streetcar school. The guy or gal sitting next to you in class didn't care if you were a football player or Jesse James. Most of them were there to get an education, and they wanted to get home as soon as the last class was completed.

"The professors were the same way. If you were mentioned in the newspaper that week they might make note of it. They'd say, 'So, you're Joe Zombek. So you're the one that blocked the punt.' Otherwise, they paid you no mind."

He remembered a game at Notre Dame.

"I was showing off, making sure my family saw me from the stands. For my family, it was like going to England or France. My parents were just old people, Polish people. My dad was so thrilled to be there, at South Bend, Indiana. They had a write-up about it in the Universal Cyclops monthly newsletter.

"They'd driven out to South Bend in a new Cadillac of mine. They were so proud. There were five of them, one brother, two sisters, and my parents. I went over and my dad's chest was sticking way out.

"That was the best team we had."

That was 1952, Joe's junior season, when the Panthers posted a 6-3 record under Red Dawson. They defeated Notre Dame, 22-19, that afternoon.

Zombek recalled that Joe Schmidt was the team's middle linebacker and leader.

That was quite a Notre Dame team, too. The Fighting Irish had Frank Varrachione and Jim Schrader on the offensive line, Ralph Guglielmi at quarterback, Joe Heap and Johnny Lattner at halfbacks, Neil Worden at fullback.

"I carried Guglielmi into the end zone for a safety in that game at Notre Dame," said Zombek.

In early high school days

During Pitt football days

Joe Zombek

Joe stands behind his family outside their home in Carnegie, from left to right, his father Joseph, his mother Josephine, his sisters Antoinette and Alberta, and brother Alfred. Only Antoinette survived him.

From the Zombek family album

Joe and Alfred with their mother

Notre Dame won the national championship the next year. "They beat us 33-0 at Pitt Stadium my senior year," said Zombek. "Nobody could touch them."

"I enjoyed doing something
for my old school."
— Joe Zombek

One of my visits with Zombek at Allegheny General Hospital took place on August 10, 1995. In two days, Pitt would be hosting Media Day before the football team went to pre-fall camp at the Pitt-Johnstown campus.

When Zombek owned the Cherry Hills Country Club, he catered Media Day at Pitt. He did it for nearly 25 years. He did it during three of the four years I worked in the Pitt department of athletics, from 1983 to 1986. He did a good job. He personally cooked the steaks over hot grills. That's when I first met Glenda, who was his constant companion at the time. Glenda helped coordinate everything at the steak fry.

Zombek was a close friend of Foge Fazio and many people in the athletic department, but he lost the assignment when Mike Gottfried was hired to replace Fazio.

"They break your heart all the time," he said of the Pitt administration.

"I lost my relationship with Pitt athletics because of Mike Gottfried. When he came in, it was the end for me.

"After Foge was fired, I went to see the new coach to introduce myself. I said, 'I'm a former Pitt football player, a Golden Panther, a long-time friend of the University, a good friend of Foge Fazio, and I've been handling some catering for the team for over 20 years.'

"Gottfried said, 'No friend of Foge Fazio is a friend of mine. So we have a problem here.' "

That was ironic, because it was Fazio who first mentioned Mike Gottfried as a possible candidate for his job. Pitt officials had the gall to ask Fazio for a recommendation after they released him from his contract, and Fazio knew Gottfried from working at some of the same football camps.

"I wanted to tell him to go screw himself, but I didn't," said Zombek. "I decided to come back a month later. I got the same response, nothing changed. It was over.

"I never made any money off Pitt, but I enjoyed doing something for my old school. I used to bring in 100 ham sandwiches for every home football game. I'd make them fresh that morning, and pass them out to the coaches, ticket office staff, the ground crew. It was my treat. Walt Cummings had a parking pass for my bus and van. I bought 14 season tickets. I gave them out to customers of my club.

Any coach could bring a foursome out to play golf at my place. The team came out and played games — bowling, golf and swimming — and (athletic director) Cas Myslinski came out several times a week. I treated everyone in a first-class manner.

"I gave up on Pitt when they gave up on me. There are 31 guys I knew of my stature who left and didn't come back because of Gottfried."

"To the greatest Steeler of them all."
— Joe's sister, Antoinette

It was Sunday, January 13, 1996, and I was just coming away from the Steelers victory over the Indianapolis Colts in the AFC title game at Three Rivers Stadium. It was starting to get dark out as I walked toward West Park, where the ground was covered with snow, and I could see the lights glowing on the facade of Allegheny General Hospital in the distance.

When I saw the hospital it made me think about Joe Zombek and I wondered how he was doing. Only the week before, I had heard that Joe was not faring well, and that doctors had told his wife that he only had a few more weeks to live. I knew how much Joe enjoyed seeing the Steelers' games on TV. I wondered whether he would stay alive long enough to see his favorite team in Super Bowl XXX.

When I got home, I was greeted by my wife Kathie. She talked excitedly about how she and our daughter Sarah had watched the Steelers-Colts game on TV, and how scary it got at the finish. Then she said, "Oh, I saw an obit today in the paper that Joe Zombek died. That's a shame."

We went together to the viewing the next day at Thomas-Litte Funeral Service in McDonald. Joe Zombek looked better than he had during his hospital stay. He was wearing a dark blue blazer, and there was a small red rose in his lapel. His wife, Glenda, said he was wearing gray slacks and white shoes, an outfit she said he loved to wear when they were on vacations.

"I'm going to miss him," she said. "We had some great times together."

Near the casket, there was a large black and gold floral display. It was gold mums, yellow roses, with black ribbon. It was a bigger version of the floral display I had seen at Zombek's bedside at the hospital. It was also from his sister, Antoinette. This time it read: "To the greatest Steeler of them all. Rest in peace."

> *"I never had a player I didn't like. I never had a ballplayer I didn't think was a star."*
> — Art Rooney,
> Steelers 50 Seasons Celebration, 1983

433

Kevin Henry
A Southern man

"Every Friday, Saturday and Sunday we were in church."

Kevin Henry has an easy-does it manner about him that belies his occupation as a defensive end for the Steelers. He is economical in his movement about the clubhouse, and always seems to be searching for a pillow so he can take a nap.

His dressing stall is the last one on the left side of the room from the entrance, and it's easy for him to stay out of the spotlight. The 1997 season would be his fifth with the team, but Henry was hardly a household name in Pittsburgh.

The departure of his next-door neighbor, Brentson Buckner, might have created an opportunity for Henry to become a bigger factor in the defensive line. Buckner was dealt to the Kansas City Chiefs for a seventh round draft choice during the spring of 1997 because he had rubbed Coach Bill Cowher the wrong way.

Henry's eyelids are always half-drawn, like window shades, his ballcap is often worn backward. So Henry has a half-drawn, backward look about him, like he's sauntering down a country road, in no hurry to get home for dinner. John Mitchell smiles when anyone suggests that Henry doesn't appear to have the necessary enthusiasm to play the position.

"He fools you," Mitchell said. "He's got a fire in his belly. He can get after people. And if you think he's quiet now you should have seen him when he first got here."

Even his name fools you. Kevin is pronounced Kee-vin, drawn out, like the way he says most words. The full name is Kevin Lerell Henry, the pride of Mound Bayou, Mississippi. He is 6-4, 285 pounds, and likes to think of himself as a basketball player as well as a football player. Some of the Steelers' other defensive linemen, Buckner, and Joel Steed, were laidback guys, but even Steed showed more emotion than Henry. He moves and talks at half-speed.

Henry prides himself on being a well-mannered Southern gentleman. His parents raised him to be the way he is, he tells you.

He played college ball over a five-year period for Rocky Felker and then Jackie Sherrill at Mississippi State University in Starkville. His dark eyes glisten when you say you know Sherrill from his days at Pitt, and he has seen some strange doings through those dark eyes.

> **Fact: Of the 40 martyrs whose names are inscribed on the National Civil Rights Movement Memorial in Montgomery, Albama, 19 were killed in Mississippi.**

Kevin Henry is promising Steelers defensive lineman.

"That's my home, my heart."
— Kevin Henry

Maybe Mississippi held the secret to how Henry seemed so low-key in the clubhouse, but had the mean streak once in battle to survive and thrive as a young pro. Greg Lloyd liked him, so he must have a mean streak. Lloyd liked to refer to him and Henry as "good ol' country boys." I'd be afraid to label them that way.

There is no winter in Mississippi, according to writer John Grisham. It goes from summer to spring. Growing up there doesn't prepare a person for Pittsburgh.

I had read William Faulkner's fiction set in his native Mississippi, but I wanted to know more, since I had never set foot in the state, so I checked out a book at our local library called *Mississippi — An American Journey,* by Anthony Walton, who had grown up in Illinois, but traced his roots to Mississippi.

Walton went there to better understand himself. He learned that Mississippi is a state of mind and the heart of the South. He learned much amid the magnolias, willow trees, sweet gum, cotton-tree, azaleas and wisteria. There is an overwhelming beauty to much of Mississippi, and, in retracing roads traversed by his parents and grandparents, Walton would discover much ugliness as well. The majority of civil rights martyrs of the '60s were slain in Mississippi. Racism was still rampant there.

Blacks and whites live in separateness in Mississippi, more so than most states, according to Walton. That was part of Henry's heritage, for sure. He grew up in an all-black community and went to a mostly black high school. Henry was not as worldly as Walton in the way he assessed situations, however, and Henry was proud to say he hailed from Mississippi. But he did fool folks back home when he chose to go to Mississippi State rather than Mississippi Valley or Alcorn State, mostly-black schools of the Southwest Athletic Conference. Henry wanted to take on the biggest challenge possible, and show he could play with the big boys in the Southeast Conference.

Mention Mississippi to Kevin Henry and he says, "That's my home, my heart, my roots. I like the warmth that it has. Everybody feels like we're related in some way. You can speak to a person down South and they don't stare at you like there's something wrong or forward about you.

"They might not know you, but they'll smile at you and say something. They'll wave to you. It's called Southern hospitality, it's something you learn when you're growing up.

"I've had women tell me when they met me, 'Where you from?' I'll tell them Mississippi. 'Oh, a Southern man. There's something just different about you.'

"They even like my southern accent. They enjoy just to talk to me. They like the way I say certain words. It makes them laugh."

Asked to describe his hometown of Mound Bayou, Henry said there was one cotton gin in town, one traffic light, one high school — John F. Kennedy High School — and two elementary schools. He said there were different clubs you could go to in town if you wanted to drink or dance or let your hair down.

"If men were lucky in their living on earth, they might win some redeeming meaning for their having struggled and suffered here beneath the stars."
— From *Mississippi* — *A Personal Journey*

His Mississippi State days were a real education in many ways. Rocky Felker was Kevin's coach until his junior year. Then he played for Jackie Sherrill for two seasons.

I asked him if he was there the night Sherrill had a bull castrated, turning it into a steer as he attempted to rally his troops before a big game with the University of Texas. It was something Sherrill had probably done, or thought about doing, when he was coaching at Texas A&M.

Henry had to smile. "Everybody brings that up when they hear I played at Mississippi State," he said.

That deed probably cost Sherrill any chance he had of returning as the head coach at Pitt when the powers-that-be were looking for someone to succeed Paul Hackett at Pitt in 1993. Oval Jaynes, the athletic director, wanted to hire Sherrill, but was turned down by Chancellor J. Dennis O'Connor. Pitt ended up bringing back another coach who'd made his mark in Oakland, namely Johnny Majors. It turned out to be a bad move. Majors had lost the magic and couldn't turn the Pitt program around. Some insiders swear Sherrill could have pulled it off. If only he hadn't been so foolish as to castrate that damn bull before the Texas game.

"It was during my senior year," said Henry. "I'll never forget it. And people won't let me forget it. It wasn't a big deal to me, because I had seen that done before in the South.

"It was done on our practice field. Jackie said he was going to do it. 'I'm going to make a steer today,' he told us. A lot of guys didn't know what he was talking about, but I knew. I was amused.

"I couldn't believe he had it done right there. He didn't do it himself; he had somebody else do it. Someone who worked on a farm. The players were whooping and hollering. It was on a Thursday right after practice. It was a hot, sunny day, a beautiful day.

"If he had known the uproar it was going to cause, I don't think Coach Sherrill would have done it."

"I don't like people getting in my face."

Kevin Henry was a fourth round draft choice of the Steelers out of Mississippi State in 1993.

"I don't know about being accepted here, being from Mississippi," said Henry. "We're behind; I didn't know how I'd be accepted here in Pittsburgh. As a rookie, I found it hard. Veterans here put a lot of pressure on rookies. I'll be honest, I didn't feel like the veterans treated me right.

"You have to know the person you're dealing with. Some people respond better to one approach. I don't like people getting in my face. I'm a person who doesn't respond well to that. I do better when you just talk to me."

A lot of the ballplayers don't like the way Bill Cowher can get in your face if you've fouled up. That was something Chad Brown didn't care for, and made it easier for him to leave town. Brown didn't care for Cowher or Greg Lloyd getting into his face.

Henry has escaped Cowher's wrath, for the most part, and he says he likes Lloyd, who gets in everybody's face, and even rooms with him at training camp and on the road. He likes Cowher, though he says, "I've never been around a coach as intense as Coach Cowher.

"Even during my rookie year, though, I can't remember Coach Cowher getting into my face. A lot of people on this team can't say that. I try not to give him a reason to get upset with me. One time I was ejected from the game, he got in my face, but he wasn't yelling or anything. He said I should have used my head; that we were already short on the defensive line. He told me it wasn't a smart move, which it wasn't."

He liked the fact that Dick LeBeau, the defensive coordinator his first four years with the Steelers, and Mitchell, the defensive line coach, didn't shout at him, either.

"Coach Mitchell . . . he expects a lot out of you," said Henry. "He's a hard-working coach. He focuses on little things. He talks about life, what to expect after football, he talks about his experiences in football. He's a southern man, too. I like that.

"Everyone from the South is raised alike. You always respect your parents, don't do anything to get yourself in trouble that will make your parents look bad."

Some of his background had a familiar ring to it, sounding a lot like Levon Kirkland's story.

"The guys from the South all have similar stories," Henry said. "My family was very conservative."

Joe Henry, his dad, worked in a factory, making ceramic products, and was a minister at a non-denominational church. He was a stern man, a disciplinarian, and he had more than ten commandments for his children.

"Being in the house by dark. Be in bed by 10 or 11," said Kevin, recalling some of his dad's dictums.

"Every Sunday you were in church. Every Friday, Saturday and Sunday we were in church. Even if you went to a party the night before, you had to be in Sunday school the next day. You had to get up early, no lying around. You definitely couldn't sleep in.

"I had an older brother, Joe Jr., and a sister, Tekeasha, who was younger. There were times when I felt like my parents didn't love me. They wouldn't let me hang out with my friends. When I think of the parties I couldn't go to. I got punished for everything I did wrong.

"I was in trouble if I brought home bad grades. My mom and dad had high expectations because my brother was a straight A student. My sister gets away with so much . . . she'd be listening to rap music, which they never let us listen to when we were her age.

"My dad wouldn't let us listen to rock'n roll, or rap music. We couldn't play cards. Every Sunday we were expected to show up at church. They were Baptists in the beginning. And Baptists sure love to go to church. We used to go on Saturday night. We'd get there around 7:30 at night, and we wouldn't leave church till 2:30. We'd get home by 3. We'd go to church at 11. It would be over at 2. We'd get something to eat, and then we'd go to another church. We'd be there for four hours. Then we'd go to another church and be there till 12. As I grew up and went off to college, I shied away from going to church.

"When I get a chance I've got to go back to worship." For the time being, he can be forgiven if he feels a little "churched out."

During his rookie season, he attended prayer meetings. He sees himself getting back to it sooner than later. It took him a while to recognize how fortunate he was to have parents like he had, and it may take a while longer for him to realize that religion can be an important part of his life again.

"I feel like my parents . . . as I grew older, I started to understand about the things they were saying. They showed me how so many of the kids I wanted to hang out with hadn't gone to college. One of my best friends ended up on drugs; my brother told me he's a real mess.

"My brother worked for the state penitentiary for five years. Now he works for Tyson Foods, in production, in Cleveland, Mississippi."

"I wanted a challenge."

Henry still fancies himself quite a basketball player. He grew up just nine miles away from Cleveland, Mississippi, and Delta State, a women's basketball powerhouse in the '70s much like Old Dominion. Delta State produced Hall of Famers Margaret Wade and Luisa Harris, the coach and star of Delta State's nationally-rated women's basketball team in that period.

439

His hometown wasn't far from Itta Bena, Mississippi, the home of Mississippi Valley State, the Delta Devils and Devilettes, where the band is called The Mack of the SWAC, the football team plays at 10,000-seat Magnolia Stadium and the basketball team at Devil's Den. That's the school that produced Jerry Rice of the San Francisco 49ers, maybe the greatest end in National Football League history and Kevin Henry's boyhood hero.

Kevin used to travel to Itta Bena to see Rice play at Mississippi Valley State. He tried to mimic him during his days at John F. Kennedy High School when he was a tight end and defensive end.

"I'd wear the long towel hanging from my waist and I'd roll my socks down like he did," said Henry. "I still do that today."

His coach at John F. Kennedy High School was Prentice James, and Henry credits him for helping him become a football player who drew the attention of college recruiters.

In Mound Bayou, everybody thought Henry would go to Mississippi Valley State or Alcorn State.

"A lot of my coaches and teammates wanted me to sign with a team from the SWAC," Kevin recalled. "Nobody from my town had ever signed to play for a predominantly white school. But I wanted something different. I wanted a challenge. I wanted to prove something to myself, that I could play with anybody."

He did a good job of emulating Jerry Rice as a receiver, even though he played tight end for his high school team. He made 13 catches in the 1987 Class AA State championship, a 21-20 loss by JFK to Enterprise High School.

So it's hard to believe that Henry never caught a pass at Mississippi State.

"Greg (Lloyd) takes football seriously."
— Kevin Henry

It's difficult to dream of anyone actually wanting to room with Greg Lloyd at the Arthur J. Rooney Hall on the campus of St. Vincent University, but maybe Henry has to have Lloyd along to make sure he doesn't sleep through the breakfast bell in the morning.

"We've all felt Greg's wrath, on and off the field," Kevin conceded. "Greg takes football seriously.

"Greg Lloyd comes to play. That's what he brings to the team. And he expects everybody around him to do the same. The defense feeds off his intensity. I admire the man. He's made me a better player.

"Greg just tells it like it is. He gets your attention. He backs up what he says on the field and he's accomplished so much. So you tend to listen when a guy like that speaks."

Lloyd seldom stops to praise anyone, opponent or teammate, so Henry has to be doing something right to rate Lloyd as a roommate.

"I'm a veteran," said Lloyd when he first hooked up with Henry, and when he was still speaking to sports writers. "You just can't put me with anybody. Kevin is one of those guys that's similar to me in that he's a country boy from Mississippi and I'm a downhome Georgia boy. "It was just luck that he got me as a roommate his rookie year up here. We hit it off. We've roomed together since. I kinda grew on him, I guess. "Kevin's come a long way. He has a great attitude, a super work ethic for a young guy, and you just have to like that."

Kevin Henry has to suck it up to stick with Steelers.

"History will not be ignored, not in Mississippi, where people live long with their memories and their grandfather's memories, where outraged and overzealous ghosts still haunt the future."
— *Ghosts of Mississippi,*
by Mary Anne Vollers

With Arnie at Oakmont
Cowher courts The King

"The thrill of a lifetime."

Bill Cowher was ripping into some golf balls at the practice tee at the storied Oakmont Country Club, one of the most respected and revered golf courses in the world, just above the Allegheny River northeast of Pittsburgh.

Arnold Palmer approached Cowher and checked out his form. "Let's see what you're doin'," said Palmer, one of the most respected and revered golfers in the world.

Cowher cracked his signature ear-to-ear smile and said, almost apologetically, "There's a lot of wrong in here."

Then Cowher cracked the ball and sent it out long and straight into a distant hillside. "Not bad," opined Palmer.

"They don't usually go that straight," conceded Cowher.

That was the ice-breaker before Bill Cowher and Arnold Palmer shook hands and actually introduced themselves.

Under pressure, Cowher had come through again. He admits that playing golf in front of a gallery at celebrity pro-am events makes him more anxious then coaching on the sidelines in the National Football League.

The Steelers' head coach was one of the featured attractions in the first day of the two-day Family House Invitational at Oakmont June 23-24, 1997.

He and Palmer were invited to play by Frank Fuhrer, the founder and patriarch of the Family House Invitational. The energetic 71-year-old entrepreneur and sports promoter is an irascible sort who can be as difficult and demanding as Oakmont itself. He's a perfectionist. He can also be charming and convincing, and he's the catalyst for attracting some of the game's greatest golfers, other sports celebrities, and corporate leaders each year for the richest non-tour event in the country. Fuhrer likes to surround himself with winners.

Fuhrer is from East Brady, farther up the Allegheny River, better known in recent years as the hometown of Jim Kelly of the Buffalo Bills. Fuhrer raised his family in Fox Chapel. He's always been a booster of football coaches, like Gerry Faust and Lou Holtz and Bob Davie at Notre Dame, and Foge Fazio at Pitt. Fuhrer is also a fan of Bill Cowher. He likes his spirit and his success since coming to the Steelers.

Cowher was paired with Palmer in a fivesome that included Frank Fuhrer III, John Paul and Jay Juliussen that teed off last in the pro-am opening day activity.

Young Fuhrer is a former pro golfer who along with his brother, David, manages Fuhrer Wholesalers, a regional master distributor for Budweiser, for their father on the city's South Side. They are out-

Steelers' coach Bill Cowher has the time of his life keeping company with golfing great Arnol Palmer and sports entrepreneur Frank Fuhrer at the Family House Invitational at Oakmon Country Club on June 23, 1997. The event raised over $400,000 for "home away from home" fo families of cancer patients at University of Pittsburgh Medical Center (UPMC).

standing young men, enjoyed and respected in the Pittsburgh business community.

Paul is executive vice-president of the sponsoring University of Pittsburgh Medical Center (UPMC), and Juliussen represented Ernst & Young, the national accounting firm which serves UPMC.

The 1997 Family Invitational was the most successful ever. Sunshine, blue skies, temperatures in the low 90s, and the presence of Palmer, Cowher, Danny Marino, and Ernie Els, who had just become the No. 1 rated golfer in the world after back-to-back victories in the U.S. Open and Buick Open, and 30 other top-notch pros drew a record crowd of 21,000. The event raised about $400,000 for the Family House, "a home away from home" for cancer patients and their families who are at UPMC for extended treatment. Fuhrer's first-class event had raised about $3 million for the residence in Oakland.

Cowher couldn't believe his good fortune in getting to play with Palmer. He came back to Pittsburgh from a family vacation at Bald Head Island, North Carolina to participate.

He's a pretty fair golfer playing with friends at the Field Club, but playing with Palmer and the big boys on the pro circuit can be a little unnerving. "As a golfer, Cowher is a heck of a football coach," wrote *Post-Gazette* columnist Ron Cook in the next day's newspaper.

Cowher and Palmer posed for some pictures. "Where's Bill and where do you want me?" Palmer said when I first approached him. "You tell me where and when and I'll be there."

And he was. He was just as cordial and cooperative in fielding a request from sportscaster Stan Savran from Fox Sports. One of the greatest golfers in history, Palmer has made more money from his sports prominence than even Michael Jordan, yet he remains one of the most gracious and agreeable celebrities for the media and his fans.

"He's just being his natural self," said Doc Giffin, a former sportswriter who serves as his administrative aide.

A lot of today's young athletes could learn a lot from Palmer about playing the crowd, and downplaying their own importance. It's not an act. "It's just me," he once told me when I interviewed him in the men's grill of his Latrobe Country Club. Palmer was wearing a pink jersey, appropriate for a man in the pink, and Cowher wore a black and gray paneled shirt with a straw plantation hat.

Palmer had risen at 6 a.m. in Latrobe and arrived by his personal helicopter for the day's outing. Palmer practiced his game with the dedication of a youngster seeking his card on the pro tour. That's why he's Arnold Palmer. He would be 69 in September, but he was still working at his game.

"I still love to play this game as much as I ever did," said Palmer. "I'm out there for the same reason I wanted to be out there when I was 40. I'm still driven for the same reasons."

Cowher, who had just turned 40 in May, embraced Palmer and spoke directly into the ear of the elder statesman of the sport. "This is the thrill of a lifetime," said Cowher in a hushed tone. "I've always admired you, and you don't know what this means to me."

Palmer patted him on the back, and said the feeling was mutual. "I've always been a big Steelers fan, you know." Palmer made Cowher comfortable right off the tee. They attracted the largest following of the day.

Both Cowher and Palmer had their problems on the golf course — Oakmont is especially demanding and unforgiving on a hot day when the greens are bone dry — but they enjoyed themselves just the same. They nearly lost some balls in the high rough, but they never lost their sense of humor.

Cowher hit his first drive off the No. 1 tee right in the middle of the fairway. Only the ball landed in the fairway of the neighboring No. 9 hole. Oh well.

It's unlikely this is what eventual winner Jim Furyk had in mind when he said, "If you start missing fairways, it's all over," after he pocketed the $170,000 first prize.

Cowher couldn't contain his enthusiasm for his long walk with Palmer on the beautiful but monstrous Oakmont layout.

"As a kid growing up in Pittsburgh and playing on the Bon-Air course in Moon Township or on the par-3 courses with my old Calloways," said Cowher, "I never dreamed that one day I'd be walking up No. 18 at Oakmont with Arnold Palmer.

"I was just happy to be able to stand next to Arnold, let alone play with him. He's a real genuine individual. When they call him The King, you know why."

To put things in their proper perspective, keep this in mind: Cowher was three years old and living in Beechview when Palmer was named Golfer of the Year in 1960 after winning both the Masters and U.S. Open titles. That's the same year that Bill Mazeroski hit the home run to beat the New York Yankees in the World Series.

Cowher's family had moved to Crafton by the time Bill became fully aware of Palmer's position in the world of sports, so he could be forgiven if he felt like a kid from Crafton again at Oakmont. Did Palmer offer Cowher any golf tips?

"I think Arnold took one look at what I had to work with," came back Cowher, "and decided he didn't have time to start from scratch with me."

Palmer is an amazing man. He was only a few months away from surgery for prostate cancer, yet he moved briskly across the Oakmont course in gruelling heat, and wanted to go back out and play some more. Thirty-six holes wasn't enough, plus he hadn't played to his own demanding standards.

At the outset of the second day, one of the clubhouse attendants asked him if he needed a cart. "No, I'm walking," replied Palmer. "All day!"

At the end of the round, Palmer told reporters, "I've never felt better after finishing a round. I could go out and play 36 more holes. I feel strong."

Jack A. Wolf, a highly-respected professional photographer from O'Hara Township who had followed Palmer for 18 holes on a special assignment the first day, is a rather fit-looking individual in his 40s. "I laid back and put ice on my forehead when I got home that night," said Wolf. "I could hardly get out of bed this morning, and he's back out there playing again after a 6 o'clock wakeup call. He's amazing."

I asked Palmer if he had learned anything about Bill Cowher on their sojourn the day before. "I enjoyed being with him," said Palmer. "I think he's a great guy. He displayed that yesterday. He thoroughly enjoyed himself and that's what it's all about. All the guys enjoyed him. And the crowd (enjoyed him) . . . that's the most important thing. We didn't talk football. We talked golf. I did offer, if he's in trouble, to play quarterback."

Later, I asked Palmer if he were aware that when Chuck Noll was the coach of the Steelers he used Palmer to make a teaching point with his players. "I've heard that," replied Palmer, before leaving to catch a helicopter home to Latrobe.

Noll was playing in a pro-am at the Latrobe Country Club once, and he watched with fascination as Palmer, long past his prime, spent an hour by himself working on chip shots while others were busy blasting tee shots to warm up.

"Here's a guy who won all the big ones," noted Noll, "and he was still working at his game, working at what he was having trouble with. When most guys practice, whatever the game, they usually spend most of their time doing what they do best, what feels good to them. You should work at your weaknesses."

Frank Fuhrer III, the operations manager at Fuhrer Wholesalers Inc., offered this observation about what he learned from playing with Palmer and Cowher & Co.

"They're both good guys to get along with," said Fuhrer, "and they're both good guys to play with. They're just like everybody else. People put them on a pedestal, but they put their pants on — one leg at a time — just like us, as they like to say in sports.

"In the five hours we were together, I gained a true appreciation of what these guys have to go through — with people crowding them, asking for the autographs, wanting a piece of them — and it's got to be tough for them just to go out on a daily basis."

"I know Chuck Noll was a great coach, but this guy Bill Cowher looks like Pittsburgh."
— Mary Bright,
Teachers Aide/Nurse
Greenville, Pa.